THE
ELUSIVE
FAN

THE ELUSIVE FAN

REINVENTING SPORTS IN A CROWDED MARKETPLACE

IRVING REIN
PHILIP KOTLER
BEN SHIELDS

McGraw-Hill

New York   Chicago   San Francisco   Lisbon   London
Madrid   Mexico City   Milan   New Delhi   San Juan
Seoul   Singapore   Sydney   Toronto

To my late parents, Ethel and Sidney Rein, who let me play
Irving Rein

To the Kotler family's six athletes:
Jordan, Jamie, Ellie, Abby, Olivia, and Sam
Philip Kotler

To Ginny and Ben Shields, the most loyal fans in the stands
Ben Shields

CONTENTS

Contents

PREFACE

Sports are in increasing danger of losing their fans. Fans are now confronted with an array of sports options never before imagined. Traditional sports—baseball, football, basketball, hockey—are under pressure to maintain market share. An entire group of emerging sports—lacrosse, paintball, NASCAR, poker—and many new extreme sports are gaining new fans and fragmenting the market even further. As the global marketplace becomes more transparent, sports that were formerly national or regional in scope are now seeking opportunities to conquer new overseas markets.

This competitive crunch exists at all levels. Colleges, high schools, and clubs find themselves in an ever-escalating battle to compete, not only against their peers but in the face of professional expectations and powerful media attractions. Add the time constraints facing most people, the rising costs of being a sports fan, and the proliferation of media channels and new technologies—and the result is the Elusive Fan crisis.

Many questions in the sports industry now demand responses. Why do fans connect with a particular sport, team, or star and ignore others? What are the challenges of retaining core fans and attracting new ones? What are the essential strategies that will enable a sports decision maker to connect to the fast-changing competitive sports audience that is splintering into numerous groups? How do cultural and political factors such as competing entertainments, emerging technologies, transportation problems, and safety and security affect the fans' willingness to spend money on sports? These questions are at the center of this book. To answer them, we develop a set of strategies that will help guide sports decision makers as they confront the competitive and fragmented sports marketplace.

These issues are important because of the huge financial and emotional stakes. Sports are growing across the globe, and estimates of the worldwide size of the sports market are nearly $100 billion. The value of the Chinese sports market alone is expected to reach $10 billion by the 2008 Olympics. In the 2003–2004 sports season, 476 million people attended sporting events in the United States and Canada, and two years later, 1.3 million fans watched live streaming video of March Madness men's basketball games online. None of these impressive numbers tell the whole story of the impact of sports. Sports have become a way of life and in many cases a principal connection to community, moral values, and hero worship. Players and teams, large and small, become the central focus of families, places, and nations as they intersect all cultures. In an industry of this size and scope, connecting to and sustaining a devoted fan base is both an opportunity and a major challenge.

This book proposes a competitive framework that will enable sports decision makers to address the critical fan connection crisis. We believe that the sports industry needs to reinvent its thinking on teams, leagues, athletes, and events in order to differentiate them from the competition. Furthermore, we advocate an action plan for building a brand for a sports product that will both retain and grow the fan base.

The central message of this book is *transformation*. All sports need to be constantly adapting and if necessary changing to accommodate a competitive and fragmented marketplace. We provide a strategic approach to change that emphasizes fan connection, innovative segmentation, brand-building, and sustaining market share. A critical component of the change process is adapting to the generational shifts in the marketplace that span babies starting life and Baby Boomers starting retirement. An agile and responsive sports brand is the solution to what has become an uncertain and sometimes confusing marketplace.

The sports industry at all levels can benefit from the framework and cases presented in this book. Whether the sport is pro football, snowboarding, or high school basketball, there are common denominators that can connect the sports fan. The concepts of escape, entertainment, and identification are universal and can provide insight and power to those competing in the often unpredictable sports marketplace.

Few sports products are perennial winners. In fact, many of them are often losers. Yet we can demonstrate that, with the proper brand-building and fan connections, most sports can not only hold onto their fans but also grow in the midst of intensifying competition for the fan's time and wallet. In this new era of competition, the willingness and ability of sports decision makers to reinvent their products and implement change will separate the successful sports products from those that cannot adapt.

ACKNOWLEDGMENTS

We benefited from the help and counseling of many people who gave us their time and effort. The manuscript was read and critiqued by Artie Bulgrin, Jeff Davis, Adam Grossman, Megan Lutz, Mark Murphy, Perry Rein, Russin Royal, and Michael Trudell. Without their insights and suggestions, this book would have been a far different read. We are particularly grateful to Barry Petersen, who made recommendations that were critical in completing the book, and to Ellen B. Pritsker, whose editing insights were invaluable. A great resource was Joe Rein, uncle and former editor of the *Chicago Daily News*, who was a constant source of historical information and perspective for the book. Lauren Rein was, as always, a source of patience and support.

We also were fortunate to have insights from Northwestern University's Department of Communication Studies graduate students Randy Iden, Brett Ommen, Chris Lundberg, and Ben Ponder. They were always insightful and rightly skeptical about issues that sometimes seemed too apparent. Irving Rein would like to thank the Northwestern University School of Communication for granting him a leave in order to complete the book. He would also like to acknowledge Cary Nathenson and Northwestern University's School of Continuing Studies Masters of Arts in Sports Administration program for developing an environment for the study of sports.

There were also Northwestern undergraduate students who contributed to the research of the book and their diligence and patience were appreciated. Gregory Pang was a key researcher and Jill Greenfield, Nicholas Lalla, and Brandon Gayler also helped in the information gathering stage. Rita Lutz, the Department of Communication Studies administrative assistant, was always saving us from equipment breakdowns and all the rest of the mechanics of preparing a manuscript. We'd also like to thank our McGraw-Hill editor Jeanne Glasser, who was into the process early and was an important resource in getting the manuscript ready, and Jeffrey Krames, publisher and editor-in-chief of the McGraw-Hill Trade division, who not only signed the book but believed in it.

REACHING THE ELUSIVE FAN

THE FAN CHALLENGE

It's an October Saturday in Chicago. On television are two MLB playoff games, two preseason NBA games, fourteen college football games, five golf tournaments, an AHL game, an international horse race, two NASCAR races, and eight soccer matches. The University of Illinois and Northern Illinois University football teams and the AHL's Chicago Wolves have home games. Hawthorne Race Course has a full card, and there's harness racing at Balmoral Park. There are twenty-nine high school football games and the final round of the boys and girls Illinois high school state championship golf tournaments. Youth and recreational league games are also being played in every community of the Chicago area. What about the Chicago Bulls, Bears, Blackhawks, and Northwestern Wildcats? The Bulls played at home last night, the Bears play at home tomorrow, the Blackhawks are away, and the Wildcats had their midseason bye. Of course, this does not include the hundreds of satellite television channels broadcasting soccer, rugby, or cricket games all over

3

the world; the millions of sports Web sites with fantasy games, insider information, and gamecasts; and a wide variety of increasingly realistic sports video games.

Sports fans have never had so many options, opportunities, places, and events to spend their time and money. Add into this mix the hundreds of other cable and satellite television channels, video games, DVDs, and interactive Web sites, and the number of entertainment options at home makes it convenient for people to never leave. And if they do, there are restaurants, movie houses, galleries, theaters, reading groups, grocery stores, lectures, coffee shops, museums, shopping malls, and concerts all vying for their attention.

In a marketplace so crowded, the search for fans has become essential to the very survival of sports. In every decade competitors in the sports industry have adapted to what they consider the pressing issues of fan attraction. A sampling of attention-getters includes:

Newspaper headlines

- "Green-Haired Woman Stalks Welterweight Champion"
- "Sox to Host Disco Demolition Night"
- "Roller Derby Star Seeks Revenge"

Targeting demographics

- Family meal deals—four tickets, four hot dogs, four sodas, and four souvenir cups
- Dog Day at the ballpark
- End zone armchair seats—buffet included

In-game promotions

- Pregame, halftime, and postgame musical extravaganzas
- Cheerleader and mascot T-shirt gunslingers
- The kiss cam

Some strategies have been outrageous successes, while others have received modest responses or failed. They all have one goal—get fans' attention; entice them to attend, watch, and buy; and encourage them to do it again with more intensity. In today's highly cluttered marketplace, the competitive strategies for attracting fans have become fiercer and the results often less certain as the sports industry continues to grow with no real end in sight.

At all levels of the industry—from professional to high school—and with all sports products—from athletes to sporting goods—we are seeing revenues and profits reach previously unthinkable heights. The top 50 highest-paid athletes in the world earned a combined $1.1 billion in 2004, with more than $400 million coming from product endorsements.[1] Fédération Internationale de Football Association (FIFA), the governing body of soccer, projects a $144 million profit and a $1.64 billion revenue stream through at least 2006.[2] The Washington Redskins have made $287 million in a year,[3] while the New York Yankees have generated $264 million,[4] and Manchester United, $315 million.[5] Sporting events such as the International Rugby Board's Rugby World Cup earned $90 million in 2003,[6] and the X Games, a decade-old extreme sports competition, has turned a $15 million profit on $70 million revenues.[7] League and team licensed sporting goods such as jerseys and hats have sold $12.6 billion worth in the United States,[8] and the manufacturers of U.S. sporting goods have generated as much as $52.1 billion in one year.[9]

These numbers only scratch the surface of the magnitude of the sports industry. They do not include the hundreds of thousands of revenue-producing high school sports programs, college team profits and losses, and the growing number of minor league teams in all sports. Nor do they include the enormous amount of money made from television contracts and sponsorships, video game and new media licensing, legal and illegal gambling, and the operating costs of the industry that include everything from travel to medical expenses. And most significantly, they only begin to place into perspective the global reach and power of the industry.

In an environment with such high rewards, the money spent to compete is escalating at every level. Sports facilities are being built at a feverish pace as high schools alone spent $440 million in 2004 on the construction of new facilities.[10] Many high schools are engaging in what Brian Holloway, head trainer of Choate Rosemary Hall, a school that recently spent $10 million renovating its athletic facilities, calls an "arms race" for professional-level medical care for their athletes.[11] The National Football League (NFL) spent $10 million on merely promoting its inaugural annual kickoff celebration of concerts.[12] The National Thoroughbred Racing Association (NTRA), a significantly smaller operation, is spending close to 30 percent of its $67 million revenue on marketing to grow their fan base.[13] In recent seasons the National Basketball Association's

(NBA) Cleveland Cavaliers have increased their marketing budget by 15–20 percent,[14] and the Arizona Diamondbacks of Major League Baseball (MLB) spent 60 percent more just on team advertising.[15] And none of this accounts for the vast amount of resources expended to brand sports stars, events, sporting goods, and new media sports experiences.

Despite the enormous amount of money and resources spent to attract fans, there continues to be a struggle for market share and profit. Major League Soccer (MLS), in an effort to establish itself as a major professional sport in the United States, is racing to build its own soccer-specific stadiums to cover its operating costs, brand its facilities, and survive in the marketplace.[16] Established professional teams in leagues such as MLB and the NBA are fighting for an ever-fragmented market share in cities with competition from other professional, college, and high school teams. In college football, while the Big Ten, Big 12, and Southeastern Conference continue to operate in the black, other major conferences such as the Big East, Conference USA, Mid-American, Western Athletic, and Sun Belt haven't made a profit in 10 years.[17] Many major Division I universities are so dependent upon football program revenue that adding a twelfth game has become a built-in budget item in order to meet expenses and subsidize other sports in the athletic program. Even high school athletic departments are becoming more sophisticated at attracting fans and revenue because they are forced to compete with college and professional teams.

In such a high-stakes marketplace with so much to gain and only so many winners, developing and implementing a winning strategy is a critical concern as the competitive environment becomes more intense and fans are harder to reach, attract, and retain. In this book, we propose a systematic approach to the fan problem based on transformation and branding—emphasizing marketplace analysis, integrating state-of-the-art communication strategies, and undergoing a change process with a central and compelling focus on fan connections.

ALL FANS ARE IN PLAY

While sports continue to occupy a great portion of fan interest across the globe, increased competition and new or reemerging sports are fragmenting the market and eroding previously hard-won gains in the sports industry. Every time a 14-year-old decides to play lacrosse instead of baseball, the economic ramifications are significant. The family will buy equipment, spend time watching games, may travel to camps for special training, and seek schools that feature the sport. After years of exposure to lacrosse, the family may well become interested in supporting a professional league, team, or player. These fan decisions create not only waves of interest but also a specific distribution channel for building a sport.

In a market so crammed with sports and entertainment options, the decision of fans to connect, disconnect, or reconnect to a sport is often overlooked. This is a critical mistake; it's as if some sports properties imagine that fans appear and disappear by magic. The temptations to adopt or convert to other activities are often nonstop. That 14-year-old who decided to play lacrosse and has managed to avoid the glamour of football and basketball still may be attracted to the rock-climbing club at the local gym, or find out that he or she didn't have much success in lacrosse and decide to join the crew team instead. Furthermore, when this 14-year old becomes a full fledged adult, how is he or she going to spend money on sports entertainment: Is it to continue to play and then watch professional lacrosse? Start a family and take the children to minor or major league baseball games? Move to a cold weather state and become a fan of women's hockey? Or will this adult forgo all sports, spend money on video games, go to movies, and take semi-yearly cruises in the Caribbean?

For the sports industry these decision points will determine if the stands are full on Saturday night and whether the television ratings are healthy. Getting inside the fans' decision-making process and understanding how they connect to sports is critical to success and survival in the sports industry. While there are dedicated fans who claim they will never abandon high school basketball on Friday night, the sports menu for competing activities continues to grow. It is safe to say that every fan is in play, and the only effective position for a sports decision maker is to manage the change process and build better strategies than the competition.

Most fans must confront two important issues—money and time. For most of them, there are only so many dollars to spend on any particular recreational activity. They might be die-hard fans of professional hockey who are willing to spend a large amount on that sport, or they might follow the high school basketball team and use their discretionary income for that purpose. The price of being a fan in many sports is an ongoing financial issue. For example, to attend an event of one of the four major professional U.S. sports, the average cost for a family of four is $164 for an MLB game, $247 for the NHL, $263 for the NBA, and $330 for the NFL.[18] Of course, not all sports are this expensive, but for the average fan the price of tickets, travel, merchandise, and equipment are increasing barriers to attendance and participation.

In a school and work environment where time factors are consistently measured and pushed, sports are also competing for the weekly allotment of recreational time, which is already scarce. Americans in 2004 spent 19 hours per week compared to 26 hours in 1973 on what could be termed leisure activities, which include relaxing, watching television, reading, attending movies, spending time with family and friends, and sports.[19] When combining both the money and the time factor, sports, leagues, teams, and athletes are in a struggle for whatever sliver they can get.

It is not surprising that in such a competitive environment a number of ingrained strategies to attract and retain fans have arisen, including winning at all costs, price breaks, targeted demographics, group promotions, community service, and direct mailings. Many in the short term have worked, and these strategies have been reused all over the world. But these are often only short-term fixes and need to be coordinated with a broader strategic plan. With the rise in competition, the margin of error has rapidly narrowed. This new environment demands more—more knowledge, more assessment, and more vision—for a product in the sports industry to become or remain successful. *The conventional strategies are in many cases outdated and inefficient. Money is spent in the wrong places and for the wrong reasons. And fans more easily shift their allegiances and change their preferences.*

In this new era, all fans are elusive; all fans are in play. Competitors are engaging in an all-out battle for the money, time, and attention of fans. Sports decision makers are facing a new level of competition, a race to survive in a crowded marketplace, and a struggle to define, attract, and retain the ever-elusive fan.

Even the most one-dimensional and avid fan is a potential target. A die-hard Ohio State football fan who graduated from the university and stayed in Columbus to raise a family, travels to and attends every game, buys jerseys, hats, and outfits for the children, and supports the alumni booster club still may remain elusive. After all, Ohio State plays only 12 to 13 games a season, usually including a bowl game, and spring practice and scrimmages aren't significant sports fillers for an active fan. The question then becomes: How does this fan spend time on sports during the rest of the year? Watching Cincinnati Reds games on television and attending a game once a year? Following the Ohio State wrestling team during the winter months and even attending an NCAA wrestling final every five years or so? When the brother's family comes to town, spending the weekend at Thistledown Race Track in Cleveland betting on the horses and visiting the Rock and Roll Hall of Fame and Museum? It's not inconceivable that pressures of age, climate, winning seasons, family size, occupation, cultural trends, gender, raising children, costs of higher education, divorce, and new sports could cut into what seems to be a dedicated Ohio State football fan package.

Our Columbus family, not unlike fans of most sports, encounters the familiar restraints of money and time. A championship season by the Cleveland Indians could seriously influence the decision to faithfully follow the wrestling season, or the sudden interest in snowboard cross by the youngest son could turn the fall's Ohio State football season upside-down. The sports that can capitalize on these shifting factors will succeed in growing their market share in this new competitive marketplace.

DEFINING THE ELUSIVE FAN

Many forces influence the decision of sports fans to attend an event, spend an afternoon watching a game on television, buy a jersey, or engage in any activity related to a sport. The Elusive Fan is a member of a dynamic marketplace that is defined by seven major characteristics:

1. Pressurized competitive environment

2. Higher fan expectations

3. Paradox of commercialism

4. New technology

5. Individualism

6. Changes in family structure and behavior

7. Time pressure

Pressurized Competitive Environment

The intensity of the competitive environment is multidimensional and can be divided into six sectors.

The first is the number of older sports such as professional football, European soccer, major league baseball, professional hockey, Formula 1 racing, NCAA Division-I football and basketball, and professional basketball that continue to capture major market share despite the challenges from the marketplace. Retaining their classification as major sports, however, has been a struggle as increased competition has put pressure on traditional fan allegiances.

A second sector is the expansion and reemergence of older sports into larger and more challenging market players. Cricket, NASCAR racing, rugby, golf, professional wrestling, and soccer have made inroads into traditional markets and developed new fans in countries all over the world. For example, NASCAR now has approximately 75 million fans,[20] and professional golf has become a significant player in television. Expanding traditional sports have capitalized on the proliferation of distribution channels to grow their fan bases and inevitably collide with other traditional sports and ones that are emerging.

The third sector is comprised of high schools, club sports, youth development teams, community colleges, and Division II and III sports that have owned a committed audience for decades and find themselves in a newly structured competitive environment. For example, it was axiomatic that Friday night was high school football night all over the United States, and it was unthinkable that college or professional sports would interfere with such a powerful, school-based family and community ritual. As children reached high school age, parents, friends, and community followers were destined to not only attend the games but to provide all the support—pep rallies, community suppers, and team fundraisers. These high school sports were drilled into the community structure. When Division I college football broke the spell by featuring games on television in the prized Friday night time slot, it signaled another chapter in the competitive sports wars. The chipping away of the traditional high school sports market is evident in the rising number of complaints of high school educators and governing associations about the infringements from the competition. High schools have countered the threat by televising their own games, seeking sponsorships for their teams, and investing in new media and elaborate facilities.

The fourth sector is the collection of new sports. These have risen quickly in a fragmented and media-driven marketplace and are attracting both young and old markets. The most obvious example is extreme, or action, sports, a category that includes skateboarding and snowboarding. There are at least 75 million extreme sports participants in America,[21] a significant portion of which comes from Generation Y.[22] Other examples of newly industrialized sports include beanbag tossing, paintball, parkour, roller hockey, and slam ball.

The fifth sector consists of older, traditional sports that have declined, such as boxing, track and field, and horse racing. These sports are now aggressively trying to remarket their product. For example, boxing, which was a dominant sport from the beginning of the twentieth century through the 1950s, has recently made reinvention efforts. ESPN inaugurated a new boxing series in 2004, and other networks have launched reality shows around the sport. Horse racing, which was a popular sport dating back to the seventeenth century in America and for centuries worldwide, has eroded primarily because of the legalization of gambling, which has expanded the opportunities for betting on other sports. Occasionally, there are spikes in attendance when celebrity horses such as Funny Cide and Smarty Jones capture the imagination of fans, but the sport still struggles to regain a competitive position in the industry.

There is a sixth sector that underscores all the issues inherent in sports competition. The sporting goods industry, which consists of team merchandise, sports equipment, and athletic participation gear, has grown into a major sector of the sports marketplace. The sporting goods producers participate in all five sectors of sports competition. Whether it is Ferrari developing a special car for Formula 1, Adidas expanding its line of running shoes, or Burton modifying its snowboards to appeal to a growing female segment, the competition is ferocious, and the stakes are huge.

In the new competitive era, there is no safe market position. Lines between sectors often merge or blur, trendy sports leapfrog over others, and some sports can decline more rapidly than anyone could ever imagine. Sports such as NASCAR have become major in the last decade, and others such as bull riding are threatening to do so. In some cases, the lines between major and minor sports can quickly disintegrate. Over the last decade, the NHL has seen a marked decline in its audience share and profits.[23] Couple this declining trend with the 2004–2005 lockout, and the league finds itself trying to reestablish its position as a major sport with rule changes, pricing strategies, and a reconfigured media mix.

In the past, these changes would not be as crisis-driven and urgent. In today's competitive marketplace, there are many more opportunities for sports fans to spend their money and time, and hockey, despite its historical major sports status, was vulnerable because of its largely regionally defined market. An example of the new competitive threats is the sport of paintball. While paintball may not be a direct threat to the NHL's fan base, it is a new and emerging sport that has the potential to attract new sports fans and challenge the traditional competitive positions of more established sports.

Will Paintball Outdraw Hockey?

For most of us, paintball is an unsupervised, immature activity pursued by young males with overactive testosterone. We drive down the suburban highways of America and we see homemade signs advertising **PAINTBALL**. The sport currently flourishes in forested, hidden, rural alcoves sometimes adjacent to **APPLE PICKING** orchards. It is often shielded from the uninformed public and as a result appears to be nonthreatening to traditional sports. We are all wrong.

Paintball has become a sport with widespread appeal. With almost 10 million people playing in the United States,[24] and another 2 million playing worldwide,[25] annual equipment sales according to SGMA International have rapidly risen to close to $417 million.[26] In essence, paintball has become another competitive sport and one that could take away players and spectators from such traditional sports as football, basketball, and baseball.

Why is that? It's clear that paintball is perfectly attuned to a society that is often characterized as individualistic and aggressive with a strong interest in the military. Like many new sports, it involves all the players in what can be best defined as a natural speed high. **POW, OW, YES!** No mom, no school, no crying. It is an opportunity for Generation Yers to get out of the house, breathe some fresh air, and blast for seven minutes at a flurry of moving targets, which happen to be other people.

Paintball also has the advantage of operationalizing military video games that are usually played in a safe, enclosed environment like a living room. Examples are theatrical paintball events, which simulate military history such as the Battle of Stalingrad. The encounter is reenacted over a 143-acre site that includes two mini-towns, downed aircraft, tank fueling stations, ear-splitting special effects, and myriad targets for the paintballers to obliterate.[27] These types of enactments integrate paintball with media, history, warfare, and athletic involvement that expand its market. As a result, the sport continues to become professionalized under the auspices of the National Professional Paintball League (NPPL). Paintball is filling sporting goods stores with elaborate gear, becoming the subject of magazines and Web sites (www.splatmagazine.com), and growing into a major force in the sports industry.

Higher Fan Expectations

At a St. Louis Cardinals ballgame 50 years ago, fans kept score with a pencil stub and scorecard, ate hot dogs and peanuts, drank beer, listened to an organist playing "Peg o' My Heart" and "Lady of Spain," and strained to hear a few factual nuggets from a terse and garbled PA announcer.[28] They didn't have a Jumbotron that replayed home runs, stadium-shaking rock and hip hop music to break up innings, diverse menu options, or an array of blinking lights, radar readouts, and executive suites. In an effort to attract fans to stadiums, venues in all sports have been forced to change their identity and adopt the latest innovations of entertainment and technology.

Sports on television have also raised the bar. Earlier sports television broadcasts placed the fan at the perimeter of the action with wide-angle camera shots, simplistic graphics, and little instant replay. Today, many fans expect MTV-like quick cuts, booming sound effects, intimate camera angles, and in-game player interviews. Television sports have upgraded their product to attract an ever more demanding sports fan, and, coupled with the new large-screen technology, the TV experience is more of a threat to attendance than ever. In this highly competitive sports marketplace, adding fan value is a daily challenge.

But it's not just sports. In all sectors, fan expectations have risen. In every industry, consumers have higher demands, and industries are racing to meet these expectations. In his book *Living It Up*, James Twitchell confirms how luxury items have become more accessible and are purchased more frequently by a larger, middle-class audience.[29] Widely sought after luxuries such as Mercedes-Benz cars, Chanel perfume, and Coach leather accessories are now fixtures in mass markets. A small economy car such as the Mazda-3 can be upgraded with heated seats and piercing xenon headlights. Even the once commodity-driven hospital industry is now appealing to a more demanding patient base with chef-designed food, rooms with garden views, and Internet access and plasma televisions throughout the facility.[30]

This shift in market expectations profoundly affects how sports products conduct their business. It is no longer reasonable to expect fans to automatically appear because they either have nothing better to do or they are so addicted to the sport that they will put up with backless seats and rude ticket takers. If a sport doesn't respond to these marketplace demands, it runs the risk of being replaced by another sports product that is more flexible and willing to accommodate shifting needs.

The Paradox of Commercialization

As sports have become more commercialized, a conflict has developed between sports as a business and sports as a game. On the one hand, sports operate as a multibillion-dollar business in which sports are products and fans are consumers. On the other, sports are games that are often associated with the innocence of youth, the spirit of competition, and the integrity of the game. The conflict between business and game is everywhere from the debates over whether games should start at 9 a.m. to accommodate television or whether advertisements should be placed on the field of play.

A major consequence of commercialization is the effect on fan-athlete relationships. The central premise for many sports fans is that the athlete truly cares, the team is totally committed, and material rewards are secondary and not primary. As sports have become more sophisticated and rewards have mounted because of more interest, larger crowds, and increased television revenues, the athlete has become sealed off from fans. Today, fans read about athletes abusing drugs, treating fans badly, spending outrageous sums of money, dogging it, and living in an airtight bubble sealed off from the community, fans, and the rest of the world. And even during public appearances, it often seems as if athletes are coming out on call and interacting with fans as an obligation. When professional athletes refuse to play in all-star games, or when large numbers of college athletic programs are under scrutiny because of criminal acts, it sends a powerful message to fans of all ages about the type of people playing the game and the type of commitment they have to it.

Contradicting the basic competitive foundations of sport is that fans find some of these contentious or self-indulgent behaviors compelling and actually instill fan interest in the sport. As a result, it becomes the task of the sports decision maker to balance the integrity and gameness of the sport with an increasingly celebrity-based culture that rewards excessive behavior and, ironically, can increase fan avidity and attendance. The purity-commercial conflict is mirrored in other entertainments, but it is more critical in sports where legitimacy is determined by skill and effort.

New Technology

The fan has never had such a large menu of sports information and games. In this new era, there is something for just about anyone, and, if you're willing to pay the price, there is no limit. The proliferation of media channels has presented the public with thousands of sources of information, mobile technology has changed the way people live and do business, and technological innovations have made the entertainment experience more customizable.

New technologies have had major consequences for sports. Nicholas Negroponte in his concept of the "daily me" argues that media personalization has the potential to narrow people's interests to their preferences and shut out the rest of the world.[31] While this may seem improbable, in this new media world, it is now perfectly possible for a Dallas Cowboys fan to tailor his or her daily input of sports to include Cowboys-only cell phone messages with injury updates, e-mails about what happened at practice on Wednesday, and insider Web site articles on the game plan for Sunday's opponent. Fans can create a world of their own in ways that were never previously imagined. The strength of this programming is total immersion in the personalized Cowboys world. But the weakness is the difficulty for other sports and media to crack through this one-dimensional sports wall.

Even more telling for the future of sports is what technological innovation brings to the sports fan experience. Sports fans can have access to a variety of sports at any time of the day and with insights from experts that were never available. Fans can sit in their living room, dry and warm, see constant replays and on-demand highlights, listen to coaches and players talk to each other, and experience almost any sporting event from anywhere in the world. With HDTV a golf fan can see the blades of grass part as Ernie Els drives off the 15th tee. With satellite television a Sacramento Kings fan in Serbia-Montenegro can watch every minute of an 82-game season. With the Internet an Annika Sorenstam fan can follow her international tournament tour, and a racing fan can play fantasy NASCAR. With Internet video games fans anywhere in the world can play as soccer power Juventus and compete against any opponent. These new technologies have broadened the scope of the sports industry to a new global level, with new rules, new audiences, and unpredictable consequences.

The unspoken fear is that fans will stay home and not go to the venues—that sporting events will become studio shows with the audience merely a staged backdrop to the important television audience. For example, the NFL has 120 million television viewers and 17 million fans that attend games annually at 90 percent capacity, which amounts to 14 percent of the television base actually going to games in a given year.[32] All sports have to be careful of the delicate balance of maintaining the integrity of the live game experience and still meeting the expectations of an expanding media market. In this competitive marketplace, however, it's not only live venues that are struggling for fans. The major television broadcasters are also under pressure as their audience base is fragmenting and being divided by new media.

Show Me the Money

Arizona Cardinals wide receiver Rod Tidwell had strict instructions for his agent in the movie *Jerry Maguire*: show me the money or take a hike. The entire sports industry is now facing a similar ultimatum, igniting a frantic search for how to find and reach the soul and pocketbook of the Elusive Fan. *The money's out there, but where?*

In the traditional media world, network television was the jackpot with venue attendance and radio also important to annual revenues. The sponsor paid the bill, the network collected a profit, and the sport received a fee for providing the content. Now, the explosion of sports media channels and the sheer amount of innovative sports information has upset the balance that defined this once reliable and straightforward sports rights infrastructure. The major networks, all sports, all the time cable providers, satellite television and radio, cell phones, video games, literally millions of Web sites and blogs, and other forms of new media have clogged and complicated the system to baffle even the most synergistic thinkers. It wasn't long ago that network executives would smile indulgently at their staffs and proclaim, "They say convergence is coming. I don't see it." Well, it's here, and now all the players in the sports industry have to reevaluate their current position and restructure in order to navigate the bursting channels of information.

What does all this mean for sports decision makers? There are two critical issues.

First, the media market will still pay, but in a different way. The real-time advantage of sports is a hole card that is unique in a media world where recorded and downloadable entertainment can be easily shifted to the most convenient time for a viewer or listener. Sports are best experienced on the spot, and for an advertiser this is still an attractive value in a competitive marketplace. Despite the advantages of sports, as in all their searches for audiences, advertisers have now begun to disperse their resources over a much wider set of advertising vehicles.

One winner that has emerged in this crowded media marketplace as a dominant communication system is ESPN. In relying less on advertisers and more on cable subscription revenue, the sports cable media giant has imprinted its brand on nine television channels, 700-plus affiliated radio

---

stations, a magazine, a Web site, restaurants, an award show, cell phones, video games, and over 180 countries around the world. The company, based on its buying power, can dole out contracts to major and niche sports seemingly without restraint. However, ESPN is now in competition with not only the broadcast networks that selectively produce sports programming and newly challenging cable providers such as Comcast, but also sports properties themselves who are increasingly seeking to become the first channel of importance for the sports fan.

Moreover, in the gold rush to reach the Elusive Fan, media turf wars now exist everywhere in the sports industry and often threaten to dilute the value of sports properties in the process. For example, XM Satellite radio is now broadcasting MLB games for all 30 clubs. As a consequence, the current rights holders of MLB television and traditional radio agreements find themselves in competition with XM. Infinity Broadcasting chair and CEO Joel Hollander, in addressing the problem of this trend, said, "We love the sports business at Infinity. We just don't love it for the price we have been paying over the last ten years. The content is not as exclusive as it used to be."[33] It is often argued that the additional exposure will only expand the market and provide more viewers so that everyone will benefit—but this position defies logic. In the end, the sports media rights, except for major events such as the Super Bowl or FIFA World Cup, will eventually become devalued, and sports properties will need to search for additional sources of revenue to maintain their current standard of living.

The second critical issue is that sports properties must view themselves not only as content providers but also as their own media centers. Sports decision makers will have to take control; assume the traditional role of media; and design, package, and distribute their own product. This is a major shift in how sports have traditionally perceived themselves. The sports model was not unlike an automobile assembly line as sports provided the information to the media centers who then wrote stories, constructed advertisements, orchestrated publicity campaigns, and did all the intermediary work to communicate to the public. Sports have not had to invest in the communication and media content to any great extent but have basically subcontracted it to a huge and rapidly growing communication-based industry.

An early benefactor of technology and the corresponding decentralization of sports media are niche sports, which have historically received little exposure on television and radio and had the most to gain. New technologies and reduced costs have combined to provide these sports with opportunities unimaginable even five years ago. The situation is more complicated for the traditional high-money sports whose contracts run into the billions and who conduct bidding wars on how their media pie will be cut up. These sports

(Continued)

17

(*Continued*)

properties are now forced to plan for the day when the media market no longer meets their revenue goals and are often starting their own networks; running Web sites with streaming video, gamecasts, and fantasy sports; and venturing into other media such as cell phones and video games.

In the often admired and related industry of film, finding fans has now become an expensive endeavor, which illustrates the problems for sports. In 2004, movie studios spent $34 million alone on marketing domestic films, a price roughly half the cost of production. These out-of-proportion budgets have forced the industry to reconsider where it should spend its money to reach filmgoers and actually turn a profit. Dawn Taubin, the president of Warner Brothers Pictures domestic theatrical marketing, complained, "Marketing costs are just skyrocketing. If we don't address this, we're going to go out of business."[34] A similar threat exists in sports. As the price of reaching fans continues to escalate and the uncertainty of how to make money mounts, moving quickly and strategically to capture fans in their new and often seemingly logic-defying media use is now a life or death issue. The answer for most sports appears to be the same: squeeze every ounce out of current media rights agreements and increasingly become both a content provider and media distributor. This dual solution will only work over the short term as the traditional rights agreements erode and the race to become the defining content provider escalates.

Individualism

On Thursday nights at the civic center, traditional community activities have experienced competition from reruns of *The Apprentice*, Internet chats about Chinese foreign policy, NBA on TNT, a seven-mile trip to the movies, long-distance phone calls to cross-country friends, or simply a relaxing evening at home with family preparing for another long day at work. People have become less group-focused in the process and have developed more specialized interests. In his book *Bowling Alone*, Robert Putnam demonstrates that since the end of World War II Americans have engaged in considerably less community interaction, choosing to spend more time in smaller, more secure groups like families and close friends.[35] Coffee klatches, borrowing milk from neighbors, and babysitting rotations have steadily decreased and with some exceptions seem all but lost.

The implications of individualism for the sports industry are most evident in the erosion of the importance and popularity of team sports. In his research,

Putnam found that participation in team sports has decreased simultaneously with the decline of community interaction.[36] It is no surprise that from 1990 to 2000, the largest growing participation sports were the individual sports of in-line skating, snowboarding, and skateboarding.[37] If you add marathon running, triathlete competitions, and swimming, the trend away from team sports and toward individualism is growing. The rise of individualism continues to fragment the traditional team sports audiences, and this powerful cultural trend is going to continue to affect major sports sectors.

Changes in Family Structure and Behavior

The family structure has undergone major changes, which have significantly affected sports participation and attendance. Over half of American families are described as "blended," meaning divorced, single parent, multigenerational, or diverse groups of unrelated people. As a result, the traditional father-mother decision-making structure of the family can no longer be assumed.

Decision making for sports participation and consumption is complicated. What authority decides who will play baseball, at what level, and if and when they should take up cross country? It is clear from research studies that spontaneous and unregulated play, which was often the traditional entry into a sport, has declined dramatically. This trend is stronger in middle- and high-income areas and less so in lower-income communities. In the last two decades, according to Dr. Alvin Rosenfeld, author of *The Over-Programmed Child*, programmed sports time has increased twofold, while children's sports free time has been cut in half.[38]

There are a number of factors that have influenced this decline. First, a growing number of children are often heavily scheduled from a very early age. This includes play dates, ballet class, soccer, after-school care, and specialty camps. The child who simply comes home after school, puts on a pair of jeans, and goes out to play playground sports is becoming rapidly extinct. Mavis Hetherington, a psychologist at the University of Virginia, identifies the parent as the decision maker by stating, "Parents essentially regulate all their children's activities."[39] Second, when children do have their own leisure time, they often spend it playing video games, surfing the Internet, or watching television. It becomes a task just to get the kid out the door. Third, if the activity doesn't have an instructional aspect to it, the parent feels it's a waste of time.[40] The cry, "Let kids be kids" is now quaint and in many communities replaced by, "Will the sport get him or her into college?"

The effect of these trends on sports participation and consumption is striking. It is estimated that 50 percent of children will quit organized sports when they reach the age of 12 and that 75 percent stop playing by the second year of high school.[41] Even more troubling is that the National Parent Teacher Association found that 75 percent of children report that they've quit a sport because parents and coaches focus too much on winning.[42] Many are being forced to play in a sport they're not interested in or want to quit. We are raising a generation of young people who may be participating in sports that are not their choice and, when they can make their own decisions as adults, could choose otherwise. Reaching young people is essential for any sport's survival, and the ever-evolving family structure is a challenge that complicates that goal.

1X to 3X through 45

The Mustang tackle football team of 1947 was made up of 26 fifth graders who attended Frances Willard grade school and lived in the same neighborhood. Every player brought his own uniform to the game, which consisted of red plastic shoulder pads, various colored helmets, corduroys or baggy sweatpants, and an assortment of tennis shoes, dress shoes, and high-top football shoes. The players were united by an oversized gray sweatshirt with **"MUSTANGS"** written on the front in crayon. The team practiced three or four times a week at North Commons, a park with an undulating grass field of unspecified dimensions. Initially, a high school student would show up to help organize and make suggestions about practice drills and play selection. By and large, however, the team was self-coached and in some version of democracy made decisions as to lineups, play calling, and arranging for games with opposition from surrounding neighborhoods.

The team's signature play was 1X to 3X through 45. 1X (the quarterback) took the ball from center, handed the ball off to 3X (the fullback), who ran between 4 (the right guard) and 5 (the right tackle). The right guard and tackle were the biggest kids on the team. Most 10-year-olds in the neighborhood played on the team, and their positions were determined by performance and consensus. It was not always a pretty process:

"I want to play end and not center because I want to score touchdowns."

"You're not tall enough, and Joel has better hands."

"All right, I'll play center this week, but if Joel messes up, I'm in."

The team played five seasons until the players reached high school, where they became the dominant force on the football team. Over a half-century later, on special occasions they come from all over the country to reconnect and recall how they grew up around sports.

Contrast the Mustangs with the current youth sports environment. The idea of kids organizing themselves, playing unsupervised a rough game for five years, and making their own decisions is virtually unheard of. Moreover, the Mustangs played basketball when the weather turned cold and baseball when the ground melted. Today, kids have many more activity choices, are supervised closely in most athletic contests and, as a result, are usually better trained and skilled. The trade-off is that many of the decisions about participation or behavior in sports have been taken out of kids' hands and are usually made by coaches, parents, and schools. Even more telling is that sports no longer follow the seasons, but overlap encourages specialization and often early burnout. For the sports industry, it was easy to predict what sports those Mustangs would play and pursue as they grew older. *In today's crowded marketplace, there is far more uncertainty as to what sports children will choose as they grow older and become adults because their experiences are more varied and controlled.* That uncertainty is a primary driver in the quest for reaching the Elusive Fan.

Time Pressure

An overview of the weekday schedule of an average full-time American employee consists of 9.2 hours of work, 7.5 hours of sleep, 0.9 hours of household activities, 3 hours of leisure or sports, and 3.4 hours for the rest of the day, which includes eating, drinking, and going to school or the mall.[43] With such a limited window for entertainment, fans have to be selective as to how they spend their time. Whether fans are going to a professional game, attending a hot-stove league winter baseball convention, or driving 50 miles to see their son play tennis, time becomes a critical factor in the fans' decision-making process.

It's not just the activity that puts pressure on fans. It's also the time that it takes to engage in the activity that causes problems. Let's look at a typical fan who has bought a ticket to an evening Los Angeles Dodgers baseball game. The game starts at 7:30 p.m., and the fan leaves work at 5:30 p.m. with a friend and proceeds to the ballpark. Suppose the fan is working in Burbank, which is 12 miles from Chavez Ravine, the home of the Dodgers. Making that trip in 1958, a fan might have made it in 30 minutes, but in today's traffic an hour and a half might be understating how long it will take. The fan, if lucky, will be in the ballpark by 7:15 p.m., 15 minutes before game time. The game lasts 3 hours; it takes 30 minutes to get out of the parking lot; it takes 45 minutes to get home; and the fan pulls into the driveway at 11:45 p.m. Not including time spent on the phone buying the tickets, conferring with friends as to arrangements of pick-up time, and explaining to other members of the family why they can't go, the fan spent over six hours on the baseball game. In one evening, the fan spent a significant portion of all available weekly leisure time on one activity. It is no wonder that at Chavez Ravine some fans arrive by the second inning and leave by the middle of the seventh to beat traffic.

Today, competition, higher fan expectations, the paradox of commercialism, new technology, individualism, family decision-making, and time pressure have conspired to make fan connection more challenging for the sports industry. In this book, we examine how sports products of all types—athletes, teams, leagues, federations, events, sporting goods—can compete in this Elusive Fan marketplace. Our goal is to provide a systematic approach to attract and retain fans and ultimately move them to higher levels of commitment and intensity.

DESIGNING COMPELLING SPORTS BRANDS

The sports industry faces a marketing challenge unlike any other entertainment. In the sports world, athletic performance has historically been the primary determinant of fan attention and connection. An athlete chasing a performance record, a team making a playoff run, and a league or event with the highest quality of competition have often guaranteed fan attention; while a slumping star, below .500 team, and lower-quality leagues and events have often received little in the way of fan interest. In dealing with a performance-based product, the best sports marketing position has almost always been winning and a high-quality competitive performance. But in a sports world where winning and losing is inevitable and sports decision makers have little control over the sports performance, this thinking must change.

The ideal sports fan connection is long term and uninterrupted by the predictable performance lapses of sports products. To achieve these sustainable fan connections in the Elusive Fan marketplace, we propose that the sports industry view its products as agile and market-responsive brands. A strong brand is a form of promise to the consumer and triggers a number of mental associations that markets can readily identify about the "product," such as reliability, level of play, personality, comfort, and access. Strong sports brands are built through *transformation*—the systematic change process that redefines and reinvents the sports product as a fan-centered brand. The movement toward branding in sports responds to how competitive the marketplace has become and the need for all sports products to constantly react to changes in the expectations and demands of the fan. Transforming into a brand not only improves the potential for fan connection, but also differentiates the sports product from its competitors and extends the longevity of the product's life.

A critical factor in brand transformation is ensuring that there is star power in the end product. Throughout the history of sports, stars have always been principal attractions for maintaining and attracting fan attention. Names like strongman boxer John L. Sullivan, the "Iceman" football star Red Grange, Olympic and all-around athlete Mildred "Babe" Didrikson Zaharias, and the skyscraper center Wilt "the Stilt" Chamberlain are immediately recognizable to fans. In fact, such stars as baseball homerun hitter Babe Ruth and tennis star Billie Jean King are credited with literally transforming their sports into important forms of sports entertainment. A major dilemma for sports properties is ensuring that a steady and predictable stream of stars is part of the brand mix.

A solution to this problem is to challenge conventional thinking on star power as limited to individual athletes. The most successful sports brands not only need star athletes but must also broaden their star power mix to include facilities, food, teams, places, events, and individuals, such as owners, who have not been a part of the storyline. Star power needs to be redefined to connect with more fans, maximize all the attributes that a sports product has to offer, and ensure a constant flow of sports branding material to convert into star status.

Branding in sports is not new. There are examples of strong brands that have established fan relationships based on a clearly delineated brand identity and its differentiation from competitors. David Beckham, Anna Kournikova, Tiger Woods, the Washington Redskins, Wrigley Field, the FIFA World Cup, Dodger Dogs, Nike, and Adidas all come to mind. English soccer club Manchester United, in particular, is an example of how a sports team can be transformed from a local club team into a global brand not unlike GE and Sony.

Manchester Unites Sports and Business

England's Manchester United was once known as just a successful soccer team. In the last 15 years, however, the team has been transformed into a highly profitable company and an identifiable global brand. As of 2005, Manchester United was worth $1.251 billion[44] and had 75 million fans across the globe.[45] To put this in perspective, the second most valuable franchise was Real Madrid at $920 million, followed by AC Milan at $893 million.[46]

How did this transformation happen? First, the organization began assembling and developing in its youth academies the best young international talent. Beginning in 1986, Sir Alex Ferguson, manager of Manchester United, honed the skills of David Beckham and many other current star players. Second, after strengthening the product, Manchester United executives altered their business strategy. CEO David Gill reflected a new type of sports executive who speaks "the language of the balance sheet and the share price, [and] see[s] clubs as brands, players as assets, fans as customers and faraway places as markets."[47] Third, the Manchester United brand was distributed through a variety of channels: team-themed restaurants, merchandise megastores, its own cable television network, a newly renovated stadium, and museums. With these marketing strategies, Manchester United's brand as the best and most star-studded team in the world resonated with a wide range of audiences.

The future success of Manchester United, however, is not guaranteed. Competing soccer teams such as AC Milan, Juventus, Chelsea, and Real Madrid and other sports such as basketball and baseball are emulating its formula. This situation has forced Manchester United to continue to improve and expand its brand. In doing so, a key component of its branding strategy has been to capitalize on new media and distribute its brand in other markets. For example, video clips, news information, and mobile video games are now delivered to fans on their cell phones through a team-branded wireless service called MU Mobile,[48] and a new Manchester United fantasy football game has been released.[49] Fueling the use of new media is the expansion into new markets such as Asia and the United States. The team has embarked several times on playing tours in both areas. In the United States, the team has also signed a marketing partnership with the New York Yankees,[50] and, in Asia, it continues to develop restaurants, stores, and soccer schools in China, Japan, and Korea.[51]

The past success of Manchester United is undeniable. Still, the new sports environment of the twenty-first century has proved that no brand is invincible. The purchase of the previously publicly traded Manchester United by American entrepreneur Malcolm Glazer initiated a furor from traditional

Manchester United fans who were offended by not only the foreign intrusion but the perceived threat of future degradation of the Manchester United brand. Simultaneously, soccer teams such as the Chelsea Football Club and other global-seeking teams are moving into the territory on which Manchester United once had a monopoly. If Manchester United is to remain a successful brand, it must manage to integrate both the playing and business sides of the franchise to satisfy its primary markets and continue to develop globally in order to withstand the increasingly competitive marketplace. The secrets of Manchester's success are out, and only better execution will fight off its tenacious competitors.

Sports branding is not limited to the highest levels of competition or the most visible sports products. With the escalating competition at every level of sports—from high schools to club sports, and colleges to the minor leagues—all sports products can benefit from branding. Transformation is a fundamental process that differentiates the sports product and connects with fans in any marketplace. Consider the example of St. John's University.

St. John's football is a dominant brand located in a small Division III Catholic university in Collegeville, Minnesota, a remote town in the northern part of the state. A perennial powerhouse, the program is easily identifiable because of the attributes that are clearly associated with its coach. St. John's has its brand icon in John Gagliardi, a high-profile coach with a very specific and attractive philosophy. Gagliardi doesn't believe in nongame tackling and practice scrimmages, carries a squad of over 100 players, and revels in the bad weather of the region.[52] As a result, players who want a Catholic intellectual experience, a principled leader, and to play on a highly successful countercultural football team pass up scholarships to larger schools to play for Gagliardi.

The response to this example of St. John's may well be, "That's great for a small college in northern Minnesota, but what does it have to do with my traveling club rugby team?" In this crowded marketplace, it is no longer acceptable to be just a run-of-the-mill small college football program or a personality-less rugby team. The sports brand with star power will inevitably emerge in any marketplace.

CONCLUSION

The sports fan is a highly prized commodity. There is only a limited amount of money and time that people have to watch and participate in any given sport. There are fans who collect every professional basketball team's jersey, but it is more likely that he or she will have one or two and the choices will be made from a large number of sports. In the end, fans have to make a choice of how they will spend their money and time. And the resurgence of old sports, the large number of new ones, and the power of media to determine financial success combine to ignite a highly competitive and volatile environment. Those sports decision makers who recognize the problem, are agile in adapting to the shifting forces, and understand how the culture and new technologies affect fan choices will be the ones more likely to succeed.

This book is organized into three sections. In the first section, we identify the problems of the current sports industry and analyze how fans make decisions on sports products. In the second section, we develop the transformation process, which includes four principal stages—brand concept generation, brand testing, brand refinement, and brand actualization—and propose brand communication strategies. Finally, in the third section, we address how sports brands can avoid decline, sustain, and prosper in this ever-changing Elusive Fan marketplace.

Chapter

$$\boxed{2}$$

SPORTS IN TROUBLE

The 1927 heavyweight championship fight between Jack Dempsey and Gene Tunney was a national event. More than 145,000 fans packed the aisles and filled the bleachers of Chicago's Soldier Field. Fifty million listeners were glued to radios, using their imagination and the announcer's description to visualize the epic battle.[1] And hundreds of journalists stood ready to deliver the fight's outcome to the readers of the latest editions of their newspapers. It was as if the entire country had paused to focus its attention on this monumental boxing match.

The drama and controversy in what became known as the "Long Count" was centered around one round. In the seventh, Dempsey knocked Tunney to the canvas and was on the brink of victory. The timekeeper, Paul Beeler, began his knockout count and reached five before referee Dave Barry started his. The referee's delay was because Dempsey was lingering over his fallen opponent and an Illinois State Athletic Commission rule restricted referees from counting until the still-standing competitor retreated to a neutral corner of the ring. With the five-second differential between the time-keeper and referee, Tunney remained down for what amounted to fourteen seconds; he finally got up after Barry counted, "Nine." Dempsey, in almost disbelief at Tunney's reemergence, relentlessly attacked him, only this time he tired while Tunney regained his strength. Tunney subsequently gained control of the fight and beat the national idol in 10 rounds.

Although the "Long Count" became one of the most debated moments in sports history, an important legacy of the fight was the number of fans it attracted. It not only captured the attention of a significant portion of the population, but it symbolized the new era for sports business. Sports decision makers in the 1920s were realizing that sports stardom and event matches could attract massive crowds and generate substantial revenue. With radio and an increasingly expanded newspaper sports section, the building and distribution of what we now call the contemporary sports industry was in full force. There was no access to the multiple channels and sophisticated Internet technology of today, but the sports industry had the advantage of limited competition and a compelling idea—the sports star and team as idolized heroes.

Much has changed in the sports industry since the 1920s. While sports have grown into a multibillion-dollar industry, *sports are in trouble*. This may seem inconceivable because there are more sports, more fans, and more revenue in the marketplace than ever before. But the reality is that the supersonic growth of the industry has resulted in more competition and a fan base that is increasingly elusive. In the contemporary sports world, sports products are threatened every day and survival is a constant challenge.

Looking back at the earlier eras of the sports industry, a number of changes have placed sports in peril:

- An explosion in sports revenue and a corresponding dramatic increase in opportunities for sports expansion
- All-pervasive and converging media covering many sports
- The rehumanization and subsequent decline of the sports hero
- A corresponding steadily growing cynicism about salaries and league, team, and star behavior

- An increasing suspicion of unfair competition including unequal salary structures, drug use, and betting cartels
- A highly fragmented audience with an increasing preference for personalization
- The institutionalization of gambling as an acceptable form of fan participation

In the midst of all this, television revenue, which has fueled the industry's growth, is increasingly defying gravity as audiences grow smaller.[2] Since 1988, marquee television sporting events have experienced a ratings decline, with the NBA Finals decreasing 56 percent, the World Series 21 percent, and Monday Night Football 22 percent.[3] Despite these ratings performances, many sports properties are still in what could be defined as a sweet spot where networks are desperately seeking quantities of fans and are willing to pay up despite declining ratings. Over time, however, many sports properties, media companies, and advertisers will find that the audience contraction will produce fewer mainstream television revenues. The exceptions are the major event sports properties such as the Super Bowl, World Series, FIFA World Cup, and Final Four, which, even if they experience declining ratings, will continue to be attractive to media companies and advertisers because of the scarcity of real-time mass audiences. Aside from these special viewing events, the once reliable television revenue infrastructure will need to change to address new audience dynamics. The record revenues, high salaries, and many competitors are making the sports marketplace less certain and dependable as media consumption and fan attendance become fragmented and move into uncharted directions.

The problems of sports did not develop overnight. The sports industry's response to the challenge of a rapidly changing and often eroding marketplace has traditionally been to do more of the same—more promotion, more marketing, and more advertising. It is not a startling discovery that more of a losing strategy only increases costs and does not materially improve the declining situation. Beginning with the professionalization of the industry and the partnership with the media, new dynamics began to develop that are the hallmarks of today's dilemmas.

The purpose of this chapter is to present a clear picture of the contemporary sports industry by looking at how it has evolved. We examine the changes that have taken place over what we define as the three major generations of the sports industry—Monopoly, Television, and Highlight—and how they have led to the emergence of the Elusive Fan. Each of the three generations has the following critical dimensions, and examining their impact places into perspective their contribution to the problems of today's sports marketplace.

- *Cultural environment*: What cultural changes affected the growth of the sports industry?
- *Products:* What sports products were dominant?
- *Distribution:* How did sports information reach audiences?
- *Power structure:* Who were the major decision makers, and what was their impact?
- *Infrastructure:* What were the economic, structural, and physical elements of the sports industry?
- *Attraction:* What were the fan attraction strategies of the various decision makers?

THE THREE SPORTS GENERATIONS
Monopoly Generation (1900–1950)

Although formal sports competition dates back to at least the ancient Greeks, we are most concerned with the period in which sports became industrialized: when sporting events became mass produced with the objective of generating profits. While in the nineteenth century there was professional baseball, horse racing, and boxing, the industry was still relatively unorganized and lacked structure. In fact, anyone would be hard-pressed to even call it an industry. It was at the turn of the century, when shortly after the American League and National League agreed to play the first World Series in 1903 and FIFA was founded in 1904 with seven founding countries, that the Monopoly Generation began to gain momentum. Over this period, there were a number of pivotal changes in how sports were produced and how fans understood them.

The culture of the Monopoly Generation was marked by rapid population growth, two world wars, the 1920s surge in consumerism and popular culture, and the Great Depression. People were moving from the countryside to the cities in great numbers and had closer proximity to the major sporting events. In this era, a growing number of fans were becoming accustomed to driving long distances to see a horse race, such as the Kentucky Derby in Louisville,

Kentucky, or taking a train to see the Army-Navy game at Franklin Field in Philadelphia. As the fan base expanded and the venues became more lucrative, the sports industry began to specialize with promotional and media departments and structured distribution for game trips and other related items for sports fans to buy. The targets were usually male because they made up the overwhelming majority of fans in this era. Sports decision makers were only beginning to understand the potential of reaching out to segmented and important markets that they overlooked.

In this generation, there were far fewer sports products that dominated the industry: baseball, horse racing, boxing, international soccer, hockey, college and professional football, and the Olympics. College and professional basketball, today huge successes, were only beginning to emerge at the end of the Monopoly Generation. As a result, there were limited options for sports fans, and each sport had its own place in the market. In essence, this scarcity-driven market arrangement enabled the Monopoly era. Most of these sports thrived in larger urban markets where there was an audience to consistently attend games. In contrast, small towns were served by minor league baseball, football, and basketball teams, company-sponsored amateur teams, and college athletics. In this era, place identified teams and athletes such as the Toronto Maple Leafs and the Finnish and Norwegian skiers became household names with huge followings.

Globetrotters Invent Sports and Entertainment

The idea of entertainment in sports was never fully realized until the Harlem Globetrotters discovered the principle almost by accident. The independent African American basketball team, owned and managed by an entrepreneurial promoter from Chicago named Abe Saperstein, redefined sports history. In the mid-1920s, Saperstein formed what became the Globetrotters from a team called the Savoy Big Five, which was named after the famous Chicago Southside ballroom that featured such stars as Louis Armstrong and Ma Rainey. Sports, like life in America, were segregated, and Saperstein saw an opportunity to brand a basketball team that not only played good basketball but was significantly more entertaining than any other in the world.

In the Monopoly Generation, teams were dominated by authoritarian owners and coaches, and players were limited not only by rules but by the

(Continued)

(*Continued*)

force of their personalities. The coaches were the boss, and the players were the employees. New York Giants baseball manager John McGraw and University of Minnesota football coach Bernie Bierman were strict task masters who insisted that their players check their egos and choke up on the bat and move the runner along or pull out from the offensive line and throw their bodies selflessly into the unfooled defense. The Globetrotters were different. Saperstein was more the master of ceremonies as his gifted athletes broke every rule in basketball. In the first generation of the Globetrotters, they played straight basketball, but by the late 30s found that comic bits turned on the audience. Combining serious basketball and humor was a novel idea at the time, and the team gradually grew a devoted following, playing in a wide variety of small towns and cities.

By the World War II years, the Globetrotters branded their star power to such an extent that they became a worldwide sensation. They had developed a type of basketball with exciting, funny routines that left the audience delighted and wishing for more. The Globetrotters stood for family entertainment, and the package attracted a large number of young people to basketball for the first time. Saperstein had also discovered the star principle and featured such players as master comic Goose Tatum and Curly Neal, the bald-headed dribbling sensation. They competed in front of huge crowds, including 75,000 spectators in Berlin's Olympic Stadium in 1951. The Globetrotters usually played the Washington Generals, a team of former second-rate college stars who were hired by Saperstein to be beaten relentlessly night after night. Despite the showy displays, the Globetrotters were a world-class basketball team. A major event was their beating the NBA champion Minneapolis Lakers in 1948, a game that captured headlines and identified them as a legitimate basketball power. During the early years of the NBA, the Globetrotters would on occasion be the opening game of a doubleheader, and the NBA team often found itself playing before an empty house after the Globetrotters finished.

The Globetrotters were the entertainment package that professional sports had unknowingly always wanted. They were a highlight reel every night, and they sent away their fans with a smile on their faces and a sense of satisfaction that belied the often one-sided scores. The Globetrotters inevitably declined once professional basketball broke the color barrier and began to hire African American stars. The purchase of the Globetrotters in 1993 by ex-Globetrotter, now entrepreneur, Mannie Jackson and his subsequent sale to Roy Disney in 2005 provided the franchise with strategic redirection as both owners promoted the merchandising and licensing potential of the team. Despite the team's current marketing challenges, the Globetrotters wrote the playbook for the modern era and forever broadened the audience for sports.

The primary means of distribution in this generation were radio, newspapers, newsreels, and magazines. If fans wanted to see the game and the players, they had to travel to the site of the encounter. It was an era in which newspapers and radio dominated sports media with celebrity sportscasters such as Graham McNamee and sportswriters like Grantland Rice who were not only the major spokespersons and interpreters of the game action, but were better known than most of the players.

The Monopoly Generation delivered the fan an often fanciful product. Staples of the early years of radio baseball were delayed teletype reports that forced the broadcaster, who was not at the game, to imagine what was going on in the game and relay it to the anticipating fan at home. President Ronald Reagan, a baseball announcer who recreated Chicago Cubs games from a studio in Des Moines, Iowa, fondly recalled how he filled in the gaps as the batter waited for the pitch and had to find words to describe the nonexistent. "I had a ball on the way to the plate and there was no way to call it back. So, I had Augie foul this pitch down the left field line. He fouled for six minutes and forty-five seconds. My voice was riding [sic] in pitch and threatening to crack—and then, bless him, Curly started typing. I clutched at the slip. It said: 'Galan popped out on the first ball pitched.'"[4]

Football announcers, who observed from their sheltered broadcasting perch, spun interpretations of the game that were frequently outlandish. Storied announcers such as Harry Wismer and Bill Stern were notorious for turning five-yard stumbling runs into hip swiveling, dancing ballets that could seemingly last five minutes. Canadian hockey announcer Foster Hewitt broadcasted National Hockey League games in Canada on Saturday night. His phrase "He shoots, he scores!" became a well-known catch phrase, and his broadcasts were the most popular program of the week in Canada. In some ways, the fans of the Monopoly Generation who didn't buy a ticket were experiencing sports as reader's theater, and it was only in the next generation when they could actually see the game that reality intruded.

This generation marked the beginning of commercialized star culture with a growing number of endorsement opportunities for athletes. Star exposure ranged from fronting for local car dealerships to working the front lobby of a resort hotel to endorsing cigarettes. Megastars such as Babe Ruth (Goodyear, Red Rock Bottlers, Fro-Joy ice cream, and Babe Ruth underwear) and Red Grange (Red Grange dolls, sweaters, candy bars, shoes, and meatloaf) were at the forefront of endorsement opportunities. Red Grange was among the first professional team sports stars to capitalize on his fame. The University of Illinois halfback, under the guidance of his personal manager "Cash and Carry" Pyle, orchestrated his inaugural season with the professional football Chicago Bears with a barnstorming tour. It was Grange, the fabled Galloping Ghost, who was marketed not only as a rare football attraction but as a cross-sector celebrity with wide appeal to non-sports fans.

The distribution of star images began to expand as the public became willing to pay for exposure to sports stars outside of their competitive performance. It was increasingly more common for established stars to appear in motion pictures such as Red Grange in *The Galloping Ghost* and *A Racing Romeo*, baseball star Lou Gehrig in *Rawhide*, boxing champion Joe Louis in *Spirit of Youth*, and horse racing iconic underdog Seabiscuit in *The Story of Seabiscuit*. In addition, newspaper sports sections and magazines began to increase their coverage of sports stars, as the public demanded more information about their heroes. This generation included the golden age of sports trading cards as chewing gum, tobacco, and other companies found a ready market for their pictures of sports stars. Wheaties, the self-proclaimed "Breakfast of Champions" breakfast cereal, began a national campaign that profiled sports stars on their cereal boxes and invited young aspirants to send in box tops for sports skill pamphlets authored by famous coaches. Many youth sports teams learned the single wing, two handed set shot, and how to bunt from these terse, but informative instructional giveaways.

The power structure of the Monopoly Generation was top down. The most influential decision makers of this generation were owners, boards of trustees, coaches, promoters, league officials, and sponsors. They largely controlled the sports industry, and the power in the management-player relationship was almost always skewed toward the former. It's also true that in professional sports there was nowhere near the money that emerged in later generations. Professional players were generally paid low salaries and had limited rights. They usually worked second jobs in the off-season selling insurance and real estate and, while often accessible to fans, saw themselves as ordinary citizens trying to make a living. While mythmaking was an essential ingredient of sports and their ability to draw fans, the athletes were treated as employees and not as independent contractors. They served at the whim and benevolence of the managers who controlled the sport. Since agents were virtually nonexistent, players, often to their detriment, negotiated directly with owners and promoters.

Sports were played during clearly demarcated, rarely overlapping seasons. Professional baseball and horse racing were the major attractions in the summer months. Football was played in the fall with college games on Saturday and professional games on Sunday. Hockey and basketball were played in the winter. Boxing matches and indoor track and field were year-round, but the big matches and races were special events that didn't disrupt the seasons of other sports. Sports such as indoor cycling, roller derby, and professional wrestling were part of any big city's sports calendar but were second-level attractions compared to the major sports.

This was also the generation in which sports facilities became important to the very existence of the games. In the teens and twenties, many of the great college football stadiums were built, and professional football teams often converted baseball parks to football venues in the fall. Forbes Field, for example, housed both the Pittsburgh Pirates and the Pittsburgh Steelers, and Wrigley Field served the Chicago Cubs and the Chicago Bears. Large city arenas were also built, and states and cities began to subsidize amateur and professional facilities. These stadiums were often intended for multipurpose use. Facilities such as the Minneapolis Auditorium hosted almost every activity in the city including roller derby, basketball, ice shows, and the annual automobile show. In England, Wembley Stadium was the centerpiece of an elaborate exhibition setting, and soccer, rugby, track and field, and greyhound and motorcycle racing were all part of its versatile use.

While these venues were often huge (such as the University of Michigan's Big House and Lisbon, Portugal's Benfica, home of soccer club SL Benfica), they lacked the amenities of facilities of later generations. The fans of the Monopoly Generation did not demand wide concourses, gourmet food, enclosed executive suites, and multitiered parking lots. If you haven't been exposed to such luxuries, it's hard to know you miss them, and the materials and skills for some of these architectural innovations had not yet been developed.

The fan attraction strategies of the Monopoly Generation foreshadowed much of what happened in the rest of the twentieth century. Sports marketing included newspaper and radio commercials, discounts at the gate, off-season events for fans, and special kids' promotions such as baseball's knothole day games. A popular strategy during this era was the use of posters plastered on empty buildings, placed inside storefront windows, and sometimes dropped into the doorways of local residents. The premiere events during this era were often the big heavyweight boxing matches that were able to charge high prices, and the World Series, which was broadcast coast to coast and was an early October ritual for most Americans. The FIFA World Cup, which began in 1930, was becoming an international obsession and joined the Olympics as a truly international sporting event.

The Monopoly Generation was the first to organize sports as an industry with major economic consequences. It also was marked by a limited number of sports products, a requirement for fans to attend the event to see it, and the emergence of media-driven sports teams and celebrities. Sports were growing rapidly and yet confined to specific markets by their lack of access and reach for broad numbers of people. All these issues were confronted when television was introduced in the next generation.

Monopoly Generation (1900–1950)

1. *Cultural:* Rapid population growth, two world wars, 1920s materialism, and the Great Depression marked this generation. Sports first became industrialized in this generation and had a male-dominated fan base.
2. *Products:* A limited number of sports dominated the industry: baseball, horse racing, boxing, hockey, and football (college and professional), resulting in fewer contests and options for fans.
3. *Distribution:* The primary means of communication were live events, radio, newspapers, and magazines. Fans had to go to the games to see the action and often experienced sports through secondhand observations of journalists and radio broadcasters.
4. *Power structure:* The power in the manager-player relationship was skewed toward the owners, boards of trustees, coaches, promoters, league officials, and sponsors.
5. *Infrastructure:* Seasons were clearly demarcated. The great football stadiums and many all-purpose facilities were built during this generation.
6. *Attraction:* Fan attractions were driven by basic promotional and advertising strategies that often emphasized access and price. The sports star culture was beginning to emerge as a major attraction.

Television Generation (1950–1990)

The rapid adoption of television in the late 1940s and early 1950s signaled the beginning of the Television Generation. In its early years, television attracted people to bars, electronics stores, and the homes of neighbors who first bought the sets to witness this new miracle. By 1959, nearly 90 percent of Americans owned a television set.[5] Popular program formats were variety shows, soap operas, sitcoms, game shows, the news, made-for-television movies, documentaries, and sports, and all of them benefited from the distribution opportunities of this new medium. Television in the home marked a key shift in how people spent their time. The home now more than before provided a personal entertainment experience. And for the sports industry, people for the first time could see the same action in their living rooms that they would see at a game.

Not only did television facilitate cultural change, but the end of World War II produced a changed American family. The post–World War II economic boom quickly affected how people spent their money. Families had more disposable income to spend and shared it with their children. With money in their hands, the youth market flourished and began influencing the marketing decisions of companies. Youth were spending money on Elvis, McDonald's, Levis, Coca-Cola, and hula hoops. In the sports world, for the kid who might have only played football in the past, there were now more things to do and less time to fit them all in. When combining the adoption of television and the tangible consumer shifts of the Television Generation, this generation in many ways set the precedent for the complexity and competition in the industry today.

The most dominant products of the previous generation experienced growth because of television. Football expanded because of its camera appeal and profitable rights fee negotiations. Olympic sports introduced a global mass audience to downhill racing, the luge, 100-meter freestyle swimming, and gymnastics. Baseball sustained its audience and grew as television increased its distribution. World Series television broadcasts, for example, were highly successful in the first 25 years of this generation.

The Television Generation also saw the expansion of two major Monopoly Generation sports—boxing and horse racing—but fan interest and attendance began to decline as the competitive marketplace changed. Even sports such as track and field in off-Olympic years began giving way to competitive pressures from other activities. Other sports appeared and capitalized on the increased exposure of television. Professional wrestling became a popular television attraction, as did basketball, roller derby, college boxing, tennis, and golf. It was becoming increasingly clear that the marketplace was simultaneously expanding and tightening for sports. The old notion that, like a city or state, a sport would last forever and have a dedicated repeat fan market was eroding.

Broadcasting sports on television had an immediate impact on fans. If they were listening to the radio or reading the newspaper, fans in the previous generation had to rely on an interpretation by a third party to imagine Ty Cobb sliding spikes up or Bronco Nagurski slamming into a concrete wall after a touchdown and declaring, "That last guy hit me kind of hard." Now people could see the game without going to the venue, and, once you bought the television set, the ticket to watch was free.

Television also created new opportunities for both monopoly sports and emerging sports to grow. In the first few years of television broadcasting, for example, sports made up 60 percent of all television programming.[6] Sports were easy to shoot, low budget, and a high-profit programming option for the networks. This prompted ABC in 1961 to produce the *Wide World of Sports*, which aired on Sundays and showcased a variety of often underexposed sporting competitions—ski jumping, cliff diving, firemen competitions, and daredevil Evel Knievel clearing 14 Greyhound buses in King's Mill, Ohio. Roone Arledge's innovation of Wide World provided the sports public with its first taste of alternative sports, which increased the awareness of less conventional sports around the globe and foreshadowed the development of extreme sports.

Another innovation in sports television was NFL Films, founded by Ed Sabol and his son Steve in 1962. NFL Films merged sports and Hollywood film and turned highlights of football games into documentaries of on-screen battles. They recreated games using slow motion, unconventional camera angles, in-game audio from players and coaches, background music that mixed symphonic orchestra and popular sounds,[7] and the deep, epic voice of narrator John Facenda. This combination of sports, storytelling, and filmic elements could make a 40-point blowout a compelling piece of entertainment or build the mythical qualities of past Super Bowl champions. NFL Films was one of the first attempts to recast sporting events in a story format and was an important signal to the rest of the industry that a market for packaged television reruns of sports history existed.

In this era, sports programming proliferated, and television audiences expanded, creating a highly lucrative market for the networks, sponsors, and sports industry. Television networks replaced radio as the primary distributor of sports, and sponsors competed to advertise their product to the growing number of sports viewers. Profits in the sports industry in turn soared as both owners and eventually athletes benefited. In the midst of this, the Television Generation saw the number of television channels expand from three over-the-air networks to seventy-four cable channels in 1989[8] and the amount of sports on television steadily rise.

With substantial television revenues now in play, the power structure in the sports industry shifted and changed. Sponsors and networks became more invested and involved in the industry with each spending increasingly large amounts of money on sports. However, in this generation it was the sports and leagues that were often in the best power position. Networks were hungry for sports programming, and the competition between them to broadcast games was fierce. In the battle for rights fees, leagues essentially went to the highest bidder. Over this period, the rights fees for all the major sports increased as new, specialized sports channels, such as ESPN, entered the competition and expanded the audience. In many regions, sports media became a primary programming component of nationally syndicated networks such as WGN in Chicago, WOR in New York, and TBS in Atlanta.

In terms of the power structure, owners and leagues ceded increasing control to players, as the boost of television revenue gave the players more leverage. This rise in player salaries was also fueled by the implementation of the free-agency system in baseball in 1976. It was an era when the players began to make enough money to enable them to work full time in the sport. A new class of specialists arose during this generation: the agent, who represented the players and frequently negotiated not only their contract but endorsement deals, licensing agreements, and cross-sector appearances. The sports star became a product, as a galaxy of support services began to capitalize on off-field performances in sectors and in magnitude of dollars that were unheard of in the previous generation. Muhammad Ali, Arnold Palmer, Pele, Joe Namath, and Chris Evert were just a few name-brand stars that emerged as multisectored attractions. In many ways, the agents became one of the key definers of the generation as most revenue sports were now forced to deal with the emerging star class.

In the Television Generation, the relationship between the fan and the sports star and team began to change. On the one hand, through media and fan promotions, sports stars became more knowable. Fans were able to have access to more information about their family life, hobbies, and scandals. The Television Generation introduced the concept that athletes' lives were an open book for intimate disclosures. On the other, the fan day-to-day relationships that were part of the Monopoly Generation began to disappear as teams and players developed a set of higher standards for their daily participation. It became routine for players to eat in private, fly on team jets, park their luxury vehicles in special lots, and live in gated communities protected by security cameras. As a result, the Monopoly Generation days of sports stars carrying on questionable or illegal behavior in anonymity had largely ended, and taking care of your off-the-field image became a pressing concern.

The traditional season boundaries of the Monopoly Generation began to erode in this era. The seasons began to overlap as more sports entered the marketplace and traditional sports expanded their seasons to generate more profit. The NFL was now ending deep in the middle of the winter. The NBA played its final championship game in the heat of the summer. And MLB was heading toward the winter equinox. The boundaries of the Monopoly Generation scheduling were quickly dissolving as each sport defined itself as a monolith. And television breakout sports such as golf and tennis increased the overlap pressure by spanning most of the year.

Facilities in this generation were surprisingly mediocre. It was as if the pressure of television forced the builders and planners to panic, lose their aesthetic judgment, and erect sterile, unattractive venues. The Astrodome in Houston, the Metrodome in Minneapolis, the Kingdome in Seattle, and even open-air stadiums such as Shea Stadium in New York and Veterans Stadium in Philadelphia were examples. If you weren't going to watch the game on television, the alternative was a stone-cold, concrete, and lifeless facility that was large, impersonal, and fan-unfriendly.

At first, television was feared by many of the sports industry leaders. It was a hard sell for those who thought that television was stealing the in-stadium audience, and, in response, they rationed the number of games and events. Sports such as roller derby, professional wrestling, and boxing dominated early television broadcasting because they often featured what amounted to a studio audience for a large television market. These sports also quickly understood the value of television and began identifying and developing sports stars such as Gorgeous George in wrestling, the former Michigan State welterweight phenomenon Chuck Davey in boxing, and Loretta "Little Iodine" Behrens in roller derby. The star culture began to shift from an on-the-field-only performer to someone who appeared in the living room and needed a persona and accompanying storyline for an increasingly diverse audience base. The difference from the Monopoly Generation was that more people could watch, and business models for extracting maximum value from on-field performance were beginning to evolve.

Television expanded the market opportunities for targeting, and a new class of communication specialists began developing methodologies to more effectively reach fans. What was once a male-dominated market of sports fans began to expand to include women as well as far broader groups than the traditional fan base. African Americans, Hispanics, and Asian Americans were not only represented on the field but also became important fan markets for the industry.

Televised sporting events such as the 1958 NFL Championship game between the New York Giants and Baltimore Colts and the Bobby Riggs versus Billie Jean King gender tennis showdown elevated these sports into national prominence. Television was now the horse that pulled the cart. It was becoming clear that without the exposure of the Television Generation, many sports would not have experienced the growth in audience and revenue that they did. However, with the increased exposure, the Television Generation both reconfigured and complicated the sports market and helped set into motion the events that would more fully develop in the Highlight Generation.

Television Generation (1950–1990)

1. *Cultural:* Television virtually saturated the market. New classes of sports consumers emerged and redefined industry practices.
2. *Products:* Football and basketball became major professional sports. Traditional sports such as horse racing and boxing began to diminish, and television sports such as professional wrestling, roller derby, and skiing found mass audiences in the early years.
3. *Distribution:* Sports play-by-play radio began to decline in influence, and television viewing became the class leader for live sports. Newspapers and magazines changed their style to compete with television and began deemphasizing game action and emphasizing personal storylines.
4. *Power structure:* The power in the manager-player relationship became both more balanced and contentious as unions, agents, and television revenue drove contracts.
5. *Infrastructure:* Seasons became indistinguishable and overlapped, threatening fan loyalties. Domed stadiums were in fashion, and large, impersonal open-air facilities were common.
6. *Attraction:* Sports programs became more specialized, adding marketing, public relations, communication, and advertising specialists. The sports industry became more quantitative, relying heavily on data from sports polls and buying trends.

Highlight Generation (1990–Present)

The explosion of new media technologies defines the Highlight Generation. In this stage, the communication marketplace is saturated with information, and attracting and keeping fan attention has become much more challenging. One response to this change in the communication environment is that media have turned to the highlight capsule, which cuts to the chase and gets to the bottom line; it has grown in popularity as fans have become accustomed to its quick pace and clear content. In this media relationship, there is a premium on speed and the visual image.

In the sports world, the highlight has revolutionized how fans receive and process sports information. The highlight is so ingrained in viewers that ESPN's Chris Berman's "Fastest 3 Minutes," which crams the action of 13 NFL games into three minutes of highlights, has become the type of condensed, time-efficient, and entertaining sports news that fans have come to expect. In these compressed enactments, all fans see is what the producer thinks is the critical moment of impact; how the teams got there is irrelevant. A highlight viewer can honestly say the next morning, "I saw Indianapolis beat Baltimore last night. Manning threw a six-yard pass, and they won by four."

In this generation, there are two powerful communication forces that are seemingly at odds with each other. On one hand, the media industry has, in reaction to fan attention spans and the need to generate more revenue, moved toward a compressed strategy that takes just about all material and reduces it in time. Commercials, for example, that may have run for 60 seconds in the Television Generation are now being miniaturized to as few as five seconds. The powerful story structure that dominates most communication has also been reduced to sometimes startlingly small, condensed, complete stories. A media-savvy viewer demands the most information in the least amount of time.

On the other hand, new media, as illustrated by blogs and podcasts, are characterized by seemingly endless conversations that are growing in popularity. The same fans who want compressed information because they're too busy for more expanded coverage are quite willing to plow through hours and hours of deeply developed and sometimes circular sports material. Much of this counterforce paradox can be explained by fans' ability to manage the different information sources and formats at the same time—a critical issue for any sports product developing messages through various channels.

The dominance of the highlight illustrates a critical shift in the culture of this generation—an increasing emphasis on youth. Connecting to youth is for many sports their lifeline, but trying to find and reach them in such a media-intense environment has become more difficult than it used to be. Much of the youth problem stems from what has been termed "media-multitasking behavior," which accounts for young people's seemingly simultaneous interaction with video games, television, the Internet, cell phones, and other new communication and media technologies. This technological interplay has become a signal to the sports industry that measuring success by attendance and television alone is a dangerous misunderstanding of what is going on in the youth world.

Tracking down youth and understanding how they spend their time and what they like to do have become a search worthy of Harry Potter. In response to the challenge, the industry has had to furiously adjust to the rapidly shifting behaviors of the youth culture. For example, Nielsen Media Research now generates ratings for video-game console usage, and those ratings have been consistently higher than those for most major cable networks. Despite youth's video-game passion, young people are watching television at record levels because of cable access in their bedrooms. As a result, television viewing for the youth market has become more of a singular and personal experience than it once was.[9] As new technologies enter the marketplace, youth media habits will inevitably change and sometimes contradict what became institutionalized youth communication and marketing strategies. The only certainty is that an enigmatic, technologically savvy, and highly lucrative youth generation has now emerged, and it will continue to affect how the sports industry thinks, plans, and executes.

This emphasis on youth does not exclude the dilemma in this generation of reaching and marketing to the older generations of sports fans. An important market continues to be Baby Boomers who are also adopting new technologies and have the resources to spend large amounts of money on sports events. *There is nothing more frightening to a sport than to imagine 50-year-olds deciding that basketball is no longer of any interest and bass fishing and hang gliding are going to dominate the majority of their time.* The traditional path—play the sport in youth, create idol relationships with stars, and then as an adult become an active fan going to games and watching the remainder on television—is in jeopardy. The challenge for the sports industry is to find other avenues and paths to create committed fans.

Sports products have had more opportunities for exposure in this generation as the number of distribution channels has increased. While the dominant sports of the Monopoly and Television Generations are still active, the infusion of new sports and the emergence of others have complicated the marketplace. The most influential new sports are extreme sports, which include skateboarding, surfing, snowboarding, motocross, and BMX. Emerging sports like poker, bass fishing, and bull riding have also made an impact and are now routinely televised with their audience share continuing to increase. Other sports properties have benefited from expanded distribution opportunities such as the Arena Football League (AFL), Major League Soccer (MLS), and K1 fighting.

Amateur sports programs such as those in high schools and Division II and III colleges are also trying to capitalize on media outlets and greater television exposure in the face of increased competition from professional and Division I sports. In order to protect their market share, high school basketball and football games are more frequently televised—an unprecedented and radical change in their "state tournament only" media philosophy. The high school coverage of LeBron James and the excitement of the great football rivalries on Friday nights have drawn attention to high school basketball and football around the United States. The whole concept in high school sports of protecting your market by restricting access to games to on-site paid admission has given way to the reality of television exposure. In this generation, the war cry is, "If we don't see you, you don't exist."

The means of distribution have also revolutionized the way fans experience sports. In previous generations, sports fans were limited to regularly reading local newspaper stories about the hometown team or watching the Saturday network game of the week. As the number of products and distribution channels increases, fans in the Highlight Generation have sports options and choices that were unthinkable in the past. Satellite radio and television, the Internet, cell phones, and video games all have changed the sports experience to make it more global, mobile, and personalized. These new technological capabilities have widened and multiplied the dimensions of being a fan, thus creating a fan experience that is unlike any of those of the previous generations.

In this technology-driven marketplace, the power structure is less certain than it once was because the various decision makers are often in conflict over revenue and exposure. As a result, media broadcasters, sponsors, and sports properties find themselves breaking away from traditional power arrangements and sorting out new ways to best maximize profit for all involved. One example is in television agreements. Some sports properties such as the Arena Football League and the National Lacrosse League are engaging in an emerging trend—a pure revenue-sharing plan with their television partners instead of a guaranteed rights fee. These new types of arrangements may symbolize the end of big media's willingness to spend an exorbitant amount of money on sports programming and a critical shift in power relations from a market with only a few players and unlimited resources to a market with multiple players and competition for resources.

The explosion of media has also given unprecedented access to the inner workings of sports. As a result, the entire sports industry has become subject to communication intensity and exposure. With increased media scrutiny, all members of the sports industry, from the players to the owners, are now under a magnifying glass for behavior. Unlike previous generations, the actions off the court or field are more explicitly exposed and can often become more important than behavior during the sports performance. The storyline, as a result, often overshadows the event itself. In this generation, it has become an axiom: If there is no story, there is no audience. This is a caution to all members of the sports industry that whether on-field or off, they're on display.

Don't Throw Chairs and Stay Away from Call Girls

At the beginning of the television era, coaches and managers were largely exempt from public scrutiny. Bud Wilkinson, the outstanding football coach of the Oklahoma Sooners in the 1950s, still holds the Division I football record with 47 straight wins in an era that his team dominated. Wilkinson's image was of a tall, blonde, blue-eyed commander who was known as politically conservative and highly moral. He was so well thought of that he almost became a U.S. Senator for Oklahoma. On the sidelines he wore a suit and a fedora, looking very much like the chairman of the board of General Motors. It was decades later that it was published that he was a big time country club drinker and sometime womanizer and that he had a large sized ego.[10]

Contrast Wilkinson's ability to mask his personal life with the litany of troubled coaching careers in the Highlight Generation: former Indiana coach Bobby Knight, former Alabama football coach Mike Price, former University of Washington football coach Rick Neuheisel, former Iowa State basketball coach Larry Eustachy, on-again, off-again, now permanently off Cincinnati basketball coach Bob Huggins, four-day Arizona Diamondbacks manager Wally

(Continued)

(*Continued*)

Backman, and five-day Notre Dame football coach George O'Leary. In each case, it could be argued that in the Monopoly Generation they would have kept their jobs and that the media and their blog counterparts would have kept their fingers off the keyboard and their mouths shut.

What has happened between the generations of the Monopoly, Television, and now the Highlight? The revenue, exposure, and outsized salaries have produced a scrutiny that is unprecedented in sports history. There is a blog, *Sports Illustrated* cover story, breaking news on ESPN's *SportsCenter*, or an unhappy spouse just waiting for a misstep.

Contrast the Highlight Generation with the lack of scrutiny coaches of the Monopoly Generation received. The life of the great Notre Dame football coach Knute Rockne was presented in the 1941 film *Knute Rockne All American*. In many scenes, Rockne's personal and professional life was distorted. For example, a major piece of the Rockne legend was his exaggerated chemistry skills, which were allegedly so strong that in coaching football he may have sacrificed a Nobel Prize. Another fiction was his claiming that All-American halfback George Gipp asked him to "Win one for the Gipper." There's no evidence that this was true, and Rockne used the plea more than once to inspire his football teams to victory.[11] There is no telling how many coaches would have lost their jobs in the early half of the twentieth century if they had to bear the scrutiny of the current environment. The lesson for the sports industry is that there is no longer any separation between the on- and off-field behavior of coaches and players.

The increasingly dominant agents, who are continuing to set the standard and stage-manage multimillion-dollar deals for their clients, are becoming more visible and involved in this generation's power structure. Agents such as Scott Boras, Drew Rosenhaus, Arn Tellem, and Mark Shapiro in the United States and Pini Zahavi and Jorge Mendes in Europe have affected the marketplace with the numbers of players they represent and the contracts they demand from owners. The criticism of agents is that they often upset the power structure by increasing the rates of player turnover, driving up costs for owners to keep star players, and sometimes becoming more of a burden than a respected business partner. At the same time, they put pressure on the industry to increase the bottom line and often serve as mediators to keep the peace among athletes, owners, and sponsors.

Agents are part of a growing subindustry in sports that is composed of a variety of support services. There are sports-related services that include personal trainers, physicians, nutritionists, and other medical specialists that are designed to help athletes improve their physical and mental performance skills. In the field of sports psychology, for example, it is now estimated that 50 to 65 percent of professional teams employ a sports psychologist to consult with players on issues of concentration and to help break slumps.[12] There are also non-sports–related support services that help manage an athlete's career away from competition, which include life coaches, financial advisers, stylists, and publicists. An indicator of the growing use of these support services is *OverTime Magazine*, which is specifically targeted at professional athletes and addresses business and lifestyle issues. The magazine's goal is, "To arm athletes with information they can use to enhance their finances and their lifestyles, their present and their future."[13] The increases in sports and non-sports support services are an example of how sophisticated and specialized the industry has become and the multiple sectors that comprise it.

The complex set of support services underscores the increasing strategic planning now occurring across the industry. Sports have turned into somewhat of a predictive science as breeding and developing new athletic talent has become a necessity to regenerate and reload the talent base. The industry's high stakes have trickled down to lower sports levels as the desperate search for the next superstar occurs in summer development camps, specialty training centers, foreign countries, and the complex databases of computer scouting programs. Scouts from colleges and professional leagues blanket the country looking for the next Wayne Gretzky who is often a fifth grader. For example, former high school All-American and University of Florida quarterback Chris Leak was offered in middle school a full athletic scholarship to Wake Forest University. Superstar swimmers Michael Phelps and Ian Thorpe, like many highly touted basketball players, skipped the college level and became professional swimmers with their private coaches, managers, and endorsement deals. That beats taking the SAT prep class multiple times to gain an edge.

Jean Carlos Chera is a nine-year-old Brazilian who tips the scales at 77 pounds and is 4 feet 6 inches tall. Most kids of his age are learning basic math and geography and wondering what's going on outside their neighborhood. Chera, who plays soccer in the south Brazilian state of Parana, is one of the hottest soccer prospects in the world. He has already been approached by as many as eight European clubs including Manchester United and FC Porto of Portugal, who have asked for videotapes of his matches.[14] How soon he will appear on the soccer fields of the major teams is hard to predict. Sports teams have moved to the old Hollywood studio model, which invented discovering young talent—Judy Garland and Mickey Rooney—teaching them to walk, talk, socialize, learn their ABCs, and perform like adults.

In this generation sporting seasons continue to expand, but the number of new competitors continues to disrupt traditional boundaries. The most influential seasonal change of this generation is that sports products have become available year round. It is now commonplace for the NFL draft, which occurs in April, to be the subject of much insider gossip in the prior December or for the MLB hot stove league to heat up the day after the World Series and stay warm until spring training. Because of high player turnover, the off-season in some sports has nearly become as important and widely covered as the playing season. In other cases, NASCAR and tennis have only two months of off-season, while golf offers events from January to December. The media and sports properties are influencing this year-round structure with the addition of team-only television channels, Web sites, and off-season meet and greets. Following the Milwaukee Bucks can now become a full-time job as team promoters and sponsors develop a 365-day calendar of events to keep the fans occupied.

The Highlight Generation saw the rapid construction of new fan-friendly venues and the rapid destruction of the concrete monstrosities of the Television Generation. The venues have become all-inclusive experience centers that now use food, customer service, and technology as attractions. Some stadium developers have traveled back to the earliest years of the Monopoly Generation in search of the right mix of nostalgia and technology. In MLB alone, there have been 18 new ballparks built since 1990 with many using this time-sensitive strategy. The throwback ballparks of Camden Yards in Baltimore, Jacobs Field in Cleveland, and AT&T Park in San Francisco attempt to re-create the past but also stay current. AT&T Park, for example, has installed wireless Internet in its own nostalgic bayside venue so that fans can stay connected to the rest of their world while they're at the ballgame. In international markets, Asian stadiums such as Japan's Yokohama Stadium and China's Shanghai International Circuit raceway and European stadiums such as Ireland's Croke Park and Germany's AOL Arena have been newly constructed or renovated to integrate more technology and amenities into the game attendance experience. These experience-centered stadiums are increasingly sports' answer to the threats of more attractive media at home as venues continually improve their amenities to attract fans.

The attractions of the Highlight Generation have centered on two major strategies: stars and events. It is an era in which stars dominated and crossed over into other sectors of entertainment. An obvious example is Michael Jordan, who revolutionized the idea of the professional athlete as a brand. He combined his outstanding basketball career with major promotion campaigns in shoes, clothing, cologne, and movies, which all made him a global star. Less visible but arguably no less successful in growing his sport is skateboarder Tony Hawk. He has promoted his name and sport through several versions of his video game, as the star competitor of the X Games, and by endorsing products from McDonald's to Quiksilver. Both the Jordan and Hawk brands were executed with a clear strategic plan with distribution carefully selected and goals distinctly outlined.

The marketing for these and other athletes is based on synergy. Building and distributing attractions around the players is a key to their success. The same principles are applied to the sporting events of this generation, in which we see the events becoming packaged and distributed over multiple platforms. Events like college bowl games or the NBA All-Star game serve as anchors for marketing and advertising campaigns, sponsorship parties, and merchandising opportunities. It is now the practice of marketers to build four-day entertainment experiences around a three-hour game to maximize the benefits an event can provide. This is all in an effort to attract the attention of fans and also provide the sponsors with an opportunity to share in the experience. The underlying fundamental strategy is that fans are not going to watch or attend if we don't make these events seem like an important, once-in-a-lifetime experience that cannot be missed. Underlying star launchings and event synergies is the willingness to institute transformation and to try new combinations of relationships that can connect to the fan.

The Highlight Generation is the quintessential new combination and offers something for everyone. It's not uncommon for a sports fan to access as many as eight different distribution channels in one day to receive and view sports information. This rapid fire, often seemingly disconnected form of sports communication is the product of a media convergence that has provided both threats and new opportunities for everyone in the entertainment industry. The sorting out of what could only be described as an embarrassment of riches leads directly to the challenge of engaging the Elusive Fan.

Highlight Generation (1990–Present)

1. *Cultural:* A new information society has evolved. Traditional sporting events become reconfigured into highlights and interactive Internet conversations, and there is an accompanying increasing focus on the youth market.
2. *Products:* Extreme sports and other youth-oriented sports become mainstream. Individualism becomes more pronounced and, coupled with technological innovations, makes the market for team sports less certain.
3. *Distribution:* New media become dominant. Almost daily, innovations appear that make the sports market more fragmented and provide fans with more options.
4. *Power structure:* The power in the Highlight Generation becomes less certain as the media, agents, players, owners, and sponsors are often in conflict with one another over revenue and exposure. There are increasing instances where ownership is taking a bolder stand against player and agent demands as the stakes become greater and the struggle over media rights continues to explode.
5. *Infrastructure:* The concept of sport seasons becomes increasingly meaningless. Fans can access information and highlights of their sport any time of the year. Facilities become all-inclusive experience centers with a strong emphasis on themes drawn from place identity.
6. *Attraction:* Everyone is seeking strategies to attain revenue from new media sources and to retain profitability in the old ones. Fans are becoming used to interaction with sports and are increasingly willing and able to participate in sports content production.

CHASING THE ELUSIVE FAN

The three generations of sports—Monopoly, Television, and Highlight—have led to the emergence of the Elusive Fan. The Monopoly Generation marked the true industrialized beginning of sports and was identified by a limited number of sports, powerful owners, and the emerging influence of sports media. In contrast, in the Television Generation, a new group of sports were introduced that were suitable to the new medium's need for programming, the fan market became more diverse, and some traditional sports began to feel the pressure of competition and consequently were threatened by decline. The Highlight Generation was defined by an increased emphasis on youth and the proliferation of technology and new media that spawned sports outlets, creating entirely new and specific genres of viewership and listenership. Over these generations, the fan gradually gravitated toward the center of attention as the industry evolved and the communication and marketing strategies became more sophisticated. The Elusive Fan now has numerous choices and cannot be counted upon for loyalty and long-term commitment. As a result, the industry today faces its greatest challenges.

The sports marketplace is the most uncertain it has ever been. For most in the sports industry, it is a perplexing puzzle with daily battles that seek to answer the seemingly ever-evolving problem. Resting at the center of this problem is attracting the Elusive Fan. This is not to say that fans have not been difficult in the past to access and to bring into the sports fold. It is simply more complicated today. Emerging technologies, changing family structures, large numbers of competing activities, and higher expectations all conspire to make the fan a cherished and highly sought-after commodity.

CONCLUSION

In 1920, pro football was besieged by a disorganized product, and owners were stealing ballplayers from college programs and complaining about out of control salaries and frequent player defections to other teams. The owners met in a Hupmobile auto dealership in Canton, Ohio, and began the process of eventually becoming the National Football League in 1922. In addition to their control issues, football was fragmented as town and city teams played each other in a helter-skelter manner. The owners were determined to create a league that was professional and that would compete with the far more successful college brand of the sport. The rewards for their steadfastness and vision are illustrated by the National Football League growing into a $5.7 billion in revenue business.[15]

While sports have always faced challenges for market share, attention of the media, and respectability, there has never been a period in sports history that combines all these factors in such a seemingly overwhelming fashion.

The problems of sports are unlikely to be solved in a Hupmobile showroom, but they reaffirm fundamental issues that those football pioneers faced: produce a market-oriented product, satisfy audiences' needs for sports viewing and participation, and distribute that sport in a meaningful and fan-centered manner. The next chapter examines an important step in that process: connecting fans to sports.

Chapter

$$\boxed{3}$$

HOW FANS CONNECT

Hal has a decision to make. He's allocated $2,000 to spend on sports events for the year. Last year, he spent it all flying from his home-town of Miami to London to watch the Chelsea Football Club play at Stamford Bridge. He had a great time, but it left him nothing to spend on sports for the rest of the year. He sat home and watched television. This year he is trying to spread his dollars for the maximum sports entertainment value. He can choose to split season tickets in the upper deck for the Florida Marlins or buy a 20-game pack to the Miami Heat. He recently received a brochure from the Miami Hurricanes informing him that he could not only afford to get season tickets to Hurricane football games, but as a graduate, he could go to special events as a member of the booster club. Lately, he's been interested in NASCAR and would like to go to the regular season and championship Nextel Cup races at the Homestead Speedway. He can not only afford to buy a pass to the infield but he could also take his girlfriend. These *are very tough decisions for a fan of sports who is typically on a limited budget.*

Hal's dilemma is a snapshot of what most sports fans face—lots of options and limited resources. There are, of course, exceptions. Some Green Bay Packers fans, for example, whose entire lives are dictated by the players in the green and yellow, may care less about the NBA, Timbersports, golf, or anything else. They buy shares in the club, go to all the games, attend fan fests, collect jerseys, are thrilled by seeing a Packer in a restaurant, and are avid, dedicated one-sport fans. But in reality, fans are not singularly committed, have to make choices, have limited finances, and are *gettable* with the right stimulus. Sports decision makers have a different agenda. They are interested in increasing fan commitment, and in general, more consumption of their sport, programming, or product.

The first critical step in reaching, attracting, and retaining fans is understanding not only who the fan is but *how the fan connects to a sport*. This chapter is divided into four parts: the connections of sports fans, connection entryways, how fans make decisions, and the levels of fan intensity. In each section, the focus is on developing a deeper understanding of the lifeline of the industry—the fan.

SPORTS FAN CONNECTIONS

A traditional way of thinking about consumers is to segment them into two categories: demographics and values.

- *Demographic analysis* looks extensively at a person's age, gender, race and ethnicity, occupation, education, and location. In sports, there is a strong emphasis on using demographics to identify and appeal to different marketplaces such as the Hispanic market or males aged 18–34. These data are often easily accessible as demographic information can be gathered from a number of reliable sources, and the next step of extrapolating to your own sport has become routine. However, no group in the United States is currently more desirable than males 18–34 years old because they are a lucrative market but not traditionally as reachable and predictable as other age groups.

- *Value analysis* examines the underlying lifestyle of the target markets. Values could include religion, patriotism, loyalty, ethics, and tradition. In sports, there are a number of connections that can be made to these values. For example, NASCAR not only markets excitement and danger but also appeals to patriotism and down-home values to build its marketplace. In contrast, professional basketball is set in an urban environment and is more individualistic and contemporary. Each of the two sports is currently reexamining its value appeal and trying to expand and present alternative sets to broaden its market. NASCAR is moving into the city, and basketball is emphasizing professionalism and globalism.

In this Elusive Fan age, the sports market needs to be segmented into additional useful and precise dimensions in order to connect with an ever-changing fan marketplace. These motivational and emotional connections are often overlooked, yet they have enormous influence on the experience. In the search for more meaningful relationships with sports fans, there have been a number of research methodologies developed that attempt to understand how fans connect with sports.

Looking for Fans in All the Right Places

- Social scientist Daniel L. Wann devised the Sport Fan Motivation Scale (SFMS), which isolates eight major motives for becoming a sports fan: eustress (positive stress), escape, entertainment, economic, aesthetic, group affiliation, self-esteem, and family needs.[1] Working with these factors, SFMS studies suggest that sports marketers pay attention to their relative importance to improve the sales of their team and products.
- GSD&M, a marketing consulting company, devised the "purpose-based branding" research program designed to discover the meaning of a brand. Once understood, the idea is to correlate the fundamental and nuanced layers of the brand in order to connect to the consumer's values and expectations.[2]
- The sports marketing firm Octagon has developed "Passion Drivers," a study which tested 12 drivers that influence fan commitment to a sport. Some of the drivers are nostalgia, athlete affinity, team obsession, love of the sport, and active appreciation.[3] The purpose is to uncover the emotional underpinnings that influence buyers' purchasing decisions.

(Continued)

(Continued)

- Brand Keys, a market research firm, has devised the Sports Loyalty Index, which is a survey of sports teams and their fan relationships. The index has four categories that determine loyalty. The most important category is pure entertainment value followed by authenticity, fan bonding, and history and tradition.[4] The intent is for professional teams to improve their revenues by assisting them with loyalty rankings that will allow them to target their markets more effectively.
- An innovation in consumer connection research is illustrated by Procter & Gamble's CEO, A. G. Lafley, who has moved out of the boardroom and into the buyer's home. He makes frequent trips to visit customers while they're washing their clothes or cooking a meal to see how they use the product in real life.[5] A sports equivalent is a brand decision maker sitting in the stands, buying food from the vendors, and waiting in line for an autograph.

FAN CONNECTION POINTS

An examination of the fan connection points often explains why people are attracted to sports products and choose one sport over another. Fans can connect to sports through a single connection or a set of multiple connections. Certain sports have natural ties that have been historically or nationalistically ingrained, integrated in the sport itself, or are products of cultural shifts and trends. Baseball, for example, has always had a strong family and historic attachment because of its deep roots in the early formation of the American sports experience. European soccer has maintained a strong place affiliation with city and country, which is often the determinant of emotional connections.

Essential Connectors

Connectors are the touch points that bond fans to sports. The connectors do not all work in the same manner because they have different origins and the fan relates to them for different reasons. For example, the two most understood and considered critical to almost any sports venture are the *essential connectors*:

star and *place*. Star is the humanized content of sports that fans can relate to and, through this relationship, express a wide number of emotions. Place is where the sport becomes deeply rooted, is played, and intersects with many emotions that relate to community identification and involvement.

Star

A star connection can be to a player, manager, team, league, facility, or any other potentially promotable sports industry product. A star is someone or something that has the name and attraction potential to connect fans. The most familiar stars are the players themselves who attract fans to the sport by their actions, personae, and playing ability. In other examples, a team can be the star, such as the Los Angeles Lakers, or a facility such as Wrigley Field. In such a crowded sports marketplace, branded names become more valuable because they differentiate the product from the competition.

In using stars as a fan connector, sports properties need to maintain a steady inventory of stars to develop and promote, be willing to support the star, place them in proximity to the fan, and reload when necessary to constantly replenish the star attractions. Reloading a star is a continuous problem, and, in the demanding and quickly changing media age, to be without a star base can be a serious disadvantage. For many sports, this requires a different view of the star culture and a willingness to broaden the possible star mix. This is especially true with the individual star when departures, poor performance, or shifting styles can undermine a permanent brand position.

Reward Star power is a clear, identifiable connection for sports in virtually every marketplace. It often serves as the centerpiece for products such as jerseys, shoes, memorabilia, road trips, and almost all other sports spin-offs.

Risk Star power has often been viewed as a volatile, temporary, and often difficult connection to institutionalize for a sports property. In professional sports, the frequent turnover of players has made management somewhat reluctant to invest in stars and has made many fans cynical about identifying with vagabond players. Even the most historic and revered facilities can become outdated or threatened by changes in surroundings or new technologies and architectural innovations that create less of a connection and make them more of a liability.

Implication Sports decision makers must be willing to select a few promising players to promote as stars, cross-sector stars into other entertainment channels, and take advantage of fantasy sports and video games by integrating them into marketing campaigns. On the broader star front, it is important to be aware of star potential when designing facilities, creating events, or even hiring coaches and management.

Place

Place connections capitalize on the presence of hometown teams, athletes, and facilities and instill in fans an allegiance to the sports that are from their area or represent the community. These connections are founded on the fans' need for community interaction, affiliation, and attachment to their place of current or previous residence. In many cases, a key aspect of the place's identity is tied up with the sports teams that represent the community. Many of the battles that occur over public funding of facilities revolve around the question of how much the place means to the citizens versus the profit gain of the institution, team, or club.

Another group of fans that is connected to sports through place is made up of school alumni. Alumni belong to a shared culture where, for a number of years, an institution had a monopoly on their attention. These fans are influenced by their previous experiences with the sports teams of their high schools or universities, and they still have attachments to their school. Supporting the school's sports teams is a way for fans to remember their experiences, stay involved with their alma mater, and remain connected to the place. On another level, there are also adopted alumni who, while not ever attending the school, exhibit alumni-like tendencies in their support of a sports program. Notre Dame and Duke are national examples of universities in which the adopted-alumni base is quite large and dedicated. At the high school level, there are schools with national reputations such as De La Salle of Concord, California, and Hoover in Hoover, Alabama, that are supported by loyal alumni who not only attend games but also actively raise funds and serve as strong emotional support for the sports programs.

Reward The importance of place provides sports with a clearly defined fan market that desires affiliation and community interaction. In turn, it provides the fan with an identity and an investment in the community that may not have existed without the sports team.

Risk The place-connected fan can be easily alienated by sports management; political decisions on access, taxes, or perceived blackmail threats of leaving; or institutional changes to a school program. There is also a constant threat that the place, city, facility, or school can lose appeal because the novelty has worn off, competition has newer facilities, unintended consequences such as increased traffic or crime reduce the attractiveness, or the sports program does not maintain the attachment to its fans. In extreme cases, a team can abandon a city, such as in the case of the NFL's Los Angeles Rams, and find that the residents never miss it.

Implication Sports properties and places need to move closer together in planning, development, and implementation. They need each other for branding, image, and economic reasons and this means more careful planning of infrastructure, tying together place activities and sports events more closely, and working with financial models that respect each other's interests. In many ways, place identity is one of the strongest connections. In a society in which people move frequently, the demands of keeping the place attachment often require excellent communication skills and an ability to use new media to connect with nomadic fans.

Communication Connectors

A second set of connection points are the *communication connectors—social currency* and *family*—which have become vital to all sports in the information age. These connections capitalize on the powerful bonding potential of sports and tie fans together through social and emotional sports experiences.

Social Currency

Sports are a universal subject of communication and are a topic of conversation that is acceptable whether riding in a taxicab or beginning a board meeting of a large corporation. They also serve as a common bond between groups of friends, communities, and business and professional relationships across all geographical regions and economic classes. Sports are a form of *social currency*, which is exchanged information that maintains and encourages social interaction. It can be gossip around the water cooler, rapport-building between new acquaintances, or an icebreaker in chemistry class. The social currency connection is not only interactive socially, but it explains in part the relationship component of the popularity of fantasy sports and other interactive sports games.

A critical component of the social currency connection is the social engagements that sports encourage. Sporting events are often social gatherings, with tailgating, parties, and other functions centered around the competition. This atmosphere often motivates fan connection, which is usually not so much about the actual game as it is about the supplementary events. One of the fundamental advantages of social currency is that it appeals to the desire of fans to be part of crowds. This factor is critical to the popularity of Super Bowl parties, pre- and postgame tailgate parties, traveling to away games, playoff celebrations, or 10 people watching a game on television. These relationship experiences not only produce social currency for the fan, but they also encourage fans to associate these experiences with the sport. What energized the classic sports comedy film *Slap Shot* was when the fans became connected to the determined comeback of the Charlestown Chiefs.

Reward Sports are the topic of the day, and often information about events spreads via word of mouth throughout the various social and business communities as a form of communication exchange and relationship building. Social currency fans often are the most easily reachable because they have a need for information to connect.

Risk Emphasizing the social currency connection could result in fans who are more interested in the social interaction than the actual sport. These fans could easily change allegiances if the social experience shifts to another sport. They could also spend more time talking about sports than buying tickets or watching an event. These fans are often referred to as "bandwagon" or "frontrunner" fans and are the most difficult with whom to establish a long-term connection.

Implication Sports properties should develop complete social experience sporting events, provide easy access through Web sites and other new media for inside information, and create forums to facilitate and channel opinions and controversy. In order to deepen the social currency connection, sports need to reach out to social currency fans on rules and strategies since they not only need to understand what they're talking about but also build an appreciation for their chosen topic. The corporate connection is a valuable pipeline to social currency, and encouraging and supporting that relationship has the additional advantage of attracting nonfans to the sport.

Family

Sports in the family environment often enable family members to bond. They are also used to help uphold family traditions and values or connect with distant members of the family tree. Rites of passage are the central connector of families; they link generations of family members with a particular sport or sporting experience. It has become an American ritual for fathers and sons to play catch, a sports activity that has spawned similar family sports bonding moments with parents and all their children. Similarly, if a parent was taken to a baseball game when he or she was a child, that parent could be motivated by that childhood experience to take his or her child to a baseball game.

The family connection breeds and raises new fans because people are often first introduced to sports through their family members. Every time an avid Washington Huskies football family has a new baby enter the family, the football program benefits from grandparents dressing the child in purple Huskies T-shirts and decorating the baby crib with pennants. Reaching youth early in the child development process imprints Washington Huskies on the child's memory channel and increases the potential for creating an enduring fan connection. In this case and others, the sports product serves as a communication connector between family members and creates lasting memories that fans can associate both with the sports experience and their families.

Reward The family connection deepens the fan's association with the sports product and creates more memorable and enduring experiences. This connection is especially effective with multiple generational relationships because sports are a rite of passage and can link families across generations.

Risk Unethical behavior and bad role modeling of sports properties can discourage the family connection. Similarly, poor family experiences while participating in or watching a sport could affect the fan and diminish the possibility of his or her following the sport.

Implication The family is one of the most powerful and meaningful connections. Positioning the sports experience as a family rite of passage is a valuable fan connection tool. In doing so, sports are increasingly competing against experience-based events such as theme parks and multientertainment retail centers. In response, sports properties need to integrate family-oriented activities into their events, build facilities such as play centers in ballparks, and use story structure to develop the family backgrounds of the participants.

Search Connectors

Search connectors make up the final group of connection points and include the *vicarious experience, uncertainty,* and *utopian connections.* These connections enable fans to satisfy a fundamental need and in doing so often construct their own sports world. They have become more valuable to the sports industry as fans seek higher levels of emotional experiences, and architectural, technological, and game theory advances allow fans to interact with sports more than ever before.

Vicarious Experience

Fans can connect to sports by identifying, admiring, or emulating the skills and performance of athletes and teams. Vicarious experiences most effectively connect people who have familiarity with the sport either by participating in it on some level or by playing video games, fantasy sports, or some other technological experiences that emulate a sport. The fan's desire to be closer and have more access to the sport and its athletes fuels this connection. Often the most avid, this fan understands the meaning of each stroke of the swimmer in the 200-meter butterfly and is running along and identifying with each pass of the baton on the anchor leg of the 400-meter relay. The vicarious fan can be attracted to the danger or perils inherent in the sport and often will at some level hope for a car crash or football injury, but usually suppresses it publicly because of the social and moral implications of the desire.

The vicarious experience connection has become more intense as the proliferation of new technologies has brought fans closer to sports. Few sports have benefited more from the vicarious experience connection than Formula 1 and the other professional racing groups that place cameras inside the drivers' cars, enabling the fan to see steering wheels turning, gears shifting, and accidents occurring in seemingly real time as if they were driving. These fans might be the first in line to pick up the latest versions of Madden and NBA Live or spend more time watching the MLB playoffs on television with the pitches intercut with 10 different shots of managers, batters, bullpen pitchers, anxious spouses, and other quick moments before the ball is hurled to the plate.

Reward This fan is in many cases the most avid and likely to pay up for the best seat in the house or buy the largest television screen with the most authentic sounding speakers.

Risk If team behavior or actions do not comport with the vicarious expectations of fans, they can easily be not only disappointed but may drop the sport. They are also more likely to switch allegiances if a sport offers innovations that are not available in their current affiliation.

Implication The vicarious experience connection has been enhanced by the advancements in television, Web sites, and video games that enable the fan to see the sport from the inside out. Continuing to provide more access to the sport through technology can establish an enduring connection with this fan if the technology modifies and upgrades the experience. Video games and fantasy sports are based on the vicarious experience connection, and on-site venues need to experiment with incorporating those interactive qualities into the sport.

Uncertainty

One of the most important attractions of sports has always been the unpredictability. The spontaneity of the action and attempts to predict the outcome keeps fans not only interested but also provides them escape from everyday monotony. Fans seeking uncertainty find the drama and randomness of the sports outcome a compelling attraction and a reason to invest money, time, and energy in being a spectator.

The fan's desire for uncertainty explains in part the popularity of gambling, which both manufactures meaning in sporting events and invests the fan's financial and emotional interest in the outcome. Will the Syracuse basketball team cover the seven-point spread? What are the chances the Los Angeles Dodgers win the division this year? Are the odds on Tiger Woods winning the Masters worth a bet? Should I draft LaDainian Tomlinson over Shaun Alexander in my fantasy football league? The wall that has long existed between most sports and gambling because of ethical issues is beginning to show cracks. NASCAR and the NBA, for example, now license their names to state lotteries,[6] and league-sponsored fantasy sports, while on the surface are not promoting gambling, have an indirect association with the activity. The amount of money wagered formally and informally on sports is in the billions, with the online gaming industry that includes Sportsbook.com and the numerous March Madness betting sites alone receiving $15 to $20 billion in wagers on sports in 2004.[7] This figure does not include personal bets, visits to Las Vegas and other on-site gambling institutions, or all the global gambling not conducted in the United States.

Reward Fans connected to sports through uncertainty will often respond favorably to changes that not unrealistically increase the unpredictability and drama of sporting events. Those uncertainty seekers who bet on sports have a financial and emotional commitment to the sporting event and are likely to attend or watch to monitor their investments.

Risk The uncertainty connection is not as permanent as others since fans linked by this connection are often interested in the most volatile and publicized event and can drift from sport to sport. Gamblers especially may remain elusive and could be content with just watching highlights to confirm whether they've won or lost. Inherent in any gambling endeavor are the risks of intentionally losing, shaving points, or unhealthy associations with gambling interests.

Implication Emphasizing the uncertainty connection is the most delicate ethical area for sports properties because its chief activity, gambling, has been associated historically with corruption. It may well be that the transparency of new media and the needs of the gambling industry to control its increasingly lucrative properties will help monitor the ethical issue. For the members of the sports industry who are watching poker dramatically increase its share of the market, it means inevitably connecting with this huge market and managing both the increasing acceptance of gambling and the undeniable certainty of its uncertainty.

Utopian

The utopian connection attracts fans to sports experiences that represent and remind them of the past; their memories of an earlier time are often idealistic recreations of the sport. They typically dislike the high salaries of professional athletes, labor issues between players and owners, cheating scandals, introduction of technologies, and new styles of play. Instead they desire a simpler, more competition-centered time without the distractions of the industrialized sports world. All the trappings of high-end college and professional sports including walls of sound and multimedia displays discourage the utopian connection, and these fans seek to downsize and pursue less intense experiences. In search of a more authentic sports experience, they may choose to go to a minor league baseball game or an amateur women's tennis tournament because it is less commercial and, "It's about the game."

The utopian connection is not just for an older demographic. Some younger fans may be looking for a sports experience that they've only heard about from family members or wishing for a sport to return to its roots. Influencing the utopian connection for any demographic is a fan's participation experience, which usually occurs when the fan was a child; it may have been sandlot games or pickup three on three basketball on a city court. It's not incidental that childhood games such as kickball, dodge ball, and capture the flag are enjoying a renaissance in adult participation. The utopian connection bonds the fan to the current version of the sport by tapping into the fan's memory channel of past sporting experiences.

Reward If their expectations are met, fans connected through a utopian memory of the sport are often willing to buy memorabilia and take cruises with retired athletes and are enthusiastic about retro sports venues. Utopian fans are a clear and identifiable target as the sports decision maker knows that certain nostalgic appeals will be attractive.

Risk Adaptations and changes to the sports product can alienate fans from the sport. They are the most likely of all fans to migrate to less commercial, more individualistic niche sports that provide intimate experiences and less pageantry—or worse, spend most of their sports hours watching ESPN Classic.

Implication The utopian connection is probably the most complicated fan base for sports properties to segment. Change is inevitable in most sports, and the fan with the utopian connection needs to be accommodated, but there will almost inevitably be issues that they find objectionable. The short-term answer is to maintain the sport's integrity, limit changes in rules that are fundamental to its credibility, and stage events that remind fans of past experiences. In the long term, the advantages of technology, ironically, allow the sports property to identify and then customize its product for the utopian connector. This includes delivering games, products, and historical information on a timely basis. It also enables fans to provide feedback so that they can connect to the sport on their terms.

Sports decision makers have a number of possibilities when examining what connection points to emphasize in their products. The fan connectors of star and place are essential ingredients of most successful sports products, and there are also communication- and search-driven connections that can deepen sports fan relationships. It is critical for sports decision makers to pursue the connection points that differentiate their product from the competition. Without them the Elusive Fan will most often move to another entertainment. The Arena Football League is an example of an emerging sports brand that is benefiting from the power of connections and is building a respectable fan base.

Roller Derby Meets Professional Football

Let's start an indoor football league, with a 50-yard field, pinball-like scoring, and a squad of NFL rejects and wannabes. Sounds like a recipe for disaster given the competition from college and professional football and a direct head-on collision with the NBA, NHL, MLB, and dozens of other sports. Well, it seems to be working. The Arena Football League (AFL) has expanded from 4 teams in 1987 to 19 teams in 2006.[8] During the 2005 season, attendance was 12,872 per game and 1.8 million overall, which is a 50 percent increase from 2001.[9] The league also has television contracts with Fox and NBC, a video-game licensing agreement with EA Sports,[10] and a minor league called the AF2.[11]

What makes this league work? The AFL had the advantage of offering a new brand of football that breaks from the traditional game. It is fast-paced and high scoring with a different color ball and lots of hockey-style checks, and it is a combination of roller derby, professional wrestling, rock concerts, and football. However, many new sports have been introduced that have combined other sports' qualities and become novelty experiences. What makes the AFL work is that it has capitalized on three connection points in its prospective audiences:

Connection Point 1 *Star:* Initially, the star connection for the AFL was the league. As the league has matured, it has developed a star connection through high-profile owners such as Jon Bon Jovi, Mike Ditka, and John Elway.

Connection Point 2 *Family:* Understanding the financial constraints of many of its fans, the league adopted a "Fans' Bill of Rights." A major tenet is, "We believe that every Fan should receive the very best in competitive football, entertainment, merchandise, food and beverage for their purchasing power."[12] Keeping their word, average ticket prices of $22 have made it affordable for a number of families and an attractive alternative to the high prices of other major sports. As a result, families buy around 60 percent of AFL tickets.[13]

Connection Point 3 *Utopian:* While the sport is high-energy and counter-cultural, it does have low salaries, an accessible indoor feel, and affordable ticket prices. It has the potential appeal to the fan seeking a utopian connection because it has at its roots the feel of a sandlot pickup game and is in contrast to the more industrialized college and professional sports.

Benefiting from the popularity of football, the AFL created a credible brand that would attract a fan base during the NFL and NCAA off-season and maintain its appeal through three fan connection points.

SPORTS FAN ENTRYWAYS

Sports products ultimately need to connect with the fan through accessible entryways. There are five primary entryways through which sports fans are reached.

Participation

The most historical and traditional connection entryway is *participation.* Participation accesses most of the fan connection points and is often the most fundamental relationship between the fan and the sport. Playing a sport provides fans with knowledge of the rules and nuances of the sport, an opportunity to bond with fellow participants, and an appreciation for the skills and performance of athletes at higher levels. It is one of the most effective tools of educating and familiarizing a fan with a sport.

As an entryway for connection, participation is particularly effective when fans are in their childhood and have the time and physical ability to play sports. This is an experimental time in which children can try different sports and discover which ones they like or dislike. Participation is also critical in adult years when fans may be introduced to a sport to which they have previously never given much attention such as league dodge ball. Golf, tennis, and racket ball, which are sports that can be played by people of virtually any age, could be described as continuation sports that are heavily represented in the adult population. Moreover, these continuation sports have meaningful adult subcultural groups that congregate around business and social engagements. These participation connection entryways not only have the advantage of teaching people about the sport, but also may convert their play into a fan at the revenue-generating levels of the sport.

The participation channel is not limited to physical activity. The increasing popularity of video games in society has created a seemingly viable alternative to participation. The graphics and playing features in sports video games have become so realistic that interacting with a joystick can teach lessons to a participant about football similar to those learned from putting on a helmet and pads. This is not to say that video games will replace the attraction of movement, sweat, and physical contact, but the competitive and educational qualities of participation in video games and other technological devices can in many cases substitute for the traditional physical world. As an example of this trend, video-game players now have their own version of the Olympics with the annual World Cyber Games, which has attracted more than 4,000 fans to watch other people play video games.[14]

Participation does not always translate into a fan connection. Sports with high participation rates at the youth level such as soccer in the United States have had difficulty converting players into fans at the higher levels of the sport. In contrast, sports with comparatively lower levels of participation such as football have a large fan base. The explanations of these differences depend on a number of factors and are often the result of technology, family involvement, or fan attraction issues at professional, college, or high school levels of the sport. All of this is compounded by a continuing trend in American life that shows a drop in participation across almost every recreational sport. This trend does not currently appear to be correlated to total television sports watching, which continues to rise, but it is certainly cautionary to sports decision makers as it could signal a long-term drop in interest.[15] Despite the seemingly unpredictable effect of participation and its current erosion, it remains a critical entryway to reach and connect with fans.

On-Site Experience

The second fan entryway is the *on-site experience*. In most cases, the sporting event takes place in some kind of facility. It has rules requirements, seats for spectators, and various sight lines for viewing the event. People encounter the sport in a wide range of environments. It can be a high-end National Football League stadium with extensive parking, complete food menus and shops, Jumbotrons and extensive sound systems, and formal introductions of players, all of which become part of the NFL ritual. In contrast, the sport can be smaller scale such as the cross-country or marathon running experience in which people are lined up on paths or streets and find themselves watching an event in far fewer numbers. The expectations of the sport are far different in the latter example, but the rewards if the expectations are met are equally as fulfilling. The marathon fan does not usually expect or could possibly experience the large stadium atmosphere of the NFL but is receiving in exchange a more personalized role in the event and intimacy with the runners.

The critical element for the relationship between the game and the fan is that expectations are met. Fans have built-in frameworks concerning what will satisfy their needs or, in the best examples, exceed them and encourage them to return. This on-site expectation is *gameness*, and it is identifiable by what the fan believes are the rules, boundaries, and satisfaction levels of the experience. Gameness includes a broad range of fan expectations: cheerleaders, sideline markers, booming announcers, flashing scoreboards, and batters pounding on their cleats. Strip away some of these gameness elements and fan satisfaction will inevitably drop. An example of a gameness conflict is the Association of Tennis Professionals' (ATP) proposed shortening of doubles matches to make them less of a second-tier event to the star-studded singles matches. While there was a certain audience that thought of gameness as a traditional tennis match with advantage points and tiebreakers at six games, the ATP believed there was a far broader market that could become connected to the sport if the matches were shortened. The proposal set off a raging controversy among doubles players and the ATP for what constitutes both a fair and attractive doubles match.[16]

Media

The *media* have become the most accessible entryway through which fans connect to sports. The impact of the media is so great that for most sports not to be on television is such a negative that the sport may well fail or lack the ability to connect to fans. There are a number of issues related to the media-fan connection such as how close the media can represent the game, the ability of broadcasters to explain it, how attractive the sport appears in media, and the willingness for the sport to adapt to the media's needs to connect to the audience.

A good example of the media-fan connection is poker, which has become a mainstream sport after the expansion of television broadcasts of the sport and exposure in films such as *Rounders*. When ESPN produced an original series entitled the "World Series of Poker," it took a smoke-filled, claustrophobic game environment into the living rooms of millions of Americans. Poker capitalized on the invention of the built-in lipstick camera that enabled viewers for the first time to see players' cards and in doing so provided the game a variety of storylines including unexpected fortune and sly, unrepentant bluffers. The ability of television to frame the tension opened up the game to a wide audience of players who didn't need any athletic ability to play along or much encouragement to connect to the excitement and rewards. Without television, poker is not a national sport.

Although television exposure has historically been the mass channel for a sports encounter, other media play an important role. Radio broadcasting used to be a mainstay medium and is still the way people driving in their automobiles or doing chores stay in touch with a game. The sports pages of newspapers are highly read in comparison to other sections and, along with sports magazines, often offer the most detailed and comprehensive coverage. New media have become the frontier for keeping in touch with the younger fan. For example, Web sites and, increasingly, cell phones not only connect the sport to the fan but they provide up-to-the-minute information and a more detailed and personalized experience than television.

Sports decision makers are increasingly faced with a paradox. The media is a dominating entryway into the fan's sports world. However, the communication responsibilities become an increasing burden to management as the entryways can become the inquisitors and the seekers of information. Atlanta Braves general manager John Schuerholz, an esteemed dean of the baseball world, laments that in the past he was responsible only for a couple of press conferences a quarter and perhaps answering as few as three inquiries a season. In response to what he terms the "media crush," he observes that it is "far more challenging even for the most intellectually competent among us, especially the young among us who have less experience."[17] The media connection to the fan is now in the process of burning out the traditional gatekeepers because of overwork and redistributing communication responsibilities across a more specialized group of people. The "media crush" is the greatest blessing the sport has ever received. It is also the most difficult to manage and requires an increasingly diligent pursuit of profit-generating venues and experts to manage them.

Word of Mouth

Word of mouth is more than ever a powerful tool for connecting with sports fans. The personal recommendation often has the advantage of credibility since it is built on relationships. Evidence of its connection potential is everywhere. In the past, a family member may have gone to a professional basketball game and talked it up to other relatives who then became interested in attending games and ultimately became fans. A hot streak of a local high school basketball team can spread through the walls and corridors of the school and build attendance.

Word of mouth has always been a staple for connecting sports to fans. It may well be stimulated by a shopping center drop-in, a sports clinic, or a fan day with handouts and player autograph sessions. The frustration for most sports is the scarcity of personal experiences as stars become less accessible and the possibility of an encounter with the fan becomes rarer.

Just in time, new media have begun to compensate for live word of mouth and fans now have unprecedented opportunities to communicate with the sport and each other technologically. A primary word-of-mouth entryway is the Internet and chat groups, blogs, and instant messaging that spread a sports experience quickly throughout the community. While no longer in person, this version of word of mouth is still relatively unfiltered, allows for democratic participation, and deepens the relationship between the sport and the fan. It is such a powerful entryway that promoters have turned to what has been termed *guerilla marketing,* which in one of its practices hires professionals to insert their comments into Internet relationships to stimulate communication about the brand. A variation is *viral marketing*, which also operates off word of mouth by encouraging fans to send information about the sports product throughout their social networks. While the ethics of some of these strategies are questionable, they do place into perspective how important entertainment marketers feel word of mouth is to building a fan base and how the Internet has reinvented the concept.

Mentoring

The final entryway is *mentoring*. When a mentor has a special interest in involving someone in sports, the connection can be very powerful. It could be a father who played football and wants his son to experience it or who spends time with his daughter on the local tennis courts and stimulates her interest in attending a tennis summer camp. It could be a gym teacher in an eighth grade class who motivates a group of girls to not only participate in basketball but to follow it professionally.

Not unlike the changes in word of mouth, mentoring has become far more sophisticated in the Elusive Fan era. Pickup games and informal mentoring relationships have often been replaced by sophisticated and targeted sports camps. America is dotted with these breeding-ground camps that discover kids at early ages, connect them to coaches, and ultimately feed them into the college and professional sports world.

The mentoring connections are probably the most complex for sports to manage because they vary situationally, are often on a one-to-one basis, and have powerful emotional contexts. However, these relationships, because of their difficulty in observing and quantifying, are one of the most important frontiers for reaching the sports fan. Mentoring can come in many forms. It can be intense like the Five Star Basketball camp, a seminal event such as a sports star appearing in a fifth grade class to talk about the value of hard work and discipline, or mediated as in a television program or film. In the movie *Remember the Titans*, Denzel Washington as Coach Herman Boone is a mentor to a segregated community that learns how to coexist. While Washington was an actor playing a coach, his language, behavior, and values portrayed in such a popular medium potentially extend across a broad and often hard-to-reach youth marketplace.

In the earlier generations of sports promotion and marketing, the communication entryways were often seen as incremental and built upon one another in a linear and often passive fashion. So, for example, a mentor relationship might lead to a word-of-mouth recommendation that produced a television experience that ultimately led to the person attending a game—or some other variation of this pattern. The relationships between the entryways of communication were independent of one another and not critical as long as they led to the next step.

In the current communication environment, this entryway experience is now becoming multidimensional. Media, for example, which have often been seen as the most distant and removed from the fan experience, are frequently becoming the most intimate. What this means to the decision maker is that managing the connection points is more complex and demands more understanding of how fans actually interact with the channels. The critical difference between today and the linear model of the past is that the entryways are becoming integrated, and fans are presented with a multiple set of experiences that no longer stand alone. Many sports products are now combining their product-fan interaction with multiple and often simultaneous entryways that are closer to a barrage than a rifle shot.

Soda, Pop, & Run

PepsiCo and MLB have partnered to offer the annual Pepsi Pitch, Hit & Run competition to youth aged 7 to 14. The event is an individual skills competition that tests the ability of a young person to throw strikes, hit for "distance and accuracy," and run the bases with speed. There are four age-divided divisions (7–8, 9–10, 11–12, and 13–14), and the competition initially takes place on the local club level with participants advancing to sectional tournaments and finally the national competition at each year's All-Star game. In 2005, 564,000 young people competed in 3,800 tournaments throughout the nation.[18]

The program is an example of how sports properties and sponsors are attempting to reach and connect with a targeted audience. What makes it effective is the integration of the five connection entryways into a multichannel experience for the targeted fan market.

Participation The program is based on young people playing baseball. It encourages participants to refine their skills, learn to have fun playing the game, and familiarize themselves with the rules and fundamentals of the sport. An advantage of the competition is that it is not nine innings and is played in short bursts, which keep the participants' interest and is a counterstrategy to position baseball as an exciting and challenging sport.

On-Site One of the incentives for children to compete in Pitch, Hit & Run is the chance to play on the same field as professional baseball players. As participants advance to the higher rounds of elimination, the competition takes place at their hometown ballparks, and if the participant makes it to

(Continued)

(*Continued*)

the national finals, at the site of the All-Star game. These on-field experiences connect the younger participants to their favorite baseball players and create lasting memories. As one participant said of the 2005 competition, "Seeing all of those people in the stands and the big Tigers scoreboard and everything, it's pretty cool. Thanks to Pepsi for putting it on for us, so we have a chance to be here and make memories like this."[19]

Media While on a smaller scale, Pitch, Hit & Run participants see themselves covered in the media in a manner similar to the way baseball players are. The MLB Kids Club Web site has a special section on Pitch, Hit & Run in which winning participants are listed and pictures are displayed. There are also programs at the All-Star game that feature the participants and an award ceremony honoring the winners. Much like the on-site channel, the chance for recognition in the media is an incentive to participate, and the experience makes young people the stars in their own version of the sport.

Word of Mouth The competition creates word of mouth throughout the community in which the participant lives. A child's advancement in the tournament has the potential to spread awareness in schools, community groups, recreational baseball leagues, and among friends and families. When a 10-year-old reaches the national competition, the local community can support his efforts, and MLB and Pepsi can benefit from the exposure on the grassroots level from the child's achievements.

Mentoring MLB and Pepsi have included special baseball skills camps during spring training that provide participants with training sessions with MLB players and coaches. One example is the Detroit Tigers' spring training camp where stars Ivan Rodriguez and Dmitri Young and former manager Alan Trammell ran skill stations with other players and coaches for the Pitch, Hit & Run participants.[20] The special training session creates opportunities for personalized interactions with youth and increases the potential for a memorable experience.

The Pitch, Hit & Run tournament has been constructed to emphasize the five critical connection entryways. It doesn't operate on the linear model of sports fan connection in which a young person would go to a game, tell a friend, watch on television, and receive coaching from a mentor. Instead, the program works based on the connectivity of each of these entryways and the access to its players, teams, and facilities that the MLB program provides for its participants. For the young people who participate, the program seeks to create memorable experiences that MLB and Pepsi hope will be associated with their products for a long period of time.

HOW DO FANS MAKE DECISIONS?

Understanding the fan decision-making process is critical to turning sports connections into active fan participation. Some sports fans make sports decisions hourly, while others once a week, month, or year. Whether it is to turn on *SportsCenter* in the morning, watch or attend a game at night, make a lineup change to their fantasy team, plan a trip to spring training, buy new hockey equipment for the family, or go to the World Cup every four years, fans make commitments that vary on a number of levels, and each level has consequences for sports.

In the sports industry, like many other industries, some of the smallest-scale decisions have impact. For example, a 38 year old woman is at home one evening flipping through the television channels. She stumbles upon a Professional Bowlers Association (PBA) tournament and decides to watch because she rented the bowling-based comedy film *Kingpin* with her two children (family connection), one of her friends belongs to a league (social currency connection), and she prefers sports that aren't very flashy (utopian connection). The event intrigues her, and she begins to root for one of the stars (star connection), learns a little about the game, and plans to watch again. After she views a few more matches, she joins her friend at the local alley and purchases her own ball, shoes, and jersey. Then, when the PBA makes its stop in her city, she attends the tournament. In this situation, a seemingly inconsequential television encounter initiated several connection points and turned an otherwise unlikely bowling fan into a paying participant and attendee. Every day, thousands of sports conversions occur. Some in chance meetings and others in planned events.

Sports products are always on display, and every minute of exposure is critical. In this highly competitive generation, each impression has the potential to affect a buyer. Because of this new decision-making environment, the question is not only when decisions are made, but also how.

The Decision-Making Process

The sports buying process begins when somebody recognizes a problem, a need, or an opportunity. A fan may be choosing between fantasy leagues or deciding between buying season tickets for the football team or taking a vacation and watching a track and field meet in Spain. However, the fan who recognizes the problem, need, or opportunity is not necessarily the one who makes the buying decision.

Sports products can distinguish from among seven buyer roles. These roles are interchangeable and fans can play one or multiple roles.

- *Initiator:* The initiator recognizes a problem, need, or opportunity and has information that introduces the idea of a sports activity. "Wouldn't it be fun to go to a ballgame? The game is half-priced on Tuesday nights."
- *Influencer:* The influencer searches for more information and validates the initiator's idea of a sports activity. "I've been to a game at the stadium. It's a lot of fun."
- *Decision maker:* The decision maker is the person who evaluates alternatives and has the formal authority to make decisions. "Tuesday night? Half price? Let's go."
- *Approver:* The approver is the person who can approve or reverse a decision. "I think we can afford it. Sounds like a good idea to me."
- *Real buyer:* The real buyer makes the final decision and must make the purchase. "I'll use my credit card."
- *User:* The user is the person whom the purchase is for. Users include family, friends, clients, or colleagues. "Thanks."
- *Evaluator:* The evaluator reflects on the quality of the experience and takes further action depending on levels of satisfaction or dissatisfaction. "I had a good time. Let's do this again."

Sports products need to consider which people are involved in the fan buying decision and what their roles are. By examining the patterns further, it's essential to find out what criteria are being used by these fan buyers and who the most powerful initiators and influencers are. A hypothetical example of a basketball decision can reveal the nuances of the interrelationship of the seven buyer roles.

Bacchanalia or Dunks?

Four male college students are considering their options for a Friday night. There are two *initiators* in the group who have information about possible activities. The first *initiator*, Peter, suggests an off-campus party with free drinks and food, some sorority sisters, and an easy walk from their apartment. The second *initiator*, Andy, suggests a local high school basketball game that features one of the best young prospects in the state. The game entails driving, a $5 entry fee, picking up food on the way, and limited female interaction.

Dave, the third member of the group, is one of the *influencers*. He has seen this high school player on television and read a few online scouting reports. He validates the playing ability, athleticism, and "nasty dunks" of the high schooler and lets his friends know that this might be a star in the making. He cites some of the player's stats—"30 points, 13 rebounds, 8 assists, 5 steals, and 3 blocks a game!"—and makes the point that it could be a once in a lifetime experience. The fourth friend, Alan, is also an *influencer* by reminding Peter and Dave that their girlfriends will be at the party.

The *decision maker* of the group on this night is Peter. Last Friday, the four young men went to a movie that three of them wanted to see, but Peter didn't. Peter begrudgingly went along knowing that their next activity would be something he wanted to do. After weighing the positions of the two *influencers*, Peter was more interested in the chance to see a future pro than spending the evening with his girlfriend at a typical college party.

Peter's role as the *decision maker* did not, however, guarantee that the group would go to the game. The *approvers* would have to deem the game acceptable. On this night, the *approvers* were Andy and Alan. Andy readily approved since he initiated the idea. But there was Alan who was interested in the party from the beginning, especially since he reminded the guys about their girlfriends to persuade them. Alan realized that he was in the minority in wanting to go to the party, so he stipulated that in order for him to approve the activity, they would have to eat at his favorite fast-food Mexican place on the way out.

As the four were leaving for the game, Dave and Andy told their friends, "We don't have any money." The *real buyers* then became Peter and Alan. Luckily, the two had enough money to cover their friends for dinner, the game, and gas. They hopped in the car and on this night each of the four friends became the *users*.

When the students arrived at the basketball arena, they were charged an unforeseen $10 to park. The parking attendant was unfriendly, concerned more with collecting the money and sending the boys on their way than anything else. It took the boys 35 minutes to get into the arena because of the long line to purchase tickets. They finally made it into the game halfway into the first quarter and were forced to stand behind the top row because all the seats were taken. At halftime Peter and Alan (the ones with the money) went

(Continued)

(*Continued*)

to the concession stand and were reminded of their freshman year cafeteria. The soda was flat, the nacho cheese cold, and the hot dogs soggy. Despite difficulties at the stadium, the star player was as advertised. He closed with 35 points, 9 rebounds, 12 assists, a steal, and a block and entertained the audience with rim-rattling dunks and a confrontation with the coach over an ill-advised shot.

As *evaluators*, the reaction after the game was mixed. Peter was annoyed at the parking attendant and having to stand the entire time, but he thought the game was entertaining. Andy saw no problem in what happened at the arena since it is what he expected at a game with such hype, and he, too, was satisfied by the game. Dave was also fine with the arena, but he was unimpressed by the game and player, whom he expected to play better defense and not turn the ball over 11 times. Alan was bitter because he originally wanted to go to the party and, as a Mexican food connoisseur, he didn't appreciate the disrespected nacho cheese.

If anything, the buyer roles in this sports decision were fluid. As the situation and the needs changed, different buyers emerged and at least temporarily were calling the shots. In addition, each person had different game expectations and that influenced their buying behavior and also how they felt after the game ended. What is critical to understand is that any buying decision model has to be examined for the context and the interplay that frequently affects the final decisions. It's also probably true that the larger the decision—buying a new car or going to the Super Bowl—has more fixed buyer roles than a typical basketball or track and field event decision.

Fan Decision Factors

There are many sports decisions that fans can make on a daily basis. In this section, we are concentrating on those that account for direct revenue for sports products such as event attendance, television viewing, radio listening, video games, fantasy sports, merchandise, and any other revenue-producing product that a sports property might offer the fan. In each activity, fans consider a number of factors before making a decision—factors that are specific to the sports product and its characteristics.

An effective assessment tool that provides a portrait of how fans make choices is the Fan Decision Factor (FDF). The purpose of the FDF is to understand which factors influence fans when they make a sports decision. It is both a diagnostic and an evaluative tool that helps sports properties determine their goals in fan connection and evaluate their progress.

To illustrate how these factors can be examined, consider a team that is looking to improve attendance by 5 percent over the previous year. The first task of this team is to identify the major factors a fan considers in deciding to attend a game. These factors can be determined by the team based on experience, intuition, surveys, feedback, and any available data that can make a reasonable approximation of fan driving issues. In the example below, they include parking, affordability, food, seat, team record, and facility.

After identifying these factors, the sports property can assign weights to each factor based on its importance to a fan when deciding to attend a game. The percentage value of the weights varies depending on the sports property's judgment and again can be determined by fan feedback and other data.

As an example, look at the importance weights shown in Table 3.1. These weights suggest that affordability accounts for 25 percent of the importance in the decision to attend the game, and the team record accounts for 35 percent of the importance. The other factors have varying but lesser importance.

Table 3.1   Assessing Fan Decision Factors

Factor	Importance Weight	Relative Quality	Score
Parking	.10	.8	.080
Affordability	.25	.5	.125
Food	.05	.9	.045
Seat	.15	.8	.120
Team record	.35	.6	.210
Facility	.10	.7	.070
Total	1.00		.650

The next question is how well does the team manage each factor. Let's assign a "1" to a factor when it has been ideally managed or achieved by the team. In the table, we assign a .8 to parking to suggest that the parking is adequate but not ideal. A small number of fans may have some difficulty finding a parking place. We assign a .5 to affordability to indicate that attending the game is quite expensive for a substantial number of fans and stands as a barrier to attracting more attendees. We assign a .9 to food, suggesting that the food is quite good as far as the fans are concerned. The next three numbers reflect how adequate the team is in the other three factors.

By multiplying the importance weights in the first column by the relative quality standings in the second column, we get a column of scores whose total adds up to .650. If the team's attraction factors were all at an ideal level, the total score would have been 1. The conclusion is that the team has some way to go to improve its attractiveness to the fans, particularly in the low rated area of affordability.

This assessment tool provides a way for the team to determine which factors will have the most impact on the team's attractiveness if they are improved. Thus if the team improved its team record from .6 to say .9, this would have a

---

Assessing Other Fan Decisions

Sports decision makers can use the Fan Decision Factor tool to assess the fan decision-making process on a variety of different decisions. The factors for each decision will vary depending on the sports property and the sports activity. Below are some of the key factors that might be involved in assessing fan decisions in other sports experiences:

Television	**Video Games**
Picture quality	Picture quality
Camera angles	Player features
Announcers	Graphics
Graphics	Music
Statistics	Statistics
Analysis	Realistic representation
Sound	Sound
Jersey	**Fantasy Sports**
Color	Information
Player	E-mail updates
Material quality	League amenities
Brand	Web site appearance
Number	User-friendliness
Historical context	Affordability

greater impact on attendance than if the team improved its food from .9 to 1, because the food is already exceeding expectations and its weight is small in the total picture.

In using the FDF, the higher the total score, the more effective the sports team is in attracting fans. The assessment is useful to management for looking at what areas need improvement and where the team most effectively can put its money to increase game attendance.

Any assessment will have inherent weaknesses that need to be factored into any decision. The factors, importance weights, and relative quality ratings are judgments and can be incorrect or misevaluated. In addition, some weights may have particular strengths in a marketplace, such as an outstanding facility or a team with a strong historical background, that can overcome any particular factor weakness. While these are potential problems, the advantage of the FDF is that it provides a total picture of the sport's assets that are critical to influencing fan decisions.

THE FAN INVOLVEMENT LADDER

Whether by encouraging fans to buy tickets, purchase authentic jerseys, or attend off-season events, sports properties ultimately need to sell their products to stay in business. In today's multichanneled sports marketplace, this task is becoming more challenging as the number of avid fans is beginning to decrease. While there are more sports fans than ever before, in many cases they are not remaining loyal to one particular product. As a result, intensifying fan loyalty and involvement has become one of the most challenging tasks for sports decision makers. The Fan Involvement Ladder (see next page) is designed to illustrate the degrees of fan intensity and help sports decision makers determine how to increase fan involvement.[21]

The ladder represents a wide range of fan involvement. The ensnared, the most extreme group of fans, is at the top rung, and indifferent fans, the most uninterested class, are at the ground level. While these two groups are important for sports properties, the fans on the middle five rungs demand most of the attention from sports decision makers. This ladder is not a foolproof expectation model of what is current, but it is a snapshot of the sports fan's world and how interest can be viewed and rewarded.

Fan Involvement Ladder

Ensnared
Insiders
Attachers
Collectors
Wallets
Eyeballs
Indifferent Fans

Adapted from Rein, Kotler, Hamlin, Stoller, *High Visibility,* 3rd ed. (New York: McGraw-Hill, 2006), p. 95.

Indifferent Fans

There are a lot of people all over the globe who could care less about sports. These people have found that opera, gardening, or simply staring into space is better than watching a season of baseball. They all have encountered sports in some fashion, but they either found it less than satisfying or even threatening. They choose not to become part of the sports dimension in society. At the water cooler at work, they remain silent as the previous day's sporting events are dissected, chewed, and then finally digested.

However, it's simply not productive for sports decision makers to view this group as hopeless. It's virtually impossible to ignore the sports world completely. The housewife who checks the newspaper for her college alma mater's football score, the history buff who appreciates twentieth-century American leisure history, the college student who runs on the track at the gym to stay in shape, and the restaurant owner who makes sandwiches for the local high school lacrosse team are all potentially sports consumers. They are the non-converted, often just in a holding pattern for some sport to whisk them into its lair.

There is another category of consumers who are under the radar but are still connected to the sports world. These may be special occasion fans who are willing to buy a scalper's ticket to attend a historic sports event like the Boston Red Sox playing in the World Series or go to the state high school soccer championship to watch their community's school compete. Or they may find that their child's obsession with rugby star George Gregan forces them to start relating to his club team of Randwick in Australia. They may dislike mainstream sports superstars, yet can be attracted to niche sports such as bull riding because they don't seem like traditional sports. They may be interested in sports, but their connections are simply not strong, consistent, or measurable. They are not hostile to sports, simply indifferent. Yet, they are a large, potentially lucrative group to attract to a sport because they often have no prior allegiance. The real question for the sports industry is whether it pays to try to attract those on the lowest rung of the ladder of interest. Given the inevitable scarcity of promotional dollars, is it better to attract sports-minded people to give more of a share of their time and wallet to sports? Like many choices, it depends on what cycle the sports industry is in and whether there is an overpowering need to invest in converting nonsports fans.

Eyeballs

Who are the fans that are the most studied, spend a relatively little amount of money, and are arguably the largest group of sports consumers? These are eyeballs, who tune in to the final round of the Masters or read Sports Illustrated. Their relationship with sports is dominated by their media sports experiences. They are observers and are not necessarily going to leave their living rooms to go to a live event. Ironically, as the largest group, they are the most profitable sector of the sports market because they are the primary audience for media-watching and are the subject of microscopic scrutiny.

They typically watch sports on television or check highlights on their cell phone, but go to games on occasion. They may or may not buy the product that is being advertised, but they may spend hundreds of hours watching sporting events, increasing the media rating level and in this way directly supporting the sports activity. In the case of the NFL, the eyeball has increased importance because television revenues are predominant in fueling the prosperity of the game. From the point of view of most sports, however, reaching out to the eyeballs and enticing them to come to a game and buy a couple of hot dogs and some sodas are important and need to be addressed aggressively. The eyeball is a "superfan" without a wallet or a cape.

Wallets

Wallets are people who will spend money to experience a sport. Wallets attend a game, fly to the cricket World Cup, buy annual versions of sports video games, or purchase a satellite season package. They are motivated to seek out the live sports venue; stand in line for an important game ticket; wait patiently in the parking lot after a game; or get a group of friends together, have dinner, go to a ballgame, and hit the bars after the game. Wallets are among the most sought-after of all sports fans and as a result are highly prized by the industry. In many ways, sports and the wallet are in the sweet spot of the business; the sports receive their money and commitment, and in return, the wallet receives attention, escape, and the satisfaction of being a fan.

The wallets are prized for more than just their immediate sports consumption because they are likely to spend money actively on entertainment decisions. They are likely to buy enhanced television sets, invest in technologies that will bring them closer to the game, and encourage others to join them. Each act of commitment by the wallets ideally earns them a return on their investment. It is the important task of the sports decision maker to make sure that their investment is appreciated and that they do not wander off into another sport or entertainment.

Collectors

A highly lucrative group of sports fans are collectors who are willing to pay for sports merchandise that reminds them of the sport. This has spawned a huge memorabilia business as illustrated by the National Sports Collectors Association, which has attracted as many as 105,000 collectors to its annual convention.[22] Sports memorabilia is an eclectic collection of goods, including almost anything that represents a piece of sports trivia or a historical moment.

There are lots of motivations for why collectors are willing to invest in sports memorabilia. It has all the elements of automobile or art collecting, which includes betting on appreciation, wanting to recall a family or personal experience, or showing off a rare find. Another important dimension of collectors is that the activity creates its own communication universe where there are numerous places to connect to like-minded fans. A walk-through of a sports collector's shop takes on the experience of an archaeological hunt. Every aspect of sports is painstakingly tagged, waiting for someone who can connect at some personal or investment level. The stores showcase autographed balls lovingly encased in glass or plastic, a variety of trading cards and portraits, and a wall-to-wall display of jerseys and other playing paraphernalia. A collector who understands the marketplace can not only engage in a fun entertainment activity but can also make some money. The prices below are a reflection of the competition and spiraling demand for sports memorabilia:

- A shoe collector spent an estimated $23,000 on a pair of Nike Air Jordans.[23]
- Barry Bonds's 700th home run ball was auctioned off for $804,129.[24]
- A Larry Bird signed, framed jersey costs $202.50 plus $19.75 for shipping.[25]
- A Honus Wagner 1910 baseball card sold for $1.1 million with an additional $165,000 buyer's premium on eBay.[26]
- Babe Ruth's dirty uniform from the 1932 World Series sells for $940,000.[27]

Attachers

The next rung on the ladder are attachers, who wish to receive communication from the team and heroes and to have the opportunity to exchange greetings or some other tangible interactive experience. Discontented with being part of the crowd and simply watching the game, attending the race, or buying the autographed ball, attachers want to interact with the stars. Teams, in response, have offered hot-stove leagues, fantasy camps, community involvement campaigns, cruises with the legends, town hall meetings, and autograph days. These strategies are critical for the attacher, but they are becoming overshadowed by new technologies.

Staples of the attacher connection were always fan clubs, which were often organized by a motivated fan who wanted to get closer to a star or team. The influence of new media has recharged that tradition by developing online forums for fan club participation. These experiences are further enhanced by the large number of sports Web sites, fantasy sports, and video games, which on some level are attachment-based. Sports properties have begun to realize that these attachment-seeking fans can also be relatively inexpensively accommodated through online chat groups, blogs, and message boards. For sports decision makers, these new connection entryways are an opportunity to vastly expand the attacher rung, and in doing so, develop relationships that were previously unavailable. The new media promises to become a base for developing avidity at a scale never before contemplated.

Insiders

The second highest rung of the involvement ladder are the insiders who enter into and often participate in the inner circle of the sports world. These fans are considered to be in the upper echelon of fan commitment. They often buy courtside seats, make investments in teams, or donate to university athletic programs. Their significant investments in sports are rewarded through seating perks, personal relationships with team executives and players, and invitations to special events.

> A Los Angeles Lakers game is encircled by insider-seeking movie moguls and stars who buy the best seats and value their closeness with the team. This insider relationship was ironically displayed in an episode of the television comedy Curb Your Enthusiasm that featured star Larry David inadvertently tripping Shaquille O'Neal as he headed for the bench. David, who was booed roundly, was later shown visiting O'Neal in a hospital, thereby demonstrating amidst a disaster his insider relationship.

The second insider category is the people who work in the industry. Sports are so attractive to these people that they choose to build their careers around it. They include television and marketing executives, journalists, agents, personal trainers, and stylists. They have access to sports in ways that other fans do not.

Ensnared

At the top of the ladder are the ensnared, who are usually the most involved of all fans. As contrasted with the insider, whose four-year-old is in a play group with Phil Mickelson's kid, the ensnared is more likely to associate his or her identity with the sport. In the best sense of the relationship, it can result in a highly charged fan base that is overwhelmingly supportive of the product. There is nothing more invigorating to a sport than a large, enthusiastic, and totally committed fan base. The ensnared is an unconditional supporter whom sports programs view as an asset and, unfortunately, sometimes as a problem.

The ensnared have centered their identity on the team or player they follow. The ultimate supporters—the Hogs of the Washington Redskins and the Silver and Black of the Oakland Raiders—are one variation of this fan. The need for such fans has become so critical to the game atmosphere that it's becoming more industrialized. In college basketball, the University of Memphis has signed up at least 150 students who are called the "Blue Crew," who sit in the front row of the basketball games and not only provide juiced up cheering but are given special practice access, travel to away games, and may even attend a high school game of a prized recruit.[28]

The ensnared often attempt to become a part of the team's identity, and they perceive their fandom to have an effect on the team, and, in the process, can become an additional fan attraction. Many of these fans dress up in Halloween-style costumes and paint their faces or bodies with team colors, acting out the vicarious experience connection in appearance and behavior. They are psychologically intertwined with the sporting event: a win or loss, player trade, or management decision resonates as if they were the players, general managers, or owners. There is an ongoing concern, particularly in basketball, that these overinvolved fans have the potential to harass or use vile language that can spoil the game for the players and fans alike. This fine line between intense enthusiasm and harmful interaction is something that has to be managed carefully by sports programs and has led to violence in some cases.

In cases like these, fans of one team may act against fans of another based on the game they are watching. This behavior, which has been termed hooliganism in the soccer world, results in violence and injuries depending on the outcome of games. Some of the most ensnared fans are those of national soccer teams. In Colombia, for example, Andrés Escobar, a member of the Colombian national team, was murdered in 1994 several days after accidentally scoring a goal for the American team in a World Cup match. Tennis star Steffi Graf's main rival Monica Seles was stabbed by a man stalking Graf, allegedly to prevent Seles from passing Graf in the tennis rankings. In increasing irony, Martina Hingis, who had exceeded Seles's 178-week consecutive record for being number one in women's tennis, was stalked by a romance-seeking fan who left his homeland in Australia to try to win her affection.[29] In the 1996 film *The Fan*, Wesley Snipes plays a San Francisco Giants all-star who is stalked by an ensnared fan played by Robert DeNiro. At first, Snipes sympathizes with his worshipful supporter, but, in the end, finds him obsessed and dangerously overinvolved. The theme of ensnared runs through not only sports but all popular culture events that seek attachment.

Intensifying Involvement

The task for sports decision makers is to move the fan from lower to higher levels of involvement. A major challenge for the sports industry is to cultivate indifferent fans and eyeballs into wallets, and continue the fan up the ladder. While sports have often had difficulty increasing fan intensity, a new set of involvement strategies are now being implemented:

- A major appeal of fantasy sports is the quasischolarship that mimics the practices of Benedictine monks and Talmudic scholars. Fantasy sports allow fans to manage their own team of college and professional athletes. Playing fantasy sports encourages fans to learn more about the teams and players by following the minutiae of their performances through close textual analysis. Internationally, fantasy cricket, rugby, and Premier League soccer are growing in popularity. Fantasy sports now have many versions not only in the major professional leagues but also in niche sports such as bass fishing and bull riding, and they continue to add more sports, increase in the numbers of participants, and intensify their degree of involvement.

- Cross-sectoring appearances attempt to reach an audience such as the indifferent fan that might not otherwise be exposed to a sports star. Agents and managers have encouraged stars to explore nontraditional media outlets to generate awareness for the star and ultimately the sport. These cross-promotional strategies have been successful in the examples of rugby star Jonny Wilkinson, who wrote his own autobiography and became an Officer of the British Empire, and Serena Williams, who has expanded her tennis stardom to include a designer fashion line by Nike and a reality television show with her sister Venus.

- Reading and other educational programs in schools not only provide exposure for sports stars and teams to a young audience but also generate goodwill in their efforts to improve literacy and learning. These programs often tie free tickets to strong reading performance or good grades. By reaching the school market, they create an opportunity to educate children, reach parents, and potentially build their fan base.

- Developing participation clinics that are essentially tutorials on the intricacies of the sport is particularly effective in involving the indifferent and eyeball fan. They are usually ground-level seminars that provide insights into the nuances of the sport and are conducted in shopping malls, community centers, parks, and other places that are convenient for the fan. The NFL has been a pathfinder in offering a wide range of programs aimed at kids, women, and other underrepresented demographics. The Ultimate Players Association (UPA), the governing body of ultimate frisbee, offers several grassroots outreach programs, which include instructional kits on how to run a women's clinic and a middle and high school ultimate frisbee curriculum for physical education teachers.

- In the new world of sports fan experiences, the combination of technology and the predictive qualities of the stock market has made athletes and events tradable commodities in such games as Protrade and Trade Sports. Protrade is a variation of fantasy sports in which participants trade athletes like stocks. Trade Sports is another version of sports gambling where bettors buy and sell futures based on sports outcomes. On game day, ten sports fans can be watching a game with six television sets broadcasting six different games, wireless computers tracking the sales of athlete stocks and team contracts, and telephone calls or instant messages to other traders across the world trying to predict the next play. The primary appeal is to the avid fan who gains social currency and a vicarious simultaneous combination of sports and financial risk and who is less interested in a single team than following the entire league or event. There is also the potential of attracting fans across all different intensity levels because the formats encourage a different dimension of fan involvement.

These developments are aimed at creating more involvement and widening the appeal of the sports market. While there has historically been reluctance from leagues and players to participate in off-field performance sectors, these walls are rapidly breaking down as the marketplace becomes more competitive and sports products are seeking revenue from a wider base of ventures. In this competitive environment, it is to be expected that sports decision makers are looking to move the sports fan up the involvement ladder. The development of devoted, high-spending fans is an increasingly scarce commodity and requires a systematic and comprehensive program to keep fans moving up the steps of the ladder.

CONCLUSION

The good news is that we know more about sports fans than any time in history. We have surveys, focus groups, intelligence agencies, interactive questions on television and the Internet, and sophisticated sales devices, all aimed at tracking the fan's habits and viewing patterns. These inquiry techniques have produced far more information and detail about fans and their behavior than was wildly imagined in earlier generations. We also are now able to segment fan groups in ways that allow for specific targeting based on connection points and entryways of communication that are far more sophisticated and precise. The bad news is that with all this information we still struggle in a fragmented market to corral significant numbers of an increasingly elusive audience. The fan base for many sports continues to erode despite the virtual avalanche of decision-making information. This chapter emphasizes fan connections and entryways, decision-making strategies, and levels of fan involvement that are clues to reaching the new realities of this difficult fan market. In the next chapter, we look at pulling the pieces together and reinventing the sports brand.

2

CONNECTING TO THE ELUSIVE FAN

Chapter

4

REINVENTING THE SPORTS BRAND

Imagine that John and Sally just moved to Atlanta and want to see a Braves game. They are not season ticket holders and not entitled to special benefits. Under a new single-game ticket plan, they buy tickets for July 18, a home game against the vaunted New York Yankees. For a special price of $250, they get two box seats; an Atlanta Braves pennant; a customized DVD sent to their home two weeks in advance that discusses the historic relationship between the Braves and the Yankees and profiles the stars of each team; an electronic traffic transponder with customized directions for the fastest, least traveled route that can be hooked up on July 18 and kept for future games; and a preferred parking space with easy entry and easy exit. Upon arrival at the game, they have a personal lunch with the guest of the day—a scout, general manager, or marketing director—which was part of the package offered to the various groups on that date. They paid a $180 premium for all the services that went with the game, but vowed to return in late August for the San Francisco Giants and add the postgame party with the manager to their package.

In the sports world, many of the elements of this hypothetical ticketing strategy are already in place. While most sports teams have not yet customized for a single ticket buyer a DVD and sending out an electronic traffic transponder, the marketplace is clearly moving in this direction because of the potential to intensify the fan connection. For example, the Chicago White Sox, through their Baseball Fantasy Experiences program, offer fans a wide variety of paid activities including a $10,000 wedding at home plate, that on occasion was officiated by the owner, and a variety of other offerings beginning at $150, including dragging the infield, handing the umpire the lineup card, and on-field access during batting practice.[1] It may seem like a lot of work to accommodate two fans who may not show up again until next year, but the search for fans has become so competitive that the marketplace demands differentiated experiences to drive consumers to one activity and away from others. In this cluttered entertainment environment, sports products must transform into strong and identifiable brands to attract attention and build sustainable fan connections. In this chapter, we discuss the special nature of brand-building in sports and the foundations for any successful brand—segmentation, involvement, ethos, and, finally, transformation. But first, let's state the branding dilemma.

THE BRANDING DILEMMA

Most sports are caught in a dilemma that is unlike any in other entertainment activities. In almost every case, the goal is to win or at the very least stage an exciting and nail-biting competition. Either of these two occurrences is historically the best marketing position for any sports product. If you squeeze a sports decision maker hard enough on why his or her product doesn't attract fans, the answer after all the excuses is often, "We gotta win," or, "We need a tight race."

In the new competitive marketplace, those responses are surefire losers. They are not exactly irrational responses but outcomes that may be impossible to attain. It is unrealistic to expect most sports products to win consistently or always offer the most intense level of competition. It is realistic, however, for sports decision makers to evaluate the current state of the sports product and use branding principles to not only reposition but also find superior ways to connect to fans. For example, a sports product can find itself in one of three positions related to the issue of winning:

1. A dominant winning product
2. A product that wins often enough to be competitive
3. A product that loses enough to disconnect from its fan base without the possibility of winning in any reasonable time frame

The first two sports products have an advantage in that they can base their drive for fans on their strong or consistent winning performances. That's the case with Real Madrid, the New York Yankees, the University of Southern California football team, the University of Connecticut women's basketball team, Tiger Woods, Michelle Kwan, the Yomiuri Giants, Oak Hill Academy prep school basketball team in Virginia, and the New Zealand All Blacks. Even these strong performing sports brands cannot rely on winning to sustain fan connections permanently. For example, in baseball the New York Yankees in the 1980s and 1990s experienced a 15-year period without a World Series appearance, and the Atlanta Braves have won their division for 14 years in a row and have struggled with attendance consistency.[2] The causes of poor fan attraction can be a market's unfamiliarity with a new sport, an overexposure or underexposure problem, an issue with behavior of the players or management, or a weak economy. These variables and others have to be addressed and are often outside the issue of winning.

It is essential that the majority of sports products brand their attributes independent of competitive outcomes. We can get clues from some sports products that don't define themselves only by winning. Programs such as the Stanford University Cardinal have an overall brand reflecting intelligence, teamwork, and resourcefulness. In winning or losing, Stanford maintains those brand characteristics. The same can be said for the Chicago Cubs, who have branded nostalgia and perennial losing. They attract a loyal fan base that comes to vine-covered Wrigley Field in appreciation of the historical and pristine nature of the experience. The Denver Broncos took 14 seasons until they had a winning football team and for most of those years drew capacity crowds.[3] A strong place connection was the key ingredient to sustaining over difficult seasons. Anna Kournikova, Vince Carter, and Bob Uecker have succeeded without much winning and have built their brands on other attributes such as looks, slam dunks, and quirky broadcasting. Whole conferences such as the Atlantic Coast Conference (ACC) basketball programs, while certainly having many outstanding teams, have built a brand on uncertainty, suspense, and the parity in the league. Other sports properties such as NASCAR and pro wrestling have branded danger, rivalries, petty feuds, uncontrolled out of competition clashes, and dirty play. They have found fans that respond to the heated mix of competition and out of control emotions.

In the sports industry, winning and losing are inevitable. There are examples of sports programs that have been winners and do not draw as well as intermittent and chronic losers that have managed to maintain a healthy fan base. Our position is that no matter what the win-loss record, all sports programs can benefit from branding strategies as fortunes turn and marketplaces change.

You Say Winning, I Say Spinning

In George and Ira Gershwin's 1937 hit "Let's Call the Whole Thing Off," they devote an entire song to arguing playfully over the pronunciation of words like potato, pajamas, and neither and either. The song is catchy and gets a knowing laugh because we all recognize that this petty feud over language symbolizes a deeper problem in a relationship. While the word *winning* in sports is rarely mispronounced like tomato, it has become for many sports decision makers one of the most disputed words in the English language and the subject of many breakups.

In 1958 and 1959, the Chicago Bears had excellent football teams that finished second in a two-division league alignment. The seasons ended as big disappointments because only the two division winners played each other for the NFL Championship. In today's promiscuous division alignments, the Bears would have been a certain playoff contender with a chance to advance to the Super Bowl, and it is safe to say that the fans would have viewed it as a darn good year. Before sports discovered the principle of inclusion, if a team failed to win the conference, division, or league, it was often curtains for the coach, players, and next year's season ticket sales.

In today's marketplace, teams are considered winners when they barely break even. All the conferences now have playback contingencies that allow for teams to work back into the championship mix through some form of postseason reward. As a result, in Division I football, all a team needs is a 6-6 record to qualify for a bowl, which for many teams now represents a winning season. At the high school level, state championships in some sports have been expanded from as few as eight to sometimes hundreds of qualifying teams, often including more than half of the possible teams in the state. The redefinition of winning affects even grade school kids because in many sports everyone gets a trophy, and there are no losers.

What does one make of this? Is it winning or spinning? In the short term, this strategy has demonstrated that expectations of winning can be redirected to satisfy fans' needs for a competitive program, instill in participants hopes for success, and expand the revenue for the sports products. The strategy does run the risk of degrading winning as a prize and also attacking the integrity of the sport itself. It's also reasonable to assume that the broadening of the term may eventually lose its potency and that there may come a time when sports begin to roll back the "everyone a winner" expansion strategy because it no longer guarantees fan support. In any case, sports decision makers need to employ inducements other than winning to attract the fan since even time-honored victories can become commodities.

WHAT IS A BRAND?

A *brand* is a synthesis of facts and images that comprise a sports product and is often defined by slogans, themes, positions, symbols, product characteristics, and a number of other tangible and intangible attributes. The attributes that arise in one's mind when a brand is mentioned constitute its identity. The brand helps us distinguish one product from another.

The word *brand* originated in the practice of burning an owner's name on livestock. Thus the brand was about ownership and property rights, not the livestock. The brand began to be seen as an organizing principle that represented a distinct identity and a set of attributes.

The concept of brand subsequently became associated with the concept of image. The development of photography in the nineteenth century made it possible for images of time and place to be captured and serve as a visual reproduction of reality. People didn't have to rely on their imagination or live experience to see something distinctive. It wasn't long after the invention of photography that the image was used to persuade audiences. In 1890, Jacob Riis, a police reporter for a newspaper in New York, published a book titled *How the Other Half Lives*.[4] Riis argued against the current treatment of the urban poor by using photographs depicting the living conditions of the city's most impoverished. Riis used the images as evidence for his argument and in the process positioned the image as a persuasive tool. For audiences who were unaware of or neglected the conditions in the slums, these images not only informed but also called for resolutions to the problem.

Images weren't exclusively used for activist purposes as they quickly began to affect the entertainment world. Coney Island, the most successful amusement park of the early twentieth century, attracting more than 1 million people on a summer day, thrived on the power of the image. Until 1920, when the park had been open for over 20 years, there was no subway access for the poorer residents of New York, which made attending Coney Island nearly impossible for a large portion of the population. These people instead had to view photographic images of the roller coasters, beaches, and fairgrounds of Coney Island to vicariously experience this so-called fantasyland. When affordable transportation finally made it possible for the poorer people to travel to Coney Island, the island experienced its busiest time in its history throughout the 1920s.[5] The images of Coney Island and all that it represented—freedom, leisure, escape—are an explanation of why families would be persuaded to save all year long in anticipation of spending one summer weekend there.

Once businesses understood the power of images in attracting customers, the marketplace became flooded with them. A company would feature one image after another, even inconsistent ones, to gain attention. But soon some companies realized that they should choose consistent images that delivered the same powerful message. Advertising executive Rosser Reeves argued that a product should be marketed with "a unique selling proposition," which served to organize the company's messages. Others subsequently called this "positioning," or "the value proposition," or the "brand essence." Thus the brand became more than a set of images. It became the driver and coherent glue that bind together all the messages.

A strong brand delivers a promise of benefit or performance to the audience. The power of a strong brand is validated when a shopper chooses Del Monte over Dole, saying, "I feel the quality is better, and I am willing to spend more money for Del Monte." Brands can bring powerful images to a consumer such as trust, adventure, reliability, or youth. A brand can become so familiar that Tropicana Orange Juice for breakfast is like a member of the family. Anything else is out of the question.

The idea of brand in sports was initially an almost accidental component of a sports product. The Pittsburgh Steelers picked up the image of a tough, gritty, punishing football team. Their practice field at South Park was remarkably primitive and resembled the practice facility of a Sunday afternoon semi-professional team more than a major NFL franchise. The Steelers benefited from their tough-guy image but rarely produced a unified brand concept to market the team. It may well be that the Steelers went out of their way to draft that type of player or that that type of player was attracted to Pittsburgh, but it was more likely that a grinding football team was a more effective style in a cold-weather market rather than a useful marketing tool.

Another example is the St. Louis Cardinals baseball team of the 1930s who were nicknamed the "Gashouse Gang" in recognition of their hell-bent playing style. The team came onto the field in the pregame workout and played pepper, which is a warm-up drill testing quick reflexes as the players throw and bunt the ball to one another. In the game itself, the team's players would bunt, steal bases, and essentially run themselves into victory. The Cardinals played a style of fast-paced, hit-and-run baseball that captured the imagination of fans across the country. They also became well known for their jug band, the Mudcats, which played bluegrass music in the clubhouse before and after games and was made up of a group of players led by third baseman Pepper Martin. We now in retrospect see their style as a set of attributes which could have been developed into a brand. Furthermore, the brand was not important enough to be sustained because, when the players retired, they were not always replaced with players of the same type. The Cardinals didn't see its brand potential as an asset they needed to protect and enhance. If they chose to continue the Gashouse Gang style as a branded team identity, they would have drafted and signed players in that image.

Today more organizations are becoming aware of the importance of building and managing themselves as a brand. This is the result of hypercompetition and the need to differentiate themselves in the marketplace. Brands can focus marketing messages to potential consumers and create long-term relationships with their markets. For the sports industry, the teams that can transform themselves into brands that offer fans a distinctive experience, one not dependent upon wins and losses, will remain competitive in the marketplace. These products will maximize the three major advantages—permanence, connectivity, and a premium—of building and maintaining a well-defined brand:

Brands establish permanence. Building a sports brand resolves many of the short-term performance issues that many sports products face. Any sports product might have a succession of losses, or lose its star players. Winning seasons and athletic careers will inevitably end. In the face of this, building a brand provides fans with more of a permanent connection to sustain the operation.

Brands have connectivity. Branding involves developing a larger number of platforms to connect the fans to the sports product. In doing so, it spreads connection possibilities to a much broader base, thus maximizing the number of potential fan connections. These platforms not only have the advantage of connecting the brand with its various entities but also provide the brand with elasticity in its branding efforts. Developing a brand provides the sports product with multiple platforms from which to communicate and deliver its product to fans. Rather than just viewing the player or facility as an individual entity, the brand organizes all its assets and presents them to fans with the advantage of moving through media and other channels.

Brands command a premium. A premium is the difference in attention and pay that an established sports brand receives over its competitors. In his prime, heavyweight champion Joe Louis could command a premium even for fights against helpless opponents during his "Bum of the Month" campaign. There are three factors that contribute to the establishment of a brand premium:

- *Visibility:* The sports brands that are more well known in the marketplace can attract more attention and a higher price. A highly visible, well-branded tennis player has the potential to receive a premium over an equally qualified competitor.

- *Sector:* Brand premiums vary based on the popularity, competitiveness, and interest of a particular sports sector. Thus the premium in U.S. markets will be greater in sports such as football and basketball and not as profitable in water polo or table tennis. Conversely, in Norway and the Netherlands, winter sports such as cross-country skiing and speed skating can attract a premium in the marketplace that exists virtually nowhere else in the world.

- *Cultural salience:* Sports brands that capitalize on key competitive and cultural trends can often command a premium. Poker as a brand has benefited from its growing number of participants, television coverage, online play, star power, and reputation as a trendy activity.

As the stakes become even higher, branding will spell the difference between the successful products in the industry and those that fold under competitive pressures. The University of Notre Dame's football program is an example of the power and influence of branding in the industry and how positioning and branding is a constant and ever-changing process.

Branding the Fighting Irish

"Outlined against the blue, gray October sky the four horsemen rode again." This line was written by the legendary sportswriter Grantland Rice who canonized the four players in the Notre Dame backfield in his account of an exciting 13-7 victory over a powerful Army team in 1924. After the team returned to South Bend, members posed dressed in their uniforms, astride four horses, wearing leather football helmets. The famous photograph was a symbol of Notre Dame's unrelenting drive for publicity, which maximized its national dominant football status and illustrated the growing emphasis on the star power of its players.

This was not always the case. Founded in 1842, Notre Dame was, for most of those early years, a small, obscure Catholic school stuck in the middle of Indiana. In the 1910s and 1920s, Notre Dame began to use football as a visibility generator to not only become the premiere college football team in the United States, but to brand its success with a set of unique attributes. And not incidentally, the fortunes of the university were inextricably tied to the football team's performance and the publicity machine that sustained its nationwide fan base.

How did Notre Dame do this? In one sense, it discovered a niche for an independent football team that could schedule a wide range of well-known institutions across the country like Pittsburgh, Michigan, Nebraska, and the University of Southern California. Other Catholic schools, such as DePaul, Marquette, Fordham, and Georgetown, also saw football as a visibility generator, but eventually they all failed and abandoned their national ambitions. Notre Dame, however, was far more single-minded, ambitious, and brand-conscious than its peers.

The team during its brand-defining years was led by a widely recognized and colorful football coach, Knute Rockne, who was the coach from 1918 to 1930. Rockne's leadership and the Notre Dame recruiting link to star athletes through the Catholic community helped produce outstanding teams. The school combined these elements with a relentless public relations effort that was able to capitalize on such stars as George Gipp, the four horsemen's linemen the "Seven Mules," and in the 1940s, legendary coach Frank Leahy and quarterbacks Angelo Bertelli and Johnny Lujack. It was Rockne, however, who was the foundation and refiner of an emerging strategy—"branding through the coach."

The Notre Dame program was also among the first to capitalize on the use of myths and storylines to popularize its program. The Notre Dame fight song "Victory" was played everywhere, mainstream films referenced the team, and the team's Chicago media connection brought the full weight of that

(Continued)

(*Continued*)

city's media power. Notre Dame also created an experience and lifestyle around attending and viewing the football games. A large number of rituals were involved, including attending campuswide masses before the game, touching sacred objects, and institutionalized pregame alumni gatherings. All this was framed by the library mosaic overlooking the field, "Touchdown Jesus." Notre Dame became the football team for not only alumni but for a huge fan base that had never attended Notre Dame. The results of the football brand could not be ignored—increased enrollment with higher-quality students, higher visibility faculty,[6] and a successful, well-funded athletic program.

Despite the remarkable benefits of the football legacy, Notre Dame has wrestled with the football brand and its effect on the academic institution, and it has tried to resolve this with mixed success. Administrators have on several occasions in the late 1930s and mid-1950s prioritized academics and were speculated to have deemphasized football. Each time, however, the shift in emphasis resulted in mediocre football seasons and a threat of losing the Notre Dame football mystique. In response, the university hired coaches— Frank Leahy in the 1940s and Ara Parseghian in the 1960s—to restore the Rockne Notre Dame brand, seemingly admitting the importance of football to the university's brand.

In the last quarter century, in addition to academic and behavioral player problems, the powerful national recruiting network, which sent many young men to Notre Dame to play football, was dissolving. College football had become a national television product, and despite Notre Dame's signing of an exclusive television contract with NBC in 1990, other programs such as those at Florida State, Nebraska, and Miami began branding their programs with competing storylines and attracting top players that might have attended Notre Dame in the past. Notre Dame responded to this new competitive environment with alleged academic leniency in recruiting during the Lou Holtz era (1988–1996), in which the team won a national championship in 1988 and temporarily regained some of the Rockne football dominance. However, in the mid-1990s and early twenty-first century, Notre Dame football, in its predictable cycle, declined in performance, and the balance between academic integrity and athletic achievement was in question once more.

It appeared that Notre Dame had again resolved its academics-football dilemma when in 2005 it hired as its head coach Charlie Weis, a former New England Patriots offensive coordinator who had earned three Super Bowl rings. The move signaled another change in direction, as Weis quickly began restoring the Notre Dame football brand. In doing so, he inadvertently restarted the dialogue over who is in charge of the school's image.[7]

The University of Notre Dame faces a branding dilemma not unlike that confronting General Motors, Coca-Cola, or any longstanding product. As

Notre Dame's market begins to erode compared to its past overwhelming national dominance, its brand constantly needs to be repositioned as new competitors enter the marketplace. It may be that Notre Dame hopes that in the long term it no longer needs its football identity to attract top faculty, high-quality students, and fervent alumni support and devotion. But in reality, football was—and still is—the primary national branding card that Notre Dame owns. It was not only the instrument that transformed the university into a national institution but it is the driver that holds everything together.

Notre Dame has created a national brand that has flourished despite losing seasons, mediocre coaches, upset alumni, and calls from within to emulate the Ivy League. The brand's strength continues to provide revenue, alumni devotion, and media adulation that will be difficult to abandon. The branding tap dance between academics and athletics is an ongoing issue that many colleges and universities will be forced to face in the twenty-first century as the competition intensifies, costs continue to escalate, and university administrations debate where sports fit in the academic universe.

FOUNDATIONS OF SPORTS BRANDING

There are four key components of sports branding that are essential to its development: segmentation, involvement, ethos, and transformation. Each plays a significant role in forming the foundation for the branding process.

Segmentation

While the modern idea of segmenting a market is relatively new, the practice originated 3,000 years ago. It began in the golden age of rhetoric in Greece. The scholars who studied communication were familiar with audience analysis and had very specific strategies in mind as to how to appeal to their citizens. The most influential and prominent was Aristotle, who was critical in developing the argument-based field of rhetoric. Rhetoric was in Aristotle's words the practice of discovering the "available means of persuasion."[8] His concept identified the importance of the sophisticated relationship between idea generators and their audiences. Aristotle was among the first to recognize that audiences varied and that certain strategies including rational and emotional appeals were more effective if the communicator understood the values, mood, and tenor of the audience. It was Aristotle who emphasized the importance of "putting the audience into a certain frame of mind."[9] However, his understanding of audience, while it foreshadowed our current practices, was quite different from our contemporary conception of segmentation.

The Greeks were generally communicating a public message to a varied audience from commoners to special members of the legislature, and the ideas were often centered on persuading audiences concerning issues of civic participation. In the Roman era that followed, rhetoricians such as Cicero also addressed audience appeal. In his admonition on public speaking to audiences, Cicero advised, "Now nothing in oratory ... is more important than to win for the orator the favor of his hearer."[10] And while the Roman audiences' situations and issues varied even more than the Greeks' did, they were still well within the realm of political and militaristic considerations. The possibilities were relatively limited in comparison to those today, but they understood adapting to an audience and, not unlike the Greek rhetoricians, were laying the groundwork for many of our current audience theories.

It wasn't until the beginning of the Age of Enlightenment, emergence of capitalism, and the Industrial Revolution that rhetoric and audience analysis began to emerge again as an important communication tool. As societies made the transition to more organized marketplaces, people were now more likely to be persuaded to buy goods and services from other members of society. In the early years of the capitalist economy, businesses had to understand what their audiences were looking for in order to be successful. They had to recognize that different people might be looking for different things within the same product class. As salespeople began to discover the need to tailor their messages to specific audience needs, audience analysis eventually became synonymous with segmentation.

Early market segmentation distinguished the audience based on demographic differences, such as income, education, religion, location, or race. The assumption was that people in the same demographic group would seek to satisfy the same need. But increasingly it was discovered that perceptions, needs, and preferences could differ greatly even within a defined demographic group. Today, market segmentation has grown more sophisticated and includes dividing people by psychographic, need, and lifestyle variables.

The sports industry has been slow in adopting segmentation techniques. Part of the reason is that it hasn't always been a requirement to attract fans. The draw of the sport and its athletes and lack of competition made segmentation an end result rather than a proactive strategy to shape the fan mix. Take

104

the fight in 1910, when the great and controversial black heavyweight champion Jack Johnson fought the white, undefeated, former champion Jim Jeffries. The fight was originally scheduled to be held in San Francisco, but because of race and violence concerns, it was banned in all other states except Nevada. Promoter Tex Rickard had three weeks to construct an arena and arrange for the fight in Reno, the divorce and sin capital of the United States. The fans who showed up were predictably almost exclusively white, hoping to see the black champion, Johnson, defeated and humiliated in the process.

Because the newspapers ballyhooed the fight as a massive confrontation between the races, Rickard was the beneficiary of mostly unsolicited free media. The fight was a smash hit at the box office, but from the attending fans' point of view it was ruined by the outcome—Johnson dismantled Jeffries. The distraught white audience filed slowly out of the arena convinced that America was going to hell in a handbasket. Riots subsequently erupted in cities and towns all over America prompted by the outcome of the fight.[11] Driven by racial hatred, curiosity, and minimal competition from other sports, the market found the fight, rather than the fight found the market. There were no marketing specialists or public relations operatives, and few direct promotion opportunities, advertisements in the media, or any other of the modern communication devices to entice audiences. The fight stirred emotions, and it was fueled by newspapers that were both fascinated and threatened by a black champion and wrote compulsively about it. This was an era in which there was a scarcity of major sports attractions, and if a league or promoter found one, they benefited from limited competition.

The trial-and-error promotional strategies of the early twentieth century were eventually refined by more calculated strategies to segment and reach audiences. The Minneapolis Millers were a Triple-A minor league baseball team until 1961 that played in a bandbox called Nicollet Park on the south side of Minneapolis. The team had a very specific audience—Minneapolis residents, who were segmented mostly by where in the city they lived. The team's most successful promotion strategies were built around the 22 annual games against the St. Paul Saints, the other baseball team in the area whose stadium was only seven miles away. The games have been termed by author Stew Thornley as the "War Between the Cities,"[12] with the winning team becoming a symbol of the superior city.

The Twin Cities created an event on a scale similar to the current rivalries between the Yankees and the Red Sox, India and Pakistan in cricket, and the neighboring Texas high school football programs Odessa Permian and Midland Lee. On the holidays of summer— Decoration Day, Fourth of July, and Labor Day—the most popular attraction in the Minneapolis-St. Paul area was the Millers-Saints doubleheader in which the teams alternated stadiums for the morning and afternoon games. The *Minneapolis Tribune* wrote stories in advance of the games to stimulate interest, and the strategic scheduling created an event that would appeal to its primary segments.[13] In this example, segmentation did occur, but it was simple and easy to define—Minneapolis residents and St. Paul residents. If you lived in Minneapolis, you hated St. Paul residents, and vice versa. It was inconceivable that a Minneapolis boy would date a St. Paul girl. And the images of each city—Minneapolis as the grain capital and Scandinavian-Protestant outpost and St. Paul as the eastern seaboard transplant and Irish-Catholic settlement—were incompatible. The baseball market was not only segmented in terms of location but also along religious lines. While the religious component was never mentioned overtly on the radio or in newspapers, it was a powerful polarizing attendance tool.

Segmentation today is much more purposeful and refined as the market has become increasingly complex and crowded compared to the Johnson and Millers examples. The expansion of channels and options gives audiences more variety and the numbers and specificity of segments are multiplied as consumers make more individualized choices on a greater number of sports products and events. As a result, there have been a number of refinements in segmentation. On one level, the segmentation practices are an expansion of what has already been done. On another, innovation in segmentation strategies has enabled more sophisticated audience analysis. And finally, techniques of audience analysis are becoming better at understanding what people do and how they behave.

Harrah's Entertainment Inc. has refined customer segmentation for its gambling customers through "decision-science based marketing" and epidemiological research.[14] Harrah's distributes Total Reward cards to its customer base, "wallets," which provide them with information on gambling activities. The program is designed to segment the gamblers on the basis of their needs and habits, which includes what they like to drink and at what time of day they like to drink it. The reward system personalizes each individual's gambling experience at the casinos and seemingly corrects undesirable behavior by rewarding actions through points distribution. The results are impressive as Harrah's Total Rewards program has accounted for an increase from 36 to 50 percent in its share of its consumers' gaming budgets.[15]

Arlington Racetrack in the Chicago suburbs is now using predictive analytics to identify microsegments in their current customer base. By examining millions of sales receipts and applying a selective set of attributes, different groups can be identified and reached. Arlington was interested in improving the performance of its gambling reward program, Twin Spires Club, and managed in one year to increase sales from $900,000 to $1.5 million.[16] Predictive analytics helps Arlington identify the best prospects for the Twin Spires Club. There is little question that sports organizations worldwide are beginning to understand and benefit from such segmentation technologies.

These growing segmentation practices that are driven by technology carry three implications. First, the sports industry must break down its audiences into more specific segments. It is no longer sufficient to aim at males aged 18–34. It is far more productive to attempt to reach 18- to 22-year-old male Asian American college students who have an uncertainty connection to sports than simply to use strategies aimed at 18- to 34-year-old males, 18- to 34-year-old Asian Americans, or even 18- to 22-year-old Asian American college students. The key need is to identify specific connection points of different groups to your brand.

Second, sports brands must prioritize their segments. This is the practice of *market targeting*, whereby brands focus their efforts on a particular segment or set of segments and try to create a long-standing connection and relationship with them. For example, if Hispanic sports fans are responding favorably to a particular baseball team, why be content with that current level of response? Why not devote more resources to create more connections that will sustain Hispanic fan interest through winning and losing seasons?

Third, the sports brand must select a set of compatible target markets. This is called *market orchestration*. In the Twin Cities example, the Millers' and Saints' market orchestration was largely reinforcing the key differences between the cities and making the game as accessible as possible to the cities' residents. Similarly, the Four Seasons hotel in targeting a wealthier market would not try to attract customers who are loud or dress poorly.

While segmentation is essential in building a strong brand, sports decision makers should be careful about how they use it. By focusing too much on one segment at the expense of others, segmentation runs the risk of neglecting some segments and alienating fans. This is especially true in major established sports such as MLB and the NFL where the fan base is wide-ranging and cuts across multiple audiences. However, the risks of segmentation are often not as significant in niche sports, which are founded on their appeal to a specifically targeted market.[17] For the sports decision maker, maximizing the benefits of segmentation requires balancing the demand for more profitable fan relationships with the needs and expectations of all fan segments.

Involvement

The second key foundational factor of a strong sports brand is the relationship the brand has with its fans. Fans can be involved in a sports product at five fundamental levels:

1. Becomes aware of a sport
2. Checks for results occasionally
3. Goes to or views events regularly
4. Follows the sport in all distribution channels
5. Integrates it as part of his or her life

In addition, these levels have a number of permutations that sports decision makers have to monitor. For example, an avid Generation Y fan may well check for results regularly and go to or view events occasionally.[18] A Baby Boomer fan may be only interested in accessing scores and statistics on an occasional basis but have regular season tickets to basketball and baseball teams. In analyzing fan involvement, it is clear that there are general patterns and also very specific consumption rituals that need to be tracked and addressed.

Involvement also comes in many other forms, and some of them are not obvious. For example, it could be that the amenities of attending a game such as front-row seats or bullpen access are a must for a certain type of fan, but for others driving four hours in snowy weather to see an away game while sitting in the nosebleed section of the visiting stadium is an intimacy high. In today's sports industry, physical closeness to the event is unlikely for all fans to experience. Sports must develop other involvement strategies to connect to the fan.

In the preindustrial era of sports, fan involvement was a relatively simple task. In fact, involvement wasn't much of a requirement for spectators; it was more of an involuntary outcome of being a sports fan. If a fan wanted to watch a game, showing up at the event was the only requirement. Fans in many cases dropped a quarter into a collection hat for admission or weren't even charged a fee. In return, they could expect to chat with the players or shake their hands after the game. The experience had an atmosphere of spontaneity, and the small crowds and the enthusiasm of the usually amateur experience overcame the frustration of leaping over mud holes.

> The first college football game was played on November 6, 1869, when Princeton traveled to Rutgers. An estimated 100 spectators showed up to watch, of which 50 were Rutgers students. There were no bleachers or folding chairs, so fans found themselves perched on a wooden fence along the perimeter of the field. The involvement factor was not an issue because the game atmosphere and informal nature of the encounter stripped away any formality. In this era, creating involvement wasn't a concern for the teams since most spectators knew the players on some level. Other factors also weren't primary concerns such as revenue, fame, or, apparently, scoring. Rutgers won 6-4.[19]

As sports became industrialized, new opportunities were created for encounters, but problems also arose with respect to fan intimacy. Charging admission to sporting events changed the relationship between the participants and the spectators, and this new form of business began to flourish in cities and towns around the world. The industrialization of sports marked a fundamental shift in how sports fans were treated. They were now viewed not just as spectators but as consumers of a sports product. The sports fan became more excluded at the intimate and interpersonal levels. Increased revenues, higher player salaries, new theme-park stadiums, large-scale sporting events, television broadcasts, and millions of fans all conspired to force a different sense of involvement. The past virtues of informality and intimacy were replaced by a whole set of experiences that offered new amenities but often sacrificed true close contact. How can a fan feel involved with a sport when the players or coaches are inaccessible, when they feel the admission price is too high, when owners threaten to move teams to another city, or when a fan is one of thousands?

In the sports industry today, sports properties seek intimacy, closeness, and personalization, but they are handicapped by the economics, stakes, and scope of the industry. On the professional level, and increasingly the college and high school levels, fans are following sports teams and athletes to whom they have no personal relationship. They don't know the athletes or the coach nor did they play on the team. And because of specialization, increasing numbers of fans haven't even played the sport. Furthermore, the chances of fans having an encounter with a professional hockey player or running into the manager every morning at the local diner are remote.

While in reality fans are customers of the sport and their relations with the players are impersonal, sports decision makers have to find a way to overcome those barriers. Compounding the problem is that fan expectations have reached an even higher standard. Fans expect a greater return on their monetary and emotional investment in a sports experience. When that expectation is not met, or that player or team disappoints the fan, alienation becomes an even larger problem.

The involvement challenge is clear. Sports brands typically entertain in large numbers and have to deal with a mass audience dynamic both in media and live attendance. For example, when 50,000 fans are pouring into a ballpark, the service questions are far different from those faced by a Nieman Marcus clerk at the cosmetic counter dealing with a single customer. The goal of getting 50,000 people into a sports facility as quickly as possible and yet creating a feeling of personal relationship with the team is daunting. At this point, consider the approaches used by some sports products to create happy customers.

Happy Customers

- The Boston Red Sox and their Red Sox Nation are indivisible. The team involves fans through a number of connection points such as *place, social currency, family,* and *utopian.* The Red Sox offer Red Sox Nation identification cards, which formally grant citizenship to the Nation, and upon winning the World Series in 2004 the team made available to the Nation replica championship souvenir rings and bottles of wine commemorating the victory.[20] Red Sox management, in order to increase and sustain involvement in the team, also capitalized on its 86-year struggle for a championship when team president Larry Lucchino declared that the World Series trophy would be displayed in every one of Massachusetts's 351 towns and cities. Upon seeing the

---

trophy, there were reports of fans crying and wishing that dead members of their families who had suffered for so many years of disappointments could be there at that moment. One fan remarked, "When I saw it, my eyes lit up. It was a dream come true. I couldn't believe it was happening. My heart was pounding. I'm *never* going to stop talking about it."[21] Obviously, the connection level between the Red Sox and their fans is quite high. What makes it work are the connections that in part resulted from the decades of losing, a stadium (Fenway Park) that is the smallest and most idiosyncratic in the league, and team owners who are not so overcome by profit motivation that they neglect maintaining tradition and closeness to the fans.

- The strength of video games is that they empower fans with a degree of ownership over their experience. While it is a *vicarious experience* connection, it can be highly personal and include members of communities all over the world. Fans are increasingly playing sports video games, which in the U.S. market generated $1.2 billion in 2004, representing 20 percent of the video-game industry.[22] Video-game technologies create new relationships between fans and players. If fans root for Vijay Singh, they can play a round on a video game *as* Singh, or if fans prefer Formula 1, they can build their own Formula 1 team and race virtually against the sport's best. Though these games are not a perfect solution, they restore some of the control over the experience that has been removed from the fan with the industrialization of sports, potentially develop fans of a sport they did not play, and provide role-playing experiences that are emotionally based and reinforce the vicarious experience connection.

- The popularity of more participant-friendly sports capitalizes on the *social currency, vicarious experience, and utopian* connections. Extreme sports, for example, attract participants because they provide many opportunities for involvement, are derived from dangerous and street-driven games, and appeal to a young, previously underrepresented market. People of all athletic skills can engage in extreme sports at the local level, which often requires only an investment in a skateboard or a bike, and players can participate for the sheer pleasure of it or attempt to emulate the stars they see on television. The televised version of the sports has an undercurrent of being nonestablishment which is appealing to young viewers who have been inundated with traditionally highly paid and often seemingly ungrateful stars. The sudden emergence of a heretofore unknown television personality of a similar age also has the attraction of fans being able to identify with peers, and it appeals to the individualism that has become so powerful among that age group.

Ethos

The third foundation of sports branding is ethos, which is the character of the communicator as understood and believed by the audience. Ethos is fundamental to creating credibility and is necessary to produce a connection. It is critical in sports because fans have to believe that the brand has integrity and that they can trust it.

Credibility has always been at the center of human interaction. The concept of ethos, which is one of the major tools of persuasion, was developed in Ancient Greece. Aristotle observed that a speaker with ethos possesses three characteristics that are valued by the audience—moral character, intelligence, and goodwill. Ethos ultimately is the audience's judgment of the communicator's reputation and message. If communicators have ethos, they will be able to communicate effectively with the audience. If the audience doesn't have it for the communicator, promises, inducements, and pledges will fall upon deaf ears.

Ethos is something the audience grants the communicator. In the end, a communicator with ethos understands the needs, expectations, and values of a community, and in return, is given the opportunity to earn their trust and attention. Communicators with ethos bond with the audience based on the belief that they will not only do them no harm, but they are acting in their best interest. In the sports world, Hall of Fame pitcher and U.S. Senator Jim Bunning, Willie Mays, and Mia Hamm have ethos because of their performance and citizenship, while despite their athletic skills, gambler Pete Rose, enraged Mike Tyson, and discredited Greek sprinters Kostas Kenteris and Katerina Thanou do not.

Ethos in sports can come in many forms, and, while it is still based on fundamental attributes, it has evolved. It can be that the game is played with all-out effort; the rules are fair, and the competitors have equal opportunities to win; the athletes do not cheat by using supplements or altering their equipment; the fans get their money's worth from the sports experience; or the intentions of the owners, teams, players, and agents are truthful and in the best interest of the fans. Ultimately, the fan decides what is credible. Credibility with fans can be established when fan expectations are met at a number of levels including reliability, quality of play, exceeding expectations, and admitting mistakes and correcting them.

In today's sports environment, ethos has different meanings. For example, World Wrestling Entertainment, while clearly a play-acting and rehearsed sport, has ethos from its fans because it doesn't deceive them on its fundamental competition premise. Pro wrestling merges entertainment and sports and is a combination of script and spontaneity. As an expression of their newfound repositioning and in response to a lawsuit from the World Wildlife Foundation, it changed the name of its organization from World Wrestling Federation to World Wrestling Entertainment. The league has a revolving door of super-star wrestlers who do everything from body slamming opponents to entertaining the in-arena and television audience with five-minute monologues on their immortality and their opponents' immorality. Although the sport is transparently overwrought with soap-opera acting and scripted fights, fans' expectations for WWE are different from those of other sports, and the league is able to meet those expectations consistently. In fact, fans can now vote for who fights during select matches[23] and draft their own fantasy WWE team to compete against other players.[24] As a result, the WWE has established credibility by not only letting the fan know up front that their sport is theatrical, but by setting high entertainment benchmarks for the experience. In turn, the pro wrestling fan knowingly accepts this proposition and in exchange receives the promised product.

Ethos is all about trust. If a sport's credibility is jeopardized, there is a threat that fans could find other sports more trustworthy and therefore appealing. When a sport is threatened by performance-enhancing drugs, player gambling charges, unethical judging practices, or even lack of loyalty to a place, team, or commitment, there is an erosion of the ethos factor. When the German soccer federation announced in 2005 that a number of players and a referee may have been involved in fixing some matches including a German Cup game, there was an immediate and strong reaction.[25] The suggestion that a soccer match is tainted strikes right at the heart of FIFA's credibility. Consider Baylor University's situation when a varsity basketball player murdered a team-mate, and the coach was alleged to have known about the murder and did not tell authorities. The repercussions to the entire credibility of the university were huge as questions were raised about not only the sports program but the integrity of the institution's control.[26] But credibility is not limited to just extreme examples such as fixing a match or a murder; it extends to the everyday encounters such as a fair price at the gate, an honest effort from the players, a management that understands and addresses fan concerns, crowd control that does not endanger lives, and simple gestures such as reasonably priced food and easy access to the event.

A major wave of the future is sports properties developing their own media content and delivering it directly to their fans. Sports properties' emphasis on distributing constant and audience-centered messages through Web sites and other media outlets in order to produce "unfiltered" information is a major ethos question. The ethos problem occurs when sports properties bypass traditional hard-sports news media sources such as newspapers and use their own channels, calling into question the credibility of the information and the intentions of the sports properties. In doing so, sports properties often run the risk of presenting information that appears planted and subjective rather than spontaneous and independent.

An example is the constant warfare between the Washington Redskins football team and *The Washington Post*, with the controversy centering on who gets news first and what does it mean. In both capitalizing on new communication technologies and responding to a history of perceived bad press in *The Post*, the Redskins have increasingly released news about the team, bypassing the traditional media filter of *The Post*. *The Post*'s sports editor Emilio Garcia-Ruiz, in response to the Redskins' self-professed unfiltered positioning, warns, "Of course their message is not unfiltered. It's from the point of view of the team. It's going to be good news. They're not going to put up negative stories. It's simply an attempt to control the message."[27] This is a classic ethos issue for sports properties. If the independent media and fans begin to feel that sports properties' messages are unremittingly uncritical and self-serving, they will dismiss them and look for alternative sources of information. A more effective, ethos-driven strategy is to aim for balanced information channels by being willing to share hard news with independent news sources when appropriate in order to maintain important media relationships. While sports properties ideally would like to communicate directly to fans without any intervention, the filters play a critical role in lending credibility to the sports properties themselves. Moreover, it only stands to reason that in a communication environment with not only traditional media but with blogs, podcasts, and message boards, sports properties must be realistic in managing their media content.

In short, if a sports brand doesn't have ethos, it has no survival rate. In this marketplace, the battle for fans is so competitive that any slip can trigger an exodus. If a sports brand has ethos, the accumulated credibility keeps fans from choosing another entertainment option during even difficult times.

Establishing and maintaining ethos is a critical factor in transformation—the final foundation of successful brand-building and the change process that actualizes a sports product into a brand.

Transformation

When Rutgers and Princeton played their inaugural game in the nineteenth century, it was pretty much, here it is, take it or leave it, for anyone who wanted to watch. Uniforms maybe matched and maybe didn't. Yard markers were not invented yet, and the game was mostly a push and shove match without much scoring or action. It was sufficient because most of the spectators identified with the players, and the game had no history for comparison purposes.

Contrast that football game with Yale visiting Harvard in 1925. By that time, fans came from all over the East Coast by car and train. They entered the cavernous 57,000-person capacity Harvard Stadium and joined thousands of other fans to watch the annual classic. Many of the fans had attended one of the two schools, but they did not personally know the players. At halftime, they milled about the concourse underneath the stadium buying hot dogs and drinks, conversing with friends, and making plans for tailgates and parties. It became a show with ticket prices, parking problems, and salaried employees relying on attendance. The players were dressed appropriately for football, and they had a coaching staff that was nearly professional. College games were now on local radio, and, when Harvard played Michigan, it was a national broadcast.

Let's now move to the Super Bowl of 2005 in Jacksonville, Florida. The event attracted over 100,000 visitors to the city and was watched by more than 86 million Americans and hundreds of millions of viewers around the world.[28] Fans were housed on luxury cruise ships; there was a pregame show titled "Bridging Generations" that offered musical entertainment to a variety of different audiences; sponsors each paid $2.4 million for a 30-second television advertisement,[29] and two weeks of nonstop, 24-hour media coverage led up to the event, which in the end lasted only 4 hours. As an illustration of how the game can now serve as the platform for social currency, the day-after talk often focuses on the ads and not the game itself. When you compare the Harvard-Yale game of 80 years earlier or even the Super Bowls of a decade earlier, the differences are dramatic. In the sports industry, change has become an annual occurrence.

In fact, many of the changes that occurred in sports over the last 150 years were gradual and in response to market forces that were not often articulated. As the marketplace became more competitive, sports became more entertainment-oriented and the expectations rose. In a sense, this evolution of the sports industry is all about transformation. But it was not always designed transformation, only evolution. *Transformation in our context is the purposeful changing of a sports industry product into a brand to heighten strengths, reduce weaknesses, and address competitive pressures.* Over time, audience expectations have changed, generations have turned over, and technologies have added new dimensions to the sports experience. In response to changes in the audience, sports have had to react by making choices on how to present their product to fans.

Many changes have already been made to accommodate competitive pressures—more frequent interviews of players; increased interactivity at the stadium with bands in the concourses, costume nights, and entertainment at every stoppage of play; a multitude of daily fan promotions and price breaks; and an expansion of sports information on television and the Internet. The problem with these strategies is that they, too, will require change and refinement to keep the fans interested and attentive.

There is, however, a fine line to walk when dealing with transformation because change can alienate blocks of fans. Transformation cannot stretch the boundaries of the game beyond what the fans can endure. When the Extreme Football League (XFL) attempted to combine football with professional wrestling, fans universally rejected it. Founder Vince McMahon of World Wrestling Entertainment (WWE) believed that an extreme version of football with a miked field, cheerleaders in the stands, and significant rule alterations from the original game, such as no fair catches, would attract football fans in the NFL's off-season. He was wrong. The league's judgment on what the audience desired was incorrect, and the league lasted only one season. The XFL was attempting to transform football into a hybrid that football fans found had no credibility. It may well be that the strategies of WWE were too early and that someday, after another few rounds of video games, *The Biggest Loser*, and Donald Trump, football audiences will be programmed to accept the hyper nonreflective XFL football product. Just not yet.

When thinking about transformation, there are four choices:

1. Simply be content with your position in the market and make no changes.

2. Make minor changes to what you perceive as a successful product and make only subtle tweaks.
3. Make major changes to the product but still retain some of its core concepts.
4. Completely overhaul the product and start over from scratch.

Considering some level of transformation is critical to approaching the Elusive Fan market today. Asking tough questions about the customers, competition, prices, and technology can only improve the strength of a sports brand and its relationship with its fans. In a hypercompetitive environment, a sports product may have to engage in some level of transformation to survive. Consider Japan's Nippon Professional Baseball.

Japanese Baseball: Old School versus New School

When Japanese baseball player Ichiro Suzuki broke the 84-year-old major league record for total hits in a season in 2004, residents in his native Japan celebrated the achievement as if the record had been broken on behalf of the entire country. Fans in Tokyo rushed to find limited edition newspapers commemorating Suzuki's accomplishment. Japanese Prime Minister Junichiro Koizumi congratulated his effort, and current professional baseball players of Japan's baseball league Nippon Professional Baseball (NPB) marveled at his talent and skill.[30] While the achievement instilled a sense of national pride for the Japanese and became a major moment in the country's sports history, the record wasn't broken in Japan and had no affiliation with the NPB. Suzuki broke it in the United States as a member of MLB's Seattle Mariners during his fourth season in America after playing seven years in Japan.

Suzuki is part of a growing list of Japanese players who have migrated to MLB for higher salaries and better competition. These defections have become a major problem for the NPB, and they contribute to the overall ills of the league. NPB, historically second in popularity to sumo wrestling in Japan, has encountered tough times in the last decade. Revenues are down, television viewership is low, attendance has declined, and fan interest is being redirected to Japanese soccer and MLB.[31] In the midst of all this, the players went on strike in 2004 for the first time in the league's 70-year history,[32] 2 teams in the 12-team league merged because of financial problems, and owners by and large have been reluctant to make changes to reconnect to their fans.

(Continued)

(*Continued*)

The problems of the NPB in part result from its original concept. The league was started by Japanese companies looking to use baseball teams as advertising tools for their products. Owners were not concerned whether the team lost money because, in the end, it was a small price to pay compared to other forms of advertising. As a result, teams did little in the way of marketing and promotion and relied primarily on box scores in the newspaper as their only media connection to their fans. They believed that putting a product on the field was sufficient for their advertising needs and that fans would find their way to the stadium. Japanese baseball owners were not unlike early twentieth-century industrialists who believed that product development and engineering were all that was needed to sell cars and ice boxes. Throughout much of its history, this strategy worked because the league lacked competitors and the top stars remained in the country. Now, the league and sport is in crisis, and like all industries the Japanese baseball league needs to become customer-centered.

To survive in its marketplace, NPB must consider transforming its current model of doing business. A first step is beginning to deal with the ownership structure. Many of the owners represent Japan's old guard, businessmen who operate by the rules of keiretsu, a business philosophy that closes off relations with any business not within the keiretsu circle. When a 31-year-old entrepreneur asked to buy the fledgling Kintetsu Buffaloes and open up the club to public shareholders, Tsuneo Watanabe, the 78-year-old former leader of the Yomiuri Giants, Japan's most popular team, definitively stated, "We can't let some unknown person in."[33]

Under the current league structure, the commissioner of the NPB is essentially a perpetual lame duck. In response to this arrangement, the league must take measures to empower the commissioner or some governing body to loosen ownership rules in order to include younger, more motivated owners with the intention of resurrecting the game and league. The league has moved in this direction by granting the sale of a new ball club to replace the one lost in the merger of 2004. The owner is Internet pioneer Hiroshi Mikitani, who plans to use his sophisticated Internet marketing schemes to regenerate fan interest.[34] Mikitani's admittance into the circle of owners was important because it infused new thinking into the league's power structure. It also emphasized the need to invent and implement new media communication strategies to compete with other global sports and entertainments.

As a second step, the league must put itself in better position to keep Japanese players from defecting to the United States, or when they do, be prepared by selecting a number of potential stars who will not be fleeing to America. Japanese baseball has long thrived on star power and must early identify, promote, and keep higher-visibility players for fans.

Finally, the league must develop new distribution opportunities, particularly on a global level. The high-quality baseball that Japan plays could be combined with other countries in the region such as Taiwan and South Korea to produce a major league level southeastern Asian baseball league. Capitalizing on its location by creating rivalries with neighboring countries through regularly scheduled games or even an extension of the league could immediately heighten awareness and brand Asian baseball in some of the fastest-growing markets in the world. The league has begun to move toward a more global strategy by agreeing, although reluctantly, to participate in and ultimately win baseball's version of the world cup, the World Baseball Classic.[35]

Japanese baseball is at a crossroads. It has a large market, many fine baseball players, and the financial and industrial potential for a substantial infrastructure. Now what it needs is a major reconsideration and transformation of its product if it is going to compete in an increasingly global marketplace.

CONCLUSION

In this chapter, we examined the issues of marketing sports brands and the four critical components of a strong brand—segmentation, ethos, involvement, and transformation. Sports, like most other industries, are building brands to compete in a fragmented and competitive marketplace. A major reason is that sports products need to develop fan connections other than winning to survive. But there are some issues in attracting and retaining fans that are specific to the sports industry. Unlike most other industries, sports products must serve mass audiences regularly, often handle all-pervasive media coverage, and manage a wide range of parties such as owners, agents, players, executives, and sponsors. Moreover, the principal product of the industry—athletic competitions—is often subject to motivational and attitudinal issues that are frequently out of the control of sports decision makers. Despite these branding obstacles, attracting, connecting, and retaining fans in such a competitive and unpredictable market can be systematically approached through the transformation process. Chapter 5 discusses the principles of brand concept generation and Chapter 6, the equally important steps of brand testing, brand refinement, and brand actualization.

Chapter

$$\boxed{5}$$

GENERATING THE SPORTS BRAND TRANSFORMATION

In the 1930s, star miler Glenn Cunningham could name his price. His sport, a track and field event, was a staple of the winter sports circuit as cities hosted indoor track meets at such premiere sites as Madison Square Garden in New York and the Chicago Stadium that drew capacity crowds and were often cosponsored by major newspapers and tied to a charity. Cunningham, a Depression-era hero who overcame a tragic fire that severely damaged his legs at the age of 12, made a good living appearing at these Amateur Athletic Union (AAU) administered events, often receiving a substantial bonus for his appearances under the table. For many young athletes such as Cunningham, the ultimate goal of running in the Olympics was supported by a vast track-and-field support system in high schools, universities, clubs, and countries all over the world. Track and field events were major sports attractions with vast followings and a strong infrastructure.

Some seven decades later, track-and-field events are greatly diminished with indoor events declining in interest in many communities and the sports being dropped by a number of higher education institutions. Track-and-field sports have also been overshadowed by emerging sports activities such as field hockey, lacrosse, spring football, extreme sports, and automobile racing. Beset by steroid convictions, major competition, and a history of decentralized and fragmented leadership, track and field's downward spiral continues. If track and field is going to regain its previous luster, it will need strong and unified leadership that understands and can relate to the Elusive Fan.

The sports in track-and-field events are an obvious candidate for transformation, but they're not the only sport in need of change. Transformation—the systematic change process that redefines and reinvents a sports product as a fan-centered brand—is becoming the gold standard in today's competitive environment.[1] As new competitors enter the marketplace, all sports products must continually reassess their market position and adapt to the changing expectations of their fans. Establishing a stronger brand through transformation is important because it differentiates one sports product from another and has the potential to extend the life of the product beyond changes in players, fortunes, or unexpected events.

The potential power of a sports brand can be realized only through adept understanding of the marketplace and willingness to undergo analysis and sometimes painful change. It is possible for a brand to develop spontaneously, from the wellspring of an unbelievable talent or the intersection of nationalism, history, or one brand-defining event. While these transformations do happen, it is more likely that a sports brand is developed over time, reworked and recrafted from a number of reasoned and intuitive situations and encounters.

TRANSFORMATION DRIVERS

The first step in the transformation model is to understand how it is initiated and who the drivers are that jump-start the process. Transformation needs a motivator. This motivation is often a deteriorating fan base, a need for financial improvement, local or global competition, or the pride of a community. In some cases, it can be a high school merging and splitting its athletic base, the dropping of a sport by a regional or national organization, or a series of unexpected events such as a strike, an injury, or player scandals. In other cases, the sports product can preempt the threat of fan erosion and proactively transform in anticipation of market demands. In any event, most sports products cannot afford to maintain their current state in today's competitive environment and as a result, have to change to adapt. This change process needs to be activated by a driver. Drivers can be as traditional as an individual who takes a leadership role or can be situational such as a crisis in television ratings or a new law.

Leadership Driver

The leadership transformer is someone in a commanding or iconic position who can orchestrate a sports transformation. In the case of the NFL, Commissioner Bert Bell in the 1950s skillfully merged competing teams into the league, recognized a players association despite ownership objections, and most importantly used television as a major distribution channel to make the sport an American institution. His successor, Pete Rozelle, continued the leadership role and the transformation of football into truly a national sport. Rozelle had a background in public relations and had been for a short period a general manager for the Los Angeles Rams. He was the unlikely designer of a massive transformation that centralized ownership and power in the NFL with the goal of competitive balance. It was Rozelle who set best-practice goals for team management and facilities, and most importantly, structured the game to appeal to the emerging power of television with events such as the Super Bowl and Monday Night Football.

The leadership transformer is not always drawn from the consensus leader as illustrated by cricket reformer Jagmohan Dalmiya, who had another vision of cricket and encouraged the sport to adapt. Whereas Rozelle was an insider and the long-term leader at the top of the NFL pyramid, Dalmiya headed an Indian construction empire and served as the chief official of India's cricket association and as the controversial one-term president of the International Cricket Council (ICC). Unlike Rozelle, he was an outsider in both style and tradition. Despite these handicaps, Dalmiya made cricket a global force, signing outsized media contracts, encouraging corporate sponsorships that began to dominate the former pristine fields of the sport, and more than doubling membership of the ICC. Unlike Rozelle, Dalmiya's reworking of cricket had many critics who were dismayed at his seeming trampling of the sport's sacred traditions. But nonetheless he was the transformer, driven by a vision that cricket could be a major force in the world of sports.

Crisis Driver

As in life itself, it often takes something negative to get attention and force change. The NBA has experienced a number of incidents of player misbehavior that have tarnished the sport. On-court eruptions, such as the Detroit Pistons–Indiana Pacers fight with fans at Auburn Hills, and outrageous comments by players, such as Latrell Sprewell who was making $14.6 million a year but claimed that he needed a larger contract extension so that he could "feed his family," only reinforced the negative image. The image problem was magnified off court with numerous charges of criminal activities against players that were captured in a book ominously entitled *Out of Bounds: Inside the NBA's Culture of Rape, Violence, and Crime.*[2] When the NBA found itself under severe criticism from the media and many of their fans in response to the off- and on-court behavior of its players, the league stepped up its punishments and fines, began redirecting its initiatives to global expansion, raised the player age minimum to 19, and enforced a dress code. All these changes were in response to a crisis and were aimed at redefining the NBA as a more international, respectable, and mainstream sports product.

If the crisis is not addressed, the sports brand runs the risk of losing both its credibility and market share. Fixed boxing matches such as Billy Fox knocking out Jake LaMotta in 1948 and suspicious fights involving heavyweight champion Sonny Liston all helped cast shadows over the legitimacy of an already questionable sport. Coupled with the televised killings of boxers in the ring and the relationship between the sport and organized crime, boxing needed to recast itself for an ever-changing marketplace. Boxing never really had a leadership structure to address the crisis, and the sport was at the mercy of state boxing commissions, promoters, and managers and handlers who all operated as independent contractors. As a result, the fight industry lost credibility, and the market declined.

Cultural Trend Drivers

Cultural trends often motivate transformation because they often have unintended sports consequences. The growing number of women who play and follow sports inspired the NBA to launch the Women's National Basketball Association (WNBA) in 1996, which continues to develop with attendance and television ratings steady and promising but not breaking out.[3] The NBA recognized the growth of women's college basketball programs and the market potential of fielding a counterpart to its all-male product. The changes in Title IX at the college level, which helped to produce the expanding pool of talented women college players, and the acceptance of women athletes in the professional sports ranks also encouraged the NBA to make the move.

Other changes in sports culture, such as how people play sports, can influence transformation. Responding to a society that increasingly emphasizes safety, some sporting equipment manufacturers have transformed their products to fit the lifestyles and playing habits of their participants. New lines of equipment have been introduced to soften certain sports and appeal to different demographics. Paintball has introduced a safer version of its paintballs that pack a lighter punch upon impact and are targeted at a younger audience. Similarly, motorized skateboards, baseballs that automatically curve, and Tamball, a friendlier version of tennis played on a volleyball court, have been created to cater to a more safety conscious market.[4]

Market Drivers

Market composition can also encourage transformation. The Los Angeles Angels of Anaheim play in a region with a growing Hispanic population. Owner Arte Moreno changed the makeup of his club to include more Hispanic players to attract interest from this Hispanic community. The team signed players such as Vladimir Guerrero and Bartolo Colon to long-term contracts and promoted these new stars as part of a multicultural brand. The strategy was effective for the Angels as the team not only made the playoffs but broke attendance records in both 2004 and 2005.[5]

While the Angels' strategy was a proactive transformation, a sport like bowling had been reactive to changing market conditions. The audience for bowling peaked in the early decades of the Television Generation, and until the twenty-first century the sport made few changes to its product to inspire younger audiences to participate or watch on television. As a result, bowling was squandering an opportunity to create the connections with the young people who could sustain the livelihood of the sport. Faced with literally a dying marketplace, a team of former Microsoft employees, who bought the Professional Bowlers Association (PBA), made changes to the competition format, signed a television contract with ESPN, and redesigned and repositioned bowling "alleys" as bowling "centers" to shed the beer-drinking, cigarette-smoking image of the sport.[6] These adjustments were intended to transform bowling, and as a result, increased its attraction to a younger audience.

Media Drivers

Some sports undergo transformations in response to media demands. NASCAR historically had underperforming television ratings for most of the second half of the racing season because the champion had usually already been decided. To generate interest for the entire season and determine the champion closer to the end of the season, NASCAR implemented new rules to the competition. It created a championship cup series that qualified 10 competitors to compete in the final 10 races for the championship. Although NASCAR received criticism from its traditional market, the move was welcomed by those in the media who saw the change as more entertaining, meaningful, and attractive to television viewers.[7] The NASCAR success encouraged the PGA Tour and the Ladies Professional Golf Association (LPGA) to introduce similar playoff formats to stimulate media viewing.

Real Madrid is a good example of a team reacting to the increasingly global audience made available through the media. It conceived a strategy of showcasing a star-powered team on the field and capitalizing on distribution channels for global exposure that helped move the team into the black for the first time in 40 years.[8] The signing of soccer superstars Zinedine Zidane, Ronaldo, and David Beckham enabled the team to use its television, radio, and Internet media outlets to not only appeal to fans within Spain and Europe but also to appeal to those in Asia and the United States. Despite an underperforming winning record,[9] the team's media-driven strategy has produced increased exposure, translating into higher merchandise sales, more international games, and increased rights fees for the team's games and other content.[10]

THE TRANSFORMATION PROCESS

Whether it is a leadership, cultural trend, crisis, market, or media driver, sports decision makers face a number of challenges to altering their sports products. Some are as psychologically complicated as the attitudes of ingrained and intransigent leaders, while others revolve around the issue of research, insight, and deep understanding of the likely consequences of a transformation.

There is a strong desire on the part of many sports leaders to hang onto fundamental concepts that have worked over the generations. However, even the most ardent supporters of maintaining the status quo have, under pressure, made numerous changes. It's been more than a half-century since the NBA adopted the 24-second shot clock before the 1954–1955 season and over two decades since the three point shot was implemented in 1979. Each new addition today seems as natural as any aspect of the game. The innovations were so successful on the professional level that they ultimately were adopted by the college game since they too sought to speed up the game, increase scoring, create more excitement, and heighten the intensity of the game's final minutes, all to enhance fan interest. In retrospect, these innovations transformed the game into a much different kind of entertainment, but the magnitude of the changes wouldn't be understood until later. During the early years of the shot clock, basketball Hall of Famer Dolph Schayes recalls, "None of us at the time realized the significance of it. Arguably, it can be said it's been the most important rule change in the history of the game."[11]

A wide range of sports products can be candidates for transformation. There are *sports*—basketball and football; *leagues*—English Premier League and Major League Baseball; *teams*—the Argentinean national basketball team and the Toronto Argonauts; *events*—the Major League Soccer all-star game and a high school state championship swimming tournament; *stars*—Yao Ming and Michael Schumacher; and *sporting goods*—snowboards and running shoes. All the products have similarities, yet each poses different challenges. League issues and star issues, for example, may be related and yet under some circumstances have different visions or goals. The PGA prefers that major stars such as Australian Greg Norman and South African Retief Goosen appear in the big money and media exposure tournaments in the U.S., while such stars often feel an obligation to build their home markets not only because of fan expectations but also because of long-term financial consequences for the sport in their region. The critical issue is that under most circumstances the underlying transformation process is similar for all sports products, and managing the transformation process successfully often has the benefit of merging seemingly incompatible interests.

Transforming sports products requires four stages of development: *brand concept generation, brand testing, brand refinement,* and *brand actualization.* In this chapter, we focus on the first stage, brand concept generation.

BRAND CONCEPT GENERATION

In many sports sectors, certain attributes are given and expected by the audience. In baseball, fans expect nine innings, four bases, a pitcher, and a rotation of nine hitters. In basketball, a 7'1" player is unlikely to change careers and become a badminton star simply because a market opportunity presents itself. However, the basketball player does have the option of becoming a different type of basketball player. He or she might become a rebounder instead of a scorer or a team player instead of a streak shooter. The player could develop a specific shot that trademarks his or her game. The same player might branch out and become a guest on reality shows or do color commentary for cable television college basketball broadcasts. This principle applies to all sports products from leagues to teams to events. There are some attributes that cannot be transformed because they are fixed and others that are malleable and can become valuable brand concept generation material.

Brand concept generation involves developing and choosing concept possibilities that will potentially attract the target segments. The change agents include all sports decision makers ranging from promoters to managers to family members. Their goal is to develop a set of brand attributes to differentiate their sports product in the marketplace.

In order to accomplish this, sports decision makers have to look realistically at the product's *capacity threshold*—the minimum talents and skills required for the sports sector. They must understand the product's assets, limits, boundaries, and stretch and reach in relationship to audience expectations, and they need to be realistic about goal setting and situations. Poker, for example, has prospered in part because it is a formerly closeted game that has opened up to television scrutiny. Its major characteristics are the lure of gambling, tension generated at the table, outsized rewards, and close-up shots of the participants' tics, behaviors, and stealth. A poker player can have any shape, weight, hair color; it doesn't matter. Within the game's parameters, the lack of physical prowess is not important, because poker will never be an athletic contest like soccer where physical skills do matter. There are capacity threshold issues for poker that may not exist for other sports such as sumo wrestling, fishing, or marathon running. The capacity threshold does not imply that one sport is better than another, but that its fundamental talent, skill, and sports requirement levels are different and require different management of the brand.

Deion Has Lots of Capacity

There have been a number of multitalented athletes such as Jim Brown, Mildred "Babe" Didrikson Zaharias, Jim Thorpe, Jackie Robinson, and Bo Jackson, but few were able to capitalize on their versatility the way Deion Sanders did. Sanders was a star cornerback in the National Football League winning two Super Bowl rings, and he played for three Major League Baseball teams and starred in a World Series where he hit an astronomical .533. Then he branched out into a multifaceted broadcasting career and launched a football comeback at the age of 37. What tied together Sanders's professional sports career was an attitude that branded brashness and defiance at a multisport level. He was "Neon Deion" and "Prime Time," and was trademarked by his fashionable clothes, outrageous behavior, and speed and skill. He resembled Muhammad Ali, who taunted the media, recited iambic pentameter poetry, and backed up his predictions with his boxing prowess.

While NFL players such as Terrell Owens and Chad Johnson dance in the end zone and infuriate commentators and officials, the pro football branding playbook was written earlier by Sanders. His multifaceted persona included rapping in a music video, broadcasting on CBS's NFL Today pregame show, and a charitable side that included many acts both noted and unnoted.

While Sanders is a gifted athlete, when he crossed over into broadcasting, he demonstrated the work ethic that underlay his brand. Jim Nance, who hosted the *NFL Today*, said of him, "No one outworked him. He was determined to become the best analyst ever."[12] Even more telling is that Sanders was never associated with drugs, alcohol, or any performance questions. He was a talented athlete who understood his skills and was willing to work hard to create his brand.

(Continued)

(*Continued*)

The lesson is that judging the capacity threshold is critical to success. The sports world is full of cross-sectoring sports stars who misfired such as NBA star Ron Artest who produced a much maligned rap album. Even Michael Jordan, whose cross-sectoring skills are legendary, failed in his attempt to make the major leagues with the Chicago White Sox. Evaluating, targeting, and executing your brand potential are as important in sports brand development as in any other field of business.

It is critical that any sports product seeking a transformation fulfill the minimum skills and ability required of its sports sector. Once the sports product surpasses this capacity threshold, the brand concept generation stage can begin. There are five steps to generating a successful brand:

1. *Audit:* Assessing the need for brand definition or redefinition
2. *Inventory:* Evaluating the brand assets
3. *Target:* Defining the target segments
4. *Plan:* Determining the scale of transformation
5. *Build:* Building the brand for the target segments

Assessing the Need

A sports product must identify what its needs are and determine what it wants to be. There are four principal steps to this process: (1) defining the current state, (2) examining the competition, (3) accounting for cultural trends, and (4) determining a vision.

The first step sports products must take is defining their *current state* through identifying their strengths, weaknesses, opportunities, and threats (SWOT). For example, if the National Lacrosse League (NLL), an indoor professional lacrosse league in North America, is looking to broaden its market share and increase its revenue, it could begin with a SWOT analysis.

Strengths:	**Weaknesses:**
• Action sport that combines hockey's physical energy and basketball's pace and frequent scoring.	• Viewed as a sport that athletes play if they can't make it in major sports.

- Strong and growing youth, high school, and college participation.
- Improving attendance and national television exposure of all-star and championship games.

- Stereotyped as an upper-class sport.
- Amateur play concentrated primarily on the East Coast.

Opportunities:

- High amateur participation rates can be converted into NLL fans.
- Potential to build star power in the league.
- Expansion into markets in other parts of the country.

Threats:

- Lack of consistent media exposure.
- Playing in other sports' facilities does not allow for the NLL to showcase its total package.

The second step is examining the *competition*. The sports property surveys the industry and other entertainment competitors to account for who's doing what, how they are doing it, and with what success. If the NLL is looking to expand its brand, it needs to understand the sports and entertainments that it is competing with and in what markets. The NLL competes from December to April against high-profile sports such as football, basketball, and hockey. The teams of the NLL are generally owned by NHL hockey franchises and are housed in their arenas and inevitably compete for a similar fan base. This stage also benchmarks some of the best practices of competitive properties and also flags their failures or other critical issues.

The third step is accounting for *cultural trends*. Asking critical questions about how people receive information, what the latest consumer buying habits are, what new technologies people are using, or how people spend their time is an important starting point in developing a brand concept. In the end, the brand concept needs to adapt to cultural trends to ensure a fan base. In the case of the NLL, the league could work with the emerging club, high school, and college lacrosse programs, build an ongoing media relationship, and capitalize on the cultural trend of high-scoring, nonstop play as well as the escalating salaries and compensation of its competition.

The final step is to determine the *vision* for the sports property. After looking at the current state of the sports product, what competitors are doing, and how the culture is affecting business, the sports property needs to develop a clear vision. It is imperative that at the vision stage the sports property be realistic as to its assets, goals, and motivation to make the brand successful. The NLL's vision according to NLL director of marketing Matt Miller is, "To become the fifth major professional sports league in America."[13] The NLL, which is now over 20 years old, is expanding into new markets, and franchises that initially sold for $250,000 are now $3 million.[14] It is in position to take the next step to becoming a major professional sports league but faces the obstacles of the emerging MLS and the continuing fragmentation of the sports television audience. Below are other examples of clear visions with realistic expectations:

> *Singapore Badminton Association:* "To establish Singapore as a top badminton nation in the world."[15]
>
> *Texas Tech University:* "Texas Tech University will be a leader in intercollegiate athletics. The Department of Intercollegiate Athletics aspires to be national[ly] recognized for excellence and performance in athletic competition, academic excellence and personal development of our student-athletes."[16]
>
> *High School Bowling USA (HSBUSA):* "It is the vision of HSBUSA to be an essential resource to school administrators, bowling centers and industry membership organizations so that all high school students have the opportunity to experience high school sports competition through a state recognized varsity letter bowling program."[17]

Inventorying the Brand Assets

Each sports product has its own set of attributes. The challenge is finding and choosing the product's most authentic and promotable qualities. In this phase of brand concept generation, sports brand decision makers gather all the branding possibilities and decide which assets to emphasize and which to discard. In the inventorying phase, three areas must be addressed: brand-forming moments, brand values, and brand synergy.

Brand-Forming Moments One of the most difficult tasks in the branding process is defining the product's brand essence—the core meaning of a brand to its consumers. A way of understanding and defining brand essence is examining the product's *brand-forming moments*. These moments often occur during competition, media exposure, or public and private history, and they instill in the fan a strong sense of what constitutes the brand. A purpose of the inventory process is to choose the brand-forming moments that will best build the brand.

The NFL, for example, had a brand-forming moment with the television broadcast of the Baltimore Colts/New York Giants 1958 NFL championship game. The game featured star players such as Colts Johnny Unitas and Alan "the Horse" Ameche and Giants Charley Connerly and Frank Gifford, and was the first sudden-death overtime game ever played in the NFL, a new rule change for the league. The game, which the Colts won 23-17, has been called the "greatest game ever played."[18] The combination of the star-based teams and television's increasing ability to transmit intimacy, tension, and suspense educated the audience on what the NFL could offer and teamed television with the NFL in a shared experience. Making this brand-forming moment so valuable was that the NFL maximized this fan connection and capitalized on it to build a very powerful brand.

Often brand-forming moments are not as transparent and must be sought out. Although the summer Gravity Games had been in operation for six years, it wasn't until 2005 that the event found its brand-forming moment—a shift back to the smaller-scale origins of extreme sports and an appeal to the utopian connection. The moment was driven by the Gravity Games' inability to create differentiation in the extreme sports market with their primary competitor, the X Games, an event they essentially cloned during their first six years of existence. Both the X Games and Gravity Games had become major attendance events at sophisticated big city venues in Los Angeles and Cleveland, respectively, and took on more of the establishment aura of big-time sports. The Gravity Games, which were held in Cleveland for three consecutive years, were a live attendance success, attracting an average of more than 150,000 fans annually.[19] But that was not what the Outdoor Life Network (OLN) had in mind when they bought the games from Octagon, Inc. The network instead transformed the Gravity Games with the expressed interest of building their sports network and expanding the Gravity Games brand to also include a relaunched winter games and a new Australian version.

To contrast their positioning with the X Games, the summer Gravity Games were held in 2005 at two downsized venues—Camp Woodward, a primitive, unrefined extreme sports venue in the middle of Pennsylvania's Amish country, and FDR Skatepark in South Philadelphia, another well-known original extreme-sports site that is under highway I-95.[20] The change in venues signaled a shift in strategy for the Gravity Games. OLN was moving away from an emphasis on live interaction to staging for television what the network terms "actionmentary coverage,"[21] which combines action sports, music, and cinematic production into an entertainment package for the television audience. The venues now became the set for a television program, and the paying spectators were the studio audience. The newly branded Games are much closer to the environmental setting of *Survivor* than the Olympics. The Games strategists are gambling on structuring a brand-forming moment that they believe the market will respond to and differentiate the event from the X Games, their main competitor.

Designing brand-forming moments often requires researching a product's history and background, monitoring sector and market expectations, and extracting a range of possible materials that could appeal to the target segments. Sports decision makers can choose from a number of sources including the players, coaches, stadium, team history, owner, and league. Brand-forming moments can be discovered accidentally, can be developed from a brainstorming session, or can be generated by a systematic, research-based process.

Brand-Forming Moments

Brand-forming moments often become the brand's signature. Following are some outstanding examples:

Brand	Brand-Forming Moment
Nike Air Jordan	Michael Jordon's slam-dunking ability transformed a basketball shoe into a social symbol.
Track and field	Roger Bannister's breaking the four-minute-mile barrier brought worldwide attention to the possibilities of breaking long-held records.
Tennis	The televised Bobby Riggs and Billie Jean King tennis match rebranded tennis as an entertaining television sport.
Starter jackets	The wearing of tough-guy Oakland Raider starter jackets by the teen market changed sports clothing into a statement of both fashion and aggression.
Houston Astrodome	The opening of the first indoor domed stadium redefined the sports arena as a multipurpose 365-day-a-year place for events.
NCAA Final Four	Underdog North Carolina State coached by Jim Valvano upset heavily favored Houston in the championship game on a last second shot that branded the tournament as unpredictable and the coach as a permanent symbol of hope.

Brand Values Brand values are defined as the principles that uphold the meaning or culture of the sports brand. They are not necessarily influenced by performance outcomes such as winning or losing and are often critical in attaining and maintaining fan loyalty. Common sports brand values are power, ritual, heritage, respect, diligence, integrity, honor, loyalty, protection, and perseverance. Sports brands need to develop a set of values that will not only help define the brand but deepen and ensure the fan connection. The Chicago Bears, whether they win or lose, are tied to the city because of fundamental values that were nurtured by historical associations and the commitment of the team's fans no matter what the obstacles or odds. The Chicago Bears create a distinct Bears culture and help bind together the entire organization, city, and fans.

Determining and refining brand values is an important ingredient for building the brand as it makes clear to the fan what the brand represents. For example, the brand values of the U.S. Rollergirls Association, which showcases all-female teams in often personal and violent matches, are clearly power, loyalty, and protection. Despite what occurs in these matches, the brand values are an important ingredient in tying the teams to the fans.

Another approach to understanding what the brand stands for is examining the purpose it serves its customers. This means looking not only at the brand *values*, but the brand *value*—or the utility of the brand. Harvard professor Clayton Christensen and industry experts Scott Cook and Taddy Hall argue that consumers have jobs they need to perform and that brands should be built to help consumers get their jobs done. They have termed the products that do this well "purpose brands" and cite best practice examples such as Federal Express, which accomplished the "I-need-to-send-this-from-here-to-there-with-perfect-certainty-as-fast-as-possible job," and the Sony Walkman, which satisfied the "help-me-escape-the-chaos-in-my-world job."[22] If marketers focus on the jobs consumers do, and not necessarily on their demographic, lifestyle, or psychographic profile, they believe that more products will survive and companies can build more loyal customers.

While applying this purpose branding concept to the leisure activity of sports may seem somewhat of a stretch, there is the possibility that a sports brand becomes so disconnected from its market that it doesn't get done what the fans want. A benefit of purpose branding is that it requires sports decision makers to uncover some of the underlying reasons why fans on the ground level engage with a brand. There are a variety of examples of purpose brands all over the sports industry. Fans play fantasy sports because the activity accomplishes the job of keeping friends connected and in touch. Paintball is an emerging sport because it satisfies the job of providing participants an outlet for aggression and a chance to perform violent acts in a controlled environment. The South Korean national short-track speed skating team does the job for the fan of symbolically representing the country's emergence as a power and a player on the world stage. In all these examples, the purpose of the sports brand is not just to provide entertainment but to satisfy a fundamental need of the fan.

What is critical is that brand values have surfaced as an important element of developing a sports brand. While there are many methods to do so, the focus on uncovering these brand values is important in sustaining a sports brand under circumstances of inevitable change, misfortune, or a cultural shift.

Brand Synergy Brand synergy occurs when the sports brands fit, support, or complement each other. Most sports products contain a governing body such as a league, conference, or federation; events; teams; and individuals, including players, coaches, and administrators. This is the group whose members must work together to not only prevent blocking each other's positioning but to reinforce it.

While it is ideal that sports branding components be unified and cohesive, sports decision makers often have control only over their specific product, be it players, leagues, or events. A coordination principle needs to structure the potential conflicts in the product mix. A useful approach to solving this problem and maximizing brand synergy is considering the branding picture from two perspectives: macro and micro.

The *macro brand* is the product that is undergoing the transformation and is under direct control of the sports decision maker. The *micro brands* serve as brand extensions to both reinforce the macro brand concept and differentiate it in the marketplace. If a league is looking to reinvent itself, it must first assess its macro brand and then address how a change would affect the positioning of its micro brands, which in this case are its teams, individuals, sports, and events. For example, the MLB macro brand embodies the core attributes of family and youth, history and nostalgia, and summer and leisure. Its micro brands include its 30 different teams, players, managers, executives, and the sport itself. While the Oakland Athletics are an MLB micro brand centered on youth, irreverence, and innovative management, ideally they still must represent and reinforce the macro brand of MLB.

Achieving brand synergy where all of the macro and micro brands fit together is the optimal result in brand concept generation. By looking at the brand synergy mix and evaluating how a transformation would fit the positioning of the other sports brand components, sports decision makers can not only measure the effectiveness of their branding choices but also maximize the brand equity already established by its fellow brands. After this point in inventorying the brand's assets, sports decision makers can look more specifically at selecting the target segments of their brand.

Defining the Target Segments

Once the sports decision makers have clearly defined their future goals, they must choose segments that will fulfill that vision. It is important to remember, however, that choosing a vision is interactive with choosing target segments. Either may be the starting point. A sports product can notice a large neglected segment and then develop its vision. Or it can develop a vision and search for segments to which the vision will appeal.

Each target segment has different characteristics and requirements. Most organizations target a mix of segments rather than one broad segment. Sports products should develop a different value proposition for each segment that is compatible, not conflicting. The four principal areas that sports products need to address in defining the target segments are their characteristics, marketing requirements, profitability, and resource availability.

Market Characteristics All segments are not created equal; some are better candidates than others for sports products to target. Market characteristics include size, demographics, values, and, most importantly, connection points. In generating a brand, these characteristics need to be clearly aligned to ensure that there is a link between the vision, the brand, and the segment.

For example, the Super Bowl draws a broader audience than a regular NFL football game. The Super Bowl averages nearly 90 million viewers in the United States alone, and a regular season national cable game averages fewer than 10 million viewers.[23] The added audience represents nonfans, casual fans, partygoers, and people who are simply interested in watching the competition for the top commercial. Monday Night Football has the added fan diversity of bar scenes all over the country, which includes typically more females and casual fans than do the Sunday afternoon games. A sports property and its advertisers recognizing these fundamental differences in audiences need to prepare material that is suitable for these differently configured segments.

There are other nuances of demographics that become increasingly complicated as a sport tries to broaden its appeal. For example, the professional golf audience tends to run older than the extreme sports fan base, which is largely made up of males in their teens and twenties. The delivery of the language, style, and material needs to take these differences into consideration when appealing to the more mature group of professional golf fans. On the other hand, golf is determined to expand to a younger marketplace, which demands developing material and events that are customized to a more contemporary, culturally sensitive group and delivering the message and pricing the product appropriately to attract it.

Marketing Requirements Special features may make the marketing of a sports product particularly difficult or easy. For example, a market may be very attractive but may already be oversaturated with competitors. For many sports products, youth represent the most important market in sports. They have substantial buying power, influence parental decision-making, and are at the stage in their lives where they can potentially form long-lasting brand loyalties. However, the list of sports products targeting the youth market is becoming longer, and the issues are becoming more complex. As a result, marketing at the high-stakes level to youth requires significant resources, commitment, and a major amount of risk. On the other hand, marketing to the older Baby Boomer audience may be more appropriate and require fewer resources because of a lack of competitors.

> The New Balance Athletic Shoe company has in the last decade made inroads into the shoe market traditionally dominated by Nike and Reebok. This is a marketplace that relies heavily on athlete endorsements and huge amounts of advertising dollars. New Balance's counterposition was to manufacture and market shoes that downplayed the fashion qualities of its competitors' products and targeted mostly an aging audience. The company's strategy has been to supply "shoes in many more widths, so that Baby Boomers with flattening feet are more comfortable as they jog or drive to the hoop."[24] Clearly distinguishing its brand from its competitors and targeting a different

audience has enabled New Balance to segment a market that was ignored by the competition and was growing. Its solid performance has also enabled it to begin offering new lines of shoes and expanding its customer base to a younger market on the foundation of its reputation for accommodating, value-driven, and unassuming shoes.

Another element that influences marketing requirements is the market's orientation to a sports product. In anticipation of the 2004 lockout of the National Hockey League, the American Hockey League's Toronto Road Runners were relocated to Edmonton for the 2004–2005 season to capitalize on the market void that would be created by the absence of the Edmonton Oilers. For the Road Runners, their new target market, NHL Edmonton Oilers fans, had the advantage of already being hockey followers, living in a city that rates hockey as its most popular sport, and desiring to watch any form of the sport of which they were deprived. In order to appeal to this market, the Road Runners had little work to do educating the fan base about the game or convincing fans that watching hockey isn't boring. They did need to provide a product that was close to the NHL in quality and performance and spur favorable word of mouth among NHL fans. To help attract these fans, the team promoted the slogan, "Pro Hockey Guaranteed," which offered the Road Runners as a hockey alternative during the lockout.[25] The requirements of their new target market were relatively minimal, but the results were not as subtle. Opening day for the Road Runners in 2004 drew a live attendance of 16,001 fans, breaking the franchise's previous attendance record by over 6,000,[26] and the team finished third in overall and average league attendance. In fact, the market's hockey orientation was so similar that in anticipation of the resolution of the NHL lockout, the team cancelled its 2005–2006 season to not interfere with the Oilers' attempts to reestablish their fan base.[27] Clearly the type of sports product that is targeted to a particular market has different requirements. It would be much more challenging to attract fans if the Edmonton Road Runners were an indoor cycling team.

Profitability Analysis Since different segments have different requirements, when choosing one, the sports decision maker must weigh carefully the profit potential of such an endeavor. The costs of reaching segments could include advertising and public relations campaigns, grassroots marketing efforts, and special events. After all these cost considerations, the revenue has to be estimated. The question is whether the profit would be adequate in relation to the considerable effort that must be put into effecting this transformation. It may very well be that suburban markets are underrepresented as fans of professional billiards but that reaching that market would not warrant the resources needed to make it profitable.

Resource Availability Even if the profit potential is promising, the sports property has to consider whether it can attract sufficient funds and expertise. It may well be that the available resources are not adequate to finance the transformation.

NASCAR is an example of a sports property with a vision that was implemented because it was able to attract and develop enough resources. Since NASCAR wanted to expand into urban markets to become a more mainstream sport, it needed facilities. In the last decade, its financial strength enabled it to acquire critical racetracks in the northern and western states. Without the tracks, there is no brand expansion, and without the cooperation of the communities, media distributors, sponsors, and the willingness of the drivers to move into new markets, there could not have been any changes.

Determining the Scale of Transformation

In evaluating how much transformation is appropriate, it is useful to examine how focused or extensive the reworking must be. We can distinguish between three potential levels of transformation: minimal, moderate, and extensive.

Minimal Transformation Minimal transformation occurs when changes are made to the sports product that are minor in scale and do not disrupt the core of the product. They are often a smaller component in a much more elaborate transformation plan and are the most frequent type of transformations in the industry. These alterations include rolling out a new communication strategy, enforcing a small rule change, adopting new technologies to enhance the television product, or making other changes to the sports product that affect the product's positioning.

Minimal transformations can come in the form of a new marketing campaign. The University of Oregon athletic department has an annual tradition of selling "Spirit" T-shirts to its fans. The color of the shirts is "lightning yellow" and was launched initially in 2003 to correspond to the football team's new uniforms of the same color. For a school known for its struggles with uniform colors, a change was in order. While the school's colors are green and yellow, the university chose "lightning yellow" for the shirts over green since yellow was more of an attention-getter and didn't blend into the green seats of the football stadium. The color yellow, despite its schoolyard association as cowardly, also was viewed as having the benefit of capitalizing on a cultural trend of bright colors as a fashion statement. Not unlike the University of Nebraska Cornhuskers "sea of red," the Oregon Ducks are trying to brand and redefine the color yellow as fierce and confident, connect fans with one another and the university's teams, and create continuity with the anticipation for the rollout of a new themed T-shirt each season.[28]

A strategic team trade can also initiate a minimal transformation by creating a new environment for a player. While NBA center Ben Wallace had the skills and ability to become a basketball star, it wasn't until he became a member of the Detroit Pistons that his brand fully developed. At the time, the Detroit Pistons needed a type of player like Wallace to reestablish their hard-nosed, bruising basketball brand in the same mold as the "Bad Boys" teams of the late eighties and early nineties. These teams were composed of tough guys such as Isiah Thomas, Bill Laimbeer, Dennis Rodman, Rick Mahorn, and Joe Dumars, who symbolically represented the hard-working city of Detroit and became synonymous with unrelenting defense, teamwork, and a warlike, take-no-prisoners attitude. The twenty-first century version of the Pistons sought to recapture this reputation and differentiate themselves from the majority of up and down, quick shooting, and defensively challenged teams in the NBA. Wallace was a centerpiece of this reinvention as he reminded fans of the Bad Boys era with his defensive-minded playing style, linebackerlike physique, and ability to play the role of the enforcer. Wallace benefited from the historic brand equity of the Pistons, allowing him to maximize the team's brand in order to build his own. Wallace's transformation was minimal since it capitalized on the synergy of his core attributes and the Pistons' historic brand, and it was not necessarily the result of a systematic reassessment and alteration of his foundational product.

Moderate Transformation Moderate transformations operate from the core sports product, but they do not make changes to its foundation. These transformations are marked by major rule changes, expansion into new markets, an altering of an athlete's appearance and communication skills, or incorporation of technologies into the product. At this level, sports decision makers generally put more effort, dollars, and personnel behind the transformation since there is often more at stake.

Soccer has always been strong in Europe and South America, but has untapped markets, particularly in Asia. FIFA substantially changed its marketing and economic strategy to reflect a strong emphasis on Asian countries. FIFA awarded the 2002 World Cup to Japan and South Korea and has moved substantial marketing into the Asian market.[29] In doing so, FIFA is maintaining European and South American markets while making an effort to expand into Asia. Soccer is becoming more global, and countries with huge markets in the Asian community are developing large numbers of participants and becoming more competitive in the soccer universe.

The PGA Tour has also moderately transformed by developing a new playoff competition, the FedEx Cup. After the conclusion of the fourth and final major tournament, the PGA Championship, in August, the PGA Tour's regular season has historically ended on a low note. It has had problems encouraging its stars to play in anticlimactic tournaments in the fall, and as a result, television ratings usually decline amid competition from the busy fall sports schedule. The FedEx Cup, which is based loosely on the NASCAR Nextel Cup model, is a points system that tracks golfers' performance throughout the regular season and seeds them in a four-tournament playoff in September. The culminating event is now the Tour Championship, which was usually played in November but was moved to September to avoid competition from the NFL and MLB.[30] By inventing the FedEx Cup, the PGA Tour is trying to sustain the momentum from its regular season and make the final events matter to golfers, fans, and sponsors. In doing so, the PGA Tour is maintaining the essence of the sport but transforming how it is organized, packaged, and distributed.

Extensive Transformation While moderate transformations maintain the core of the sports product, extensive transformations make changes to the core to redefine the product. The sports products that consider extensive transformation are generally in financial trouble, the integrity of the product is in severe jeopardy, the market is on the verge of collapse, or an athlete is crafting a brand from scratch. An extensive transformation consists of a serious examination of the sports product and making decisions that may result in struggles between factions. Extensive transformations are the most risky but potentially are the most rewarding.

Sports products are often caught in trying to satisfy conflicting market segments. On the one hand you may find the traditionalists who love the game for its nuances and its essential gameness. On the other are the reformers who want to reach out to the non- and less-committed potential fans and who petition for increasing the sport's pace or drama, becoming television friendly, and building star power. A candidate for extensive transformation was the National Hockey League, which found itself struggling with pressures from fans, media, and its own players. The sport failed to capture a significant television audience and needed to consider major changes not only to make the game more attractive but to redefine it as a major winter entertainment. The league implemented rule changes to speed up the game and increase scoring, instituted overtime shootouts, redesigned its logo, and launched its reemerging season with a five-part series advertising campaign resembling a movie trailer.[31] All of this moved its profile closer to a combination of international-style hockey and the Arena Football League than old-time hockey. The transformation resulted in some impressive fan attendance figures[32] and increased regional television viewership in some markets but did not help the league's lagging national television ratings.[33] The next stage in the transformation is going to require making the redefined game and its players even more accessible to the television viewer. This may include more sophisticated camera angles, personality-driven storylines, and speeding up the game even further by reducing the intermissions.

The Indiana High School Athletic Association (IHSAA) decided in 1997 that it needed to create a multitiered division for its state basketball tournament and needed to utilize extensive transformation to achieve it. The continuing movement of the population to the large cities and the increasing disadvantage of small schools competing in the one-division tournament forced this controversial move. The film *Hoosiers* captured the drama of this single state tournament when the small school Milan (Hickory) mesmerized the state with its improbable wins against big city schools. The IHSAA created four divisions based on school size and, in doing so, completely changed high school basketball in the state by eliminating the small school's single championship hopes.

The annual state title competition was transformed from a throw-the-dice, one-shot-for-all-the-marbles, win-or-lose frenzied quest to a lower-key, equal-opportunity, bureaucratic-trophy bonanza. There were some downsides to the transformation as total attendance continues its downward trend. But many of the attendance issues can be attributed to other factors such as more sports, consolidation of schools, and the competitive marketplace that defines this book.[34] However, the transformation created more opportunities for schools that would have been excluded under the old system and was a critical component of an evolving IHSAA high school sports television package that now reaches every area of the state.[35]

Michelle Wie has the talent to become a champion golfer on the professional level, but she will need extensive transformation to continue to build her brand. Wie, who began playing LPGA Tour events at the age of 12 and PGA Tour events at 14, has a seemingly transcendent vision—redefine golf as an androgynous sport with her brand as the instrument of change. Wie has been positioned in the early years of her career to fulfill that vision. Her father, B.J. Wie, a professor at the University of Hawaii, and her mother, Bo, a realtor and former amateur golfing champion, moved to Hawaii from Korea in the 1980s and have since been spending thousands of dollars on Michelle's career. In 2003 alone, B.J. and Bo invested $50,000 in Michelle, which included tournament travel, instruction, and all other golf-related expenses,[36] and that amount increased to an estimated $70,000 per year, which her parents subsidized with a bank loan.[37]

While Wie has been impressive with her playing ability, her brand future is still uncertain as her recently formed extensive team of decision makers faces a number of challenges to fulfill her vision. For example, she needs to perform well enough in men's tournaments to establish a foundation for her vision. In addition, she has personal issues that need to be resolved such as her reputation for being a challenging interview for the press. She also has had a revolving door of caddies, who seemingly have a difficult time coexisting with the demands of Wie and her father.[38] And there is growing feeling that Wie's strategy is too ambitious in her attempts to play on the PGA Tour without first establishing herself as dominant on the LPGA. Despite all these obstacles, Wie has already signed multimillion-dollar deals with Nike and Sony.[39] It is a testimony to the eagerness of sponsors and the media for star power and how they are willing to pay in advance for someone's potential.

The long-term transformation of Wie will need to balance her youth and attractiveness with her toughness and athleticism, refine her communication skills, and establish strong relationships with the media and potential sponsors to fully realize the potential of her brand. If she is going to be a pathfinder, all these elements will have to be examined, refined, and distilled into a clear brand identity. If not, she will still retire as very rich.

Reworking Cricket

Cricket, long known as a five-day, elitist, white-suited, stuffy, incomprehensible game, continues to transform itself. A game once played largely by the English and their colonies, it symbolized Anglo-Saxon dominance and an aristocratic approach to the often messy world of sports. It was with extensive transformation accompanied by much political maneuvering that cricket arrived in the twenty-first century as one of the hottest sports in the world.

Beginning with the introduction in 1975 of a World Cup tournament and the innovation of one-day matches, the International Cricket Council (ICC) has steadily reinvented the sport for a global audience. Cricket has been particularly strong among the former British colonies—Pakistan, Australia, New Zealand, India, and the West Indies. The India-Pakistan cricket rivalry, for example, draws some of the largest sports crowds in the world and often transcends the political animosity between the two countries with leaders crossing each other's boundaries to watch matches.[40] A major television breakthrough for cricket was in 1977–1978 when the late Australian media empire builder Kerry Packer drastically changed the image of cricket by offering it on satellite television. In doing so, he innovated by assembling star players from their home teams to play all-star international competitions in primetime.[41] Packer's influence eventually enabled the ICC to organize its participating countries into a strong global brand resulting in a $550 million television contract from News Corp. and $188 million in revenue from the 2003 Cricket World Cup.[42]

Other changes to the game unassociated with the ICC are remaking the sport and attracting new generations of fans. It was ironically in England, the mother of all cricket, that it continued to lag in popularity as soccer was the sport of the masses and cricket remained a sport for the leisure class. In response, the England and Wales Cricket Board developed in 2003 what is called the Twenty20 format to appeal to a younger, family-oriented audience and attract a wider range of television viewers. This version of cricket takes only about three hours to play compared to the seven to eight hours

(Continued)

(*Continued*)

of one-day cricket matches and emphasizes run scoring and power hitting. The format is the equivalent of adopting baseball's nine-inning structure, and it signaled another step in adapting cricket to audience behaviors. Players wear multi-colored jerseys, demonstrate wildly after victories, and in doing so completely break the staid traditions of classical cricket. While the ICC has not yet embraced Twenty20 as an official international competition, this version of cricket has been successful in England[48] and is gaining increased attention on the international stage.

It is fair to say that without extensive transformation, cricket would have remained an obscure sport that appeared only on the international scene as a quaint oddity. Instead, because of aggressive rule changes, adaptation to audience needs, and the maximizing of television's power to communicate a sport, cricket has become a major player on the world scene. Other sports can learn from the cricket model as there were many squabbles and conflicts over these changes. In the end, the traditionalists and the innovators found a way to work together.

Building the Brand

After defining a vision, inventorying the brand's assets, selecting target segments, and determining the degree of transformation, the critical phase in the brand concept generation stage is to develop the brand. The brand serves as a common umbrella for all the chosen segments, attributes, images, and the product itself. This phase consists of selecting the type, developing the character of the type, establishing points of parity and difference, and creating the star power that drives the brand.

A fundamental driver for brand-building is for sports decision makers to decide upon a type that will drive transformation. Why are types so important to this change process? The *type* is an organizing concept that gives a sports product identity, texture, shape, and context. Most importantly, type is a fundamental connector to which fans can identify and relate. Type transformation is at the heart of the branding process and often constitutes the brand itself. In approaching type decisions, sports decision makers need to research, connect, and ultimately invent an enduring and buildable type.

Selecting the Type Psychiatrist Carl Jung defines archetypes as the universal content of the unconscious that exists in all people. Jung identifies many

146

different archetypes that exist in the unconscious including the self, the shadow, the anima, the animus, the mother, the father, the child, the family, the hero, the maiden, the witch, the magician, and others. Archetypes can be activated through different stimulations that audiences identify with such as commercials, a supermarket display, or even someone else's baby's picture. They are so universal that an audience member will recognize and reframe a person or product on the basis of specific types.

A type is a pattern or imprint derived from archetypes that audiences understand and recognize. Sociologist Orrin E. Klapp, in his book *Heroes, Villains, and Fools,* expanded typing theory to include an extensive list of types of people that is surprisingly wide ranging. He identified three major classes of types: heroes (winners, independent spirits, charmers), villains (rebels, rogues, sneaks), and fools (incompetents, boasters, weaklings).[44]

There are similar types in sports that have historically connected fans with a sports product. While they don't necessarily represent Jung's fundamental conception of archetype, the overarching principle remains the same—whether conscious or unconscious there are types to which sports fans are attracted and connected. The first step in selecting and developing the appropriate brand is to define the type that the sports product should present to the target segments. Below are possible type choices.

Sports Type Imprints

In developing types, a useful connecting device is to look at broad categories and the possible patterns that will appeal to the targeted segments. While these types are certainly not inclusive, they are suggestive of the generative process of selecting and rejecting the most plausible choices for transformation.

People
   Hero (Michael Phelps)
   Phenom (Michelle Wie)
   Natural (Mickey Mantle)
   Tough guy (Ray Lewis)
   Genius (Billy Beane)
   All-American boy/girl (Matt Leinart, Jennie Finch)
   Love goddess (Anna Kournikova)
   Brat (Drew Rosenhaus)
   Achilles (John Daly)

(Continued)

(*Continued*)

Teams

  Superstar (Michael Jordan and the Chicago Bulls)
  Nomads (St.Anthony's high school basketball team in Jersey City, New Jersey)
  Leader (Pat Summitt and the University of Tennessee Women's basketball team)
  Underdog (George Mason University)
  Galaxy (AC Milan)
  Spoiler (Gonzaga University)

Facilities

  Promised land (Madison Square Garden)
  Father (Allen Fieldhouse)
  Mother (Athens Olympic Stadium)
  Palatial (University of North Dakota's Ralph Engelstad Arena)
  Insane (Stadio Olimpico in Rome)

Leagues

  Egalitarian (National Football League)
  Rivalry (Rugby Football Union)
  Generations (Major League Baseball)
  Jester (Arena Football League)
  Nationalistic (Japan Sumo Association)

Events

  Gentility (the Masters)
  Holiday (Super Bowl)
  Rap (And 1 Street Ball tour)
  Tribal (European Champions League Cup)

From tennis rackets to the sport of bass fishing, distinct types can be associated with all sports products. Consider the marketing director of a club soccer team with several potential stars. The team has the range of talent to emphasize either the "family" type or "superstar" type. The marketing director thinks the team has greater potential as the former than the latter and begins developing material to move the campaign in that direction. "Family" and "superstar" are sports types that are imprinted in our unconscious and can be accessed by the appropriate brand strategies.

One of the best personifications of the family type was the New England Patriots who won three Super Bowls in four years. The Patriots became known in the media as the consummate team, consisting of regular guys who bury their egos and come to work every day and play hard every down. They were lauded for being well prepared by a diligent coaching staff and managed both passionately and efficiently by an involved owner and experienced personnel executives. The team's mantra was straightforward and in many ways a sharp contrast to the current culture of major professional sports: sacrifice individual accomplishment for the good of the team. The Patriots played a brand of football that was different from most other teams in the marketplace, and the fact that they were winners provided exposure to the brand and further credibility. And even during the most tempting times to promote the individual, the team stayed on message. Super Bowl XXXIX MVP Deion Branch, on accepting his award, said, "It doesn't matter who gets what. Our plans were just to come in and win the game."[45]

The Patriots didn't have to settle on a family type. After the team won its first Super Bowl, quarterback Tom Brady had the potential to become a superstar that overshadowed his team. Brady took over the quarterback position earlier in the year and surprisingly catalyzed the Patriots' winning season and eventual Super Bowl title, being named the Super Bowl MVP in the process. After such strong performances, potential stars often use their achievements as a launching pad for wider distribution of their own brand. Instead, Brady, who embodies the all-American boy type to make a substantial dent in the celebrity market, downplayed his starring role and continued to emphasize team achievements even during his commercials and interviews. After his third Super Bowl victory, Brady again reinforced his team-first strategy by submerging his importance and restating team modesty, "We've never really self-proclaimed ourselves anything. That's not our style."[46] Consistently redirecting questions about himself to talk about the Patriots fulfills the family type that has been successful in creating and sustaining fans and promotes cooperation and teamwork that reinforces fundamental values of team sports and a community ethic. As a bonus, Brady, by emphasizing commitment to team over individual stars, reinforces his own typing as the all-American boy who accepts the role of star reluctantly.

That sports products need to adopt a type is a critical component to developing the brand and competing in the sports industry. Chase Austin is a teenage African American race car driver who is one of the top future prospects for NASCAR. Austin has the talent to be very competitive and has already been signed by Rick Hendrick Motorsports, the same racing team that manages Jeff Gordon and Jimmy Johnson. With such high competitive expectations, NASCAR, Hendrick Motorsports, and Austin's personal managers have to prepare an

Austin brand for when he reaches the circuit, which by NASCAR's rules will not occur until he's 18. This gives Austin time to build a brand, but it also means that tough choices need to be made about his type.

Despite his talent, he has different attributes that could be emphasized—most notably, his race and age. He is an African American driver in a sport that is trying to improve its diversity through the NASCAR Drive for Diversity program. He is also young and talented and could become NASCAR's version of Freddy Adu in soccer or Donald Young in tennis, who, through their appeal to diversification and young star power, are potentially attractive to younger and emerging generations of fans. In addition, there are a number of type possibilities for Austin—"boy next door," "pioneer," "stubborn brat," or "child prodigy." The right type needs to be selected so that his potential impact as a sports brand will be effective and maximize his unusual opportunity. Austin's mother acknowledges that he needs practice time, "Our focus is seat time—taking a driver with raw talent and developing that. Who knows? No one has ever been down this path before."[47] In today's industry, however, developing that raw talent for competition on the track must not only be "seat time" but be accompanied by building a competitive brand to compete for the Elusive Fan.

Type Transformations

Sports Product	Type Before	Type After
Ronaldo	Local hero	King
American soccer	New kid on the block	Social climber
Girls high school basketball	Little sister	Big sister
Triathlon	Superman	Corporate warrior
1960 U.S. Olympic hockey team	Underdog	Overlooked underdog
Oakland Raiders	Bully	Senior citizens
Wimbledon	Aristocrat	Proletariat
Chicago Cubs	Loser	Social butterfly
Ivy League	Patrician and winner	Gentleman and scholar
Headband	Perspiration protector	Personal expression

Developing the Character After selecting the type to emphasize, such as the tough guy type for an athlete or the tribal type relating to the Argentina and Brazil soccer rivalry, the second step in building the brand is developing the type with a multidimensional character. For example, the "tough guy" type is only a blueprint; it has to take shape and be filled out. Different sports products might brand tough guys, but the specifics in the difference of athletes such as baseball home run hitter Jim Thome, hockey top scorer Jeremy Roenick, and basketball icon Shaquille O'Neal are significant. Thome plays baseball as a down-home tough guy who was born and raised in the Midwest, eats meat and potatoes, and is just your natural, brawling old school, Clint Eastwood in *Dirty Harry* variation of a baseball player. Roenick is an urban tough guy who works the media with expertise and is a fashion model in his selection of clothes, sunglasses, and slicked back long hair. He is hockey's version of Michael Douglas in *Wall Street*. O'Neal is very outspoken and charitable, who can intimidate an opponent with one flying elbow. He is also a dichotomy tough guy. While cracking heads and slamming bodies, his public persona is of a gentle, kidding, soft touch. In some ways, O'Neal redefined tough guy into a basketball version of *Spiderman*.

Author Richard Dyer in his book *Stars* identifies nine qualities that constitute a checklist for character development.[48] They can be adapted to a brand since person and brand characteristics have become increasingly interchangeable. The nine characteristics are

1. *Particularity:* The brand should have differentiated traits.
2. *Interest:* The brand's core traits should attract attention.
3. *Autonomy:* The brand should not appear planned or scripted; it should create "the illusion of 'life' in front of us."
4. *Roundness:* The brand should not be dominated by one trait but rather should have a multidimensional set of traits.
5. *Development:* The brand should evolve and reveal new traits over time.
6. *Interiority:* The brand should communicate its messages and values not only through its verbal material but also through its behavior; audiences should be able to understand these messages and values based on the brand's traits and overall character development.
7. *Motivation:* The brand's behavior should have a rationale, rather than appear incidental or uninspired.

8. *Discrete identity:* The brand should develop an identity that is separate from the main role.

9. *Consistency:* The brand should maintain a predictable set of behaviors despite having multidimensional traits and experiencing inevitable changes.

A good example of developing character in a sports product is the Louisville Slugger, the wooden baseball bat that is entrenched as a baseball institution. The Louisville Slugger's typing is well set; it is a sports type of the "trusted accomplice" needed by baseball players to perform and succeed. It helps fulfill the archetype of the hero as his weapon for battle. It is not incidental to the typing strategy that Louisville Sluggers are seen as a source of stability, dependability, and necessity for the heroic goals of all baseball players.

The example of the Louisville Slugger illustrates the significance of developing unique traits in a brand. Although Louisville Sluggers are just baseball bats, Dyer's nine characteristics apply just as well to an object as a human being. For one, Louisville Sluggers have *particularity*. The bats are all custom-made depending on the type of wood, length, diameter, and weight, and they can also be personalized with a player's signature. Fans have the opportunity to buy the same bats the players use—for the same price—to use in their baseball tournaments or Little League games.

The bat also has *autonomy*. Each Louisville Slugger is different from every other Louisville Slugger even if it is made according to the same specifications. The bat is made of natural wood and no two pieces of wood are the same. It is not as predictable as an aluminum bat, a more mass-produced and manufactured piece of equipment. In contrast to the reliability of the aluminum bat, part of the character of the Louisville Slugger is that it can break and is not invincible.

The Louisville Slugger also exhibits *roundness*. It is more than a bat, but a brand that symbolizes baseball's history. It has been used for over 120 years and is a symbol of baseball's authenticity. To emphasize its roundness, the bat has been immortalized in a Louisville Slugger museum in Louisville, Kentucky, that features films of historical hits such as Bobby Thomson's home run in the 1951 playoffs, batboy confessions of their experiences with star sluggers like Stan Musial, and a factory tour to showcase how the bats are actually made.[49] During the factory tour, the museum-goers are saturated with the smells of the wood and the associations of watching baseball outside in the spring and summer and hearing the Louisville Slugger bat meet the Rawlings baseball, another distinct sports brand.

The Louisville Slugger also has *consistency*. The bat has branded the crack of the bat hitting the ball, which recalls a fundamental association with the game. The museum's Web site reminds, "A visit to the museum shows you how the sport has changed a bit between then and now, but the 'crack of the bat' remains one of the sporting world's most thrilling moments."[50] In addition, it has been trademarked as the official bat of Major League Baseball, which helps to ensure that 80 percent of professional baseball players use Louisville Sluggers every season.[51] Keeping the bat in the hands of the players and providing continuity for the sport of baseball with its feel, sound, and even smell, build and sustain the brand of Louisville Sluggers.

The first two steps in building the brand consist of choosing the sports type and then differentiating the type by developing a multidimensional character. The example of the Louisville Slugger illustrates how critical character development is and that even sports equipment can come to life by creating a believable and interesting character.

Gorgeous George Turned on Television

Gorgeous George lit up early 1950s grainy, 12-inch Dumont television sets like no one could or ever would again. Born George Wagner of Seward, Nebraska, Gorgeous George was a 5'9", 210 pound, run-of-the-mill wrestler before he transformed his identity. During the 1940s professional wrestling was declining, and to break out as a star, the anonymous and average-skilled George needed more than a half nelson to attract attention. In a strategy that differed sharply from his very masculine competitors, he began wearing to his matches eclectic, effeminate, custom-designed robes, which were made with such materials as lavender turkey feathers, apple blossoms, and horsehair lace. One evening during a match in Oregon, an awed female fan, in response to George's garments and appearance, remarked, "My! Isn't he gorgeous!"[52] George had found the marquee name for his stage act, and he began adding refinements to his character.

The invention of the Gorgeous George brand, which was a variation of Klapp's "villain" type, struck an electrifying chord in the American consciousness. His persona was of an androgynous, strutting, blond-wigged, royally robed, pompous taunter who had no regard for conventional behavior—an antagonist that not only repelled and appealed to a still very conservative America but attracted a large number of female fans. Women identified with Gorgeous George's put-on femininity as he thrilled the underrepresented in

(Continued)

(*Continued*)

sports female audience during his bouts. He also thrust into the sports world an evil recognizable character much like the foreign spy in radio dramas or the archetypal 1940s film noir homosexual mobster character.

Gorgeous George was in Dyer's terms a fully developed character, with two qualities standing out. He had a strong emphasis on *particularity*, because his character was distinct as a sexually threatening, arrogant, self-proclaiming aristocrat who threw good Americans around the ring with seemingly unfair abandon. All this was stirred by George's comedic and almost mocking of not only the sport of wrestling, but of the fans themselves. How could an upright, straight, hardworking American athlete be so demeaned by this elitist "pansy"? He also demonstrated Dyer's concept of *interiority*, because his actions spoke louder than his words. He had platinum-dyed hair festooned with golden bobby pins that he threw into the crowd. His managers also sprayed the ring and opponents with perfume and disinfectant that nonverbally enabled the fans to understand George's intentions.

Gorgeous George, of course, started out as an act but became that character. It took a branded character to leap out of the television set and into the living room to connect with multiple audiences all over America. In perfecting his brand, he created the blueprint for wrestler Ric Flair, boxer Muhammad Ali, soccer star David Beckham, and other risk-taking, nonconforming athletes. Gorgeous George was the first to understand that being a sports star in the new era of television demanded not only a well-developed and differentiated character, but one that had an emotional dimension as well.

Establishing Points of Parity and Points of Difference The brand should have characteristics that everybody else in the market has (*points of parity*) and characteristics that can be emphasized to influence why people would choose your product (*points of difference*). For example, the sport of freeskiing is a new brand that is a variation of the more conventional sport of downhill ski racing. The sport's points of parity are that it takes place on a ski mountain, the same skiing equipment is used, and there are men and women divisions. These fundamental components of the brand serve to legitimize freeskiing as a sport.

However, the points of difference in freeskiing distinguish it from downhill ski racing in a number of ways. Freeskiers are not confined by the boundaries of a course and are encouraged to use all the aspects of the mountain to score points. In addition, whereas ski racing is for time, freeskiers are judged on a point system that considers "line choice, control, fluidity, technique, and aggression."[53]

Finally, the snow on the mountain is not manicured as it is in ski racing and instead is left in its natural form for the skiers to navigate.

The brand of freeskiing essentially applies extreme sports to traditional ski racing. In the process, a distinct brand is created to appeal to target segments different from the segments traditional skiing reaches. It would be unwise in the brand concept generation phase to conceive a brand that is too close to the original. On the other hand, deviating from the original brand too much could also be problematic. In the case of freeskiing, freedom and individuality were added to the traditional brand to emphasize an appeal to a younger market, a concept that has experienced success in the related sport of snowboarding. In the end, without the points of parity and corresponding points of difference, a brand cannot be accepted or differentiated in the marketplace.

Creating Star Power In developing the brand, star power is essential. In the crowded marketplace, in order to complete the fan connection and compete with other sports and products, stars are a critical component. As earlier discussed, stars can be drawn from a wide array of product possibilities, not just players but teams, coaches, facilities, and events.

The Boston Celtics of the 1960s and 1970s had an unusual four points of star power: individual players, the coach, the team, and the facility. In the case of the players, Bill Russell and Bob Cousy were recognizable stars who stood out in what was a strong team concept. Russell was the template for the dominant defensive center who both physically and psychologically intimidated his opponents. Cousy was a smooth guard whose between-the-legs dribbles, behind-the-back passes, and calm leadership steadied the team when it was under pressure. Coach Red Auerbach was the ultimate congenial manipulator who understood team chemistry and ceremoniously lit a cigar to signal the moment the team sealed the victory. In doing so, he trademarked the professional coach as an identifiable star. The team itself was a star power draw because it not only won the most NBA championships in league history (11) but was also self-sacrificing, won nail-biting games, and invented the role of the sixth and seventh player as critical elements in wearing down an opponent. The team's home court, Boston Garden, also took on star quality as the unusual parquet floor became a symbol of the Celtic brand as it was the only floor of its kind in the league. Upon entering the Garden, there was a combination of smells, sounds, and visual stimulation that built the anticipation of watching the Celtics. The Garden was for adults and had more in common with a pool hall than the more contemporary arenas such as American Airlines Center in Dallas, the new home of the NBA Mavericks. The Garden's concourse was a combination of cigarette and cigar smoke, overcooked hot dogs slathered in mustard, beer spilling over paper cups, excited males in Harris tweed coats doused with cologne and aftershave, and the carnival barking of East Boston Irish program sellers. It was a powerful star constellation that was critical to remaking the image of the NBA.

Star power can come in many forms. It is the task of sports decision makers to develop and discover those qualities in their products that stand out and build differences in the marketplace. A flat horse racing track is ultimately a pack of thoroughbred horses running different distances around a dirt or grass oval. The brand builder may find star power in the track's glamour (Churchill Downs, Santa Anita), in the horses (Secretariat, Smarty Jones), in the jockeys (Johnny Murtaugh, Julie Krone), or even the type of bettors who show up at the track (Saratoga, Royal Ascot, or Harry the Horse from *Guys and Dolls*). The star power step demands that sports decision makers make choices and build star capital. Failure to build stars is not an option. It's needed by fans for them to connect to the sports brand.

BRANDS ARE ABOUT FAN CONNECTIONS

In the Barry Levinson film *Diner*, the Baltimore Colts fanatic Eddie Simmons makes as a condition of marrying his girlfriend her ability to pass a test based on Colts history. The situation is frustrating for the poor girlfriend and her bridesmaids-in-waiting as she struggles with a 140-question quiz typified by the question on the amount of money the Colts spent on the phone call to Pittsburgh for the rights to sign Johnny Unitas.[54] Eddie and his devoted Colts buddies were totally immersed in the fortunes of the Colts. The team was the hometown hero type and represented the city, its values, its lifestyle, and in the case of Eddie and his fiancée whether they were going to get married or not. While somewhat extreme, it does place in context how important a team, player, or sport can be to fans.

In this chapter, we focus on developing brand concepts that can connect with fans. In the next chapter, the final three stages of the transformation process—brand testing, refinement, and actualization—are defined and discussed. The emphasis is on completing the transformation and ensuring that the brand becomes an identifiable and powerful symbol for the sports product.

Chapter

$$\boxed{6}$$

IMPLEMENTING THE SPORTS BRAND TRANSFORMATION

Few sports teams in the world are as successful or more integrated into their country's culture than the New Zealand All Blacks national rugby team. The team is noted for its winning, innovations in game strategy, and the performance of a menacing pregame dance ritual called the Haka. The Haka, based on a Maori legend from the early nineteenth century, became a symbol of the team's confidence, rage, and ultimate dominance over other teams and is its brand-forming moment. In fact, when international rugby is mentioned, the team that inevitably comes to mind is the All Blacks.

What connected the All Blacks to New Zealanders was its emergence as a colony team that could beat the Brits and the Europeans with surprising ease and intimidation. This contributed to a nationalistic spirit that became ingrained in New Zealand culture as the team became the instrument for respectability and stature in the colonial hierarchy. Furthermore, many international sporting events took the team's players away for long periods of time, which produced comradeship and team chemistry. While some rugby opponents scoff at the Haka and the accompanying New Zealand mystique, they add tradition and cultural connection to the event. "It's a wonderful tradition and still thrills me to see it," said an Australian World Cupper in 1999. "I wasn't in fear of it, more a sense of awe."[1] The New Zealand All Blacks are a powerful brand that is not only a symbol but is internalized by its players, fans, opponents, and country.

This was not always the case. When the All Blacks began serious commercialization and branding efforts in the 1990s, the team ran into inevitable conflicts in fan expectations. While the team was an intimidating force on the field when facing cowed opponents, it lacked emotional appeal to expand the brand and needed to be able to withstand losing. It also became the center of a controversy because it was seemingly abandoning its national authenticity for global appeal. Moreover, according to author Paul Temporal, the brand image that was surfacing after the team became professionalized and a television and commercial commodity was increasingly seen by fans as arrogant and distant. He points out that this image ultimately came to be seen as negative by All Blacks management, and part of management's coordinated plan was for the team to become warmer and more accessible to their increasingly global fan base.[2] This regeneration included a consistent brand strategy of making the players friendlier and more accessible in all their encounters with their various markets—except opponents. This particular change in direction was critical as its major sponsor Adidas and television provider News Corp. needed more rounded and fan-identifiable players. While the All Blacks began with a ferocious image, the team has gradually broadened its image as the marketplace demands called for a different set of characteristics.

The All Blacks' continued brand dominance is not by chance. From top to bottom, the brand is intended to be unified, reliable, and credible and is constantly monitored by a group of independent and team-based experts. The management of the brand includes every piece of communication including player Web sites, press conferences, all media output, and even the most localized, small-distribution brochure. The New Zealand Rugby Football Union marketing manager, Fraser Holland, says of his all-pervasive control of the All Blacks, "My biggest job is managing adversity and triumph. Because the team can win or lose, and I have no control over that. When the team is winning, the brand is strong. When the team loses, it's a challenge."[3]

Holland also makes an insightful differentiation between what he calls team values, not brand values. He argues that the All Blacks' fundamental *team* value is winning in contrast to the *brand* values, which are "respect, humility, power, heritage, inspiration and commitment."[4] He pointedly leaves out winning as a brand value and in fact will drop a star player if the brand values are violated. That differentiation is a critical one, and, if fans are going to be involved in a brand through a typical winning and losing cycle, building core attributes is essential.

The All Blacks brand is an example of successful transformation because the team institutionalized its nationalistic, "street" brand concept of rugby, made it more fan-friendly, and implemented the new positioning with state-of-the-art branding strategies. The brand unifies a distinct set of attributes that fans identify with and which players, coaches, and management have come to represent and consistently reinforce. The All Blacks capitalized on their heritage and underwent a full-scale transformation to make the brand successful. The success of the All Blacks is a testimony to generating a new concept and under real-world situations testing, refining, and making the brand a unified one.

How can other sports products become a market-responsive and unified brand like the All Blacks? The first stage is *brand concept generation*, which we develop in Chapter 5. In order to fully develop the brand so that it will be energized in the marketplace, it needs to be tested, refined, and actualized. In this chapter, we place these factors in the transformation process into perspective: *brand testing*, testing the brand concepts to identify their appeal, problems, and audience needs; *brand refinement*, refining the brand in response to testing, state-of-the-art practices, and market innovations; and *brand actualization*, making the sports brand and all its participants become one.

BRAND TESTING

Once the sports product has selected the most promising brand concepts, the next step is to test these concepts for feasibility. Fundamental questions need to be asked:

- Does the brand represent a unified and identifiable image?
- Do the brand and target segments fit?

- Does the brand differentiate the sports product from those in the rest of the marketplace?
- Does the brand create involvement?
- Is the brand fan-centered?
- Does the brand have ethos?

A sports brand can be tested in a variety of ways to answer these questions. Three formal brand-testing methods—focus groups and interviews, surveys, test markets—are most often utilized. In addition, there are informal methods, such as scanning the media environment, conducting on-site field research, and walking-around techniques, which include interviews with players and fans or just hanging around some out-of-towners discussing their experiences at the stadium. Combining formal and informal testing procedures can round out the process of assessing the brand concept's potential.

In current sports brand testing, the foundational testing methodology is often standardized. However, sports decision makers are now demanding more specific and detailed information that will help them refine their brand and be more specific as to audience desires and needs. For example, connection points have to be tested in some manner. This means often adapting methodologies from fields, such as sociology, psychology, and the neurosciences, in order to obtain the information that will allow action steps with a reasonable expectation of results. Given the increasing suspicions of fans to testing methods and their increasing reluctance to participate, more sensitivity and use of newer distribution channels are required to reach them. Focus groups and formal interviews are the first testing method we discuss and are a logical step in the drive to obtain deeper and more detailed information because they involve small groups and allow for a range of logical and emotional responses.

Focus Groups and Interview Techniques

To test the brand concept with focus groups, the sports brand can invite a small group to participate in a formal discussion about its product. Usually the setting is casual, and participants are rewarded with beverages or food and sometimes an honorarium. In most focus groups, the sample of participants matches a targeted segment that the brand wishes to understand or attract. A skilled moderator leads the discussion and keeps it focused on the branding aims. The group members may give their permission to audio- or videotape the discussion for later analysis by skilled interpreters. Focus groups are commonly used to generate feedback on a concept, and the information from the participants has the advantage of often being personal and detailed. Depending upon focus group reactions, a brand concept can be either refined or discarded.

The focus group model is widely used in the sports world. Focus groups are conducted by public relations firms, sports marketing companies, specialty sports development organizations, and leagues and teams. Companies such as the Bortz Media and Sports Group and Bayer Sports Consultancy, as part of their research efforts for sports organizations, conduct focus groups in addition to pursuing other research strategies.

The Massachusetts Institute of Technology (MIT), in considering launching a new athletic brand to redefine the athletics physical education and recreation department, used a brand focus group to help guide the process. The department's mission statement attempts to create an image, style, and competitive spirit that will redefine MIT's reputation in athletics.[5] In inviting students to participate in focus groups, the department was not only hoping for useful feedback but also to stimulate word-of-mouth among the student population about the new brand efforts.

In professional sports, rarely are major incentives initiated without focus group input. The United States Tennis Association (USTA) has begun the U.S. Open Series, which is intended to provide 10 summer USTA-sponsored tournaments that will be directly related to the late summer U.S. Open. The USTA conducted focus groups to test ideas on scoring systems, star power, television ratings and scheduling, and the effects of building momentum and heightening the awareness of the local markets through the summer tournaments. In launching its summer tournaments and new television programming, it specifically cited the focus groups as evidence of the organization's thoroughness and commitment to a more coordinated professional tournament schedule.[6]

There are also a number of interview techniques that can be used to deepen the search for sports brand meaning. Some researchers use *word associations*, which ask participants what words they think of when they hear the brand's name. The primary purpose of such free association tasks is to identify the range of possible brand associations in consumers' minds.

In *projective* techniques, participants are presented with an incomplete stimulus and asked to complete it, or they are given an ambiguous stimulus that may not make sense in and of itself and are asked to make sense of it. In doing so, the goal is for people to reveal some of their true beliefs and feelings.

Brand personification is a method in which respondents are asked to describe what kind of person they think of when the brand is mentioned. For example, if tennis were to come alive as a person, what would it be like, what would it do, where would it live, what would it wear, who would talk to it if it went to a party, and what would it talk about?

Another technique to help decision makers better understand a person's motivation is *laddering*, in which a series of "why" questions is used to tap into the deeper, more abstract goals consumers are trying to satisfy with the brand. In this method, researchers would ask people who are buying season baseball tickets why they are making the purchase. If the answer is "I will have a good time with my family," the next question would be, "Why is baseball so important to your family?" The subsequent questions would build on one another to help the researcher better understand baseball as a brand. These probing techniques can be used in focus groups and their variations and are essentially devices to deepen and understand brand motivations and directions.

The Zaltman Metaphor Elicitation Technique (ZMET) is another probing technique, which seeks to understand the role of the unconscious in decision making and is primarily a *visualization* method. Arguing that 95 percent of all thinking occurs unconsciously, the ZMET provides another perspective on what explains consumer behavior by researching this vast area of brain activity. The method typically involves in-depth interviews of 12 to 30 participants who are asked to bring 8–10 pictures that represent their emotions and opinions regarding the research subject. Interviewers prompt participants to discuss what metaphors the pictures evoke, and at the conclusion of the interview a digital image is created to symbolize how the participant feels about the topic. Using the interview data, analysts deconstruct the information and draw conclusions about the participants' emotional connection to the product.[7] When applied to sports, this method could be useful, for example, in determining why fans connect to a team or why parents encourage their children to play sports.

Yahoo has developed what it describes as *immersion groups*, a small number of people whom it involves in the product development process by not using the traditional moderator. The purpose of this strategy is to limit biases of participants and to work more closely with the group to identify consumer needs. It seems like a leap of faith to ask professional football fans to participate in the design of a scoreboard or a parking lot, but there is no question that that information from them may be useful in closing the connection gap with fans. Other variations include using the Internet to receive feedback from online panels that are like focus groups but that are far larger. The main appeal of this variation is that it gets larger numbers and more information in less time than do traditional methods, and it eliminates the effects of group dynamics on outcomes.[8] All these innovations have the potential to allow sports decision makers not only to collect important information but to enable the fan to participate in the actual design of the sports experience.

Surveys

Researchers often follow focus group work with surveys in order to capture a more comprehensive picture of the public's attitudes. Even though a sports decision maker can run several focus groups to obtain a larger picture, this is not the same as launching an orderly survey in a defined population.

It is important to distinguish between casual surveys, in which fans or non-fans are stopped on the street or in the stadium and asked some questions, and scientific surveys that attempt to assess the true state of mind of the target population. Casual surveys are less expensive to conduct and are quite useful for finding and refining ideas. But they are exploratory in nature. On the other hand, scientific surveys start with defining the target population and then drawing a random or stratified sample. If all the people questioned responded, one can even state the range of accuracy of the findings. This is what happens when a scientific political poll states that one candidate is winning 65 percent of the vote with a margin of error of 3 percent.

Of course, many people who are selected to answer a scientific survey may not cooperate. Surveys by mail or telephone are getting lower response rates than they used to because people are busy or suspicious. More surveys are being done online, but these have similar problems. Other biases can creep in from poorly worded questionnaires to weak or dishonest field workers. Market research firms use a number of tools to try to control and improve the quality of the research and findings.

In the sports industry, survey data are widely available and commonly incorporated into decision making. There are myriad examples of surveys: informal sports opinion polls conducted daily by espn.com, Harris and Gallup polls that release audience reactions to the most prevalent sports issues, and sports marketing research firms that manage audience feedback and segment markets according to various criteria. A long-standing survey methodology is the

Q rating, which measures the appeal of a sport or sports personality to a targeted demographic group based on familiarity and likeability factors. One of the most comprehensive surveys is the annual ESPN Sports Poll from TNS Sport. For over a decade, the poll has provided data on fans and sporting events to a wide-ranging and influential list of sports leagues, events, and sponsors. A particularly effective resource for youth marketing is the Kids Poll from this ESPN and TNS Sport research base.

Surveys have become so critical to the industry that companies have been founded for the purpose of providing statistical information for sports brands. Sports Marketing Surveys is an international research firm that evaluates brand exposure and market preferences through surveys. For example, a sports activewear producer was considering five logos for its product. To test which one was the best, Sports Marketing Surveys conducted a survey that polled a sample of 10,000 subjects in the United Kingdom, Brazil, and Australia. The results of the survey provided the client with clues on how certain markets might respond to the logo and critical evidence to justify its logo choice.[9]

In some cases, independent surveys enter the marketplace and often become a good test for a sports brand. Market Tools, Inc., an independent marketing consulting firm, conducted a survey on the image of the six major professional sports in the United States—MLB, NASCAR, NBA, NFL, NHL, and PGA. The study found that the PGA had the most positive image overall, while MLB was rated most positive in community initiatives, and the NFL in its support of charities.[10] The survey, while not commissioned by any of the six groups, is a useful perspective for organizations to evaluate their brand against the competition.

Survey interpretation has always been disputed because the samples are sometimes too small or large or too similar or different. It's important that sports decision makers maintain a perspective on any survey data. For example, after the NHL canceled its season, ESPN *SportsCenter* followed with a poll asking viewers whether the owners and the players union should patch up their differences and still run a shortened season. Sixty-six percent of the respondents said no. This poll was voluntary, and the respondents were ESPN viewers and Internet users and were most likely composed of avid fans of some sport. How should this poll be interpreted? That a shortened season is simply not a good idea? That hockey is in deep trouble and it would be very difficult to bring back as a major sport? That the NHL is finished and those polled don't want to see it again? Evaluators of sports products need to ask probing questions of the methodology and findings before they make judgments on how their brand should be developed and modified. Despite these limitations, that quick and fast survey was a momentary but important insight into what was a fast-developing story that needed remediation from the NHL no matter what the interpretation. Surveys have the advantage of scope and efficiency that can provide an overall picture that few other methodologies can match.

Test Markets

Before launching a brand concept in the marketplace, sports decision makers can test it in a smaller market with less risk. While surveys provide quantifiable answers to specific questions, small-market testing is often the most useful and realistic source of feedback for the sports industry. The technique allows the sports property to place its brand in real environments to see how it fares in different markets. Small markets are versatile testing grounds as sports properties can test new marketing and advertising strategies, technological innovations in stadiums and on television, a star's brand or media skills, and essentially any other promotional strategy that might be associated with the brand.

Consider the case of cricket, where a change would have to be tested carefully in a small market to minimize the risk of agitating traditionalists who are set against disrupting the traditional format and rules. When the England and Wales Cricket Board introduced its new format of cricket, Twenty20, it served as a test market not only for England, but also for the entire world of cricket. The format was played on the county level and remained far removed from international team competition that played one- and five-day matches. The success of Twenty20 in England built momentum for the format in the country and the rest of the world. Other countries such as Australia, New Zealand, and Pakistan adopted the new version of the game, and the first international competition was played between Australia and New Zealand on February 17, 2005, in front of 30,000 fans, the largest crowd to watch a cricket match in New Zealand in three years.[11] These test situations in local markets and on a limited international scale serve as valuable evidence for other countries and the International Cricket Council in their decisions to adopt the format.

Small-market testing can also serve as a launching pad for new trends in sporting goods. The Nike One Black golf ball was tested during the FBR Open in Scottsdale, Arizona, and received immediate attention from golf fans. Nike's small-market testing strategy was to have only four of its contracted endorsers play these balls on the par 3, 16th hole of the TPC at Scottsdale, a hole that attracts a gallery of 7,000 people and the attention of television cameras and home viewers. While the testing market was strategically limited to four players and one hole, Nike chose the hole that would attract the most attention and provide the most feedback. The response was favorable, as fans almost immediately called the TPC and Nike headquarters in search of the ball.[12] In this case, Nike chose a golf tournament that was not the Masters, players who were not Tiger Woods, and only 1 hole rather than 18 to test its ball. It was a strategy that minimized risks but also put the product in a position to make an impression on audiences and receive significant feedback.

Small-market testing is also an effective strategy for executing the brand experiments of potential stars. It's far better to try a new concept on Sunday morning radio in a small market than to appear on *60 Minutes* and risk a fatal glitch. Dylan Oliver started skateboarding at the age of three in Louisville, Kentucky, and was sponsored by the age of four.[13] Oliver did most of his skating at the publicly financed Louisville Extreme Park, a facility where the city's skateboarders go to practice and compete. As a precocious little skateboarder, he developed into a popular local attraction because of his skateboarding capacity, young age, size, and appearances on several local news programs.

Oliver's attention-getting ability encouraged Nice Skateboards to sign him to a sponsorship deal to use its skateboards and wear its logo. The Nice sponsorship was successful, and, as Oliver traveled to tournaments outside of Louisville, he became a national story. He received increased brand exposure with a cover story in the *New York Times* magazine and television appearances on the *Ellen DeGeneres Show*, *Good Morning America*, *Inside Edition*, and *54321*.[14] By the age of six, Oliver had a number of sponsors, including Jones Soda Company, Kicker car stereos, and Von Zipper sunglasses, and his own agent to orchestrate his brand.[15] His management team created his own Web site complete with pictures, videos, and a schedule of his future appearances.[16] The branding of Oliver is another indication of how the fan marketplace is being driven down in age to mirror who's participating in the sport. In this case, the average five-year-old sidewalk skateboarder has a star to emulate and products to buy. Oliver's brand is not only an example of taking a locally successful concept and gradually breaking it out into bigger markets but testing how a young skateboarder can attract peer fans.

Informal Observation

Informal observation techniques can provide a different perspective and often supplement focus groups and surveys with in-depth information. Walking around the stadium and observing a promotional event and fan reactions can be telling for a sports team. For example, the Chicago White Sox, like most professional teams, have autograph days as part of their youth marketing strategy. It is a day that parents make a special effort to take their children to the ballpark early to get autographs from their favorite player on trading cards, hats, or baseballs. In the summer of 2003, the hottest player for the White Sox was pitcher Esteban Loaiza, who was leading the league in wins. Fans were promised that he would appear to sign autographs on a sunny Sunday afternoon at U.S. Cellular Field. The families waited patiently in the large Loaiza line, but as the other players came and went, Loaiza was nowhere to be found. When the event manager announced the end of the session, the parents comforted their children and were visibly upset. It is unlikely that a focus group or survey would have picked up the emotional impact of this small but significant event. Informally observing the implementation of brand strategy is not only illustrative of fan reactions but also offers insights into how the brand is executed at the ground level.

An alternative is using a more structured informal technique. Many sports organizations have created forums in which fans can ask questions, voice their opinions, and react to changes. The NCAA national office hosts town meetings on issues such as women's sports that encourage open discussion and feedback on critical issues. Professional franchises such as the NHL's Carolina Hurricanes hold town meetings that are specifically targeted to significant stakeholders such as season ticket holders, sponsors, and suite owners. The Metropolitan Sports Facilities Commission, a government agency of Minnesota that was responsible for building and managing the Metrodome, holds meetings with the citizens of Minnesota to discuss the future of sports in the state. These meetings are generally unrestricted, and fans are encouraged to ask questions of the decision makers. The interactive nature of this format encourages feedback about the sports brand, provides the fan with a sense of involvement, and is a testing ground for the sports meeting planners. Besides town meetings, sports properties can run consumer and fan panels on a more continual basis.

Informal observation has become even more complicated and intense as competition requires uncovering the most unquantifiable and not obvious details in order to construct an appealing product. For example, Volkswagen, in order to better understand the automobile market in the United States and China, has devised what is termed a "cultural immersion project." It is a form of tailing the customer and requires that company members follow the customer in their everyday routines including filling up at the gas station and going to the grocery store. A sports team wishing to use this technique would follow the fans in purchasing seats for sporting events, commuting to the stadium, and to where they eat and drink. DaimlerChrysler AG, in a similar attempt to get closer to their customer base, has built rooms for a prototypical imaginary customer, which includes furniture, food, and daily activities. The idea is to watch this customer in order to discover those previously undisclosed cues that will build a better car experience for the company.[17] A sports product could adapt this concept to different fan avidities and study the customary behaviors of a target fan group. In this example, a sports brand looking to improve attendance could construct a type of targeted fan in this lab setting and observe how they interact with its product.

All these informal observation techniques have strengths and weaknesses. It's not unusual for an observation to simply be too idiosyncratic to draw any conclusions from, or for certain biases to enter into the observations that invalidate them. Some of the deeper observational techniques suggest a mouse-in-the-cage lab experiment and may well run into the same ethical issues faced by animal experiments. Despite these drawbacks, what is crucial to understand is that we are now in an era where experimenting and digging deeper for previously uncovered cues to fan behavior has become an essential part of the sports decision-making process. It will not go away as the fan becomes more difficult to define and harder to find.

Brand testing is the evaluation stage of the transformation process in which the sports product decides to proceed with the brand or try another one. It is the stage that determines the potential of the brand and how it needs to be refined before a large-scale rollout. The three formal methods and several informal techniques can be employed independently, but they should be combined when possible for optimal feedback. Testing can reveal if the brand concept has potential and whether it is worth the investment to transform the current brand into something else.

Starting Small in Le Mans Racing

The Le Mans racing circuit in Europe draws massive crowds and receives large amounts of media attention. The names of Juan-Manuel Fangio and Pierre Levegh are legends that rival any sports star in the world. In the United States, European-style auto racing has always been secondary to NASCAR, open wheel CART racing, and even county fair dirt stock car racing. When the American Le Mans Series (ALMS) was initiated in 1999 as a four-class timed event, its prospects seemed dim. The idea of exotic foreign makes—Ferraris, Porsches, Audis—running a timed event did not seem appealing to the American slam bang, get out of the way, bump you to the finish line style. The results, however, have been promising and are an example of focused segmentation, careful brand building, small-market testing, and connecting with a small but influential market.

The ten-series race concentrates on an affluent, automobile-savvy fan base. Scott Atherton, ALMS president and CEO, says of its segmentation strategy, "NASCAR is the Wal-Mart, while the American Le Mans Series is the Nordstrom of racing."[18] The entire experience is directed to a premium motor sports fan and attracts upscale sponsors such as JeanRichard Watches. The races are usually on challenging race courses such as Sebring International Raceway in Sebring, Florida; Road America in Elkhart Lake, Wisconsin; or Laguna Seca in Monterey, California.[19] The venues are often star attractions, setting a mood for the race. Road America is a large, geographically challenging race course with hairpin turns and uphill climbs, all framed in a country setting of grassy hills and numerous trees. The Le Mans Series is often more of a picnic in the park than the football stadium atmosphere of oval racing.

A key market differentiation strategy for Le Mans is its concentration on the premium car as the centerpiece of the event. The events are small enough that fans can walk around the race preparation staging areas and watch the mechanics prepare the luxury cars and interact with their drivers. The drama of the race preparation builds alliances between the fans and their favorite cars and drivers. The race becomes more than just a viewer or media event seen through the filter of distance or cameras. The results are encouraging. Television ratings were up by 24 percent in 2004 over 2003, and crowds of up to 100,000 spectators have been attracted to the races.[20] It does not have NASCAR numbers and probably never will, but the series is slowly building an enviable fan base that is involved and has the money to buy the sponsor's products.

BRAND REFINEMENT

After the sports product generates and tests a brand concept, the next stage is to refine it. Refinement is the process of defining the brand's *core attributes* to make it consistent and believable with the new brand identity. The goal of refinement is to take the brand blueprint developed in the brand concept generation stage and begin constructing and solidifying the brand. The brand refinement stage addresses four critical core attributes: name, appearance, material, and behavior.

Name

A sports brand's name is a particular sign that conveys important brand images. The name is everywhere—stamped on merchandise, printed in the newspaper, advertised on television, and spread by word-of-mouth. The name should not only attract attention but also evoke familiarity and identification within the target audience. A name should evoke the associations and attributes that the sports product wants to project. If the name does not trigger any associations, it is weak. If the name triggers contradictory associations, it is also weak. A name should trigger a rich set of associations with the target public that hold together and deliver some key distinguishing ideas. The name is often the audience's first exposure to the product and can symbolize the essence of the brand. The name is a part of the sports brand's market positioning, an argument that informs the audience of the product, its goals, and what it represents.

Every sports product—players, teams, leagues, sporting goods, conferences, coaches, events, tournaments—faces naming issues. The sports product may be limited as to choices because of historical, geographical, or sponsor restraints, or the existing name may be facing serious wear-out from overuse or lack of differentiation from new competition. Some sports properties may have more latitude as the name choice factor might involve not just the principal product, such as the team's primary name, but might include a series of new products such as special dugout seats, stadium boxes, promotional tie-ins, or a wide range of new opportunities for identification. *The competition between sports brands is fierce, and the name is the front door of the property.*

Once names are generated, they can be evaluated according to three criteria:

Recognizability: Names should attract attention and be memorable.
Fit: Names should reinforce the sports brand's type and character.
Contrast: Names should differentiate the sports brand from its competitors.

A new franchise that faced this set of criteria was Houston 1836, a transplanted professional soccer team from San Jose. The name 1836 was the winner of the name-the-team sweepstakes, which included an online poll on franchise owner AEG's Web site.[21] The choice emulated the European tradition of naming teams after the year of the team's founding. The modification was that it was the city, and not the team, that was founded in 1836, which was also the year other seminal events occurred in Texas' statehood, such as the storied assault on the Alamo and the rout of Mexican troops led by General Antonia Lopez de Santa Anna, which ultimately led to Texas seceding from Mexico. The name choice was celebrated with confetti and balloons at a middle school with 200 students cheering the selection.[22] But it was met with a seemingly unexpected response from the large Hispanic population in Houston who are big supporters of soccer. In this case, the name was certainly recognizable and clearly differentiated the team from its competitors. It failed in fit as many Latinos in Houston saw it as an insult and a symbol of remarkable insensitivity to their history. Tatcho Mindiola, a Mexican-American scholar at the University of Houston, asked, "Do they think we're going to wear a T-shirt with the year 1836 on it?"[23] In defending the name choice, team president Oliver Luck acknowledged that he was aware of the "double entendre" but saw the virtues of the name as overriding any objections. Despite Luck's seemingly unconditional support, the Houston 1836 survived for only a month until the protests from various offended communities encouraged the team to change their name to the Dynamo.[24] Name choices are about identity. Sports decision makers need not only to do the polling and research, but to make sure they select a name that will withstand the inevitable public pressures of representing a place and community.

An example of accommodating the issue of fit are the choices the Women's National Basketball Association (WNBA), the sister league of the NBA, made when the league was inaugurated in 1996. In naming the league, the WNBA

171

was chosen instead of coming up with a new name or resurrecting the names of previously failed women's leagues such as the Liberty Basketball Association, Women's World Basketball Association, or the American Basketball League. In selecting team names, of the eight original teams, five chose a name that resembled closely the NBA team's name of the same city: Phoenix Mercury (NBA Suns), Sacramento Monarchs (NBA Kings), Utah Starzz (NBA Jazz), Charlotte Sting (NBA Hornets), and the Houston Comets (NBA Rockets). The league and team-naming strategy was clear—capitalize on the brand equity of the NBA by transferring its exposure and familiarity to the newly founded league. As new sports properties, the league and its teams needed ethos, and the overt association with the NBA through the team names symbolized the legitimacy of the WNBA.

In some situations, an already established team changes its name to accommodate new market forces. Owner of the NBA's Washington Wizards Abe Pollin understood the power and reach of the team name and changed it from the Bullets to the Wizards for the 1997–1998 NBA season, but not without dissent from among many of the team's entities. Motivated in part by the assassination of friend and Israeli Prime Minister Yitzhak Rabin, Pollin thought that the name "Bullets" was too violent for a safety-conscious American society and sought a more politically correct and family-friendly name. The timing of the name change was also important. The team was moving into a new arena, the MCI Center, and tying in the name change with the team's move would be an opportunity to reinvigorate ticket and merchandise sales.

How did Pollin decide on the Wizards? He encouraged fans to suggest a name by filling out a ballot at local Boston Market restaurants during a 36-day period. The voting period produced more than 500,000 responses and 2,996 various entries from which to choose. Pollin then created a seven-person panel including Bullets executives, members of the media, a Bullets player, and the president of Boston Market. The panel narrowed the list to five names: Dragons, Express, Stallions, Sea Dogs, and Wizards.[25] After revealing the choices, the response to the five chosen names in Washington was unenthusiastic, and some fans wanted simply to keep the old name. One fan said, "It seems like these are the five worst names they could come up with." Another lamented, "I hated all those names. I think they should stay the Bullets. They have been around a long time. I wish they would leave it alone."[26] In the end, Wizards was chosen, reportedly the favorite of Pollin, and the brand was repositioned as uniforms, brochures, billboards, media sites, and merchandise were all refashioned to support the name change. Pollin changed a name that many fans in Washington preferred and identified with in the interest of redefining his brand to capitalize on a specific target market—families—and to avoid pressure groups that could tie up his marketing efforts. Even if the Wizards do not benefit financially over the long term because of the name change, the importance of the renaming was its building of goodwill in the community.

Names are an important source of involvement, as they often personalize the sports brand. Player nicknames, for example, create special relationships between players and fans that often lead to a strong connection. Nicknames give fans the perception of closeness with players and a feeling that they really know them. There are some nicknames that are etched in sports history and suggest a superhuman persona such as the Babe (Mildred Didrikson Zaharias), the Manassa Mauler (Jack Dempsey), the Splendid Splinter (Ted Williams), Slingin' Sammy (Sammy Baugh), and the Big Dipper (Wilt Chamberlain). In contemporary times, however, the mythic nickname continues to redevelop through initials (MJ, Michael Jordan; TO, Terrell Owens), abbreviations (Shaq, Shaquille O'Neal; Alex Rodriguez, A-Rod), or word plays (Swiss Miss, Martina Hingis; the Big Easy, Ernie Els). Snowboarder Shaun White is called the "Flying Tomato" to signify his style and red hair, and it, like all nicknames, serves as a convenient hook for a set of brand attributes that are too numerous to reference constantly. Nicknames often come from the media or fans and not the sports product and then are subsequently incorporated into the sports product's literature and promotional activities.

Almost the reverse occurred when snooker legend Jimmy White changed his name to James "Jimmy" Brown, "the godfather of snooker" in association with a food company to elevate the profile of the sport.[27] The name change was funded by HP, a British food company that sponsored the important four-point brown ball in snooker as part of a promotional campaign for its Brown Sauce. Brown signed an endorsement contract with HP, changed his name officially, and even replaced his trademark match attire of a black and white tuxedo with a brown suit. Brown said, "The sponsorship of the brown ball really puts the fun back into snooker and, given my previous surname, I wanted to follow that lead. I think it is also up to the players to help liven up snooker's image and raise its profile, and I feel good to do my bit with the help of HP."[28] The governing body of snooker, in what could be termed a British moment of restraint and nostalgia, rejected his branding redefinition and forced him to play under his own name.

Some name changes do work. Rod Smart nicknamed himself "He Hate Me" in response to people who disrespected his playing ability. His brand-forming moment was the XFL's inaugural game as a member of the Las Vegas Outlaws where he had his new nickname embroidered on the back of his jersey instead of his last name. The name attracted attention to the league and helped build his brand as a football cult figure. Smart continued to use the name to capitalize on the larger stage of the NFL as a special teams player first on the Philadelphia Eagles and then more permanently with the Carolina Panthers. During the 2004 Super Bowl as a member of the Panthers, Smart was arguably the most sought after media interview, and custom-made Panthers jerseys with his nickname were a major seller.[29] In a strategic extension of his name, he later changed it to "He Love Me" to reflect his newly achieved respect as an NFL football player and integrate it with an advertising campaign for Alltel communications company.[30] In the case of Smart, the nickname maximized the profit potential of an athlete without standout skills or performances, differentiated his product from his competition, and served as another attraction for his teams and leagues.

Facilities can also have their own nicknames that serve as an attraction for fans. The incorporating of facility nicknames in brand development is important because fans can feel more involved in the game rather than as passive spectators. College sports are good examples of involving the fans through nicknames of stadiums or student sections. Football stadiums such as the University of Michigan's "Big House" and the University of Florida's "Swamp" create a persona for the home crowd, connect the fans to one another, and combine to make the stadium an intimidating place for opponents. In these cases, the media—ABC Sports broadcaster Keith Jackson—originated the name for the University of Michigan,[31] and the Swamp came from the football coach, Steve Spurrier.[32] In some cases, the sports facility is identified with a subgroup of ensnared fans such as the University of Illinois "Orange Crush" who symbolize their devotion with orange faces, shirts, and special cheers. The most extreme example of including the stadium crowd in the game itself is Texas A&M's "Twelfth Man," nonrecruited football players who play on special teams and for decades have been the fans' surrogates. These nicknames, while going beyond the conventional naming strategies of sports products, illustrate that name changes are powerful and sports brands need to take tighter control of the process.

Top Ten Sports Team Nicknames*

1. *Murderer's Row*—1927 New York Yankees.
   Batting lineup that included Babe Ruth and Lou Gehrig.
2. *Steel Curtain*—1970s Pittsburgh Steelers defense.
   Won four Super Bowls, dominated by Soviet Union-like defense.
3. *Gunners*—Arsenal, English Premier League soccer team.
   Named after gunmaking factory in south London.
4. *Monsters of the Midway*—1930s and 1940s Chicago Bears.
   Rough and tumble football teams led by George Halas.
5. *All Blacks*—New Zealand's national rugby team.
   World rugby standard team with menacing black uniforms.
6. *Four Horsemen*—Notre Dame from 1922 to 1924.
   Backfield symbolized Knute Rockne-era football.
7. *Dream Team*—1992 U.S. Olympic men's basketball team.
   The most dominant all-star basketball team in history.
8. *Los Galacticos* (Galaxy of Stars)—Soccer team Real Madrid.
   An entertainment variety show reference to Spain's premiere, talent-laden soccer team.
9. *Broad Street Bullies*—Philadelphia Flyers in the mid-1970s.
   An aggressive Stanley Cup championship team with a reputation for a hostile home advantage.
10. *Phi Slamma Jamma*—University of Houston college basketball team of 1983–1984.
    A clever play on Greek terminology, jazz, and slam dunks.

*Authors' debatable selections

Appearance

Appearance is the visual expression of the brand that symbolizes and reinforces the brand concept. There are some brands that, because of historical or place associations, are so powerful in their marketplace that they do not need appearance alterations. The St. Louis Cardinals' red bird symbol, Green Bay Packers' green and yellow uniforms, Chicago Bulls' menacing bull logo, Toronto Maple Leafs' blue and white maple leaf logo, or Manchester United's red and yellow patch are powerful symbols. They are permanently etched in the minds of their fans and serve as expressions of past victories, defeats, and heroes. For many other sports products, they lack the history or tradition that demands such a fan premium and need to seriously consider in their brand efforts tying in image appearance changes that will solidify the brand. Even in the case of the Cardinals, in moving into a new stadium, the historical significance of the past appearance symbols needed to be incorporated into the present environment to sustain the brand.

When refining the brand, choosing an appearance that will support the brand is a key objective. Too often in the sports industry the brand does not fit its appearance. In these cases, the brand often overextends its reach in an effort to represent something to all audiences, which is not always possible and can often backfire. As part of the NBA's strategy to redirect its brand to a more upright, professional look after a series of behavior problems with players, the NBA instituted a dress code. The code insisted upon business casual dress and, by exclusion, banned T-shirts, baggy pants, jewelry, and headgear in team-related appearances. Understanding that appearance was not only symbolic but also suppressing their need for personal expression, some players objected. Superstar Tim Duncan said of the code, "I think it's basically retarded . . . I don't like the direction they're going, but who am I?"[33] While personal appearance will not by itself change the brand concept of the NBA, it is an example of how appearance can serve as an integral part of a change in the branding of a sports property.

Appearance attributes vary depending on the sports product, but the underlying importance of appearance remains the same—appearance must fit the positioning of the brand. A brand can be refined through *personal*, *organizational*, or *structural* appearance attributes.

- *Personal appearance refinement* addresses the clothing, hairstyle, body type, or accessories of people associated with sports brands such as players, coaches, owners, or league executives.
- *Organizational appearance refinement* considers logos, colors, uniforms, or mascots that represent sports brands such as teams, sporting events, or products.
- *Structural appearance refinement* focuses on the environmental communication of the facilities of the sports brand.

Personal Appearance Personal appearance is often a critical starting point for many sports and an important way to attract fan attention. For example, the success of beach volleyball in the summer Olympics and its growing popularity in the United States can in part be related to the physical appearance of the sport's participants. The sport has evolved from a predominantly family sport in the 1920s to a *Sex in the City* style entertainment-type sport with sex appeal, blasting music, and nonstop action between sets. The women competitors often have tan, tall, and toned bodies and are dressed in bikinis, while the men are often shirtless or wearing tank tops with their own version of the tan, sculpted body. Sponsorship expert Kim Skildum-Reid observes, "It's not about contrived six-foot stick figures who don't eat or exercise. This is really an athletic sport, but at the same time it has a 'pure' factor. The setting is gorgeous. There's a combination of healthy sexiness with extreme fitness and athleticism."[34] The sport thrives on the appearance of its athletes whose bodies are more exposed than most other athletes. It is not surprising that, in terms of popularity, beach volleyball is more successful than indoor volleyball.

In some cases, personal appearance attributes can become more influential in the sports brand than sporting achievements. David Beckham's playing ability has often been in question as late English soccer legend George Best, who was also known for his flamboyance, once said of Beckham's game, "I don't think he's a great player. He can't kick with his left foot, he doesn't score many goals, he can't head a ball and he can't tackle. Apart from that, he's all right."[35] To be fair, Beckham is an outstanding soccer player who has often played well under pressure. However, Beckham has built his brand on more than just his soccer skills and has done so with his personal appearance refinements. He uses changes in hairstyles, clothing, and accessories to keep his brand fresh and generate high visibility for his own personal brand independent of the soccer field. He has become the icon for *metrosexuality*, a term used to define the heterosexual, masculine, and successful male who appreciates shopping, fashion, and appearance. Throughout his career, he has built unpredictability and excitement into his hairstyles, a defining attribute of his brand, as he has worn Mohawks, ponytails, cornrows, braids, spikes, and clean-shaves.

Beckham's appearance refinement through fashion has also attracted attention. He designs his own line for Marks and Spencer clothing, endorses a number of products that showcase him as a model in various media settings, and has been seen wearing unconventional clothing such as a sarong, a traditional women's garment that is often used as a bathing suit cover-up. He has been credited with reinventing the hat as a fashionable accessory in Britain and also has received controversial exposure for wearing rosary beads as an item of jewelry. Beckham carefully monitors and refines his personal appearance characteristics and has actively used these attributes to complement his looks and body type. He thrives because he surpasses the capacity threshold for his sport and he consistently refines his personal style to create a differentiated brand. It is a reminder that an aspirant who does not meet or exceed the capacity threshold is not in position to execute many of the branding strategies.

Organizational Appearance Organizational appearance attributes are often most evident in sports uniforms, which are defined by colors, logos, and styles. For teams considering changing uniforms, the colors and logo are often important symbols. The NFL's Seattle Seahawks changed their uniforms to coincide with their division realignment and move to a new stadium. At the center-piece of the refinement was the trademark Seahawk logo. Redesigned with "a more aggressive, forward-looking posture," the bird symbolized the Seahawks' brand transformation into a fiercer, cutting-edge, and more modern football team.[36] The color of the helmet was also changed according to a fan poll from silver to blue. The total effect was to reposition what was an essentially frag-mented brand identity into a futuristic concept, taking advantage of a new stadium and other appearance changes.

In addition to uniforms, logos are also an important organizational appear-ance attribute because they often symbolize the positioning of the brand. The Iraqi National Olympic Committee introduced a new logo amidst the turmoil of war and occupation to foreshadow a new identity. The logo had a date palm tree and the five Olympic rings at its center, which was bordered by palm tree leaves with the "National Olympic Committee of Iraq" in English and Arabic as the sub-script. The date palm tree and tree leaves symbolized the vitality of life in Iraq that existed in spite of the war.[37] It also presented an image of Iraq that was dif-ferent from the ones in popular media such as dry deserts, dilapidated buildings, and civil conflict. In this sense, the logo was a powerful symbol, justifying the Iraqis' participation in the Olympic games and serving to unify and represent the entire Iraqi population through sport. For the Iraqis, the Olympic games were an important stage on which they could exhibit strength and commitment to the world community, and the logo unified and organized this brand image.

One of the most enduring examples of organizational appearance is the University of Southern California's football team's symbolic package. Designed by USC's director of special events and a USC junior, it incorporated a Trojan soldier on a white horse named Traveler. The horse and rider enter the stadium accompanied by horns playing "Conquest," a signal of an oncoming massive destructive force. The fans rise in a unified roar, the USC players appear energized, and opponents recognize that they are confronted by a warrior spirit. Traveler is so important to the USC brand that it has a $2 million endowment, is a frequent parade star, has appeared on television and in film, and shows up for chats with grade school students all over Southern California.[38]

Structural Appearance Facilities have structural appearance attributes that attempt to make the brand distinct and also represent the team, city, and state. For example, Minute Maid Park, home of the Houston Astros, is a retractable-roof ballpark that is intended to evoke the spirit of Houston as a city and Texas as a state. Upon entering the ballpark, the feel and spirit of Houston, Texas, is everywhere—through the smells of Tex-Mex food, the cowboy bar ambience of jacked-up music and blinking lights, and the left-field train that traverses back and forth as a symbol of early industrial Houston. The park is an auditory and visual miniaturization of the state of Texas. By contrast, the team's former stadium, the Astrodome, despite the name affiliation, was more like a multipurpose convention center than the personalized home of the Astros. Minute Maid Park fulfills the vision of the Astros' brand and personalizes the stadium in ways the fan can identify.

Structural appearance is a critical factor in branding and how audiences perceive the product. For example, in London's bid for the 2012 Olympics, the British branded the city as a capable host based on their elaborate plans for a structural appearance renovation. Their proposal included a $2.375 billion budget to build a new 80,000-seat stadium, finish constructing a new subway system called the Javelin that would transport fans from central London to the Olympic village in seven minutes, and make additional extensive transportation infrastructure improvements throughout the city. Critics of these infrastructural improvements cited the current structural appearance of the city as evidence that the proposed investments might not turn out as planned. The British had a recent history of problems with large building projects such as the Millennium Dome, the Millennium Bridge, and a proposed sports stadium to hold the 2005 world track and field championship that never was built.[39] In addition, transportation problems in London are well known as the subways are expensive and inconsistent and roads are overcrowded and sometimes unwieldy. Although the British had a clear plan, the city had a poor track record with planning and construction. However, London countered with a political and economic commitment to structural improvements that included the largest infrastructure budget of the bidders and the assurances that it could host the transportation and hospitality demands of the Olympics and meet the IOC's perception of its Olympic brand. This counterstrategy combined with the star power of Prime Minister Tony Blair, famous Olympic athlete Lord Sebastian Coe, and David Beckham, and a persuasive final presentation that emphasized the potential of the London Olympics to motivate youth world-wide to play sports helped win the 2012 games for the city.[40]

Whither Joe Paterno

Joe Paterno, the legendary Penn State football coach, has been a dominant figure in college football for five decades. His teams rarely lost, and he won two national championships—in 1982 and 1986. What distinguished Joe Paterno was his brand defined by his 1950s nostalgic look that featured a brush cut, large Buddy Holly–like glasses, rolled-up pants legs, and white socks. His brand was further expanded by his ethical standards, an unwillingness to give in to the pressures of big-time sports, and an ability to cross over into politics and civic leadership because of his highly principled positions. He combined the types of warrior and boy scout, becoming a national legend who won numerous awards and was arguably the most venerated coach in American football history. Former president Ronald Reagan said of Paterno, "[He] has never forgotten that he is a teacher who's preparing his students not just for the season, but for life."[41] The president could have added "battle."

Now, the dilemma. As Paterno's teams began to deteriorate in his last years, a controversy began over whether he should stay or leave. Confusing the situation was that Paterno had been very generous to the university by donating large sums of money for academic buildings, was considered the university's leading fund-raiser for its many research and building projects, and was adored by generations of Penn State fans. To fire him could easily set back the football program at Penn State for a decade. On the other hand, there was the overwhelming need for a more competitive product to fill the gigantic Nittany Lions' Beaver Stadium and keep attracting top-notch athletes to the school.

The solution was a transformation, not in Paterno's brand but in the university's positioning of his final years. The theme for Paterno's last curtain call was "make Joe's last years great ones" and was serendipitously reinforced and perhaps prolonged by an unexpected return of Penn State's football dominance with a Big Ten championship in 2005. This repositioning was sold not only to incoming athletes but also to alumni, and it subtly shifted the "forever" brand's principal identity. The university's ongoing celebration of the end of Paterno's tenure enabled it to reposition itself for a future without

Paterno on the sidelines. It held in place a very difficult situation for the Penn State administration as it tried to deal with the what-to-do-about-Joe problem. The exiting coach or player is an issue for an institution when so much energy and goodwill have been invested in his or her tenure. The retirement and graceful passing of the adored leader poses a different problem in an era when these icons become major fund-raisers and the very symbols of the team's performance and future.

Material

Material is the content of the sports brand. When a sports brand inventories its material, it is evaluating both its on-stage formal performances and its usually more numerous supporting off stage informal performances. Material includes all elements that are related to a sports' performance, such as an athlete's specific playing style, a coach's strategies, the makeup of a team, and a league's rules and regulations. It also includes the messages, press conferences, Web sites, and charity events, all of which carry the content and style of the sports brand. It is critical that the material refinement respond to fan expectations of what the sports brand ought to be or represent, and in doing so, reinforce the sport's essential gameness, be consistent with the brand and all its entities, and differentiate the brand from its competition.

Many sports products have the same material such as the sports that athletes play or sporting events host, but it often requires differences in material to stand out. Anna Kournikova and Maria Sharapova are alike in many regards—both are supermodel/athlete, blonde tennis players from Russia who have become popular global stars. However, a major difference is in Kournikova's and Sharapova's on-stage formal performances—ground strokes, serve, and court strategy. As a consequence, while Kournikova is a mediocre professional tennis player, Sharapova has won a number of tournaments including Wimbledon. Kournikova's brand has stereotyped her as a glamour queen who happens to play tennis, whereas Sharapova is a champion tennis player who happens to be a glamour queen.

In a material refinement, the sports team can often bring in new players. The Oakland Raiders and owner Al Davis have been known for hiring expensive, established, name brand players that reinforce his slogan, "Just Win Baby." What stays consistent is the Raiders' historic brand of toughness, outsider status, and willingness to challenge the leadership of the powerful NFL.

As a result, the constant player turnover, which represents a commitment to the brand's no-holds-barred mentality, fits in with the traditional Raider brand. Other examples of material refinement through players and staff include football owner Daniel Snyder's impatient, win-now demeanor and his brand-supporting, ever-shifting expensive cast of Washington Redskins football players; media baron and former Italian Prime Minister Silvio Berlusconi and his building of a star-studded, global media attraction AC Milan soccer team; and Dallas Mavericks basketball owner Mark Cuban, who reinforces his innovative, quick decision, Internet background with personnel changes that disregard salary caps, confrontations with referees, and a futuristic, if hard to decipher, battle plan.

An additional benefit of material refinement is the opportunity to expand the brand. A good example is sports journalist Bob Costas, who has a reputation for candor and jewel event broadcasting. Costas's original on-stage formal performance was play-by-play broadcasting for NBC. While he still broadcasts prestigious events like the Olympics, he has expanded his brand as an author of the best-selling book *Fair Ball: A Fan's Case for Baseball*, host of HBO's *Inside the NFL* and his own talk show, *Costas Now*, which covers a broad array of topics (some not sports related), and narrator for the audio books *And the Crowd Goes Wild* and *The Fans Roared*. In addition, enhancing his material are his outspoken opinions and comments, distinguishing Costas as not just a sports broadcaster but a social critic. Costas's material was essential to promoting a major brand expansion from a narrow, team-hired announcer to an influential definer of sports and cultural events.

An example of an extensive material refinement is the school-yard sport dodgeball. The sport was played in school yards all over the world for generations and had no identifiable identity other than hit someone and you're out. In 1996, the International Dodge Ball Federation (IDBF) was founded, and it transformed the sport by changing the material of this loosely defined school-yard game. The federation had as a mission making the game safe and quantifiable—meaning it could be officiated and judged. It also had as a mission (and as a necessity) of choosing one ball that was to be used by everyone. The ball was critical because it was designed to avoid injury and was light enough to encourage spirited play. In addition, instead of playing the game in circles or kicking the ball or other variations, the federation established rules on the number of players allowed, standardized the court of play, and allowed only throwing instead of kicking to propel the ball. The association projects that by 2007 there will be 300,000 players certified by the IDBF, and currently it has chapters in all 50 states of the United States and is rapidly becoming an international organization.[42]

Tennis Anyone?

In the late 1940s, two of the legendary male tennis stars were Jack Kramer and Pancho Gonzalez. Tennis fans looked forward to their matches, which featured stirring rallies with deep backhands, occasional lobs that just skimmed the back line, and serves that were sharp, but returnable. The two stars played with hefty wooden rackets that limited their potential for overpowering an opponent with their serve.

The game of men's tennis has changed dramatically in the past 50 years as titanium rackets have replaced the wooden versions and the power game has taken over. In many matches, star players such as Roger Federer and Andy Roddick serve as fast as 140 miles per hour, making it virtually impossible for anyone to return a serve. In fact, a ball hit at that speed allows the opponent less than a tenth of a second to return the ball. The game, now dominated by the new racket technology, has been accused of becoming "tedious, and even boring,"[43] while women's tennis, which is marked by longer rallies, is often seen as more entertaining to fans. There is a raging controversy over whether men's tennis needs to be transformed. On one side are the evolutionists who argue that whatever speed a ball can be hit is the purest form of the game. On the other are the fan-friendly realists who feel the sport needs to be reborn.

The solutions that have been proposed by the International Tennis Federation (ITF) include various modifications of the tennis ball including making them larger in order to slow down the game. Other modifications include standardizing grass courts with rougher grass surfaces that will slow down the ball.[44] Proposals to modify the rackets so they are less like boomerangs and more like the rackets of 50 years ago are under consideration. The changes suggested for professional tennis are not unlike those that were instituted by the International Table Tennis Federation (ITTF), which increased the size of the Ping-Pong ball to slow the game down. This transformation altered the material of the players. It has encouraged longer rallies, more emphasis on defensive strategies, and made the game more accessible to fans in terms of their playing the game themselves.[45] If men's tennis is going to flourish in the twenty-first century, it will have to make a major change in the material that constitutes the game and be willing to withstand the criticisms that it levels the playing field. If the changes aren't made, the question "Tennis anyone?" may be answered with, "I'll take a pass."

Behavior

While material constitutes the content of the sports brand, behavior is the actions of the sports brand participants that give the brand fire and texture. Behavior can take place both during on-stage formal performances such as arguing with a referee or leading the fans in a cheer and away from competition such as in media interviews or community service projects. In each environment, behavior serves to personalize the brand and add an identifiable and sometimes controversial dimension.

In sports, behavior is the one component of a brand that is the most difficult to manage. This is in contrast to the traditional business environment, in which corporations can have relative control over their personnel and can fairly easily model their behavior components in two ways. First, except for the top managers and public relations material, there is relatively little the public sees about the internal mechanisms of the corporation. Second, company hierarchy often dictates how behavior will play out in not only the public but in the private lives of its employees. In contrast, attention-getting behavior in sports is sought by the media and rewarded by exposure, endorsements, and licensing arrangements. In this sense, handling a brand in sports is different from any other endeavor, and that difference needs to be understood when branding behavior. *Sports are covered like an entertainment, often operated like a big business, usually set in a political environment, and are different from all of them in that it's a competition with a specific set of rules of play and a fan base with different expectations.*

The behavior of people affiliated with a sports product such as players, coaches, employees, executives, endorsers, and announcers directly influences the way fans perceive the brand. How these sports properties conduct themselves on a daily basis is a window into the brand's integrity. In the contemporary era, behavior both public and private is increasingly subject to scrutiny and can threaten the brand's integrity. In refining a brand, determining what the brand communicates and what fans learn about the brand is often understood through behavior. In fact, behavior as a brand-building tool is often overlooked and needs to be carefully monitored by all managers of sports products. Behavior must reinforce:

- The promise of the sports brand
- The ethos of the sports brand
- The cues of the sports brand

The actions of participants in the sports industry can easily undo a *brand's promise*. The brand's fundamental concepts such as sportsmanship can be compromised easily by the behavior of the participants. A fundamental principle of most sports is that participants will respect the effort of opponents. The idealized version of this behavior is reflected in the enforced shaking of hands after the contest and the language of victory and defeat that is usually couched in weary anticipation of the next encounter, admiration of an opponent's effort, and reluctance to overplay a winning performance. In the television age, counter types such as the sportsmanship renegades have become fixtures in the behavior mix. For example, taunting and scoring celebrations are commonplace in sporting competitions, media wars break out between teams and players, and players and agents openly speak out against their current coaches and teams. It is good theater because it gives emotional context to the encounter and personalizes the efforts of the participants. It also gives the fans the impression that the brand promise of teamwork and respect for one another is not consistent and that the brand promise is unclear and diffuse.

The conflicts are everywhere. When Barry Bonds appears publicly unrepentant and defiant on steroid use, he affects baseball's brand attributes of integrity and family values. When figure skater Tanya Harding is associated with a plot to disable a leading competitor, and an Olympic figure skating judge confesses to biased rankings, it undermines the sports' competitive integrity. The behavior of owner Donald Sterling of the Los Angeles Clippers, whose drafting and personnel transactions were erratic and often ineffective, has historically harmed the franchise's brand. Former Indiana and now Texas Tech basketball coach Bobby Knight and longtime Temple coach John Chaney with their on-court intensity and contentiousness can potentially conflict with their universities' brands.

This is not to argue that all participants need to sign on to a sports brands' promise in order for it to work, but it does recognize how individual behavior can damage the brand's intent and often force the sport into a crisis mode. The message is that brand behavior cuts across all lines of sport participation and can come unglued at any level.

For example, many sports fans want to believe that the love of the game for sports participants is the highest priority. This may have always been somewhat of a fiction. It is hard to believe that baseball legend Ty Cobb would have played for free or that miserly owner Charles Comiskey and his Chicago Black Sox of 1919 World Series fixing infamy cared only about the game. However, there has been a fundamental shift since the early nineties in fans' feelings about the sports industry's commitment to the game and its fans. The sports sections and various media channels are often dominated by reports of high salaries of professional players, special dormitories for college basketball players, sneaker deals for high school powerhouses, all of which may give the impression that the fan is not first.

It is conventional wisdom that any brand refinement needs to emphasize the sport and not necessarily the rewards of its participants. However, some fans are increasingly attracted to the business side of sports. When a fan is dealing in a sports fantasy league, it is an extension of the business practices of sports. This trend and intersection demand that sports decision makers make choices as to what elements of behavior are going to be emphasized in any sports mix and recognize that on-field performance is a platform for many fan activities.

In today's sports industry, behavior after the competition can be as important to the *brand's ethos* as behavior during it. Swimmer Michael Phelps became an international star athlete and endorser during the 2004 Athens Olympics. In competition, he won six gold medals and two bronze medals and selflessly gave up his chance to tie Mark Spitz's Olympic record for gold medals so his teammate Ian Crocker could win a gold. At this point, he was the all-American boy who mothers would love to have their daughters bring home. Phelps's model behavior positioned him as the savior of swimming; his modesty, wide smile, and passion for 7,000-calorie breakfasts only added to his strong brand. Companies reacted favorably to Phelps's brand as he appeared in Visa commercials, on Wheaties boxes, and as a Speedo spokesperson after receiving a $1 million bonus for his achievements. For Phelps his brand was accentuated not only by his strong performance but also by his all-around good behavior.

Just over two months after Athens, Phelps's carefully developed brand capsized as he was pulled over for drunk driving, an offense compounded by his underage drinking at age 19. His coach, Bob Bowman, said about Phelps's behavior: "He had everything going for him. Such a lapse in judgment. I'm sorry for everyone who supported him, which is everyone. He let himself down. He let us all down."[46] In response, Phelps acknowledged publicly his misbehavior and capitalized on his youth and the public's willingness to forgive. "I wanted to look at people in the eye and tell them, you know, I made a mistake. I want to reach out and affect as many people as I can."[47] Phelps's behavior jeopardized the credibility of his brand, forcing him to respond with something that would help fans reconnect with his image. In the end, Phelps recovered because of the goodwill he generated at the Olympics and his willingness to quickly confront a threat to his brand.

An often overlooked aspect of behavior management for sports brands are the *cues* that are often embedded in behavior. The *movement* of the participants, often subtle, can have an important effect on a brand's perception. Michael Jordan moved on the basketball court with a coiled athleticism that could seemingly be optimistically purchased by a fan through his Air Jordan brand. In most player introductions of team sports, the entrance of the team is foreshadowed by smoke bombs, breaking through a paper wall, and acrobatic cheerleaders, all of which are intended to signal to the fans that the team is eager and ready to play. In boxing and wrestling, the walk down the aisle and the leap into the ring are often indicators to the fans of the contestants' confidence and ability to take on their foe. In baseball, batters approaching the batters box have routines that fans recognize, such as swinging several bats aggressively over their head, grunting at the plate, or fixing their batting gloves, all intended to signal to the fan that they're ready and poised to hit the ball. Bench movement in sports is also watched closely by fans as coaches who move indecisively are often questioned, and players who take cell-phone calls or are looking for friends in the stands are considered problems.

Trying to orchestrate a participant's cues in order to build the brand on one level seems like a futile endeavor. It's almost impossible to program a new Michael Jordan and expect him to move on the court with Jordan's fluidity. On the other hand, there are many cues that are simply expected by the fan and, when not delivered, damage the fan connection to the sport. Many of these cues are built into the sport's fundamental makeup such as how sprinters in track and field approach the starting line or how amateur wrestlers move cooperatively and effortlessly into their starting position on a mat. If those movements are not consistent with fan expectations—whether it's vigor, determination, understanding of the fundamental rules—it's unsettling and gives the impression of brand fragmentation.

Behavior can be brand building or brand destroying. A major campaign can be launched to reposition a sports brand as audience-centered only to be thrown off track by the behaviors of hot dog vendors or parking lot attendants. Careful monitoring of the behavior of the brand from top to bottom is essential and perhaps the most overlooked component of brand development.

BRAND ACTUALIZATION

Brand actualization is when all the elements of the change process become second nature to the sports brand that has been altered. That is, in the everyday conduct of the sports product, the transformation is seamless and not strained or forced. It is essential to the transformation of a sports product that the change be internalized by all the participants. Generating and testing the brand concept and refining the core attributes—name, appearance, material, behavior—represent the ingredients of the transformation. In actualizing the sports transformation, the participants in the process have to believe and act within the brand plan. In the end, how credible the transformation is to the fans will determine whether it succeeds in the marketplace.

Actualization is often overwhelming because of the many different components in the sports brand—players, coaches, teams, events, leagues, vendors, and parking lot attendants. An obvious goal in actualization is for the most visible people to embody the brand, but in many cases if all the other brand entities don't buy in, the product will fail to connect with fans. However, actualization is not just about the top-priority products of the sports brand such as the way an athlete or team performs. It's also about when fans pull into the parking lot and how they're greeted, order food and how they're served, and walk the venue and how they feel about the cleanliness of the facility. And it's about when fans read a newspaper, magazine, or Web site, watch television, and play video games that feature the sports brand and how fans perceive the information. All these points of contact become part of what the overall brand represents to fans.

Achieving quality control over all these brand elements is a principal goal of the actualization process. The key is to put together an actualization plan that includes all the various brand constituents. While it is unrealistic to expect that equal time will be spent on actualizing players and parking attendants, it is imperative that all of the brand's components be informed on some level of the brand's positioning, standards, and visions. If some of the brand's entities are unaccounted for, the transformation process and the goals of reaching out to the fans are ultimately going to be less successful.

Actualizing the transformation is usually implemented by the following four strategies:

1. Behavior modification
2. Mentoring
3. Role modeling
4. Calculated risk transformation

Behavior Modification

Behavior modification is the use of rewards and reinforcements to influence actions. The purpose of behavior modification is to condition brand participants to behave within the parameters of a brand's promises. Behavior modification is an actualization technique most commonly used with players and coaches, but it can also be applied to most other brand participants such as general managers and food vendors.

One method of behavior modification is the use of contracts, which in some professional leagues are written with stipulations for appearances at community- or team-sponsored fan events. In addition, contracts often include provisions against riding motorcycles and playing other sports during the off-season; they may also have weight restrictions; and they may refer to a general category of behavior that includes using drugs and other criminal activity.

In colleges, clubs, and professional leagues alike, media training has become a fixed part of brand development. Participants are taught what to expect from the media, how to answer questions, and how to incorporate specific delivery techniques. Other seminars include life skills in which participants are taught how to cope with the pressures of the sports industry. In each forum, specific behaviors are emphasized, and the rewards and penalties are clearly outlined for participants.

Suspensions are another method of behavior modification. Single-game suspensions, indefinite suspensions without pay, or permanent dismissal are ways of deterring certain behaviors. For example, the antidrug policies of many sports leagues clearly specify the suspensions and fines that correspond to an offense. In cases such as these, indirect pressures from the media also serve as a deterrent because of the public knowledge and embarrassment of a publicized offense. Suspensions can also be effective when brand participants violate team rules or when product endorsers are involved in a questionable legal situation.

Behavior modification can work only when the penalties are stiff enough. All levels of the sports industry can use behavior modification, but it is often on the professional level where behavior modification may not be the most effective. The financial state of many professional athletes makes fines and suspensions without pay often not strong enough to deter bad behavior. Upon the notice of receiving a $10,000 fine for mimicking mooning the fans at Green Bay's Lambeau Field, the former Minnesota Vikings wide receiver Randy Moss countered with, "What's ten grand to me?" This is not to argue that all professional athletes respond to fines in this manner, but that for behavior modification to work, the penalties have to be harsh enough to resonate with the person being reprimanded.

Behavior modification can also occur in the way sports personnel are treated by peers and management. For example, a player who does not represent the team well on the field or breaks certain codes of conduct in an event is often given the silent treatment or shunned by teammates who want the bad behavior modified because it threatens their own performance. Management—whether coaches or other officials—also reinforce or punish behavior through congratulatory comments or making sure that preferable player behavior is noted in the media or given priority in contract negotiations. Other behavior modifiers are the sports brand's selection of personal appearances, all-star nominations, and the entire universe of public notice that can affect a participant's career. These often subtle behavior modification techniques do not always affect the superstar who has the agent, marketing, and media contracts to override whatever the team decides to promote, but it still serves for most participants as a restraint.

If contracts, behavior training, suspensions, fines, and informal communication techniques don't work, the ultimate behavior modification is to dismiss the participant from the sports brand. This final step is being used more often than it was in earlier decades as sports become more aware of the damage that a nonbrand participant can cause. For example, the Chinese National Sports Bureau, an arm of the Chinese government, expelled gold medal diver Tian Liang from the national team for his actions after the 2004 Athens Olympics. He agreed to appear on the front of a Taiwanese noodles box, signed contracts to be an actor or singer, and participated in many celebrity gatherings.[48] The problem with Liang's activities, according to the government, was that they ran counter to the Chinese national sports brand, which is founded not on individual accomplishment but on nationalism. In addition, Liang had gained weight during his celebrity tour, and that did not fit in with the country's goals especially with its hosting of the 2008 Olympics in Beijing.

His dismissal served as not only behavior modification for Liang but also sent a message to the rest of his teammates that that type of behavior would not be tolerated. With this action, the Chinese National Sports Bureau used behavior modification with Liang as a deterrent for the entire national team. While the expulsion fueled an ongoing heated debate in China about an athlete's freedom to pursue individual commercial activities, it still fit into the goals of the Chinese Olympic team—to bring the best and most competitive team to compete in the Olympics on its home turf. Liang was reconsidered for reinstatement to the national team in anticipation of China's desire to excel in the 2008 Olympics—[49]a caution that behavior modification works even better when the modifier is willing to forgo gold medals.

- *Strength:* Behavior modification has the advantage of quickly and relatively inexpensively effecting a behavior change.
- *Weakness:* The sometimes superficial behavior training and the threat of an insincere commitment by the participant can damage the brand over the long run. Enforcing behavior has historically been inconsistent in sports teams and leagues, sometimes reinforcing negative behavior and disappointing fans.[50]

Mentoring

Sports brand participants are often counseled by mentors from whom they can get advice and whom they might even benchmark. It can be somebody from the organization or a consultant or an outsider who provides the service. This actualization strategy is often one-on-one and highly interactive. Unlike behavior modification, this style of actualization is often less direct and demands more patience. When it connects, it can be more long-lasting for the brand because the participant may feel potentially less manipulated and have come to his or her own conclusions about brand transformation.

There are a number of versions of mentoring. The mentor may be directly related to the team or player's performance such as a coach, psychologist, or fellow player. In many sports, the most common mentor for competition is an older player who encompasses the values that the sports property wishes to brand. In professional sports, veteran players such as PJ Brown of the New

Orleans Hornets and Marshall Faulk of the St. Louis Rams volunteer to mentor younger players on performance savvy, work ethic, and unselfish devotion of the team.

Another set of mentors has specialties that relate to brand expectations. For example, when NFL football teams convert to passing attacks, they have often brought in passing experts such as Bill Walsh or Jim Fassell who work intently on rebranding the team's offensive personality and strategy. In some cases, individual athletes in sports like tennis or golf have private coaches with established reputations for building a certain style of play. Tennis coach Nick Bollettieri, for example, is well known for his emphasis on both the physical and mental molding of his young athletes.

There are other mentors such as parents, friends, agents, or hangers-on, who for one reason or another are involved in the brand actualization process. The parent as brand manager is seen in Richard Williams who early molded his two tennis playing daughters, Venus and Serena; Earl Woods, who was an enormous influence on the early precocious years of his son, Tiger Woods; and Bob Leinart, former USC quarterback Matt Leinart's father, who was instrumental in the management of his son's career. While agents have mixed reputations for mentoring their clients, Leigh Steinberg for many years was noted for his emphasis on his clients performing community service, getting involved in charitable foundations, and becoming model citizens. He reinforced his mentoring by insisting on contracts with those provisions.

In some cases, the parent or friend can influence a team's brand such as Wilma McNabb, mother of Philadelphia Eagles' quarterback Donovan McNabb, who has her own endorsement contract with Campbell's Chunky Soup. This parent-child relationship in this case has helped define the Philadelphia football team's brand identity as an assembly of prolonged adolescents—not necessarily a positive brand image in such a rough and tumble sports world, and certainly not one that Eagles management would have chosen.

- *Strength:*. Mentoring often requires a more serious buy-in of participants and gives them more of a sense of control in their participation with the brand.
- *Weakness:* Mentoring is a broad-based category that can range from intense concentration to a form of distance learning, which is more difficult to monitor for brand effectiveness.

Role Modeling

Role modeling is a strategy that uses leaders who personify the brand's core attributes to actualize the sports brand. Role models through their persona embody what the brand represents and serve as an example that other brand participants can emulate. The role model can be the president of the organization, a particularly skilled performer, a media star, or a wide variety of other people in a sports organization.

The advantage of role models is that they often have the power to shape and reflect the total sports brand. For example, Bob Hurley, who worked as a police officer during the day, is head coach of St. Anthony's High School basketball team in New Jersey, a school with dire financial problems and a student body of underprivileged minority students. He serves not only as the team's basketball coach and mentor but also as the school's figurehead. He sets the example of discipline, persistence, and hard work that educated his players in basketball and academics and came to define the team's brand. Similarly, George Steinbrenner, who has created an all-star brand as the controversial New York Yankees owner, is a role model with his unrelenting desire for excellence at any cost and his demands for professionalism within his organization such as requiring his players to be clean-shaven, appear well dressed, and live up to his perception of the Yankee image. When Steinbrenner would fire a manager, sometimes the same manager over and over, he was demonstrating that performance at all levels was expected and that the manager was not exempt.

In other cases, the media serve as a channel to enable role modeling for sports brands as the brand aspirant can emulate the models portrayed in the media. The media are constantly doling out lessons on what is acceptable and successful behavior in the sports world. Some coaches' behavior can be wildly celebrated, while other coaches can be dismissed as inadequate strategists and managers of their team or stars. The point is that viewers are learning lessons about coaching from what they see in the media, and this has proven to be a very powerful modeling tool. It is incalculable how many young men were influenced by Michael Jordan, and as a result his sports brand became a universal style for young, aspiring basketball stars. His role modeling was so successful that when the 2004 U.S. Olympic team failed in Athens to win the gold medal, it was blamed on Jordan's model that emphasized athleticism over shooting and finesse.

A similar role modeling strategy is a trademark of sports films. In the film *Bull Durham*, Kevin Costner demonstrated to Tim Robbins how to act in a game and even what clichés the young pitcher would need for successful media interviews. Other sports films are also lessons in modeling such as *Hoosiers*, which preaches a strong team community ethos as a proper brand for the school team, or Academy Award–winning *Million Dollar Baby* that emphasizes the gritty, tough nature of boxing and at the same time extols the celebrity possibilities and the tragic consequences. In these examples, there is no direct interaction with the role model and the subject. It is the viewer who completes the role modeling arrangement by identifying those characteristics of the media figure that they wish to emulate.

- *Strength:* Role modeling can often influence a greater number of brand participants in a relatively short period of time.
- *Weakness:* There is infrequent one-on-one interaction with the role model, making the actualization process difficult to control and the results often less sustainable.

Calculated Risk Transformation

In some cases, the brand is not afforded the luxury or the time of using behavior modification, mentoring, or role modeling to transform the brand. An alternative is the more risky strategy of placing sports brands in situations that will force transformation under combat conditions. In a classic example, the football team decides that a short passing game is its new identity; the rookie quarterback is given real game experience, and the short passing game may be a hit or a failure. The change in strategy may be backed up by a complete marketing campaign including press conferences, advertisements, and a new slogan capturing the transformation. In this calculated risk transformation, it may be all or nothing as many of the elements have not been orchestrated or practiced.

The advantage of the calculated risk transformation is that there is a moment of truth that can be evaluated and quickly discarded if it fails. While the risks are considerable, if the short pass brand fails to catch on, it will be obvious and a new brand choice is next on deck. In the real world of sports brands, calculated risk is probably the most prevalent. Many sports programs would not like to admit that, but it is the most efficient and most revealing, and it can establish a brand under fire.

After the National Hockey League lockout, many fans felt that the league and the players didn't care about them. The players were often portrayed in the media as continuing to live their extravagant lifestyles, playing in Europe, and generally not caring about the fans who pay their salaries. The Chicago Blackhawks implemented what could be termed a calculated risk transformation by issuing what they termed "business cards." If a player gives a fan a card, there was a code that would enable the fan to receive two free tickets to a game.[51] The transformation strategy placed the player and the fan in direct contact. On one level, the player has to talk to the fan in order to give the card. On the other, the fan is likely to seek out the player to receive the card and in doing so may well develop a more sympathetic and closer relationship with the professional player. The risk is that players or fans will not seek each other out and, when they do meet, they will find out they dislike one another.

- *Strength:* This form of actualization has the quickest results and enables the brand to move on in case of fan resistance.
- *Weakness:* As in any roll of the dice, it may result in a superb branding moment or, in the worst case scenario, a breakdown in fan expectations.

The four actualization strategies are not exclusive of one another. Given the demands and time facing the sports product, one or another in combination may be utilized. For example, a sports team may use behavior modification on critical aspects of a player's behavior and use calculated risk in instituting its basketball team's fast-break offense. In the end, a failure to buy-in on the part of the participants will potentially destroy any brand plan.

SPORTS BRANDS ARE ALWAYS EVOLVING

Developing a sports brand is not an easy task. The stages that are involved— brand concept generation, brand testing, brand refinement, and brand actualization—are all critical. Ideally, all these components will be implemented and used in a systematic manner. However, brands can find themselves in many different situations that may require spending more time on one stage than another. It is essential that the brand identity be clear and that all the participants are fully aware of and have bought into the identity. In the next chapter, we take the sports brand out of this manufacturing stage and move it into the public arena.

7

COMMUNICATING
THE SPORTS BRAND

The Hartford Wolf Pack, an American Hockey League team, succeeded the National Hockey League's Hartford Whalers in 1997 and has constructed and communicated a brand with mixed results. Like most high-level minor league teams, it has the usual communication programs of promotions, local media events, Web sites, and newsletters that are devised to communicate with the fan base and connect with the media. A major component of the Wolf Pack's brand communication strategy is its large-scale emphasis on working with community needs. The team has a number of community initiatives including the Community Foundation, Golf for Kids, Bowl-a-Thon, Chariots of Hope, NHL Street Wolves, the Acoustic Café CD, and a Speakers Bureau. The Community Foundation, for example, supports 25 organizations including the Connecticut Special Olympics and the Salvation Army, and Chariots of Hope is a program centered on a version of ice hockey called sled hockey, a game with different equipment that enables disabled children and adults to play the sport.[1] *The Hartford Wolf Pack has a limited adver-tising budget and, by emphasizing community needs programs, it attempts two major fan connecting objectives. First, it is trying to generate free media to help create the kind of excitement and inter-est in the team that doesn't appear to be bought. Second, if members of the community find that the team's involvement and commit-ment to its cause is worthwhile, they may reciprocate by going to the games.*

Despite these community-oriented communication initiatives, the Wolf Pack has experienced limited results as evidenced by a decline in attendance figures over the last several years, despite eight straight playoff appearances. In fact, at one point during the NHL lockout season of 2004–2005, the Wolf Pack's attendance decreased by 9 percent from the previous year, while the rest of the league's atten-dance increased by 9 percent.[2] *There are plenty of excuses—the competition from University of Connecticut's basketball and foot-ball programs, resentment over the NHL franchise leaving for North Carolina, an outdated arena in a poor location, and suburban fans' reluctance to go downtown for games. It may well be that the Wolf Pack is in an increasingly competitive market and that these are unfortunate circumstances, but the team also needs to reposi-tion its brand by reexamining outreach programs and focusing on its total package of communication strategies.*

The Hartford Wolf Pack is an example of a sports property that, in the face of competitive pressures, is having difficulty connecting with its fan base. In this case, what seems like a well-designed sports brand communication plan with charity initiatives, promotions, media events, and advertisements has struggled to bring fans into the venue or get them to watch on television. The Wolf Pack's problem is not unique. The sheer number of sports and the amount of money being spent to communicate is growing yearly, forcing brands to nav-igate through a difficult maze to achieve brand differentiation and distinction. As a consequence, sports brands must now reevaluate how to communicate in a modern era where budgets are often restrained and expectations are high.

Choosing a strong brand concept is only part of a fan connection; being able to communicate it meaningfully with fans brings another set of challenges. A major task in many brand communication strategies is to understand fan expectations and deliver a differentiated brand that will persuade fans to support it. An important obstacle in making the brand a singular standout in the sports world is simply the number of messages that potentially bombard fans day and night. As Minnesota Timberwolves' senior vice president and CMO Chris Wright observes, "In a very cluttered marketplace, we've got to find more ways to communicate with our consumers."[3]

WHAT DOES IT MEAN TO BE FAN-CENTERED?

An important task in communicating to the Elusive Fan is to place the fan in the center of the message. Fan-centered strategies should encourage and enable fans to identify and become involved at some level with the sports brand. Accessibility, interactivity, and responsiveness are core components of being fan-centered.

Accessibility means that the fan has access to the sports brand and is able to fully experience the sport. Accessibility is fundamental and can mean making sure that the city cooperates with the roads and public transportation for getting people to the game. In the stadium, it can mean adequate parking, wide concourses, and not too many steps to the top of the stadium. It also means having a media policy that supports transparency in its message delivery at all levels. An effective sports brand will constantly monitor all its personnel and media channels to make sure that the message is clear, interesting, and appears reasonable to fans who want to understand the sports brand better.

Interactivity is when the fan plays a participatory and involved role in the sports experience. It can include dinner at the tournament clubhouse with professional golfers after the second round, an Internet chat with a general manager about free agents, or a fantasy sports league that closely binds the fan to athletes. Interaction creates events in which fans actively participate, connecting the sports brand to the fans around their own experiences. Sports brands have to balance the need of protecting the time demands on their participants and the need for fan interaction that enables bonding and exposure.

Responsiveness means that the sports brand listens to the feedback of its fan base and is willing to make changes when applicable. It might be a simple gesture such as making sure that different prices in the parking lot are clearly demarcated or something even more central to the team's ethos like addressing pricing packages and other concessions to accommodate different economic groups that want to attend the games. A fan-centered response also ensures that a player's comments or behaviors are addressed and that uncomfortable fans are convinced that the association, team, or league is listening. While responsiveness can appear to be a routine and easy communication device to keep fans happy, in some cases sports brands simply do not see the problem or have become so caught up in their own activities that it is not promptly or ever remedied.

What's Your Image?

The possibilities for fan-centered communication are often based on how the sports brand is perceived. Image is shorthand for a cluster of attributes, and fans can have four images of the brand—favorable, unfavorable, mixed, and indifferent. Each image calls for specific strategic responses.

Favorable A sports brand has a favorable image when the fan perceives the brand's attributes as positive and feels that the brand consistently satisfies his or her expectations. Examples of favorable images include the NFL's designation as America's sport and NBA star Dwyane Wade's persona as a young, well-rounded, and hard-working family man.

Sports brands that have favorable brand images need to monitor closely their behavior for potential unfavorable situations, ensure that lines of communication remain open, and continually search for new channels to distribute the favorable image.

Unfavorable A sports brand has an unfavorable image when the fan perceives the brand's attributes as negative and feels that the brand does not satisfy his or her expectations. Unfavorable images can be situational such as the Minnesota Vikings' alleged sex cruise or continuous such as Mike Tyson's problems with his personal life and the law.

A sports brand with an unfavorable brand image needs to understand the criticism, reshape the product and communication message to reflect a more positive brand positioning, and in general actualize all participants, internal and external, on the new image positioning.

Mixed Most sports brands fall into the mixed image category, which includes favorable and unfavorable images. Fans who perceive sports brands with mixed images may feel that their expectations are not being satisfied.

An example of a sports brand with a mixed image is NCAA Division I college basketball where some fans might have a favorable image of the Final Four tournament but also have an unfavorable image of the brand because its star players often forgo graduation and leave college early to enter the NBA.

Sports properties with mixed brand images need to improve their favorable image by reexamining their product's perception, refocusing their image efforts on positive qualities, trying to reduce or eliminate the negative qualities, and making sure that all participants understand the refocused brand.

Indifferent A sports brand has an indifferent image when the fan does not perceive the brand in any meaningful way. It can be a general problem in which the sports brand such as the newly launched National Pro Fastpitch softball league needs to move from indifference toward a state of awareness and interest. It can also be a geographically-based issue. For example, hockey has an indifferent image in Latin America, and baseball is in a similar situation in most of Europe.

In many ways, an indifferent brand image is the most challenging of all and demands that the brand segments the target markets into real prospects. If not, the brand is relegated to living with its indifferent image problem and being content to retain and satisfy its present fan base.

COMMUNICATORS OF THE BRAND

There are three major sports communicators: *sports brand participants, media,* and *sponsors*. Managing the movement of the sports brand through each communicator is critical to a fan-centered communication strategy.

Sports Brand Participants

The ideal situation for a sports decision maker is that the launching of a new communication strategy fits seamlessly in a predetermined timeline, is understood by all involved, and is approved by everyone in the organization. In this perfect world, all communication programs complement the brand framework and the resources are in place for implementation.

Yet in the sports industry, the ideal is hard to achieve. In implementing a communication program, there are often timing problems that push up the schedule for execution, dissension within the organization that challenges the direction of the brand, and economic realities that can alter significantly the communication rollout. All of these force the sports decision maker to make tough communication choices often in a rush or during times of crisis. But the results do not have to be disastrous.

How should one approach these conflicts? The answer is being realistic and reasonable about setting priorities. Sports decision makers need to be aware of their priorities upon entering implementation and be prepared to eliminate or modify programs that do not fit the brand framework or the target segments. In the brand communication process, certain programs, initiatives, or events are more important to a target audience than others.

Even more telling and sometimes more difficult is evaluating what you already have and deciding what you're going to keep, expand, develop, or drop. The vested interests are often going to dispute or feel diminished by the disappearance of their program. This argues for two strategies. First, critical participants of already existing programs should be included in the deliberation concerning fundamental communication and branding issues. Second, clear lines of leadership should be developed for making decisions on what programs will expire and what will be developed.

Blogs: Sports Talk by the Billions

Web logs, or blogs, are the fastest growing communication channels in the world and are an effective tool for sports decision makers. Blogs started out as personal journals on the Internet, have rapidly expanded into the world of commerce, and have great potential for sports brands. The growth in the blog industry is supersonic; in a two-year period from 2003 to 2005, it jumped from 100,000 blogs to 14 million, according to Technorati, a search engine that specializes in blogs.[4] Blogs are rapidly becoming a part of the brand portfolio along with advertising, public relations, brochures, and Web sites. The blog provides three strong assets for brand building. One, it creates a personal relationship between the brand communicator and the consumer. Two, it is the one place where the brand can express a position, correction, idea, or any other information without the threat of being misinterpreted. The blog becomes an unretouched communication message that is controlled by the brand communicator. Three, it provides flexibility, which allows insider talk, daily updates, and other insights not usually covered in other media.

The keys to successful blogging are not much different from successful writing or speaking. All blogs should have a beginning, middle, and end, like any

---

other well-written story. The messages should be tied to the sports brand and yet not have the overt, self-serving associations connected with advertising and other forms of paid media. The blog should favor a conversational style and not create a logjam of data. It should be authored by communicators in the sports brand operation who have a specific voice and persona.

The NBA has integrated the blog as a major component of its online communication strategy. The league has created the "Blog Squad," a group of current and former players, team and league executives, members of the media, and Hollywood entertainers. While the NBA does not control the content of the Blog Squad, it filters this fan communication channel by managing its list of bloggers. Past bloggers have been retired star Scottie Pippen, Detroit Pistons guard Richard Hamilton, Portland Trail Blazers general manager John Nash, Israeli journalist Yaron Talpaz, and actor Jaleel White.[5] Each has provided a different perspective on the NBA, deepening the blogging experience for the fan. The Blog Squad also expands the league's global reach by featuring international bloggers and offering Spanish, Chinese, Brazilian, and Taiwanese versions of the Squad. The Blog Squad reflects and reinforces the NBA's vision to become a global sports and entertainment brand. In doing so, the blogs support the brand's communication efforts and provide a fan-centered experience for their readers.

For all of their advantages, blogs and other interactive Web sites have the potential to damage or call into question the goodwill of the brand. There are thousands of independently managed sports blogs on the Web that are not fully under the control of a sports brand. These blogs are occasionally the instigators of rumors, false accusations, or other controversies that can spread in the media and hurt the brand image. In these situations, sports decision makers obviously only control the information that they develop but must respond to inaccuracies in a different fashion. Information clarification has to be conducted on a regular basis, and sports decision makers must develop an ongoing daily response program to deal with them. Blogs are an open communication system that can deepen associations, but they also demand that brands become more accountable for what they deliver and how they respond to unsubstantiated or negative information.

Media

The traditional sports media is the most prolific and least controllable ingredient in the sports communication mix. The sports brand-media relationship has historically been reciprocal—sports brands need the media to reach the public and the media need story lines, news material, and programming from sports brands. While the sports brand can't control all of its relationship with the media, there are communication steps that can help the brand's chances of developing a reasonable relationship. For example, sports brands are obligated to provide timely and accurate information. They are also obligated to build good personal relationships with the media managers. The frequent breakdowns that occur in the everyday handling of story lines affect the fan directly. In many sports, the fan experiences the sports brand only through the lens of the media and the media have the potential to reshape the product through their camera angles, editing, placement, and point of view.

It's just not accessibility anymore that is a major stumbling block to good coverage. There is also a crisis in the infrastructure of the sports media-sports brand relationship. The traditional sports media is now in competition with many sports brands that are developing and distributing their own media content directly to the fan. As a result, communication conflicts have emerged all over the industry. An issue is the onslaught of competing channels both institutionally and individually driven. For example, when there is negative information or a problem, the sports brand is often accused of not sharing it with the media. It becomes an ethos issue when the only information coming out of the sport is excessively positive, which makes the media skeptical about its quality. Who gets what and when is no longer always in the control of the sports brand. This means that sports need to reshape their media relationships to make clear what they are willing to share and ensure that they build credibility to withstand the sometimes powerful and embarrassing revelations from nontraditional media.

Who's Driving Coverage?

We can distinguish five different communication-driven *media coverage* situations.

Continuous Coverage Major sports properties normally have all the media attention they can wish for, but it is not always favorable. Continuous-coverage sports such as basketball, football, and baseball in America and soccer, cricket, and rugby in other parts of the world are covered on a daily basis and receive exposure from a number of media outlets including newspaper box scores and stories, spots on the evening television news, radio programs, and magazine cover stories. These sports are reported in minute detail by the media, and as a result fans have access to the internal workings of the sport.

Continuous-coverage sports are often kept busy just keeping track of the daily communication volume and need to be aware of deteriorating relationships with beat writers, broadcasters, and reporters that can be potentially damaging. They also need to make efforts to ensure that coverage is truly continuous and monitor the quantity and quality on a regular basis.

Event-Driven Coverage Event-driven sports experience a spike in media coverage during marquee events and weak or nonexistent coverage during the rest of the season. Examples of these sports properties are major tennis and golf matches, high-stakes horse races, and cycling events such as the Tour de France.

Event-driven coverage demands a lot of communication activity in a short period of time, and event communicators need to ensure that there is enough personnel to handle the tasks, that all the media centers are aware of and anticipating the event, and that everyone in the organization is given a clear sense of priorities to manage the barrage of coverage that will occur.

Niche Coverage Niche-coverage sports receive very little mass coverage but have a very strong channel that reaches a defined and targeted market. These sports are often television-based and rarely appear in other distribution channels such as mass circulation sports newspapers or magazines. Professional wrestling, bass fishing, and extreme sports fall into this category where coverage is limited to only a few channels. These sports may be very strong in a particular market but overall are not as extensively covered as the major seasonal sports.

Niche-coverage sports brands are particularly committed to their avid fans and have to increasingly provide a full menu of events and opportunities for feedback and participation in a variety of forums to satisfy fans' demands and keep them from going elsewhere.

Struggling Coverage These sports struggle to increase their exposure in the media and in some markets simply do not exist. In place of media coverage, these sports properties often communicate with their fans through newsletters, Web sites, and local events because none of these sports are considered mainstream, except in a few markets. Traditional sports such as amateur wrestling, field hockey, and water polo fit into this category.

The struggling-coverage sports have the most to gain with the development of new media channels such as Web sites and other Internet-related content, which are often low cost and can simultaneously broaden interest and generate word-of-mouth.

Fan-Driven Coverage In the new media environment, there is now a rapidly emerging category of coverage that is fan-driven. This shift in sports coverage is the result of new media technology that enables fans to define,

(Continued)

(*Continued*)

personalize, and direct coverage of sports. In a media society with blogs, Web sites, satellite television and radio, interactive television and radio shows, podcasts, and numerous video games and fantasy sports, fans can now drive coverage. Fans are able to determine what they're going to hear and what they're going to see in increasingly growing numbers. The coverage, therefore, of some sports is determined by whether the sports brand connects with fans in some manner that compels or encourages them to shape a coverage world around their preferences. It also means that a sport that is in other traditional coverage categories may well find itself irrelevant if it does not stimulate fan-driven coverage.

Fan-driven coverage demands two responses from the sports industry. The first is the need for constant monitoring of these new technologies for trends and issues that are important to the sports brand, and the second is to coordinate and cooperate with these fan-driven developments.

Sponsors

Sponsors are another communicator of the sports brand because they provide financial support and exposure through the advertising and marketing of their products. Sponsors are increasingly taking a long-range view that their partnership will mutually benefit their organization and the sports brand. Companies are continuing to raise their investment in sports properties with an estimated $2.4 billion spent in 2005 on sponsorships, which is a 29 percent increase over 2003.[6] The advantages of these sponsor–sports brand relationships are that sponsors can reach many connection points of the fan base; capitalize on the strong affinity of sports fans to their athletes, players, and leagues; and sell their products and services with messages that don't appear as manipulative as conventional advertising. In essence, sponsors borrow the emotional capital of the sport and seek to transfer it to their own product. It is an emotional heat that a financial investment company or a potato chip manufacturer cannot generate on its own. The downside of the sport-sponsorship relationship occurs when the sponsor's product or service does not fit the brand values of the sports property, or the sponsor becomes so dominant in promotion that fans begin to see its involvement as exploitation. In some cases, stadiums have taken names off the property, or advertisements on players' uniforms have been debated and discarded.

Many sponsors have a product that is not directly related to sports, but they use the sports brand as a promotional platform. For example, the Allstate insurance company, a major advertising sponsor of college football, has extended its reach to product placement by branding field goal nets with its slogan, "You're in good hands with Allstate." In addition, Allstate has sponsored half-time field goal contests and scholarship funds.[7] The strategy has the benefit of not only generating goodwill for the company but also reaching a loyal group of fans that support their alma maters or favorite programs. The disadvantage for the sponsor in this case is that the product being advertised is not in daily use or possibly being purchased in the near future by the target audience, and the exposure effect may weaken over time.

In contrast, there are also "tools of the trade" sponsors that often fit seamlessly within the sport itself such as Reebok, Adidas, Prince, and Under Armour. These sponsors have sports-related products that athletes and teams use during competition, and the vicarious experience connection allows fans to emulate their models. The benchmark is the sports apparel and equipment brand Nike, which has grown into a $13 billion a year global business.[8] The brand combines high-profile superstar athlete endorsements with a local grassroots marketing strategy to remain a powerful communicator in sports. Not only are world class athletes such as Tiger Woods, LeBron James, Maria Sharapova, and Michael Jordan top Nike endorsers, but the Nike logo can be seen on the uniforms of high school, college, and club teams around the world. The big thrust is international as the U.S. athletic footwear market is no longer growing. Nike has responded to this trend by making spectacular international sponsorship deals with organizations such as the Indian national cricket team for $44 million over 5 years and 21 Chinese sports federations.[9] In doing so, the Nike brand is attempting to counter the increasing competition from the Adidas acquisition of Reebok. Its strategy is to continue to integrate its product and messages into the sports performances of its star athletes and teams at highly visible international, regional, and local levels. Fans see the Nike brand in action and can identify with the athletes who wear Nike shoes by purchasing and wearing the same pair.

Former star professional golfer Greg Norman is an example of how super-star athletic endorsements can be redefined in a fast-changing sports climate. In earlier generations, famous athletes were exclusively represented by management firms who took their cut and often made the important decisions. Norman dropped his agency, IMG, and has set out to build what he intends to become a brand that will endure beyond not only his career but his life. His $300 million business includes a clothing line called the Greg Norman Collection,

Greg Norman Estates, a co-venture with Fosters Wine Estates that markets Australian wines, Norman's large-scale coventure golf course and home construction company that operates in three countries, and book deals.[10] Norman has a macro vision of his brand that encompasses not only the conventional endorsement, licensing, and sponsorship relationships but transcends them all into a lifestyle package. He has taken control of his name and owns it on a scale that is unprecedented in the sports industry.

Making the sports-sponsorship relationship fan-centered is a critical communication question for sports properties and for sponsors. There are perfect marriages that no one would dispute. A product like Papa John's pizza, which bought naming rights to the University of Louisville's football stadium, is not only seen in public and media events, but can be munched on while the game is in progress. It's easy to measure and has direct, if not immediate, results. Other products that may seek long-term affinity goals such as Charles Schwab or Century 21 are not as easy to measure, but they keep their name in play with a target audience that is often loyal to the sport. The sports property also has decisions to make on the desirability of how much sponsorship and to what degree. If the sports brand allows too much sponsorship control, the fans may view the sponsor's involvement as a commercial intrusion. On the other hand, without sponsorship support, sports brands often cannot financially survive. The challenge for sports brands is to not only attract responsible and committed sponsors but to ensure that the decisions made are based on fan interest and not solely on survival.

THE SPORTS BRAND'S STORY

Whether the communicator is the sports brand participant, media, or sponsor, they all have in common the need to connect to fans. What often makes sports so compelling is the drama that is created—the tension in the final round, the controversy over which player will start, and the rivalry between two towns. Fans can escape their everyday lives and experience vicariously the fortunes and failures of their athletes and teams.

The relationship between story lines and sports brands is a powerful one. Story lines are potentially interesting, suspenseful, and controversial. They are critical in a marketplace in which sports brands are trying to engage an audience that is frequently overwhelmed with messages and that demonstrates increasingly fragmented media use.

Rather than leave the creation of story lines to chance, the communication industry has begun to consciously design and promote them by using *dramatic reality*.[11] Dramatic reality is the restructuring of reality into a narrative format to strategically heighten the drama of real events. The integration of dramatic structure to frame real events provides fans with an emotional context to understand, interpret, and identify with sports. As the line between sports and entertainment blurs, the implementation of dramatic reality is critical. There are five goals of dramatic reality:

1. To engage the fan's interest
2. To imprint the sports brand's identity for a longer-lasting impression
3. To humanize the sports brand
4. To encourage the fan to identify with the sports brand and feel that he or she has a personal connection with the participants
5. To place the outcomes of competition in more than just a winning context

In an information society, audiences are increasingly accustomed to receiving and understanding content delivered in story form. The "Road to the Final Four" is an example of an unending series of stories that provide the emotional context for a compelling tale of a quest for a championship. This reframing of the sports event is now expected, and any sports product stripped of dramatic reality is bound to fail. This turn of events is the product of four factors.

1. Stories historically are the most effective way for audiences to understand and be involved in any activity whether it is sports, entertainment, religion, or politics. What we have now is the institutionalization of story culture as an accessible connection point for most activities.
2. The rapid expansion of technology delivering basic sports information in quick and real time has forced print media to respond with more dramatic story lines for a value-added interpretation of games and events. The time element in story structure has been compressed because of channel costs, the shifting behavior of audiences, and the corresponding need to tell the story in as little as 10 seconds. The compression factor has altered the pace and the visual elements of story lines but has not changed the need or fundamental premises.
3. In a communication society where choices are everywhere, stories are one of the few message forms that can claim audience involvement.

Because a story has a beginning, a middle, and an end, the audience is often compelled to stay engaged until the final outcome.

4. In a sports environment with so many conflicting messages, stories have the potential to personalize and provide color and texture to an event or a game. Stories are one of the most effective means to delay the remote control fan from switching off your program.

Most stories have common elements, often involving lesson-giving and moral issues, and discovering those links is critical to developing the sports brand story. Consider the story line of Toby Willis, the owner and creator of Real Pro Wrestling, a league of eight teams across the United States competing in Olympic-style wrestling. A newspaper story about Willis describes how and why he decided to establish the league:

When Toby Willis lost five brothers and a sister in a gruesome traffic accident that had a bitter political aftermath, he knew of two places to seek solace. Both had been shown to him by his father, Rev. Scott Willis, a Baptist minister. One refuge the younger Willis sought was "in the Good Book," the Bible. The other was in wrestling. . . . He has put millions of dollars from the traffic accident settlement into wrestling, the sport he loves. "I lost one set of brothers," he said. "Now I'm trying to help another set, my wrestling brothers." To do that, he has invested in Real Pro Wrestling.[12]

The story continues with a description of how Willis and his partners created the Real Pro Wrestling league. The story line suggests to the audience that Willis's attempts to launch the league are to serve a higher purpose—remembering his family and helping out his sport—rather than to make a profit. It provides texture and depth to the launching of the new league, encourages audience members to feel sympathy for Willis, and creates a memorable story line to associate with the league, all offering a reason other than the wrestling matches to tune in.

As illustrated by Willis, most sports brand stories can be distilled into six components:

1. *Drama:* a story-based construction with a beginning, middle, and end. Willis's family tragedy forced him to cope with his life and channel his money and energy into wrestling.

2. *Adversity:* a barrier that presents a challenge. Willis's coping with the memory of the family tragedy, trying to start a new league from scratch, overcoming competitive pressures and the influence of staged professional wrestling in fulfilling his vision for Real Pro Wrestling.
3. *Crisis:* an uncertain event or series of events that magnifies the challenges. Willis's unsuccessful attempt at establishing the league will affect his ability to get over the loss of his family, and resources limit the amount of time available to test the league
4. *Mentors:* the support system that offers advice to overcome the obstacles. Religion and Willis's father guide his actions and have contributed to the formation of his values and ethics.
5. *Persistence:* a commitment to solving the problem. The hard work and dedication that Willis experienced as a wrestler have been applied to making the league succeed.
6. *A final reward or climax:* the payoff of the quest and the culmination of the story. For Willis the very act of the league's launch is a rewarding conclusion to the story line.

The most effective story lines are often extended over time and expanded to heighten the original drama for the fan. There are strategies that can be used to increase the drama of a story line. One strategy is for the sports brand to undergo transformation, which can produce a new set of story line possibilities. For example, when the NBA instituted the three-point shot, the MLB speeded up the game with new pitcher and hitter time restrictions; both leagues benefited from the story lines that were created by the altered style of play. Another example is Tiger Woods, whose story line has evolved from a California child prodigy dominated by his father to an articulate, poised, multisectored brand who sets the standard for sports stars. In both examples, the transformation process altered the sports product and as a result stimulated the developmemt of expanded and enhanced story lines.

Another strategy is to reconfigure the story line by gradually disclosing new information and details about the sports brand. A brand communicator for a team might go beyond the conventional profiles of its players to include information about moments with their families, former loves, how they spend their time in the off-season, and detailed accounts of their playing experience. New media provide an excellent communication channel for this particular strategy because it enables a wide variety of brand participants to communicate with micro audiences.

It's important that the sports brand and its managers are able to have control over their story content. While it is understood that stories in the sports world can come from myriad sources, there is story material that can be generated from the sports product itself. That material is often underutilized and can be a vital communication link to the fan. Since story lines are strategic communication units for interaction, use of dramatic reality can help establish the fan connections that are so universally sought. (For major sports story line possibilities,[13] see the end of the chapter.)

The Enthymeme

One of the fundamental challenges in delivering any kind of message in the crowded sports marketplace is getting a meaningful audience response. There are millions of slogans, themes, positions, advertising campaigns, and Web sites, all screaming for attention. Designing a message that will resonate amidst such clutter is a matter of understanding and respecting the fan's experiences and needs.

As early as 350 BC, the Greek philosopher and rhetorician Aristotle was struck by how direct appeals were not as effective as ones that were more centered on audience responses. He called these audience-centered rhetorical arguments the *enthymeme*. Aristotle expressed the concept as a syllogism with the speaker strategically setting up premises that were then resolved by the audience. He further observed that if the message is constructed in a way that the members of the audience discover the key idea on their own, there will be a connection that will last longer with more intensity and more conviction. He also cautioned about the difficulty of setting up the enthymeme because the speaker had to make sure that he or she understood what triggers would resonate with the audience because if the enthymeme failed the audience would miss the point.[14] It's not overstated to claim that Aristotle was the first to understand the difference between the hard sell and the soft sell and the rewards and risks of each.

Twentieth-century communication specialist Tony Schwartz expanded Aristotle's enthymeme. In his provocative book *The Responsive Chord*,

Schwartz updated the enthymeme to include the electronic age and the need to be more specific in evoking what he called the "responsive chord" from the beliefs and attitudes of the audience. Schwartz wrote, "To achieve a behavioral effect, whether persuading someone to buy a product or teaching a person about history, one designs stimuli that will resonate with the elements in a communication environment to produce that effect."[15] Schwartz's famous example of the responsive chord is a commercial he developed for Lyndon Johnson's presidential campaign in 1964. The commercial featured a little girl plucking petals from a daisy until she reached a count of 10. The next frame contained a nuclear explosion with another countdown accompanied by a statement from Johnson: "These are the stakes, to make a world in which all God's children can live, or to go into the darkness. Either we must love each other or we must die." Finally, a black screen appeared with white letters and the words "on November 3, Vote for President Johnson."[16] Although the commercial aired just once because of charges of unfairness from the Republicans, it was highly effective in implicating Johnson's opponent, Barry Goldwater, as an advocate of using nuclear weapons without even mentioning his name. Schwartz understood the audience's objections to nuclear war and created a message in which audience members came up with their own conclusion—Johnson could keep the country safe; Goldwater couldn't.

Today, new inquiries into how biological and psychological factors influence audiences are often aimed at understanding how people are persuaded. For example, studies have begun examining how human pheromones such as androstenol affect product purchases[17] and how "consumption dreams" about products during sleep affect consumer behavior.[18] The sports industry has also moved in a similar direction. For example, Octagon's "Passion Drivers" study argued that sports marketers and sponsors ought to understand underlying fan motivations when designing messages.[19] In each of these studies, the focus is on reaching deeper into the audience, searching for how they make decisions, and understanding what they want, all in an effort to construct more persuasive messages that will evoke a desired response—concepts not far from Aristotle and Schwartz.

In a communication environment that is increasingly dominated by media, reduced message exposure, and an audience base that is increasingly more difficult to reach with longer messages, the enthymeme becomes a critical device. These audience- and media-driven changes account for the increased focus on stories, visuals, and other communication message forms that not only depend on audience involvement but demand it. The best designers of sports messages will master these forms and be willing to take all the risks and subsequent rewards that using them entails.

COMMUNICATING DRAMATIC REALITY

There are a number of strategies that emphasize dramatic reality, but the most important and effective is often star communication. In this section, we first focus on star communication and then discuss a number of other strategies that can be used both together with star communication and independent of it.

Star Communication

Star communication uses the star as a lever to connect with fans and differentiate the brand. Stars have the advantage of most effectively communicating the dramatic story lines that fans can understand, relate to, or admire. Most sports products—players, coaches, leagues, teams, facilities, events, sporting goods—have the potential to be stars, but not every product can be one. "Star" by its very nature means that the product possesses some outstanding attributes and has the potential to attract fans. In analyzing the brand's star aspirants, there must be a careful selection process and the willingness to put maximum effort behind star development.

Star selection can be both market-driven and producer-driven. Market-driven stars are discovered by the fans themselves, and the brand has to be willing to acknowledge their wisdom and build from that platform. With producer-driven stars, the brand must choose from a number of possibilities and often make difficult decisions. Sports brands often have to take into account the behavior and maintenance of a star. Compounding the problem is that fans often like the star who is most unlikable to management, and it is more likely that a star athlete, unlike facilities, leagues, or events, will be difficult to manage.

It is around these star issues that brand managers must work and find an effective compromise to satisfy the experience for the fan. This particular problem becomes more difficult as other revenue sources such as media and sponsors become more important to the star's income than the sport itself. While that is a reality that is difficult to undo, sports decision makers have to begin thinking earlier about their star inventory. They must begin to develop strategies to encourage brand integration and reward systems without coercion but with enough rewards for all the participants to retain brand loyalty. An integrated sports brand needs to make star decisions on the brand's integrity that include not only performance skills but also communication and marketing issues that affect the fan and not compromise for short-term star gain.

Star individuals, in particular, often require communication training to develop their star potential and improve their interactions with the media. This includes staying on brand message and clearly developing key ideas as well as stylistic issues such as voice inflection, eye contact, and gestures. NASCAR is an example of a circuit that has made star development and communication a priority. According to NASCAR media trainer Rick Benjamin, "It's a different world for drivers trying to break into the top echelons of racing today. Twenty years ago, if you could drive the wheels off a car, that might be enough to get you to the big leagues. It certainly made you a star at the local level. Today, speaking well and projecting yourself positively is essential if you want to be successful in racing. That's true no matter how old you are, from the local tracks right up to the top levels of the sport."[20] With this perspective on the importance of the media and public communication, NASCAR's star power is driven in part by the ability of NASCAR's drivers and teams to cooperate with the media and communicate clearly and often theatrically with their fans.

A star facility obviously has different characteristics from individual star development. The facility might need a slogan or a positioning that reflects whether it's a state-of-the-art architectural achievement, a historical landmark, or an important part of the community. In many cases, the major communicators are the architects, interior designers, and other planners of what the facility will look like, what it will represent, and how fans will interact with it. The facility is one of the most powerful visual symbols that a sport can offer and accounts for the increasing emphasis of teams on demanding either their own facility or their ability to customize it.

The San Francisco Giants' ballpark, AT&T Park, is an example of how critical decisions by the planners have created a facility that combines important qualities that the team wanted to express to its fans. The team answered the question: What would it be like to build a park with the charm of Wrigley Field and the up-to-date amenities of twenty-first-century architectural innovations? The response was a park site built on San Francisco Bay, which symbolizes the city's signature image and drives all the visual experiences. The park makes every attempt to connect baseball's past with its future. For example, it has a liberal use of old-fashioned brick, a statue of the great Giants slugger Willie Mays at the main entrance, and a novel homage to another Giants star

215

Willie McCovey, a water inlet called McCovey Cove that sits outside the stadium and is often full of fans waiting in kayaks and other flotation devices for home run balls. In addition, the ballpark was built to be very children-centered with numerous slides, the "world's largest baseball glove," and other attractions that suggest a sports entertainment park.[21]

It was early in the decision-making phase that the park became a superior brand symbol. The communication in the park was imprinted when the team's planners and designers decided what communication experiences the fans would have. When it comes to facility planning, star power needs to be embedded early and with the recognition that it will define the brand experience for the life of the venue.

Implications

- Choosing the star communicators of the sports brand is probably the most important decision for a sports brand.
- Increasingly, star brands are an integrator of other connection points. The star power of the San Francisco Giants' park potentially connects with place, social currency, family, and vicarious experience.
- Stars exist at every level and in every marketplace. The increasing challenge for sports decision makers is to seek out those star possibilities and then apply them with an awareness of the entryways and connection points that are critical.

Cultural Trend Communication

The cultural trend communication strategy capitalizes on the behaviors and rituals of fan cultures. Sports brands need to search for key fan cultural codes and integrate them into the sports fan experience. For example, the Big Ten conference has institutionalized a tradition of fans traveling to road games by supporting ongoing road show promotions for the fall football seasons. The proximity of the schools across the Midwest and the numbers of fans already traveling to away football games from their home university makes this a natural communication strategy to develop. It capitalizes on what fans were already doing and expands the ritual to a much broader and more sophisticated operation. Home universities accommodate the visiting fans by institutionalizing areas to tailgate at the stadium and by offering group ticketing options and related social activities. The Big Ten conference, Southeast conference, and others have branded the road trip, and all the schools have benefited from the fan activity with the growing popularity of traveling to see basketball games or other conference sports.

Another example of cultural trend communication is bling-bling culture, as visual a symbol as one could imagine. Bling-bling culture is characterized by fancy, high-priced diamonds and other jewelry; large SUVs with tinted windows, chrome hubcaps, and interior gadgets such as DVD players and video games; and clothing items including throwback jerseys, bright colors, and fashions from urban designers. The culture reflects the extremes of materialism and is most closely associated with two interconnected entertainments—hip-hop music and the NBA. Although the NBA did not produce nor does it necessarily support the bling-bling, hip-hop connection and seems to now be condemning it, the league benefited from the cross sector exposure it created. Rappers mentioned NBA players in their songs and would regularly attend NBA games, and NBA players made appearances in rap music videos and at hip-hop social events. The hip-hop–NBA partnership was the result of a cultural connection in which many of the rappers and athletes had similar story lines—growing up in poverty, living in single-parent homes, and now making excellent livings. The association with hip-hop was an advantage for the NBA because of the music's appeal to younger generations. As one of the most popular genres in contemporary music, hip-hop gave the NBA a direct line to reach and engage key sectors of the youth market. This cultural connection with bling bling demonstrates the power of popular cultural trends that can intersect with the sport.

Implications

- The place to find cultural trends is not always within the sports industry itself but rather in other trend-conscious sectors such as fashion, music, film, consumer goods, or foreign markets.
- Sports brands need to integrate other types of cultural experiences into the sport such as encouraging young people to film games from their perspective and staging a contest to select the most compelling video representations or making an iPod playlist around the theme of the sport and the team.

- Some of the best cultural trends are already in place and are being played out on the street or in other places. Sports decision makers can search for these trends and then institutionalize them within a communication agenda.

Community Communication

This strategy builds fan support for the sports brand by involving community members. Key to this strategy is that community members feel invested in the sports brand. The strength of community communication is that it makes it much more likely that sports fans will open the newspaper to check for scores or go to a game if they know the athletes or have some sort of investment in the brand. The Nova High School baseball program in Davie, Florida, has built its brand on the community communication strategy. Each year, head coach Pat McQuaid sends his players into the community to solicit team sponsors, who, in exchange for a donation, receive a banner on the outfield fence advertising their product or service. This community strategy accomplishes two important goals. One, it encourages members of the community to invest in the team. Two, it generates revenue to improve the program. This strategy has helped the program build a state-of-the-art facility with updated player locker rooms, batting cages, and training equipment. As a result, the program attracts top-quality players, media members, and scouts to the school and annually hosts tournaments with local, regional, and national participants. The Nova High School baseball team has benefited from tapping into the community and forming profitable relationships and has branded itself as a university-level program.

The center of the Green Bay Packers community involvement strategy is the public ownership of the team. The team became a nonprofit corporation on August 18, 1923, after several years of financial trouble. The team now has 111,921 stockholders consisting of many community members and others from all over the country who have a personal investment in the Green Bay Packers in the form of shares.[22] The investment encourages an emotional connection and more closely binds the team with its fans and community. In addition, the Packers have redefined their home stadium, Lambeau Field, as a historic landmark and an important community center where the team holds special kids' nights along with meetings and weddings. The Green Bay Packers with its shareholders and Lambeau community center are perhaps the gold standard for fan connection as it solidifies the power of its place as a connector.

Implications

- Community communication operates best when the sports brand asks for something from citizens such as contributing their time or money. Trying to manufacture community without the involvement of its citizens is a common error and will inevitably fail.
- Effective community involvement strategies can demonstrate what the contributions will bring, which is usually something tangible such as a building, facility, or scholarships.
- Community communication is most effective when it has permanence and generational connections. Sporadic community efforts are not enough to establish a connection that has enduring value for a sports brand. Some of the most effective community communication strategies are not only outreaches to insiders or avid fans but to multigenerational family connections or unaffiliated community members who are given opportunities to participate.

Setting up the Season: Communicating Renewal

As each season's play ends and the losers clear out their lockers, calls to anticipate and hope for the following season are soon to follow. It is an axiom of sports decision makers to begin seeding fan attention and interest for the next year through a number of strategies that are loaded with the basic emotional need for renewal. Most of us like to think of ourselves, our heroes, and our teams as getting better and not deteriorating. In the sports universe, next year the team ideally has new spirit, athletes are quicker, and the facilities are upgraded. All this, of course, has to be communicated in a story format to a marketplace that may well have become immune to prior failed calls for rejuvenation.

In most sports, the strategies for renewal are drawn from a familiar group of slogans such as "The Future Starts This Fall," "Buckle Your Seat Belts," "This is a Whole New Game," or "Back Where We Belong." A variation are themes which often visualize the future by operationalizing anticipation and hope such as a team in transition, rebuilding through youth, and a franchise building brick by brick. A second set of strategies is the use of media, advertising, and other

(Continued)

(Continued)

media channels to deliver team story lines such as a star athlete being rehabil-itated, interviews with the coach, and insights into league and event details. Third are the traditional and newly developing interactive sports experiences that are intended to engage the fan both in-season and off-season such as hot stove leagues, fantasy games, and cruises with iconic former stars. And finally are the major infrastructure changes such as moving the team, hiring a new coach, changing ownership, and building a new facility. These major changes have the highest potential impact and are consequently usually the most expensive and riskiest. However, all of these run the risk of overpromising wins as slogans such as "Expect the Unexpected" can often result in a winless season.

What should the sports decision maker be looking for in terms of max-imum exposure and not overselling the public when communicating renewal?

- Make sure that the marketers and public relations staff understand the condition of the sports product. And, in doing so, monitor com-munication expectations to reflect a reasonable outcome and not experience disappointment and backlash.
- A new season is an opportunity to introduce the fan to a new set of expectations. Targeting connections such as family, social currency, and place can expand audience expectations and reorient the fan to not expect only winning appeals.
- Using new media such as podcasts, blogs, fantasy sports, and other highly interactive channels is particularly effective in reaching younger groups. Many sports programs perform the necessities—refrigerator schedule magnets, posters in store windows, bumper stickers, or pre-season media day. But without responding to channel innovations, sports can lose their youth market.
- The renewal appeal can connect the fans to a variety of communica-tion platforms that combine participatory events, special promotions, invitations to personal contact with players, and other activities. The crucial element is that the appeal be multidimensional and connect on a number of levels.

Experience Communication

B. Joseph Pine II and James H. Gilmore in their book *Experience Economy* argue that products have become commodities and that creating experiences is the most effective differentiator.[23] The key is not using a direct selling approach to the consumer because it is the enthymatic communication environment that the consumer is placed in that creates the desire for the product. For example, doll company American Girl, Inc., uses experience communication to connect with consumers. At its store American Girl Place in Chicago, the emphasis is not just on selling dolls, but also on selling an experience. Consumers can attend an American Girl theater production, have tea or a meal, get their picture taken and placed on the cover of *American Girl Magazine*, or get their dolls' hair done at the doll hair salon.[24] In this case, the connection is based not just on the dolls but on the total package of social and emotional connections that the store encourages. The in-store theater approach in sports is illustrated by the ESPN Zone, which combines the sports experience with intense media saturation, a restaurant and bar, and an arcade. Similarly, Niketown and Adidas stores stage their products and athletes in a reverential, theatrical environment that suggests superhumanness and iconic worship.

An example of how experience communication can build market share is sporting goods company WL Gore and Associates, Inc., which makes the waterproof Gore-tex fabric and entered the Chinese market in 1997. Since the company and its products were new to the market, it needed to create awareness for the brand. In doing so, it used a form of experience communication in which it provided consumers with free classes in surviving outdoors and built special "weather chambers" in their stores so consumers could try out the products.[25] These promotional strategies were not necessarily designed for consumers to buy the brand on the spot, but to create a connection with the consumer that could eventually result in a purchase.

Sports properties have been forced to provide a more holistic and less generic fan experience to compete. It wasn't so long ago that banners, pom-pom girls, and some musical accompaniment was all that was required to create an expectation-meeting, in-game experience for a fan at a venue. As entertainment values have escalated and fan expectations have risen, programmed anticipation, architectural venue integration, and an overall entertainment experience are now expected. An example are the newly built football stadiums, which are expected to incorporate visual symbols such as fan meeting sites, elaborate player introductions, massive scoreboards, and new media that are more compelling than the living room. Experience communication is essential for fans to be convinced that leaving their television sets and computers for a trip to the venue is worth it.

Implications

- The experience is not generic and should be something that fans can't get elsewhere. It should have a delight factor that connects to an essential need of the fan.
- The most effective experiences use theatrical communication devices such as scenery, music, and sound to make the environment more effective and differentiate the product.
- Communicating through experiences has the advantage of taking the longer view of consumer relationships. The central focus is upon building emotional bridges that will make the sports product an integral part of the fan experience.

Viral Communication

Viral communication is a strategy that capitalizes on the influence of word-of-mouth to plant and connect with potential customers. This is the new communication frontier. Driven by technology and fragmentation, old-fashioned word-of-mouth is now an industry.[26] Like a virus, messages are injected into selected consumers and then are quickly spread to the consumers' peers, a communication process that has become especially effective with the Internet. In some cases the viral messages do not overtly sell a product or even mention a brand. The key is creating a buzz about the product and getting a core of people talking about it. A good starting point for successful viral communication is targeting the best disseminators of information such as avid and influential fans who are most likely to diffuse the message to their peers.

A successful example from the fast-food industry was Burger King's viral communication campaign called the "Subservient Chicken," a Web site that allowed users to control a man in a chicken suit by making him peck and putting him into motion. The Web site was very successful in that it drew at least 16.5 million visitors.[27] This interactive Web site had links that enabled viewers to see pictures of the man in the chicken suit, download a replica of the chicken mask, send the Web site to a friend via e-mail, and a link to Burger King's Tendercrisp chicken sandwich. Rather than focusing on the direct selling of the Burger King brand or its Tendercrisp sandwich, the most important component of the strategy was that the user was entertained and would tell a friend. The advantage of viral communication is that it appears to be consumer-driven rather than producer-driven advertising and marketing messages.

Sports brands have been moving in the direction of viral communication. The NBA during the 2004–2005 finals sent 3 million e-mail messages reminding fans to watch with the hope that they would forward the messages to friends and family.[28] The University of Texas Longhorns football program has created an Internet video magazine (Vmag) that provides fans with insider video footage of players and coaches and has included viral communication in its promotional strategy,[29] which has resulted in 22.5 percent of the Vmag's recipients forwarding the Vmag to their peers.[30] Wigan Athletic, a soccer team in England, uses viral communication through meshcards, which are digital business cards that advertise a brand on a person-to-person basis and have the advantage of collecting information about the fans that use them. Wigan fans can register for 20 cards at a time, and the fans can personalize them based on their own preferences to express their devotion to the team and share their allegiance with other fans.[31] In all these examples, viral communication seeks to capitalize on the influence of peer communication in sports and the potential of the Internet to reach and connect with a great number of fans.

Implications

- The most effective viruses draw from fundamental experiences like kids drawing pictures, the need to send cards, or the experience of just simply connecting to people with similar interests.
- Viruses don't have to be complicated. It's best if they're visual, active, and connective.
- Viruses, while often substantial, can be short-term in impact. The use of viruses demands a coordinated package that has a follow-up set of strategies.

Controversy Communication

Sports fans like to debate major and minor issues related to their sports. For many fans the involvement comes from the dustups, scandals, and petty behavior that are among the principal characteristics of sports. When participants engage in competition, it is inevitable that charges of unsportsmanlike conduct, unfathomable calls by referees or umpires, or a management decision to fire a coach become the material of important sources of dramatic reality. In the past, with the exception of sports such as NASCAR and professional wrestling, sports properties have historically stepped back from controversy and allowed the media to program and orchestrate this vital communication connection. It may well be former Washington Redskins quarterback Joe Theisman criticizing, from his snowstorm-protected booth, a quarterback's work ethic or ESPN host Stephen A. Smith ripping an innocent audience member's question about the contract status of a holdout. While there is no stopping the onslaught of colorful analysts and media critics finding fault with an athlete's or a league's actions, this is no excuse for the brand to surrender the main stage of fan controversy. Controversy fuels sports and is a principal entertainment factor that drives attending and watching.

Even more critically for the brand's ethos, the seeming informality and spontaneity of the controversy interaction often appears to the fan as a truer indication of intentions than public statements and advertising. When there is intense scrutiny, fans often feel that it is likely to produce a reaction that is most revealing of the sports brand's character. Therefore, sports brands should manage controversy, provide forums for the exchanges, and ultimately embrace the use of it as a vital part of the communication strategy.

Implications

- A willingness to engage in controversy should be a fundamental sports brand value. How the brand responds to a set of issues gives the fan insight not only into whether the sport cares about them but the sports brand's true character and integrity.
- Controversies are ultimately interactions. They reflect common communication needs—frustration, alienation, need for resolution, or simply disbelief. It's best when the needs are addressed rather than countered with silence. Encouraging the sports brand personnel to deal with these needs and not be defensive is critical.
- There's no such thing as a limited controversy, and avoiding the difficult ones is a sure brand destroyer. The brand has to be open to minor spats and major drug issues alike and find experts when necessary, be willing to conduct research, and be able to respond to these controversies with knowledge and confidence.

Spoiled Brand Relationships

In developing a communication program, there are always spoiled brand relationship issues that arise. These issues fall into two categories: The first relate to permanent or recurring situations that need to be addressed in any communication program. An example is a team like the Hartford Wolf Pack, which moved in after the departure of an NHL franchise and inherited a certain amount of opposition because of it. Another example is the Minnesota Twins who communicate their brand in an indoor dome, the Metrodome, which has driven away some fans who would like an open-air experience and who feel stifled on a nice summer day.

In communicating with alienated audiences, these feelings need to be anticipated and addressed. In the Wolf Pack case, this may include attempts to develop outreach programs such as management speeches, players hosting special events, charitable activities, and other community-building relationships to help ease the transition from the NHL. For the Twins, it means ownership communicating with the governor, state legislature, and fan base about the necessity of a cooperative financial agreement for a new state-of-the-art facility experience. Other examples of this type of spoiled brand relationship include past scandals that are long-lived and raise questions about the integrity of a sport, team relocation to a previously failed market, and importing a sport to regions that do not lend themselves to participation.

The second category of spoiled relationships is the issue of a one-time occurrence that is serious and threatens to be brand damaging, or even worse, a long-term brand communication problem. These issues include player suspensions or other incidents, work stoppages or lockouts, or cheating scandals. The University of Colorado football program was the center of an alleged series of recruiting violations and accusations of sexual assault. The aftermath was intense criticism from the governor, unrelenting media criticism, and the eventual resignation of the athletic director and the school president. In response, Colorado has changed its recruiting and disciplinary policies but finds itself still trying to convince fans that its brand has been transformed. The danger of one-time occurrences is that if they are not handled properly, they can turn into permanent or recurring issues.

Many situations can be avoided by anticipation and good planning. However, when damage occurs, it is critical to audit the information, evaluate communication choices, personalize messages, and, in general, move quickly and decisively to remedy the spoiled relationship. When Yankees first baseman Jason Giambi's grand jury testimony on his alleged steroid use was leaked, it immediately damaged his image as a dominant power hitter. The idea of his using any performance-enhancing drug worked against the sport's ideal

(Continued)

(Continued)

of fair competition and implied that the fans were cheated when he performed. Before he faced the onslaught of media questioning at spring training, Giambi responded with an apology: "I feel I let down the fans. I feel I let down the media. I feel I let down the Yankees."[32] In doing so, he spoke in a controlled press conference with his manager, agent, and general manager by his side and at least began the process of rebuilding his image. In the short term, Giambi became the target of considerable criticism for his alleged behavior and was accused of not fully disclosing. However, his initiative to respond in some fashion was in contrast to some other players who were even less forthcoming about their alleged drug use; and, over the long term, Giambi recovered some of his lost credibility. Giambi's response combined with his improved play the following year and his dedication to rebuilding his game began to neutralize the criticism of some media, fans, and critics.

In any spoiled brand relationship, it is always best to not have anything spoiled in the first place. In brand communication, problems are always going to occur. Understanding your communication options and being willing to confront them quickly and decisively is important for converting a spoiled brand relationship into an enduring fan connection.

CONCLUSION

We began this chapter with two goals—differentiate the sports brand and connect with fans. But today's communication environment has presented a number of difficult obstacles to achieving them. The marketplace is not only cluttered with messages and channels, but audiences have become more savvy and sophisticated in how they communicate. To compete in this environment, sports brands must become more fan-centered in their communication—understand the expectations and appropriate stimuli of their fans, devise messages that will resonate, and choose channels that will reach them. While the communication environment stands to become even more intense, there are fundamental communication techniques based on creating effective story lines and connecting to fans with specific strategies such as star, cultural trend, community, experience, viral, and controversy communication that will cut through the clutter to differentiate the sports brand. In the next chapter, we discuss how a differentiated and connected sports brand can remain competitive and sustain its position in the marketplace.

Major Sports Story Lines

1. *First of a kind:* swimmer Gertrude Ederle, tennis player Althea Gibson, Jackie Robinson, softball player Lisa Fernandez.
2. *Talent wins out:* Jack Johnson, LeBron James, Secretariat, Pele, Mark Spitz, Jackie Joyner-Kersee, Michael Johnson.
3. *Success/adversity/success:* Kobe Bryant, Jennifer Capriati, Rick Pitino, Seabiscuit.
4. *The fatal flaw:* Maradona and drugs, Ben Johnson and steroids, Bobby Knight and anger, Bode Miller and off-the-cuff.
5. *Restrained from greatness:* Mark McGwire, Michelle Kwan, Josh Gibson.
6. *A great rivalry:* Texas and Oklahoma football, Brazil and Argentina national soccer teams, Montreal Canadiens and Toronto Maple Leafs, India and Pakistan national cricket teams, milers Roger Bannister and John Landy.
7. *Mom or dad's footsteps:* Dale Earnhardt, Jr.; Ken Griffey, Jr.; Laila Ali, Brett Hull.
8. *The great teacher:* Amos Alonzo Stagg, Vince Lombardi, Pat Summit, Phil Jackson.
9. *Moved by religious power:* Muhammad Ali, Kurt Warner, Sandy Koufax, Ray Lewis.
10. *The miracle:* Doug Flutie's last-second Hail Mary, Dave "Miracle Boy" Mirra, 1980 U.S. hockey team's defeat of the Soviet Union, 1986 New York Mets.
11. *Young dramatic death:* Reggie Lewis, Steve Prefontaine, Pat Tillman, Maggie Dixon.
12. *Small person takes over big job:* Jeff Van Gundy, Muggsy Bogues, St. Louis Browns' dwarf pinch hitter Eddie Gaedel, Daniel "Rudy" Ruettiger.
13. *The pure archetype:* Jim Thorpe, Jim Brown, Mildred "Babe" Didrikson Zaharias, Diana Taurasi, Wilt Chamberlain, Junior Johnson.
14. *Revenge:* Boston Red Sox winning the World Series, Joe Louis's knock-out of Max Schmeling, Billie Jean King's defeat of Bobby Riggs.
15. *Needs to prove something:* Phil Mickelson, Kerri Walsh and Misty May, Michelle Wie, Chariots of Fire sprinter Harold Abrahams, Indian female tennis player Sania Mirza.
16. *Risks all:* injured gymnast Kerri Strug's Olympic gold medal landing, Bill Romanowski, Olympic wrestler Rulon Gardner, bassmasters legend Rick Clunn.
17. *Tumbling from the top:* Shoeless Joe Jackson, Pete Rose, Ryan Leaf, Marion Jones.
18. *The natural:* Albert Pujols, Annika Sorenstam, Roy Hobbs, Tony Hawk.

(Continued)

(*Continued*)

19. *The bad actor:* John Daly, Jose Canseco, Ty Cobb, Marty McSorley.
20. *The workhorse:* Lou Gehrig, thoroughbred John Henry, Vijay Singh, Cal Ripken, Jr.
21. *Gentle giant:* Shaquille O'Neal, Primo Carnera, William "the Refrigerator" Perry.
22. *The showboat:* Babe Ruth, Gary Hall, Terrell Owens, Ric Flair.
23. *The talented underachiever:* Derrick Coleman, Michael Chang, middle-distance runner Mary Decker Slaney.
24. *The Cinderella story:* Villanova NCAA basketball team; Milan, Indiana, high school basketball team, Jim "the Cinderella Man" Braddock; amateur golfer Francis Ouimet; poker champion Robert Varkonyi.
25. *The unflappable leader:* Tom Brady, Bob Cousy, Joe Torre, Phil Jackson, American Eagle skipper Ted Turner.
26. *Social influencer:* Arthur Ashe, Brandi Chastain, Allen Iverson, Danica Patrick.
27. *Sex symbol:* Maria Sharapova, Gertrude "Gorgeous Gussie" Moran, David Beckham, Natalie Gulbis.
28. *Out of control:* Ron Artest, Woody Hayes, sumo wrestling yokozuna Dolgorsuren Dagvadorj (Asashoryu in Japan), Wayne Rooney.
29. *Ambassador:* Wayne Gretzky, Tiger Woods, Yao Ming, Arnold Palmer, surfer Kelly Slater.
30. *Perfect couple:* Steffi Graf and Andre Agassi, Kris and Anna Benson, Nomar Garciaparra and Mia Hamm, Jake and Vicki LaMotta.
31. *Medical marvel:* Lance Armstrong, Tommy John, Tedy Bruschi, Italian auto racer Alex Zanardi.
32. *Family connection:* Boone family, Williams sisters, Andretti family, Perry brothers (Gaylord and Jim), Dean brothers (Dizzy and Daffy).
33. *Angry warrior:* Michael Jordan, John McEnroe, New Zealand All Blacks, Dick Butkus.

SURVIVING IN THE SPORTS FAN MARKETPLACE

8

SUSTAINING THE FAN CONNECTION

The 1947 film Body and Soul *tells the story of the rise, fall, and redemption of boxer Charley Davis, played by famed method actor John Garfield. Davis, originally an amateur boxer, begins fighting professionally to make money for his family after his father's death. A hardworking, quick, and overpowering boxer, Davis convincingly beats every opponent he faces on the professional level. Roberts, a corrupt boxing promoter and mafia boss, notices Davis's winning streak and moves ruthlessly to get him on his payroll. Enticed by the financial rewards, Davis accepts Roberts's offer—the turning point toward Davis's eventual moral crisis. Under Roberts's control, Davis wins fights, makes money, becomes a star, and is seduced by Alice, the film's temptress. In the process, Peg, his idealistic girlfriend, and Shorty, his best friend and manager, lose their patience with the new Charley and abandon him. It is not until Davis is asked by Roberts to lose in a fixed fight that he realizes how far he had fallen. In this final fight, Davis disobeys Roberts's instructions and wins. He then reunites with Peg, and the audience is left to believe that he will return to his old self.*

The film captures the sport of boxing in both its finest and darkest moments. It portrays the distinct physical and emotional dimensions of boxing, but it also is a snapshot of what contributed to the sport's decline. In many ways, the film is a metaphor forecasting the struggles of boxing throughout the second half of the twentieth century. In Body and Soul, *the sport suffered from inept regulation, gambling and corruption, and questionable medical supervision. These factors contributed to the sport's precipitous decline worldwide. What was once a major sport with a strong grassroots foundation became a special event sport that attracted widespread attention only when star boxers fought. The sport's decline symbolizes the new reality for sports brands—market position is not fixed, fans are always in flux, and the combination of competition and new media channels makes sustaining a fan base even more challenging. In the era of the Elusive Fan, boxing is still looking for its own redemption.*

After a sports brand is successfully established, it must be kept fresh and must adapt to new conditions such as audience changes and emerging distribution channels. Otherwise it will experience setbacks. Some of the setbacks may be temporary resulting from competing events, adverse weather patterns, or ticket price increases. The sports product can change its pricing, improve its communications, or try other ways to reinvigorate the brand. Other setbacks may be more challenging and longer-lasting. Fans of the sports product may have been turned off by players' arrogance or a strike, or fan interest in playing the sport has declined. There is nothing more troubling to sports decision makers than entering their own practically deserted stadium, walking around the paddock ring and seeing no crowds, or sitting in a once jam-packed basketball arena with only a few loyal patrons looking on.

To avoid decline, the sports brand needs to identify the decline problem and determine its causes, understand the specific challenges, and devise sustaining strategies to ultimately retain and grow the fan connection.

CAUSES OF DECLINE

What does it mean to be in decline? Generally, in the sports industry there are two categories of decline. First, there are measurable decline indicators such as attendance, television ratings, merchandise sales, or overall revenue figures. As the primary indicators for a brand's health, these are often the most widely cited measures of market position. The second category is made up of often less quantifiable indicators of decline, which include a weakening brand image, reduced media coverage, and, most tellingly, a diminished connection with the fans.

Whether the decline is easily measured or not, when decline indicators begin to emerge, sustaining issues become urgent. At this point, sports brands must isolate and understand the factors that contribute to decline. Here are nine of the most common causes.

Underperformance

The most common cause of decline is underperformance, which occurs when athletic performance expectations are unmet. Underperformance is not necessarily related to wins and losses. A basketball team that finishes five games over .500 might technically have had a winning season, but it can underperform because its lineup of all-stars failed to meet fan expectations of a championship. In contrast, a perennially losing football team may exceed performance expectations by winning four out of twelve games instead of its usual two games per year. In every sport and athletic performance, there are some measures of what an acceptable or outstanding performance entails. At a private university like traditionally underperforming Vanderbilt, a 7-5 football season, which included a bowl game and victories over some traditional powerful rivals, would be considered an outstanding performance. In contrast, the same record for the public state university powerhouse Louisiana State football team would be considered an underperformance and could jeopardize the status of the coach and send the team's fans into revolt. All sports properties need to evaluate what their capacity for underperformance is because when they fall short of those expectations, fans may lose interest, especially casual or nonfans who would be attracted by a spectacular winning season or outstanding performance.

Participation Downturn

A participation downturn can signal a major problem for sports brands. A decline in participation could threaten the long-term strength of a sports brand. While professional golf has strong television ratings and overall viewership, the number of golf participants is decreasing. The National Golf Foundation reports that almost 3 million golfers stop playing the sport each year, with financial and time costs as major reasons for quitting.[1] While there are people who take up golf each year to help compensate for the loss, there has been a steady decline in rounds played, and sales of golf shoes have dropped 8 percent and clubs, bags, and balls 7 percent since 2002.[2] Annual declines like these are not just random spikes in participation, but are signals that a more systematic problem is affecting the entire sport.

Eroding Financial Support

When a sports brand experiences eroding financial support from political or economic decisions, one common solution is to cut budgets and, in doing so, create additional causes of decline. The Olympic sports of gymnastics, wrestling, swimming, and diving are good examples. NCAA universities often drop these sports when they face tight budgets for their athletic programs or have to respond to gender inequalities. Men's gymnastics, in particular, have been in decline with only 19 teams currently on the collegiate level,[3] down from 202 in 1972.[4] A similar problem exists on the high school level where participants are joining club teams or seeking increased opportunities in regional amateur leagues rather than competing in school because of reduced budgets. In another sector of financial support, much of professional sports support is dependent upon corporate sponsorships. Without this source of revenue, sports properties could have difficulty surviving as in the case of the Women's United Soccer Association (WUSA).[5]

Weak Leadership

Weak leadership is a cause of decline because it can affect all aspects of a sport including internal brand operations and brand ethos. For example, the Olympics have historically suffered from leadership issues. There were questions about the fairness and judgment of long-time Olympic leader Juan Antonio Samaranch. In addition, corruption affected the International Olympic Committee (IOC), with some members allegedly accepting bribes during an

Olympics site selection process.[6] One of the hallmarks of the resurgence of the Olympics is the realistic, yet visionary leadership of IOC president Jacques Rogge and the firm antidrug stance of Dick Pound, the chairman of the closely related World Anti-Doping Agency (WADA).

The quality of leadership has always been a controversial issue and plays heavily in the selection and retention of general managers, athletic directors, coaches, and players. *Leadership* is a magic term in the vernacular of the sports world, and its failures are bandied about with little restraint. The media often relay these problems with headlines such as, "Cavalier Attitude Costs Silas His Job," "Leadership Still Missing at CU," and "Leadership Void Haunts Jays." Many of the successful coaches such as John Wooden, Lou Holtz, and Joe Torre not only had long tenures but also wrote books highlighting their leadership principles as a guide to managers in all sectors.[7] Holtz's book, *Winning Every Day: The Game Plan for Success*, is illustrative of how powerful leadership is identified with a single person's success in sports. Often these books are formulaic with difficult childhoods, unusual barriers to success, a breakthrough mentor or lucky break, and finally a long run of uninterrupted victories.

Despite these popular commercializations of the leadership principles in sports that often deify individuals, a more social network model is essential in order to prevent decline. Besides a strong and confident personality, a leader needs to also have capable and empowered assistants and an ownership or institutional leadership that is committed to supporting the sports brand. It's essential that leadership runs throughout the entire organization, and it is a flaw of many programs to invest all their hopes in one person. In the end, sports leadership is based on a cooperative venture, and leaders need to be able to share their vision, convince everyone in the organization of the common goals, and instill the brand values through a combination of persuasion and understanding.

Overpricing

Overpricing can cause decline when the price does not reflect the fan's willingness to pay for the sport. In some sports, such as minor league baseball, inexpensive seats are a critical factor in fans choosing it over other sports. The value equation is perceived as high because fans feel they are getting a good return on their investment. In some professional and college sports, it has become a common criticism and an attendance decline factor when seats are not priced for families and other fans who can't afford the escalating costs. The perception that the pricing reflects high-priced salaries for overpaid players and that only corporations can afford tickets often encourages fans to stay home and watch the event on television or on their computer.

Missing Star Power

Missing star power is devastating to a sports brand. Stars generate attention and are often the most effective fan connectors. The decline of amateur wrestling in America can be attributed to not only Title IX issues but the lack of a star such as Dan Gable. Gable, who was a college and Olympic legend and subsequently a colorful and dominating coach at the University of Iowa, drove record interest and coverage in amateur wrestling in the last decades of the twentieth century. The media coverage of Gable spurred dramatic story lines and continuous coverage of the sport, and without someone of his stature, the sport has struggled for attention.

A decline in star power demands development, breeding, and state-of-the-art communication strategies to increase the chances of finding a new generation of stars in that sport. Conferences can also be missing star power, as the departure of college football powers Miami, Virginia Tech, and Boston College from the Big East sent the conference into an identity crisis and a frantic rush to add some football teams. Despite adding some fine football programs such as Louisville and Cincinnati, the football secession was a major brand hit as critics questioned the conference's inclusion in the Bowl Championship Series bowl, its legitimacy as a powerful conference, and even whether it would continue as an organization.[8] However, the Big East has countered the football exodus by building a 16-team all-star basketball conference.

The Indy Racing League (IRL) had experienced declining television ratings for three consecutive years, and much of this stems from the lockout of its star racers, a classic case of missing star power. Even a specifically targeted campaign in the largest media markets of the United States emphasizing the circuit's races resulted in a ratings decline.[9] This absence of new stars is especially conspicuous because of the IRL's past star power with drivers Al Unser, AJ Foyt, and Mario Andretti as major draws. The emergence of female driver Danica Patrick at the 2005 Indianapolis 500 received unprecedented media coverage and resulted in an increase in television viewership, demonstrating that a new generation of stars was critical to the IRL's comeback.

Shifting Demographics

Shifting demographics in both the sports brand and the audience can cause a decline. The number of African American players in Major League Baseball decreased from 27 percent in 1974 to 9 percent in 2004.[10] The effect of this decline on the African American fan base has been significant, with only 5 percent of African Americans from 2000 to 2002 calling baseball their favorite sport compared to 43 percent in 1960.[11] While the demographics of athletes don't always reflect the fan base, baseball's decline in this traditionally strong market is a reason to refocus. Other demographic shifts, such as the increase in participation of women in sports, could signal a decline in some male-dominated sports. The number of girls playing high school sports has risen from 1.9 million in 1990 to 3 million in 2004,[12] creating new fan connection opportunities and forcing some male-dominated sports to dwindle in popularity because of the competition from the emerging women sports.

Cultural Shifts

Cultural shifts can affect a sports brand's market position. When America still had a strong rural population base in the early 1900s, harness racing was a major sport with superstars such as trotter Dan Patch. The sport of hunting has also been affected by changes in rural society with the growing emphasis on urbanization and an increase in single-parent homes, which diminishes the traditional father-son channel for the sport.[13] Other changes in culture such as the decline of community involvement have contributed to the rise in individual sports participation and the decrease in traditional team sports. The sport that does not stay tuned in to cultural shifts is bound to decline.

Mishandling Scandal

Mishandling scandal can destroy or severely damage a sports brand. Scandals often involve incidents of criminal behavior, rule violations, or inappropriate actions. Events such as the Chicago Black Sox betting scandal of 1919 live on in sports memory through film, novels, and even a curse on the team itself. Alleged incidents such as Kobe Bryant's sexual assault charges, Rafael Palmeiro's steroid use, and the rape scandal at Glen Ridge High School in New Jersey[14] all threatened personal and team brand ethos. While a team or star may survive a scandal, gambling charges destroyed the once dominant college basketball powerhouse City College of New York (CCNY) and doping allegations of Olympic gold medalist Michelle de Bruin led to her ultimate banishment from the sport.

While decline dynamics are often centered in these nine categories, the range of possibilities is so extensive that a venue such as the University of New Mexico's basketball arena can demonstrate the variety of major decline factors.

Unpacking The Pit: Stopping Decline

The University of New Mexico men's basketball team has historically owned Albuquerque. The program is the university's most celebrated team sport, and it has become the hometown team for the city's residents in the absence of a professional franchise. Since 1966, millions of Lobos fans have attended games at The Pit, a venue with a branded fan experience that is trademarked by its sunken court and boisterous crowd.[15]

But after the 1999–2000 season, the Lobos' attendance dominance began to unravel seriously for the first time. By the 2004–2005 season, attendance reached its lowest point in the history of The Pit.[16] There are several causes for this decline in attendance:

Underperformance The sports brand sets up a performance proposition for the fans that is not met.

The University hired Fran Fraschilla in 1999, considered a talented and reputable head coach who "promised Sweet 16 trips."[17] Not only did the team not make it to the Sweet 16 during Fraschilla's tenure, but its players had off-court issues. The Lobos fans became discouraged by the failure of the coach and team to follow through on their promise to win and to represent the university with dignity.

Action: The basketball program has undergone major changes under new head coach Ritchie McKay. While fan expectations for McKay were significantly lower than they were for Fraschilla, the program's ethos is being restored with a new group of student athletes and an NCAA tournament appearance in 2005, which served as a launching pad.

Venue Erosion The infrastructure is inconsistent in accommodating fan expectations.

The Pit was built in 1966 and is still functioning with its basic infrastructure. Although the stadium is in good condition, the university is often challenged to accommodate fan expectations. A major issue is the size of the concourses. During sold-out Lobos or NCAA tournament games, the size of the crowd is often difficult to manage, especially during halftime. The concourse congestion when fans go to the restroom and wait in line at concession stands

---

often keeps fans from leaving their seats. It also creates a comfort and safety issue as the bumping and jostling in the concourse often make it unappealing even for those willing to seek a hot dog.

Action: The Pit is a college basketball institution and a popular choice for NCAA tournament games. While there are no plans to replace The Pit, the university has already expanded women's restrooms and intends to widen the concourses to make the stadium more fan-friendly. The most significant venue change has been the addition of a new practice facility for the men's and women's teams next to The Pit. It will include state-of-the-art training facilities and media rooms to help offset some of The Pit's limitations.[18]

Unfulfilled Expectations Changes in the branded fan experience do not meet fan expectations.

One of the recent criticisms of The Pit is that it has lost its ferocity and piercing volume levels that create an experience that fans have come to expect. A possible reason for a more tamed Pit is the fans who are attending the games and where they are seated. The Lobos have a very loyal fan base with many fans holding season tickets since the early years of the building's existence. While these fans are valuable to the program, it often has weakened the home crowd experience and excluded some of the university's students from more actively participating in games.

Action: The athletic department is trying to reenergize The Pit experience by involving its students more while also satisfying its loyal older fans. In doing so, it has addressed this decline issue in two ways. UNM has installed handrails for older fans to help them walk down the aisles to their seats. In addition and most importantly, understanding that student participation is critical to the fan experience at The Pit, the university reinstituted the student section, which had been removed over a decade earlier, and placed the students and the band closer to the court to reinvigorate the home crowd at the risk of inconveniencing some season ticket holders.[19]

There are other threats to the program's once dominant attendance as competition grows more intense from the improving football and women's basketball teams, low-priced and easily accessible high school football and basketball markets, and better-quality television broadcasts of Lobos men's basketball games. The Pit, not unlike Fenway Park or Lambeau Field, now has to balance preserving the building's history with competing in the modern, technological world of higher fan expectations. By making changes to the team, improving the facilities, and accommodating its multigenerational fan base, the University of New Mexico has begun to reestablish The Pit as a major attraction. Without the value added in the attendance experience, however, Lobos fans could stay at home and watch the games on television, shift their allegiances to another team within the university, or worse, do something else.

There are numerous factors that can cause a sports brand to decline. Sports decision makers must identify these factors early to head them off. In the next sections, we discuss how brands can halt the decline and restore a sports brand to health.

THE SUSTAINING CHALLENGE

Sustaining is the process of retaining and growing the fan connection. Ideally, once the fan is attracted to a sports brand, a connection is formed, kept for a long period of time, and grown to higher levels of intensity. However, in sustaining the Elusive Fan, there are four major challenges that threaten fan connections: participation, attendance, media, and crisis.

Participation Challenge

Sports participation is an entry point for prospective fans for many spectator sports. It educates the prospective fan about the game, provides experience with the difficulty of mastering it, and allows the participants to form bonds with peers and family involved in the sport.

The effects of participation vary depending on the sport. For team sports such as baseball and basketball, player participation could have a profound effect since participation is so critical to long-term interest in the sport. In other sports such as horse racing, boxing, bull riding, or women's roller derby there is little chance of spectators having ever been participants. Fans of these sports are driven by other factors such as utopian or vicarious experience connections.

It is essential for many sports that intend to sustain themselves to address the following participation issues:

- A central issue is encouraging kids to play. Opportunities for participation include clinics, school activities, junior programs, parent-children activities, and a host of other programs and initiatives. It is another matter for parents and children to select a sport from the vast array of possibilities. A sport looking to the future must market its appeal at those points of age-centered entry. These entry points can be as early as age two and can continue all throughout childhood.[20] These are *sports connection windows*, which are those periods in which the buyer is listening to the message. A targeted sports program should be addressed specifically to these windows and, when they open, strike with a great deal of effort because in most cases these windows will not open again.

In this modern age of heavy parental and institutional control of youth sports activity, understanding this relationship is critical. Sports have to be mindful of the disconnect between forcing children to play a sport and the inevitable counterforce that leads youth to rebel against parental direction. As earlier discussed, this particular point is critical because an overwhelming number of children quit a sport because it focuses too much on winning,[21] which often reflects parental pressures. This is an unacceptable trend and indicates that relationships between parents, schools, and youth programs are potential land mines in youth participation levels.

A forward-seeking sport might position itself not as an entry level participation experience but as a countersport that would appeal to a 12- to 13-year-old rebelling against traditional sports or heavy institutional control. Up until now, when that occurs, it's been more accidental than strategic, but extreme sports are a textbook case of capitalizing on the counterforces of youth rebellion against authority. Another possibility is that sports decision makers might consider institutionalizing and supporting pickup games such as the NHL's sponsorship of the North American Roller Hockey Championships (NARCh) that have the potential of appearing less establishment-based.

- A clear signal that parental and institutional control has begun to backfire is the growing movement to lower the level of control and make parents and coaches more aware of sportsmanship and fair play and not concentrate so much on winning. This is in part a response to the mounting pressure in youth sports that has caused concerns about injuries, time commitments, and the loss of unstructured play. Organizations such as the Maine Center for Sport and Coaching, National Alliance for Youth Sports, and Positive Coaching Alliance[22] are actively promoting good sportsmanship, civic pride, and a more value- and less winning-centered experience. A reflection of this countermovement is the rise of bowling at the high school level, which is a response to the demands of sports overspecialization and the need for young people to find a participation outlet that is more congenial and less physically demanding.[23]

- There is a growing movement toward opening or refining new markets for participation. For example, hockey has benefited from women who, often stimulated by their children's participation, have formed leagues and play regularly.[24] In corporate America the sport of marathon running has been adopted as a testing bed for prospective executives to exhibit their work ethic and drive. It is inevitable that as new configurations emerge, there will be new rules, refinements in equipment, and enhanced potential for spectator support. It is in the best interests of sports brands to be monitoring grassroots modifications of their sport and find ways to facilitate the innovators.
- A new definition of what constitutes sports participation for children and adults is essential. New sports media technologies such as fantasy leagues, video games, and Web sites can be just as powerful in bonding to potential fans as playing a sport. Participation should ideally include live action, but the overwhelming growth of electronic participation must also be emphasized as another critical connection point.[25] It also enables the sport to educate the youthful participant on the history and records and controversies and interplay that fill out a sport's profile.

Attendance Challenge

Attendance has traditionally served as a barometer for the popularity of a sporting event and its athletes. Today attendance runs the risk of becoming less attractive for a number of reasons—pricing issues, time commitments, transportation difficulties, work and family obligations, and other entertainment options.[26] In response, the sports industry must start planning for the communication issues that will inevitably impact the fan's willingness and ability to attend sporting events.

How will fans get to an event when traffic congestion is epidemic, oil spikes diminish their willingness to travel, and a ballpark trip can take longer than the game itself? Finding new and more economical ways to transport fans to the stadium, and more importantly, integrating transportation considerations into all facility design plans are essential. Whether it is the use of high-speed trains or dedicated highway lanes to access the park, sports decision makers must insist that every new sports development before it's even built has a traffic plan attached to it. This requires cooperation among public officials, sports decision makers, and taxpayers and a willingness of all parties to devise new transportation infrastructure and systems to satisfy the needs of the entire community.

If fans cannot get to the venue, the alternative is to bring the event to the fans, which means finding attractive or suitable sites around the target locations that can serve as satellite venues. This strategy may seem counterintuitive given the multimillion-dollar investments in venues and the push for single sports sites. However, if the predictions on traffic and congestion in the future are true,[27] sports decision makers will have no choice but to move their events to more accessible sites for their target markets. This is somewhat ironic as this "bring the event to the fan" strategy resurrects the barnstorming tours of the Monopoly Generation. Sports brands might take a cue from the modular building industry, which is fast-growing and has introduced new building technologies that could give sports brands more flexibility in hosting their events in satellite venues.

Fans are increasingly forced to make a choice between a compelling sports television and media experience and attending the venue. For example, major corporations who traditionally pack the Super Bowl city decided that rather than traveling to cold-weather Detroit for Super Bowl XL they would attend "viewing parties" in Las Vegas and the Caribbean with all the accoutrements of casinos, beaches, and large HD television sets.[28] In these new spectator environments, the venue itself is competing with alternative sports media experiences that have the television broadcast as the centerpiece. As a result, the event becomes decentralized and dilutes the importance of actually being at the game. The fan makes these kinds of venue decisions every day, and as the Super Bowl example illustrates, the event itself for some fans is not enough to overcome the objections, and money and time can be more productively spent elsewhere.

Another solution to the attendance challenge is to construct venues with many of the advantages of the new media technologies. This strategy is intended not to force fans to make a choice between a compelling media experience and the camaraderie and excitement of the event site. An example is NASCAR, which in order to capitalize on the large number of race-goers who listen to audio feeds of races, introduced a NASCAR Nextel branded multimedia handset called Kangaroo.TV. The device is a wireless mini-television set with a remote and headphones that provide the in-race attendee with customizable statistics, video camera angles, audio options, and a different point of view from their otherwise fixed stadium seat.[29] Kangaroo.TV seemingly has all the benefits of watching the race on television such as access to tight turns, the pits, and driver-team communication. The NASCAR strategy attempts to satisfy both the venue and home media needs of the fan, and in doing so, potentially keeps the fan from wanting to stay home and watch on television.

There will always be people who will go to an event whether the temperature is 20 below or the event is held in a shacklike site with burnt-out lights and a 2-foot-wide corridor. Unfortunately, these dedicated fans are a small portion of most sports brand fan bases, and the competition for the remainder has never been more competitive. Looking into the future and preparing and adjusting to political, environmental, and cultural shifts is essential for the surviving sports brand.

Media Challenge

The threat of losing attendance for sports brands is one reason that sports are looking for other channels to attract revenue. In many cases, sports are implementing and exploring the development of their own media programming and sites that directly compete with traditional television networks. Moreover, contracts between the media and sports are now beginning to shift the emphasis from network, cable, and sponsor dollars to a revenue-sharing model that makes the sport a marketer and promoter of its own performances. As the major media market becomes more competitive, sports that lose or cannot receive major market penetration on television have to drive their media in a multichannel manner using state-of-the-art new media. The new media opportunity is a once-in-a-generation chance for emerging and struggling sports to segment audiences and deliver media messages in a personalized and often cost-effective fashion. It also requires that these sports either hire information technology specialists or outsource to specialty consulting companies that can manage the new media at a sophisticated level. An example is CSTV.com, which manages the Web sites for over 250 college and university sports programs and provides exposure for previously anonymous sports such as equestrian events, fencing, and cross-country running.[30] Without this third-party involvement, the colleges' minor sports are unlikely to reach potential markets.

The dominating presence of media in the sports world calls for a rethinking of what defines attendance. In this new attendance world, a 30-year-old playing the Madden 2006 video game is essentially part of the attendance picture as is someone picking up 20 minutes of a college game on a cell phone. It is no longer sufficient to consider only game attendance as the single factor in the attendance relationships between the sport and the fan.

This newer configuration can be summarized in the following manner: attendance = total of time spent in all channels. A more refined approach would be to assign different weights to the different channels, such that venue attendance is given the most weight. (See the table below) The task for sports brands is to increase the fan time spent in channels that increase revenue, develop long-term fan relationships, drive venue attendance, or any other determined need. Video-game creators, cell-phone providers, and highlight packagers are important potential connectors for sports, and, while venue attendance is still important, connecting at the technological level is essential.

This configuration demands that sports brands make their products media-friendly. Ensuring that the sport is appealing on television, makes for a compelling video game, and inspires active blog entries is critical. Sports brands without a strong media presence will only suffer against competitors that have it.

Measuring Channel Attendance

There are many channels that can connect the sports fan. Some sports might be more heavily experienced at their venue, while others may thrive on television or video games. Sports decision makers can use weighted averages to compare across channels the time fans spend on the sports brand. The goal is to understand in what channels the fan is "attending" sporting events and how to allocate resources to improve the channel mix. While it is hard to quantify revenue, these measurements can stimulate the brand to reflect on the present channel mix and to see the trends in the future channel mix and its revenue implications.

This assessment is a cross-channel indicator of revenue with the key elements of time spent and revenue weight. Time spent is the percentage of the total sports attendance time that the target segments or overall fan base engages in the channel. A revenue weight is then assigned to each attendance channel, which could be based on two factors—real revenue

(Continued)

(*Continued*)

or revenue goals. For example, if the sports brand prioritizes live attendance and would like to make it 50 percent of its revenue stream, sports decision makers could weight the attendance channel as 50 percent and the other channels accordingly. The following table illustrates how this model works.

Fan Channel	Time Spent (percent)	Revenue Weight (percent)	Score
Venue	20	50	.1
Television	40	25	.1
Radio	5	5	.0025
Video games	25	10	.025
Internet	10	10	.01
Total	100	100	.2375

In this channel comparison, the goal is to maximize venue attendance, but most fans spend their time with the sports brand by watching television. Brand decision makers have several choices in this situation. They could capitalize on their healthy television channel to convert viewers into venue attendees or realize that they are not driving enough revenue from their television market and shift their revenue goals to reflect their fan base. Or they could see that fans spend a quarter of their time on video games and yet they only have a revenue goal of 10 percent for this activity. Whatever the decision, sports decision makers can look holistically at their fans' experience and understand the various ways fans experience a brand and how these channels relate to revenue.

The purpose of this table is to help the brand decision makers see which channels are succeeding and which need to be improved to reflect their financial goals. The measurement is often most effective as both a diagnostic and evaluative metric with sports decision makers calculating a diagnostic score, using it as a benchmark for setting goals, and finally testing future performance against the initial score. It may well be, for example, that in some sports the venue importance weight may be less than the television or video game weight, and that would have to be reflected in any table. Channel attendance will continue to become much more complicated in the future, and monitoring how fans experience the sports brand is a critical ingredient in sustaining fan connections.

Crisis Challenge

In a media-driven culture, a sports brand often experiences unexpected events that can amount to a crisis. The number of crises that affect sports brands seems to grow as the financial stakes increase and the media seek more access and information. Sports brands need to anticipate the issues that ignite crises if they are to protect their hard-won fan relationships.

A crisis is defined by three elements: threats, uncertainty, and lack of control. Participants, the media, and the fans are usually either involved in the crisis or are influenced by its outcome. Participants include the aggrieved parties, prominent opinion leaders, and the political players. They are often either the targets or the decision makers involved in the crisis. The media filter the crisis for the fan by providing coverage and perspective on the issues.

The protection and improvement of the brand's fan relationships need to be addressed in crisis communication. The crisis situation should be seen as a fan connection opportunity for the sports brand—a chance to show goodwill, demonstrate the resolve of the sports brand, and ultimately retain and grow fan relationships. Fortunately for the sports brand, there are not an infinite number of situations that define the crisis-fan relationship. It is possible to isolate the main types of crisis and come up with possible solutions as the examples below illustrate:

Blackhawks Down—*Losing Touch with the Fan Base*

The Crisis: The National Hockey League locked out its players for the 2004–2005 season. The owners demanded that a salary cap be employed to limit player salaries. The players union refused to accept salary limitations, claiming that employee rights protected players from such provisions. The league argued that it was losing millions of dollars each season and that the owner-player salary dispute must be resolved before the games would resume. The crisis was that there was a growing concern that the fans did not miss the sport, and the stalemate between the league, owners, and players called into question their ability to solve the problem.

The Response: In one club's repsonse during a press conference address-ing the lockout, Chicago Blackhawks owner Bill Wirtz and then general manager Bob Pulford took the ownership position that they had been gener-ous with the players and wished that the players were more like the players of 50 or 60 years ago. Pulford reminisced about how the players of his generation used to drive Chevys and that, "Today's players drive Mercedes-Benzes." Pulford also observed that power has shifted to the players and that the "pendulum has swung too far the other way."[31]

The Remedy: The Blackhawks needed to realize that the sports market had changed dramatically and that the fans were looking for solutions, not blame. The fans were left with the impression that the ownership had a vendetta against current players and were out of touch with the contemporary sports environment. Instead of personal attacks laced with emotional overtones, the owners should have expressed a desire to work with the players to determine what the fans wanted and made clear how an equitable agreement was foremost on their minds.

"I Would Never Join a Club That Would Have Me as a Member" (Groucho Marx)—*Solving the Problem and Creating New Ones*

The Crisis: Martha Burk, chair of the National Council of Women's Organizations, accused the Augusta National Golf Club, the home of the Masters, of sexual discrimination by not allowing women to join the club. Hootie Johnson, the president of Augusta National, took the position that private clubs had the right to choose their members. Johnson remained firm on his position saying at one time that he would not allow women into the club even "at the point of bayonet."[32] The crisis called attention to not only the conflicts over the right to privacy and gender discrimination but also potentially tarnished American golf's most hallowed tournament.

The Response: The initial response ignited a media circus with many parties involved and lots of charges. The personal exchanges often overshadowed the more important controversy of Augusta maintaining its private club rights as the host of an event of international magnitude. Burk and Johnson became trapped in a wide array of arguments, removing the focus from the core issues and prolonging the crisis. Burk even admitted, "The only regret I have is that this has turned into a story about me and Hootie Johnson."[33] The rancor expressed in the side arguments ran the risk of alienating people who were sympathetic to both Burk's and Johnson's positions. Instead of each side winning supporters, it became a question of which side alienated fans the least.

The Remedy: Augusta National addressed the crisis by broadcasting the next Masters tournament without sponsors or commercials. This gesture was an attempt to place them on the high road by not exploiting their commercial interests and in a sense purifying their privacy position. They were also aided by support from anti-Burk women's groups and professional women golfers who saw the attacks as a threat on their sport. In the end, the crisis weakened and stands as evidence that unrelenting attack styles as well as ill-considered defenses can seriously damage a cause.

Good Knight—*Reacting and Not Enacting*

The Crisis: As coach of Indiana University's basketball team, Bob Knight became synonymous with Indiana University. His iconic image was built on a combination of winning, drill-sergeant discipline, and a reputation for running a clean program. However, his high-profile outbursts in the press room and on the court, while sometimes entertaining, too often compromised the university's authority. There was also a videotape of him allegedly choking a player in practice that became a national story. All of this conspired to produce a series of public disputes between the administration and Knight that finally forced a confrontation that resulted in his dismissal.

The Response: The university made a number of efforts to solve the Knight problem, which included periodic threats of dismissal and eventually a zero tolerance policy. However, the administration held off too long and lost institutional control of the basketball program to the coach by not decisively dismissing Knight for his behavior. A standing media sports storyline was the question of whether the coach ran the university or the president ran from the coach.

The Remedy: The lesson is clear for crisis managers: no action is action, and moving early and swiftly was the solution to reasserting university control and preventing the basketball program from becoming a soap opera. The university lacked timely execution, seemingly surrendered control to Knight, and became embroiled in an endless crisis over institutional leadership. After Knight was finally terminated and the crisis abated, the mishandling of the issues made it very difficult for the program to reestablish credibility with its fan base and its national reputation as a basketball power.

Sosagate—*Fast Reactions Can Put Out a Fire*

The Crisis: Sammy Sosa, a venerated slugger for the Chicago Cubs, broke his bat during a game, and cork spewed onto the field, setting off criticism and ridicule. Sosa was involved in one of the most celebrated and now questioned home run record-chasing seasons in the history of the sport but at the time was still easily one of the game's most marketable and popular players. Any indication that he was a cheater could seriously undermine his past achievements and damage his commercial appeal.

The Response: Sosa's position was that he made an honest mistake. He apologized quickly and profusely, accepted his punishment without protest, and vowed to never allow the mix-up to happen again. Sosa said, "I was just trying to get ready and go out there and get ready for the game, and I just picked the wrong bat. I feel sorry. I just apologize to everybody."[34]

The Remedy: Major League Baseball arranged for all of Sosa's 76 bats to be X-rayed. and they were all found to be without any foreign substance. This enabled executive vice president of baseball operations Sandy Alderson to claim, "We're happy with [the X-ray results] and that is consistent with Sammy's explanation of the incident last night."[35] While the suspicion among some fans and media members remains, all parties appeared responsive, and the incident dissipated rapidly. The quick response demonstrates the importance of a quick apology. While some fans may not have been satisfied by the crisis resolution, Sosa and MLB's response ensured that the situation didn't get any worse.

Friday Night Lights Out—*Overexposing the Brand*

The Crisis: The crisis erupted after the release of a book about Permian High School in Odessa, Texas, in 1990. Author H.G. Bissinger spent an entire season with its football team and documented the academic and sports culture of the high school. The school's administration thought it would benefit by a book written on what it believed to be an exemplary high school and athletic program. What the author delivered, however, was much different from the administration's expectations. As one citizen recalled, "I thought he was writing a Hoosiers-type book and it didn't turn out that way."[36] Bissinger wrote about the alleged racist and lax educational underside of the community, embarrassing its citizens and attracting undesired national attention to the school including a *60 Minutes* report by Mike Wallace examining the validity of the charges.[37]

The Response: Odessa administration and town citizens were mostly outraged and complained that they were duped by Bissinger. The author received death threats, and the general feeling of the citizens of the town was that they had been betrayed. The school's administration did respond to the charges, but the most effective response was the district's tightening of the educational requirements of the school and exerting more control over the relationship between athletics and the overall goals of the school.[38]

The Remedy: The administration, in giving Bissinger access, did not accurately evaluate Bissinger's motives or its own program. The success of the football team overshadowed practices that could appear to the outside public as unacceptable. The most effective strategies were the school's decisions over the long term to fix the problems. The "Mojo Madness" of Permian was another side of high school sports that needed to be understood and remedied. Fortunately for the school, the 2004 film *Friday Night Lights* overshadowed the book's accusations by presenting a largely favorable image of the town and school.

A Quick Guide to Fan-Centered Crisis Communication

Stage 1: Governing Plan
Designate who has the authority to act, in what time frame, and with what powers. Leadership should be determined in advance, and leaders should be empowered to coordinate and make unilateral decisions on who will speak, timing issues, and delegation of authority. The plan should be written out in detail and made clear that there is backup support in every major category of communication during the crisis. A common failure of these plans is that key players are unavailable and the execution is incomplete or nonexistent.

Stage 2: Problem Analysis
Gather, synthesize, and analyze all the facts to most effectively solve the crisis and satisfy public expectations. At this step, it is important to inventory your assets, assess your situation, and look realistically at potential problems.

(Continued)

(Continued)
Stage 3: Targeted Message
Develop a message that is clear and forceful and that begins to resolve the crisis. It is crucial that all communication be focused and not contradictory. The targeted message should include the major arguments that will be used. This step includes anticipating counterarguments and practicing answering questions. The message ideally should provide a concrete resolution to the crisis, and, if that's not possible, it should enumerate the steps that will be taken in order to achieve a resolution.

Stage 4: Implementation
Determine a budget, time frame, and message distribution plan that includes all the intended constituents including media, local agencies, and grassroots efforts. During the crisis, all information should be coordinated through the predetermined governing plan. Without this step, the plan will inevitably sit on the shelf, and the crisis may well be handled on an improvised basis.

Stage 5: Feedback
Institute a feedback process that responds to questions and provides guidance to the participants on unexpected developments. The entire feedback mechanism should be guided by two principles: adaptability (a willingness to adjust to unexpected circumstances) and flexibility (address unexpected circumstances quickly and with evidence). The feedback phase should always include an analysis of how well the plan worked and how it can be improved.

THE RULES OF SUSTAINING

Many obstacles confront the sports brand during its quest for longevity. In addressing the various causes of decline, there are universal rules that can be applied to any sustaining strategy.

> *Rule One: The more competitive and fragmented the industry, the more dependent the sports brand is upon fan connections.*

As new competitors enter the marketplace and fragmentation continues, market boundaries will consistently dissolve and re-form. The sports brand that fosters the strongest connections with its fans will most often withstand this rapid and inevitable changeover. In contrast, the volatility of the sports marketplace will penalize the brands with underdeveloped and weak fan relationships.

Rule Two: Sports brands must prioritize and manage their core markets.

Maintaining and cultivating connections with core markets is the seed corn of all sports brands, and it is shortsighted to take them for granted. After all, during a decline, the most likely supporters are often the fans who have season tickets, call in to radio shows, and attend off-season conventions. Without the proper care of core markets, any sustaining strategy loses its foundation. Even for the most avid fans, support is not always unconditional.

Rule Three: Sports brands must understand fan expectations and be reasonable in setting them and consistent about meeting them.

The sports brand should make promises to fans that can be fulfilled. If the promotional material for a professional hockey team conveys a hardworking, well-behaved, and community-minded group of players and the team members turn out to be lazy, badly behaved, and selfish, the differences in what the fans were promised and the product they actually experienced can result in an unsustainable fan base. Such unfulfilled promises reduce the brand's ethos and can be damaging to any sustaining efforts. Brand consistency is much easier to achieve when in recruiting and signing participants they reinforce fan expectations.

Fans' expectations should not only be met consistently, but they should be exceeded routinely. It can be as basic as an unexpectedly good-tasting, well-priced chicken sandwich or as sports-centered as an autograph session with a friendly star pitcher. This "delight factor" occurs when fans experience something that is unexpected and appreciated, reaffirming their investment of money and time in the sports activity.

Rule Four: Sports brands must stay within their "gameness" by maintaining core values and controlling the change process.

In any sustaining strategy, the brand must operate within its own gameness, maintaining its core brand attributes. In a saturated market, sports brands must establish clear points that distinguish them from their competition. The specific gameness of each sports brand represents that differentiation.

There are certain gameness attributes that are set up that must be met—how hard the athletes will play, how the players and coaches will carry themselves, what language will be used to describe the game, or what the field will look like. Fans even have expectations for the smells and temperature of the indoor arena. The sports brand cannot abandon these fundamental attributes and must emphasize them in any sustaining strategy.

Rule Five: Sports brands must understand the dynamics of a constantly evolving marketplace and be proactive in forming new connections.

In order to have longevity, a sports brand requires a long-term vision of the fan marketplace. The market changes regularly, fan preferences vary, and the dominance of a sports brand is often cyclical. There is no guarantee that a traditionally loyal fan base will support the brand forever. Retaining the fan base requires a strategy of maintaining ties to the core while forming new connections with other fan markets. New segments will ultimately form, and it is critical that the brand be proactive in identifying and pursuing them. The key is maintaining current connections while forming new ones to make the transition from generation to generation seamless.

Rule Six: Sports brands must balance best practices with a willingness to experience and reach out to new relationships and concepts.

It is often not enough to imitate the best practices of other sports. At a certain point, many brand practices become commodities, and newer, more innovative strategies need to be implemented. There are synergies related to sports marketing that have yet to be fully explored, such as combining an event with an interactive fantasy game, multi-city global tours, and other multilayered marketing initiatives that attract the fan to the sport.

The Case of the Cold Hot Dog

It's the third inning of a baseball game. The fan is having a great time, the teams are playing hard, the seats are good, and the fan is ready to indulge in a big, juicy hot dog. The encounter at the concession stand runs smoothly—the concession workers are friendly, the line moves quickly, the service is fast. The hot dog is $4.50, a diet drink is $3.50, a jumbo pretzel is $2.50, and a tray of nacho cheese is $4.50. Total $15.00. Eagerly, the fan dresses the dog with packets of mustard and a sprinkle of sweet pickles, and takes a huge bite. *The hot dog is cold.*

If fans have a bad food experience at the event, it might only keep them from buying food, but it could also so sour them on the experience that they never return. It could trigger a series of responses such as management doesn't care, players make too much money, or the food concessions are rip-offs. To complicate the problem, management doesn't even know that the hot dogs are mishandled and that fans are dissatisfied.

How can sports brands receive feedback from the fans to prevent such unpleasant experiences? One promising area is the Internet, which has opened up new ways to receive consumer feedback. For example, Ford Motor Company has developed FordDirect.com, which allows consumers to state their preferences clearly, and the company can use this information before it starts producing cars.[39] Similarly, the baseball team can not only receive feedback on the cold hot dog, but it could also ask for preferences from baseball fans in terms of what they would like to eat, drink, and buy. In addition, fan feedback mechanisms can be incorporated to include viewpoints on the team and its players. A weakness of sports brands is that they understand the need for feedback, set up the channels, but often do not respond to the complaints. If the sports brand is determined to be fan-friendly and provide the mechanism to articulate displeasure, resources need to be allocated to promptly and in real terms produce hot, hot dogs.

STRATEGIES FOR SUSTAINING

There are a number of sustaining strategies a sports brand can implement to reinvigorate the fan base.

Eventize

To generate broader awareness of a brand and sustain fan markets, "eventizing" applies the strategies of special events such as championship or all-star games to more routine events. Underlying the strategy is the belief that ordinary events can be transformed into blue-chip attractions and give fans a reason to watch, attend, or care about a meaningless preseason scrimmage, insignificant regular season game, or inconsequential off-season event. Eventizing manufactures events that break through the normal clutter to reach the fan. Midnight Madness, an invention of college basketball programs to institutionalize the first moment of college basketball practice, is an example of eventizing.

Another example of a packaged event that has taken on a life of its own is the NFL draft. The draft occurs in April during the NBA and NHL playoffs,

MLB's first month, the PGA's regular season, and a host of other competitors' schedules. The draft, a selection of mostly little-known college football players, is not in itself a compelling event. The NFL in conjunction with ESPN has eventized the draft with several goals—attract attention, encourage fans to watch 17 hours of live coverage, and sustain fan interest in the NFL during the off-season. The draft has succeeded in its eventizing strategy by capitalizing on its unpredictable, pseudoscientific qualities and packaging the entire event on television. It has also promoted the importance of every pick in the draft, emphasizing the potential of rookies to instantly turn around a team, and it has even packaged the often-ridiculed second-day draft of unknowns with a compelling theme of this is where the scouts earn their keep. Combining these strategies with lead-in promotional advertisements, star player profiles, and fan hopes for a quick fix, the NFL manages to accomplish its goals with the draft and sustain fan interest.[40]

Ride a Star

Star power can single-handedly sustain a sports brand. People can identify with and relate to the star, and they often find the star's quest compelling. In the past, stars were sometimes cross-marketed, but the driver of visibility was usually a combination of sports skills and media- or fan-discovered interest. Larry Bird from Indiana State University was drafted by the Boston Celtics and, combined with some outstanding teammates, his small town persona, and shooting skills, became a marketable star. He also benefited from a rivalry with Magic Johnson of the Lakers who frequently met Bird in dramatic games. The public found Larry Bird and the encounters with the Lakers a compelling meeting of the stars. These kinds of instances of star branding were powerful, connected to fans, and have historically fueled interest in a sports brand. It's always most effective when the marketplace discovers a star, and that makes it easier for any sports decision maker to construct a star brand configuration. In the new environment, the machinery is more sophisticated, the stakes are higher, and the star products are not usually waiting on the shelf for market selection.

In the current branding world, more sports properties are interested in personality development and are packaging personalities to feed their various market segments. As a result, the sport or the league is increasingly promoting stars on the basis of segmentation and potential fan appeal. This has become a major sustaining strategy because it ensures a steady star flow and less problematic inventory. For example, MLB identified a number of players that became the centerpiece of an advertising campaign titled, "I Live for This." In this star model, the league is making decisions as to which stars to deliver to the market because they need them as an essential part of their branding position. The new level of interest in star power demonstrates how valuable the branding possibilities are and how leaving any element to chance is no longer an option.

Venture into Foreign Markets

Expanding into foreign markets can be highly profitable and a long-term investment for brands with an established domestic fan base. If the sport is the first to reach the market, there is a necessity to educate potential fans about the sport and this provides an opportunity to create brand loyalty. In reality, the foreign markets are in various states of invasion ranging from virtually untapped to a small and tentative penetration or a full-scale conquest.

Global expansion is a major component of the marketing strategies of many sports brands including NASCAR, MLB, the NFL, and the NBA. The NBA, for example, is capitalizing on a growing sports market in China where approximately 300 million of the country's 1.3 billion people play basketball—more than the total population of the United States. Interest in the NBA from the Chinese market has increased as the league promotes a Chinese version of its Web site, markets the nation's superstar center Yao Ming, and broadcasts live games via satellite throughout the country. During the 2004–2005 NBA Finals alone, at least 115 million television viewers in China watched game 2 between the San Antonio Spurs and the Detroit Pistons.[41]

Foreign markets can also be used to promote a sports brand if it does not succeed in primary domestic markets. For example, Bob "the Beast" Sapp was an NFL football player for several years, but injuries, steroid use allegations, and being released by four teams cut short his NFL career. After an unsuccessful attempt at becoming a professional wrestler, Sapp was discovered by the Japanese K1 fighting league after he fought William "the Refrigerator" Perry in a made-for-television boxing match. Sapp then moved to Japan, and after six months of training, he began competing as a K1 fighter.[42] From that platform, he became a celebrity in Japan, appearing on television shows, endorsing products, publishing books, and making music. His successful and controversial career in Japan has presented him with opportunities to come back to the U.S. market. Appearances in the Hollywood films *Elektra* and *The Longest Yard*, while limited, were his first major moves back into the U.S. market. For Sapp, the choice to move into a foreign market not only generated more revenue and fame for his brand than staying in the United States, but he positioned himself for a potential relaunching in his home market—just not as a football player.

Connect with New Segments

When a decline occurs within a specific set of segments, it may be time for the sports brand to rethink its segmentation strategy and move to form new connections with other markets. Repositioning the brand to appeal to another set of segments can stretch out the brand's longevity and tap into previously undeveloped markets.

As we have seen, boxing has experienced its own set of decline issues. Its current and more traditional target segments are largely unresponsive and are not providing the foundational strength the brand needs to regenerate. Where can boxing go for new connections? One possibility is a shift in its gender target. Cultural trends suggest that boxing may find a new, viable, and highly profitable market with women. Female participation in boxing has steadily increased not only on the professional level but also as a fitness fad.[43] The increasing emphasis on safety, self-defense, and staying in shape has empowered the female boxer with an incentive to participate. In addition, the Academy Award–winning film *Million Dollar Baby* capitalized on this emerging market, featuring a woman boxer in a role historically reserved for men.

The opportunities in segmenting are not always obvious. Many sports have rightfully sought the youth, family, and promising ethnic markets for targeting. In some sports such as horse racing, there is an obvious target such as the senior citizen market, whose members have more time to attend the weekly afternoon races. Even in a rapidly segmenting marketplace, it is rare that targets include blended families or promotions aimed at divorced men and women. The issue is that segments are becoming more specific, markets are more fragmented, and opportunities to connect to a segment abound—but not always in the familiar places.

Appeal to Nostalgia

The marketing of the past can resonate with multiple generations of fans, but it has historically been the older fan who more easily connects with past experiences. Nostalgia, a utopian connection, is effective because, seen through the lens of time, the sport may appear less commercial and more personal, and it serves to counter prevailing attitudes about the mercenary state of the industry.

An undervalued advantage to nostalgia is its newfound appeal to the younger markets. Avid fans, often interested in statistics, fantasy sports, video games, and memorabilia find that the historical perspective enriches the sports experience. Throwback jerseys, 1941 game day uniforms, card auctions, sports trivia, baseball bats, old lacrosse sticks or the robe that Gorgeous George wore in the 1950s have increasingly become valuable connections to a sport's past. What was once a fairly one-dimensional connection to an older market has evolved to include younger and more diverse segments with great potential for expansion of the brand. Sports brands in response can organize clubs around vintage sports interests, arrange trips to historical game sites, sponsor Web site auctions, and in general own the nostalgic market for their brand.

Create a Rivalry

Rivalry is one of the most powerful ways to generate awareness for a brand. The public's natural attraction to conflict is what makes it so successful in sustaining fan interest. In sports, controversies can come in a variety of forms: player-coach arguments; player-player feuds; owner-city disagreements; scandal; or player, team, or conference rivalries. Rivalries are special occasions that in turn create story lines that make the sporting event a deeply involving experience.

The North Carolina–Duke basketball rivalry is built on more than just the competition between two college basketball teams. It symbolizes the battle between two towns, two universities, two student bodies, and two alumni bases. The outcome of the game is not just important to the teams' records, but to the reputation and self-esteem of everyone involved. The strength of rivalries is that it fully involves fans, turning the sporting event into a highly recognizable reflection of themselves.

The sports brand can seek out and promote potential rivalries and in doing so connect the fans to the event. There are geographical (Florida–Florida State), personality (Shaquille O'Neal–Kobe Bryant), institutional (Midland Lee–Odessa

Permian), historical (Auburn–Alabama), class (Lazio and Roma), and incident (Little Brown Jug, Michigan–Minnesota) rivalries. The recently developed Big Ten–ACC Basketball Challenge is an example of creating a league rivalry out of thin air and has become a highly publicized early season event.

Develop Synergistic Experiences

Market synergies bring together multiple products and essentially create one-stop shopping for a variety of fans. They combine sectors such as sports, music, fashion, food, soft drinks, and new media into one entertainment experience. The strategy aims to market not just a product, but a lifestyle—one that integrates a variety of products that involves the fans in a complete experience.

The sports brand can explore new marketing relationships with products to maximize potential fan markets and connect on a number of levels. The Tony Hawk Boom Boom Huckjam Tour combines extreme sports with alternative music, video games, fashion, and an overall youth-centered lifestyle that attracts young fans. The tour has merged entertainment and sports into a new synergistic mix to attract a fan base with multientertainment desires. The emphasis now is to segment a market and combine a number of experiential relationships that often end up in a prize, an award, or a special experience. A sports brand may sponsor a form of street ball, combine a story contest with the making of a movie about the sport, or provide blogs that create friendships that may result in a face-to-face trip.

The staging of the 2006 Citgo Bassmasters Classic on television is an example of developing an entertainment synergy that lifts the sport into a concert environment. The Classic is an annual event that is owned and televised by ESPN, which showcases the top bass anglers in a competition for a $500,000 first-place prize. On the surface, the event doesn't appear to have much audience appeal, as the actual fishing occurs before the awards ceremony and the audience only sees delayed highlights. Not only that, but fishing is not historically seen as a fast-paced action sport. What makes it work is a combination of music, lighting, and the WWE-style promotion of the competitors. Each angler arrives into the arena in a boat towed by a pickup truck, is miked to speak to the fans, and is greeted by a loud and cheering audience. The weighing of the fish, an activity that seems rather mundane, takes on center-stage proportions as the crowd is prompted by the master of ceremony's breathless commentary and the fisherman's intricate account of the pursuit. The winner is showered with a mountain of confetti, greeted by his family, and bestowed gifts. Angling is a growing sport in part because its promoters understand that connecting to popular culture trends can transform their sport. As evidence, the ratings continue to improve as the 2006 Classic was the highest rated in the history of the competition.[44]

Sports brands are compelled to link the fan to a number of interconnected experiences and not merely a random advertising campaign or a single direct promotion. The multilevel experience strategy has the advantage of providing a satisfying experience and also the potential to reach the fan in a variety of ways that are nontraditional. There is always the risk that the combinations can so distort the actual event that it becomes a distraction rather than a complement. However, in an age where entertainment forms are moving seamlessly across sectors, use of this strategy is critical.

CONCLUSION

In this chapter we discuss a number of causes of decline and how they might affect a sports brand's ability to sustain. In an era in which communication feedback is commonplace and the tools to connect with fans are available, the potential for sustaining is in many ways easier than it has been in any other period. At the same time, however, the competitive environment presents participation, attendance, media, and crisis challenges that a sports brand must continually address to survive.

In this competitive marketplace, it is important for the sports brand to inventory its strengths and weaknesses and understand the fundamental rules of sustaining. The brand can avoid decline and sustain fan connections with targeted strategies such as eventizing, riding a star, venturing into foreign markets, connecting with new segments, appealing to nostalgia, creating a rivalry, and designing synergistic experiences. In the next chapter, we illustrate and analyze some of the most successful brands in the sports marketplace.

9

SUCCESSFUL CASES
OF SPORTS BRANDING

The first Saturday in May is dominated by America's premiere horse race, the Kentucky Derby. Inaugurated in 1875, the Derby continues to be a major fan attraction. The 2005 Derby attracted its second largest crowd in history of 156,435 people,[1] a 7.3 national Nielsen rating,[2] and a record $103.3 million was bet on the race.[3] These figures are only part of the story as racing fans congregate at the Derby in low and high fashion, attend wild and fancy parties, and are for one week totally absorbed in the Churchill Downs southern hospitality horse racing culture.

None of this is by accident. The Derby projects a modernized old south image that is acceptable to visitors from all walks of life. The race symbolizes spring, rebirth, and a return to gentility that is branded and communicated by the entire state. Crystallizing the event is the Churchill Downs multimillion-dollar rehabilitation, which retained its trademark twin spires while completely modernizing its interior. The Derby has a number of brand extensions:

the freshly trained three-year-old thoroughbreds and their owners, trainers, and jockeys; the historic racetrack facilities; and the distinct social and cultural environment promoted by the fans themselves. This entire package brands Derby Day, which creates enduring fan connections, commands a premium for the experience, and remains one of the blue chip attractions in sports.

While the Kentucky Derby has more than a century of history, its position in the marketplace has never been guaranteed. Threatened by a constantly changing competitive environment, the Derby, like all other sports products, has been forced to identify core assets and build a brand that will attract and sustain the Elusive Fan. In this chapter, we analyze a number of cases of various sports brands that have achieved differentiation in the marketplace. Each case illustrates how sports branding is operating in specific sectors and how branding can increase the potential for long-term fan connections.

THE BRANDED ATHLETE

An athlete has the advantage of being the principal performer in the sport, and that usually means that the athlete's image is constantly before the fan. Because there are a growing number of distribution opportunities available, the athlete has the potential to enter into a variety of sectors and use his or her sports career as a platform for other endeavors. Critical to brand expansion is the athlete's ability to construct a brand that identifies and connects with specific target segments.

Maria Sharapova won Wimbledon at the age of 17 and in doing so became an instant star and a full-fledged brand seemingly in one stroke. In Sharapova's case, however, her stardom was a long process in the making that included not only mentoring on the tennis side but early intervention in brand development on the part of her agency, IMG. In many ways, she is a textbook case of investment brand marketing and how the modern athlete can be packaged to connect to the Elusive Fan.

Sharapova has a dramatic story line that is a combination of Cinderella and the unlikely immigrant. Born in Siberia she was moved by her parents in her grade school years to Florida, where she was at first rejected by the exclusive Nick Bollettieri Tennis Academy because she was too young for training. After two years of self-financing and self-described tough years, she was given a scholarship to train at Bollettieri's camp where she was mentored by some of the leading tennis coaches in the world.

In what could be described as a combination of the discovery and molding model of sports marketing and branding, Sharapova was signed by IMG at the age of 11. This relationship was clearly a development strategy as her early modest endorsement deal from Nike enabled her to begin developing her talents with the tools of the trade such as training clothes and shoes. Her management team and her father found themselves turning down endorsement contracts, wanting to focus more on developing her tennis skills and gradually bring her along as a commercial attraction. Max Eisenbud, her IMG agent, claims, "It was never really about the money. We were all in agreement that something big was going to happen, and we needed to be clean." Of course it was about the money because IMG spent a half-million dollars in development costs for Sharapova[4] and was banking on an eventual long-term payoff.

The reward for all of her tennis training and IMG's incremental promotion was her win at the 2004 Wimbledon. The branded athlete that emerged from this victory was a tall, smooth tennis player who was not unlike the much maligned Anna Kournikova in physical attractiveness. The commercial activity that followed, however, positioned her to become more like Tiger Woods than her fellow blonde Russian émigré. Within a year of her major victory, Sharapova signed 10 endorsement contracts with an annual income of between $15 and over $20 million.[5] Sharapova, with one grand slam championship win, had become a powerful brand, generating more endorsement income than other more accomplished women tennis players such as Lindsay Davenport (three grand slams) or Justine Henin-Hardenne (four grand slams) or any other female athlete. Sharapova is now a brand, merging the attractiveness and story line of a film star with the competitiveness and focus of a professional athlete. She appears on magazine covers, stars in television commercials for her many clients, and is followed by the paparazzi like any other Hollywood starlet.

None of this is intended to dismiss the fact that Sharapova had the capacity to become a top tennis star in a highly competitive sport, worked extremely hard to develop her game, or won the most prestigious tennis tournament in the world. Or that she has the physical attractiveness and youth to contribute to her success. It is clear, however, that Sharapova and her team of managers and coaches developed and molded her talent in a strategic manner to capitalize on her skills and attributes and transform her into a tennis superstar. After a slow and gradual development phase, the Sharapova brand launched. To sustain, she needs to win enough to avoid becoming another Kournikova and convert her visibility into opportunities in other sectors such as fashion or entertainment to take advantage of her brand name.

Maria Sharapova

Brand An international brand that combines world-class tennis playing with intelligence and glamour.

Transformation She systematically evolved from a nine-year-old Siberian tennis protégé to a top tennis star and prolific product endorser.

Involvement She has created many channels to experience her brand, and her overall package of undeniable tennis skills, Hollywood-star royalty, and glamour appeals to a wide range of fans.

Ethos Audiences clearly respond to her strong brand because they recognize her work ethic. Also the combination of her skills and appearance makes her attractive to younger demographics. If her performance declines, she is always in danger of becoming another Anna Kournikova and needs to concentrate on tennis skills first.

THE BRANDED OWNER

Branding an owner of a professional sports team not only makes the owner more visible but also resolves the sometimes contentious relationship between owners and fans. Fans have often linked owners to greed, selfishness, isolation, and a general lack of concern for their needs. Transforming the owner into a selfless brand attraction is an effective strategy to build the franchise's worth on a platform that is more permanent than free agent athletes.

Mark Cuban connected sports ownership to the media age. Up until Cuban, a controversial billionaire, bought the Dallas Mavericks, the public by and large perceived owners of major sports franchises as older, often dour, and somewhat distant from their product line. Fans could look up into the rarefied luxury boxes and see the owner and family sitting behind a glass window, drinking chardonnay, and appearing only marginally interested in the game. While there were exceptions such as baseball owner and marketing innovator Bill Veeck, the owners were generally low key and reluctant to play a central role in their team's persona. Even iconic team owners of the Monopoly and Television Generations such as the Washington Redskins' George Preston Marshall and Philadelphia Warriors' Eddie Gottlieb were characterized as secretive and curmudgeonly in their behavior.

Cuban had a different playbook, and when he began instituting it, he upset not only the ownership establishment but baffled the media. He didn't seem austere, made comments that were often provocative, and built a world-class environment for his players. All of this, however, was only a backdrop to what was his image-turning ownership persona. He was an avid fan and signaled to his team and everyone in the Mavericks universe that he was having a great time, loved being in the arena and working in the sports field, and could cheer and jeer just like anyone else. In doing so, Cuban turned one of the NBA's historically most embarrassing franchises into a modernized brand with a new arena and a competitive team.

It's not surprising that Cuban, who made his fortune on the Internet, has centered his brand communication strategy on new media. He has his own blog (blogmaverick.com) and has made himself available on e-mail for fans to send their comments and criticisms. His Internet presence lets him explain his reasons for making decisions regarding the fan experience, generate controversies with blog entries such as one titled "I Own Phil Jackson,"[6] and receive constant feedback from his fan base.[7]

Cuban has helped spawn a new generation of professional team owners, such as Robert Sarver of the Phoenix Suns and Zygi Wilf of the Minnesota Vikings, who are willing to promote themselves as symbols for their team. They too have recognized that an owner's enthusiasm, energy, and willingness to delight and surprise the fans can pay off in terms of fan loyalty and market share. As Cuban observes, "There is nothing smarter than a CEO enjoying his or her product and encouraging their customers to do the same."[8] The approach of these new owners is not only about running a profitable franchise but also enjoying the trip and the visibility of being the team's most avid fan.

Mark Cuban

Brand The unpredictable ringleader who wants everyone to have fun.

Transformation He combined calculated risk transformation with a strategy that countered the staid persona of owners. He played the role of the new kid on the block who was going to push the system until it gave way.

Involvement Cuban constructs a Mavericks fan experience with which his fans can identify and interact. He understands the new age of fan interaction, and whether he is right or wrong, his commitment is unconditional. He connects the sports world to emerging technologies and the more casual style of popular music, film, and other art forms.

Ethos The fan base responds to his total devotion to the team's welfare. He is their advocate, and while the players, league, and society may let them down, Cuban will always have a smile, a quip, and a solution to getting things back on track.

THE BRANDED COACH

In an era of rapid player turnover, a branded coach can provide continuity to a team and become a major fan attraction for a team, program, or league brand. Branding a coach is important on all levels of sports since players have short careers and many coaches serve over longer periods. The coach serves an important role in not only coaching the team but in marketing the program to its fan base.

University of Vermont basketball head coach Tom Brennan was not even close to being the winningest coach in the NCAA, but he accumulated enough support throughout his career that his win-loss record became secondary to the strength of his personal brand. He began his career at Yale University where he compiled a 46-58 record in four years. He then moved on to Vermont where he won only 8 of his first 58 games and retired after 19 years with his record under .500. This amount of losing would not be tolerated in most college programs, but Brennan developed a brand that endeared him to the fans of Vermont and fully integrated him into the culture of the state. In the process, Brennan transformed himself from a marginal college coach to ultimately a national celebrity.

His brand was built by differentiating himself from the majority of college coaches. He openly acknowledged that he was not responsible for Xs and Os and team strategy and that he served more as a figurehead. He was known for his humor, laid-back mentality, and—as Hofstra coach Tom Pecora described him—"everyone's crazy uncle".[9] And he made clear that making people feel good—or as he puts it, "filling up people's buckets"[10]—was one of his missions in life. He even went as far as taking opposing coaches out to dinner the night before the game. Brennan's brand positioned him as the antithesis of the slick, corporate, and micromanaging college coach—a strategy that worked with his audience in the historically liberal state that spawned not only Brennan but the inventors of Chunky Monkey, Ben and Jerry.

The primary platform on which Brennan communicated his brand was not on the sidelines but as cohost with Steve Cormier on *Corm and the Coach*, the most popular morning drive radio show in Vermont. He became an iconic figure in the state and was well known for his poetry readings, political rants, and phone calls to opposing coaches at 6:30 a.m. the day of their game. The radio program provided Vermont residents with access to Coach Brennan and allowed them to form connections with him independent of the basketball arena. At points in his career, it could have easily been argued that he was a better radio host than a college coach, and he remained popular despite his losing record.[11] He also converted his radio celebrity into other communication opportunities as a public speaker at "charity events, business seminars, youth sports functions and high school graduations."[12]

Brennan maximized his public appearances and capitalized on his differentiation in ways that resulted in visibility benefits for him, the university, and the state of Vermont. In a place that is traditionally dominated by hockey, Brennan became synonymous with the entire state. Vermont's governor Jim Douglas observed, "Tom is Vermont's coach. He epitomizes the spirit of the university and the state. I just hope he doesn't want to run for governor too soon."[13]

Brennan eventually used his branding power to turn the Vermont program into a winner. His brand enabled him to recruit better players such as Vermont native Taylor Coppenrath who helped the team reach three straight NCAA tournaments. During his tenure he was able to retain all of Vermont's homegrown basketball talent that received scholarship offers from other Division I schools. He also promoted a program of quality student athletes in which each of his starters during the 2003–2004 season had at least a 3.41 grade point average.[14] By the end of his career at Vermont, he and his team attracted capacity attendance at the 3,266-seat Patrick Gym, generated media attention for the school and his players, and ultimately turned the program into a winner. In Brennan's case, winning did not create his appeal since he barely managed to meet the capacity threshold; it was the product of a strongly built and well-managed star brand.

Tom Brennan

Brand An Andy Griffith-meets-Bill Murray type who was unpretentious and smart, but able to play a number of unconventional roles. Brennan was a daily presence in the lives of the citizens, and his true talent was connectivity combined with an antidictatorial basketball stance.

Transformation Discovered at a Rotary Club luncheon by a general manager of a radio station,[15] Brennan was the beneficiary of a calculated risk strategy. Thrown into a talk show format, Brennan's candid, surprisingly revealing personal observations attracted a curious and large radio audience. He was able to express his political, artistic, and personal side because of his lack of inhibitions and unwillingness to be stereotyped as an uptight basketball coach.

Involvement Brennan used multiple channels to reach the Vermont consumers. Unlike other coaches, he accessed his fan base through his non-sports radio show by creating a familiarity and intimacy that connected with the everyday affairs of Vermont citizens. It was a risky strategy that expanded his story line, enabling him to become an ESPN college basketball analyst after his retirement.

Ethos The coach earned the trust of the citizens of the state through his willingness to be transparent in his personal and professional life, and his candor and use of humor served to make him interesting and believable. In a state that prides itself on unpretentiousness and nonslickness, Brennan was a reassuring symbol of their values.

THE BRANDED EXECUTIVE

Front-office sports executives can be branded. As the media cover more frequently the business side of sports, exposure opportunities for executives have increased with their role in player contracts, roster transactions, stadium negotiations, marketing, and day-to-day operations. The strategy of branding an executive is particularly effective with the high rate of professional player turnover and the financial realities of many sports teams. Connecting on the executive level enables fans to become more involved with the team's decisions and provides fans a more stable face of the franchise with which to identify.

Billy Beane is the general manager of the Oakland Athletics and has become a star attraction for the team and Major League Baseball. Since taking over the position in 1997, Beane's task has been to put together a winning team in a small market with a limited budget. In doing so, Beane differentiated himself from the rest of baseball's decision makers who were slow to adopt computer-based analysis, continued to solely rely on scouting reports, and emphasized conventional practices such as paying large signing bonuses to high school stars and ignoring more mature college players. Beane, the principal in the best-selling book *Moneyball* by Michael Lewis,[16] built his brand on an approach to constructing a team that emphasized on-base and slugging percentage, drafting college players, and using quantitative research methods to predict performance. While statistician Bill James established the science of statistical analysis in baseball, Beane's approach applied James's theories to outsmart baseball's big spenders. Combining his baseball "innovation" with his casual appearance and diverse interests from European history to punk rock,[17] Beane built a counterculture baseball brand.

The establishment of Beane's brand was not by accident. As a highly recruited baseball player in 1980, Beane was drafted by the New York Mets in the first round. He played six years in the major leagues, but never really fulfilled his promise. After he retired as a player in 1990, he joined the Oakland Athletics as a scout and in 1993 was promoted to assistant general manager under Sandy Alderson. It was under Alderson that Beane refined his skills and, when he took over as general manager in 1997, he expanded the foundation Alderson set in place. In 1999 and 2001, Beane won executive of the year awards from *The Sporting News* and *Baseball America*, respectively, and his team made the playoffs four straight seasons from 2000–2003.[18]

Throughout his tenure, Beane has often traded his best players away or let them leave through free agency because the team could not afford to keep them. In most markets and with most teams, such actions would be considered intolerable and would result in a fan backlash. But Beane, who has established ethos with his fan base, has been able to pull off what seems like an annual fire sale of the team's best talent and still run a profitable franchise.[19] In the process, many fans have connected with Beane's brand. Athletics merchandise has been created with the logos "In Billy We Trust" and "What Would Billy Do?"[20] which symbolize how Beane's seemingly irrational transactions are supported and ultimately reinforced by many Athletics fans. Beane has also been able to lessen some of the effects of his transactions by interacting with fans on Web sites such as the Athletics Nation.[21] By making himself accessible, Beane can justify his actions and also form connections with fans, reducing the possible repercussions of his roster moves.

The ability of Beane to sustain his brand, however, is obviously in question as he continues to run the team on a tight budget and trade away his best players for younger prospects. In the winter of 2004–2005, Beane traded two of the team's star starting pitchers—Tim Hudson and Mark Mulder—under the same cost-saving rationale. At a certain point, the patience and understanding of fans could erode, leaving fans to question Beane's brand. But in a move to further center the franchise around the face of Beane, new owner Lew Wolff extended Beane's contract till 2012 and made him a part owner. The Athletics have clearly focused their branding strategy on Beane as Wolff asks and answers, "Do we pay $100 million for a player or do we extend Billy's contract? We think, if the past is prologue, we're very comfortable. We think we've made the right decision in getting Billy to stay with us long-term, just like you'd like to have a player finish his career with you."[22] This shift in focus is a critical lesson for all sports properties as the market becomes more competitive, the faces of teams change more rapidly, and fan expectations increase. A branded executive can help stabilize these types of situations and expand any sports brand.

Billy Beane

Brand A baseball counterculture brand that is based on technological innovation and quantitative analysis. Beane has taken the Silicon Valley, informal "genius" style and adapted it to one of America's most traditional sports.

Transformation Beane had the advantage of a mentor in Sandy Alderson who understood the changing economics of the game. He added his own personal style in contrast to Alderson's button-down, corporate demeanor. Beane maintained his casual appearance and no-time-for-frills, sun-baked style, which served as a connection for his core fans.

Involvement Through his unconventional personal appearance and behavior and his accessibility to fans, Beane has a special appeal to Internet-surfing, video game-playing contemporary fans. Fans can identify with Beane's strategies of outsmarting the establishment, and they can utilize similar computer methodologies to judge his decisions and either confirm or deny his risk-taking ventures on the basis of their own computations.

Ethos Beane is a straight shooter without much money, which resonates with the average fan who doesn't have much either.

THE BRANDED PROGRAM

Why can't a high school athletic program benchmark itself against the top college and professional teams? At first glance, the idea seems unlikely because high schools often have limited budgets and different fan expectations compared to college and professional teams. High schools have historically developed as local attractions, and the sophisticated world of college and professional sports programs seemed not only unnecessary but extravagant. That trend is beginning to change.

Southlake Carroll High School outside of Dallas, Texas, has built a brand for its football program by benchmarking the top college and professional programs. The school is a good example of how branding and benchmarking top programs can broaden appeal, cultivate fan connections, and form new ones.

The school district, in campaigning for funds to reposition the school's athletic program, not only instilled a sense of pride in the community but also joined a few first-in-the-channel high school athletic programs to redefine the role of high school sports in the athletic universe.

With the hiring of head coach Todd Dodge in 2001, the program took the first step in remaking its brand. Dodge implemented a spread-passing offense that broke with the more traditional run formations of Texas football such as the wishbone and the I. By using a passing attack, Dodge developed a football team that was more wide open, higher scoring, and ultimately more entertaining and appealing for fans to watch. It was this critical transformation that not only made it challenging for other teams to defend against and beat Southlake but also attracted more attention to the faster-paced style of play.

In addition to hiring the coach, the Carroll school district also funded a new facility, a $15.3 million football stadium that seats over 10,000 people and an adjacent indoor practice field. The Dragon Stadium complex is positioned by the school as state-of-the art in fan seating, locker room amenities, field condition, and even parking accommodations. Professional teams such as the Dallas Burn of the MLS played its 2002 season home schedule at the stadium, and the Dallas Cowboys of the National Football League often used the practice field in 2001.[23] While there was some controversy over the main playing field's surface,[24] these professional-caliber facilities positioned Southlake as a star-quality operation and created another set of attractions for the program. In this way, the program is creating synergy. It's not enough just to hire the coach. In building the stadium, it not only encourages fan involvement opportunities but generates media exposure.

The support of the Dragon's football program by its fans and alumni also contributes to its brand. The fans often describe themselves as being a part of "Dragon Nation," and many participate in what is called a "Green Out" for the games. During a Green Out, fans show up to games wearing green, with some fans painting their bodies and hair green. Fans often tailgate outside the stadium for games, travel to away games, and, if they're not Southlake residents, follow the team on the Internet or try to stay in touch through old friends and neighbors. For many fans that have attended Southlake Carroll High School or lived in the community, the fortunes of the team are intertwined with their identity. The school has even formed a Dragon Council, which establishes a connection with the often overlooked market of residents who do not have children in the school system.

A booster operation and an alumni support base help fund the team and seek to maintain the star quality of its program. A gift shop at the stadium called the Dragon's Den has evolved into a substantial business as it is the principal seller of Green Out merchandise. Debra Kinser, the manager of the shop said, "We have a total interest in Dragon apparel year-round. People from other teams come in the shop, and they just step back. It's close to a college-level interest with some people." The profits from this store and a Dragon store at a local photography business go to the school's booster club and help fund the athletics of the school.[25]

Southlake Carroll effectively transformed itself from a local community football team to an integrated brand that won the state championship in 2003 and 2005. As a community with only one public high school, the program benefits from limited competition and a devoted group of citizens. It is, however, committed to a breeding model for maintaining a competitive program that mandates that all Southlake football youth programs use the Dragon name and play the same system as the high school. At any time in the program, there are as many as a dozen young quarterbacks being groomed to run the offense at the high school.[26] Despite these competitive strategies, if the Dragons are going to continue to maintain their strong brand, they must look for other distribution opportunities, expand their fan base to non-community members, and monitor fan expectations just like teams on the professional and college levels. For other high school programs, the Southlake Carroll model is an indicator that the low buck, minimal resources high school athletic programs are giving way to competitive pressures. The future is in developing integrated, synergistic programs with innovative coaches, state-of-the art stadiums, and modern Internet merchandising.

Southlake Carroll High School Football Program

Brand A suburban high school football program that consistently exceeds expectations by benchmarking itself against college and professional programs.

Transformation Convincing an upper-middle-class community that a program can be redefined through a total focus on integrating leadership, facilities, and community involvement is what drove the transformation. The program also made the extra effort to benchmark all its football activities at professional and not high school levels of expectation.

Involvement The homegrown, community-funded program enables citizens to realize their investment on almost a daily basis. This includes raising kids to play on the team, supporting the team on many levels, and enjoying being the envy of communities that do not have its success or facilities.

Ethos The citizens of the community can identify with the strong commitment to excellence of the Southlake Carroll football program, which reinforces their community's value system.

THE BRANDED LEAGUE

If we were going to make bowling relevant to an MTV, videogame-trained generation, we had to make it exciting.[27]

—Rob Glaser, co-owner of the Professional Bowlers Association

After Glaser and his two co-owners, all former Microsoft employees, bought out the Professional Bowlers Association, their mission was clear—transform bowling from an over-50 sport to a youth-centered entertainment. To do so, the new owners had to not only remodel the PBA brand but develop a communication strategy that fully recognized how to connect with a younger demographic. As technology-trained business executives, they understood that owning the platform was critical to transforming the bowling league into an aggressive startup.

After selecting its new target, the PBA needed to develop the bowlers that would promote the brand. A first step was to reposition the image of professional bowlers from overweight, out of shape men to presentable twenty-first century athletes. The PBA found a new superstar in Pete Weber, son of bowling legend Dick Weber, who was young and eccentric and had the skill to compete. He even developed a signature move, the "crotch chop," which was not unlike football touchdown dances or soccer goal-scoring celebrations. Weber and other bowlers were encouraged to promote their different personalities by taunting their opponents and playing to the crowd, all of which took place on television broadcasts during which the bowlers were wired. In addition, they hired a former Nike executive group that developed player rivalries, one-on-one competitions, and a stunt shot segment. And they made the obvious move to include women in competition with the prospects of expanding that market.[28]

The PBA capitalized on two major distribution channels to reach a younger audience. First, the league signed a television contract with youth-centered ESPN, which created exposure for the league on a cable network with younger male-skewing demographics. A set of advertisements were developed that were usually humorous, sometimes cynical, and often sarcastic, which helped to reverse the image of bowling as bland. A second measure was the relaunching of the PBA Web site, which before the takeover by the Microsoft trio was maintained by a member of the association in his den. The owners revamped the site to include Web casts, detailed player profiles, and message boards for fans to provide feedback. The home page emphasizes current stars and, on the day viewed, the only reference to past stars was to Earl Anthony's record of 41 titles.[29]

Bowling is still a sport that does not receive continuous media coverage. Part of its strategy, however, is to build its core markets such as Detroit and Rochester, New York, and continue attracting younger generations by emphasizing social currency, star, and utopian connections. The PBA has also cooperated with the independent documentary film *A League of Ordinary Gentlemen*, which benefits the league by showcasing bowling in the contemporary, more artistic genre of independent filmmaking. Is bowling now cool? The numbers say it has made some major inroads. Viewership in the 18- to 34-year-old male segment was up by 80 percent in 2004, the PBA's Web site receives 300,000 visitors per year to watch Web casts of bowling tournaments, and membership in the PBA has increased by 75 percent in a five-year period.[30]

Professional Bowlers Association

Brand A retro sport that maintains its traditions and provides an entertaining and compelling experience for a media-accustomed generation.

Transformation The PBA identified a younger demographic as its target market and chose stars, story lines, and distribution channels that would make bowling relevant in pop culture.

Involvement Bowling is a high-participation sport that simultaneously needs to accommodate its avid players and build the spectator fan experience through media. Access to star bowlers during television broadcasts and on the Web personalizes the stars and connects them with the participation base.

Ethos Professional bowlers, unlike many other professional athletes, have an everyman quality and an athletic prowess with which fans can often identify.

THE BRANDED FACILITY

Facilities, like star athletes, can have a distinct brand that can provide differentiation in the marketplace. The advantage of a branded facility is that fans are attracted to the event not just because of the competition but because of what the facility offers to the overall fan experience. Despite which athletes compete, how a team performs, or what the outcome is, a branded facility encourages fan involvement through multiple platforms and connection points. Offering these various connections removes some of the importance of the on-field outcome and spreads the connection base to a much broader experience.

Racing began at the Daytona International Speedway in 1959, and its popularity grew with NASCAR's. It holds the "Great American Race"—the Daytona 500—and calls itself the "World Center of Racing" as it hosts nine racing competitions each year. The track has also become an attraction for other events such as "civic and social gatherings, car shows, athletic games, photo 'shoots,' production vehicle testing and police motorcycle training."[31] In 1996, capitalizing on its popularity, it introduced Daytona USA, a theme park that includes an IMAX theater, driving simulation rides, and exhibits providing fans a behind-the-scenes look at the racing world.[32]

Despite all these fan attractions, the rapid popularity growth of NASCAR began threatening Daytona's dominant status. One major challenge was NASCAR's building of new tracks near big cities such as Los Angeles, Chicago, Las Vegas, Miami, and potentially New York to expand and urbanize the sport. These tracks ironically created competition for NASCAR's own premiere Daytona brand and inevitably established new fan expectations for the twenty-first century NASCAR race experience. Another problem was that the traditional casual, laid-back Daytona atmosphere that gave fans access to the inner workings of the event, including admission to the pits, had diminished as concerns about safety and security increased. The new era of superstar drivers, corporate sponsors, and national media attention drew previously nonexistent boundaries between the fan and the race, and as a result Daytona began to lose the intimacy of its bump-and-liquor-run racing culture. To address these threats and remain NASCAR's marquee, southern-style track, Daytona needed to reinvent itself.

Daytona underwent a massive, multimillion-dollar renovation that included the establishment of a Fan Zone, which opened in 2005. For a more expensive ticket, a fan could gain additional access to the infield, view the pits from a newly built observation deck, and peek through glass windows to watch pit crews work on their cars.[33] The new infield arrangement allows drivers to emerge from the pits to sign autographs or pose for pictures. One journalist called this architectural intimacy "contrived closeness,"[34] a label acknowledging that 200,000 people are going to be in the stands and that the sport needed at least an illusion of closeness.

The effect of the Fan Zone is significant as fans are up close with their favorite drivers, view how teams prepare the cars, and feel involved with the race experience. One fan said of the change, "Last year, if you didn't have a garage pass or a pit pass or anything, you had no access to what was going on behind the scenes. You didn't even get close to the cars. This way people feel more a part of it."[35] This entire all-access Fan Zone experience, including the sidewalk entertainment of circus performers and bands, provides a value-added experience for the fan who attends Daytona. Mike Mooney, Nextel's NASCAR director of corporate communication, emphasized Daytona's distinction: "If you look at other sports you can't get on the playing field before the game."[36] In essence, Daytona has built a multichannel experience, creating reasons for the fan to attend the event that go beyond the importance or outcome of the race.

In sports entertainment, looking back at the last hundred years, the focus has been to grow the sport, attract more fans, build a bigger facility to house them, and, in doing so, ignore some of the qualities that built the sport in the first place. A major attraction of sports such as poker and marathon running is the ease of involvement and intimacy that encourages the formation of a deeper connection with participants and followers. These qualities enhance the sports experience and are particularly attractive not only to the traditional fan but to the youth market that has grown up in a more individualized environment. It's been only in the last ten years that NASCAR and other major sports have begun to understand that developing pockets of fan intimacy is critical to long-term success in such a competitive marketplace.

Daytona International Speedway

Brand A world-class racing facility that enables fans to experience the sport from a close-up vantage point.

Transformation Daytona redefined the sporting event experience by adapting the world of aquariums and zoos to its sport—where it's permissible to view but not actually interfere with the everyday workings of the operation of a live sporting event.

Involvement The Fan Zone enables the drivers, cars, and fans to connect. While it is not the same as pit and garage passes, it provides large numbers of fans access to the inner world of car preparation.

Ethos The facility renovations were made in an effort to rescale the mass audience NASCAR experience to a more intimate connection with its fan base.

THE BRANDED PRODUCT

In the early years of sports development, sporting apparel was very limited. It was not yet a cultural trend to wear a jersey or a cap with the name of some commercial or public enterprise of which you were not a member or participant. If fans wore an identifiable hat or jersey, it was often ratty, and it wasn't unusual to have to go to an embroidery shop to have one made up. The need for identity, the story connection with the apparel, and the integration of sports brands with fashion completely retooled the sports industry.

Mitchell & Ness Nostalgia Company is a sporting goods company that now specializes in the reproduction of authentic jerseys, hats, and other sports clothing. First opened in 1904, the Philadelphia-based company was under pressure to survive in the 1980s. To avoid bill collectors, owner Peter Capolino hid above his shop in a bookstore, which had the most expansive periodical collection in the United States. During his time at the bookstore, he read sports magazines dating back to the 1940s and "noticed the detail of each baseball jersey and team logo."[37] After finding 12,000 yards of the same wool flannel used for old-time baseball jerseys, he experimented and made jerseys of his past heroes such as Mickey Mantle, Babe Ruth, Joe DiMaggio, Henry Aaron, Warren Spahn, and Satchel Paige. The baseball jerseys became a good seller for Capolino, who was profiled in a *Sports Illustrated* article in 1987.[38] Two years later, Capolino signed a licensing agreement with Major League Baseball to exclusively manufacture and sell his jerseys. After a decade of producing baseball jerseys, he received permission from the NBA in 1999 and the NFL in 2000 to recreate their players' jerseys.

Capolino invented a sector that didn't exist and created demand for the type of sports jerseys that used to be hand-me-downs. He built his brand on good quality, accuracy, novelty, and nostalgia, and his company became an outstanding performer in a limited market. What established Mitchell & Ness as a powerful brand, however, was its transformation from a novelty sports memorabilia brand with a target market of "middle-aged white men looking to reconnect to their youth"[39] to a mainstream designer clothing line for a young, fashion-conscious, urban demographic.

Capitalizing on several brand-forming moments led to the transformation and distribution of the Mitchell & Ness brand. Starting in 1999, rap stars from Atlanta such as Scarface, Jermaine Dupri, and Big Boi and Andre from the group Outkast began to wear these "throwback" jerseys in their music videos. Capolino said, "All of a sudden, these hip-hop artists in Atlanta became loyal customers of my stuff. . . . They liked the funky colors and liked that these were the sports heroes of their childhoods. So they were wearing my jerseys and putting them in videos. People were calling me, 'Hey, I saw your Nolan Ryan on MTV.' I was in shock. I had no idea."[40] In 2001, long-time customer Rueben Harley understood the potential of this trend and convinced Capolino that more strategic marketing to the hip-hop sector would generate significant rewards.

After Capolino hired him, Harley focused on grassroots distribution, spending much of his time in New York where he would make visits to night clubs and record companies to promote the jerseys. He also encouraged other rap stars such as Jay-Z, Sean "Diddy" Combs, and Snoop Dogg to wear throwback jerseys in their music videos and public appearances, and some began mentioning throwback jerseys in their songs. The brand's "big break" according to Harley was during the 2002 American Music Awards when Diddy, the show's host, wore a variety of Mitchell & Ness merchandise throughout the event.[41] In addition, athletes themselves wore the jerseys in their press conferences and other public appearances. As a result, Mitchell & Ness benefited from product placement and celebrity endorsement that resonated with a younger market and propelled the brand to star status.

The brand commands a premium for its product with jersey prices ranging from $250 to $350,[42] whereas a regular jersey might cost $50. Mitchell & Ness sold $2.8 million worth of nostalgia clothing in 2000,[43] and by the end of 2003 the brand had generated $40 million in sales.[44] As president Peter Capolino said in a celebratory moment, "Rolex, Gucci, Versace and Mitchell & Ness. Those are the names."[45] But sustaining this popularity is a major challenge as the nostalgia trend has slowed and unlike Gucci and Versace, Capolino doesn't create new fashions and has to sustain market interest in a form of vintage clothing. Therefore, the product must maximize its brand by continuing to develop a steady stream of new variations in its product line. A product expansion strategy was to market blazers worn by stadium ushers in different eras for different teams[46]—a move to capture the sports trend into more formal dress. It was also an admission that while they must maintain their brand premium through exclusivity and price premiums, they must at the same time expand their line in order to reach new markets.

Mitchell & Ness

Brand An authentic and ethical recreation of team and star products that enables fans to travel first-class to the past.

Transformation Mitchell & Ness transformed from a company that made authentic sports clothing to an institution that invented a new sector. In doing so, it capitalized on hip-hop artists' discovery of the merchandise and in turn segmented its marketing approach by building a systematic network of artists and sports figures who wore their clothing and served as strategic product placement.

Involvement The clothes are a form of exchange between the buyer and the team and star worn. When you buy the product, you're honoring and reconnecting to history and expressing to your peers your understanding of its significance and your willingness to pay a premium for it.

Ethos The buyer receives a product that has no compromises in authenticity, quality, or detail.

THE BRANDED EVENT

It's 60 miles in the middle of nowhere, and anybody would tell him he's crazy to do that. He's in this little town of 1,563 people and he's telling me to build an 18-hole golf course. Now there are four courses and you can't get a tee time.[47]

—Course designer Pete Dye on Herb Kohler's proposal to build a world-class golf course at his American Club

The 86th PGA Championship was played at Whistling Straits in Kohler, Wisconsin. The event commanded a premium and attracted attention from fans around the world. The tournament set all-time records in both tickets purchased (94,470) and fan attendance (over 300,000). The impact on Wisconsin's economy was $76.9 million, almost two times that of the 2003 tournament in Rochester, New York, and over $25 million more than the previous record in Chaska, Minnesota, in 2002.[48]

The driving force behind the success of the PGA Championship at Whistling Straits was the course itself. Built in 1998 by designer Pete Dye, the course is an updated reincarnation of the old links courses, which were the historical foundations of the game in the British Isles. Located on Lake Michigan, the course seeks to recreate the same feel and windy playing conditions of the seaside British links. Like the courses in golf's birthplace, Whistling Straits must be walked—modern conveniences like golf carts are not allowed—and golfers and spectators can even find Scottish blackface sheep roaming the course. The layout and design also imitate the British model with its "huge sandy areas, deep pot bunkers, grass-topped dunes, big and undulating greens" and "natural fescue fairways."[49] While the majority of U.S. courses are more pristine, finely manicured, and often predictable, Whistling Straits was constructed as an authentic, organic, and unpredictable golf course that appears to have been in existence for 400 years.

In essentially uprooting a golf course from the United Kingdom and planting it in Wisconsin, the course not only has utopian fan connections but adds star quality to any event held on its grounds. In fact, both the United States Golf Association (USGA) and the PGA of America have competed to secure the course for its major tournaments such as the U.S. Open and PGA

Championship, the latter of which is already scheduled to return in 2010. The appeal of Whistling Straits has also increased the visibility of the entire state of Wisconsin and attracted the golf world to the state's golfing opportunities and offerings. As one Wisconsin journalist observed, "Suddenly, we're Pebble Beach with cows and corn fields."[50] There is no question that the attraction of Whistling Straits, which is built on a clearly differentiated brand in an American market, is the primary influencer of the golf events in Wisconsin. To sustain its brand, the course must continue to reinforce its first-of-a-kind status, and in doing so, withstand the inevitable replications of its model in the United States, while continuing to attract major golf events to complement its premiere course.

Whistling Straits

Brand U.S. golf's version of Epcot, which sets a new standard for tournaments, challenge, and surprises.

Transformation The decision to break from the traditional American style of manicured golf courses and faithfully recreate a British Isles links course that was more challenging for the players redefined the golf experience.

Involvement In either playing the course or watching the tournament, the course connects golfers and fans to the sport's past and provides a historical perspective on the game's challenges.

Ethos In recreating a more difficult course, it repositions golf as more unpredictable and rewards both a more strategic and athletic-driven game.

THE BRANDED TELEVISION SHOW

The avid fan is a much sought after commodity in a fragmented sports world. An important ingredient in maintaining and developing avid fans is connecting them to the insider and detailed universe of sports. Sports talk shows, Internet chats, insider scouting reports, and draft extravaganzas are all targeted to this sports-hungry segment. It could be argued that sports are an entertainment and that the real world is about work and other more serious topics. The new trend in branding sports products is to take the opposite view and make sports the centerpiece of an intense and compelling lifestyle and wrap it in controversy.

Washington Post sports columnists Tony Kornheiser and Michael Wilbon host the ESPN talk show *Pardon the Interruption* (PTI). The show airs most weekdays in the afternoon for a half hour of one-on-one argument and debate. On the show, Kornheiser and Wilbon exchange views on the sports headlines of the day, play argument games accompanied by props and costumes such as "Good Cop, Bad Cop," "Role Play," and "Psychic Hotline," and spend "Five Good Minutes" with a special guest interviewee. The debates are framed like a boxing match with time limits and "dings" signaling the end of each round. Viewers are also provided with visual sidebars that include the menu of topics, the time remaining in the round, and current topic reminders so that they can follow the debate. With this format, PTI capitalizes on the marriage between sports and controversy and showcases on a television program what often occurs among groups of friends discussing sports—arguments.

The brand of the show was established following the principles of transformation. Kornheiser and Wilbon generated a brand concept based on sports debate and their distinct type and character. Kornheiser is a Caucasian New Yorker who graduated from SUNY-Binghamton, plays the role of comedian and older brother, and is dressed traditionally with a sport coat and tie. Wilbon is an African American Chicagoan who graduated from Northwestern University, plays the role of the cooler and younger brother, and is dressed in a more contemporary style often without a tie. Both are veteran sports columnists with experience and credibility in the field, but they often argue like stubborn siblings who are set in their views.

The two tested their personal concepts and the show in their local market of Washington, D.C. They appeared with two other journalists on a television program titled *Full Court Press* during basketball season and *Redskins Report* during football season, which followed a similar argumentative format as PTI. But it wasn't until ESPN began airing PTI in 2001 that they became a national sports attraction. In the process, Kornheiser and Wilbon have actualized both their distinct personas and their television concept by maintaining the differences in their characters and establishing ethos with viewers for their knowledge and opinions of sports. In fact, the stars and their show have become so popular that a CBS sitcom called *Listen Up!* was based on Kornheiser and starred Jason Alexander as Kornheiser and Malcolm Jamal-Warner as Wilbon.[51]

In the end, the successful brand creates fan involvement, and PTI effectively serves as an intermediary to plug fans and sports into a meaningful exchange. While there is a segment called "Mail Time" when Kornheiser and Wilbon answer e-mails, the real involvement is in the argumentative nature of the show itself. The hosts serve as initiators of the arguments, which encourages television viewers to agree or disagree and expand the debate with their fellow viewers. The show becomes not just about sports but the argumentative performance of the two stars and the interaction that it stimulates with its viewers. The appeal of their performance and the frequent debates on topics other than sports make the program attractive to a wide range of viewers. While the show's format is an important selling point, it is personality-driven, and every effort is made to emphasize and promote the distinct characters of Kornheiser and Wilbon.

Pardon the Interruption

Brand The show is a combination of MSNBC's *Hardball with Chris Matthews* and the *Fox NFL Sunday* studio show. It is designed as a nonstop, unpredictable, entertaining half hour of sports controversy.

Involvement It connects the fan to a highly charged and controversial sports dialogue hosted by two outspoken experts who take different points of view.

Transformation PTI evolved from a local Washington, D.C., television show to a national venue that emphasized the refinement of the type and character of the two main players.

Ethos The show is full of insider sports opinion that is authenticated by the experience and reputation of the journalists and their willingness to argue sensitive and sometimes unexplored topics.

THE BRANDED TEAM

*Fifty years ago, most female sports participants were Olympic ath-
letes, a small number of professional women tennis players and
golfers, and high school girls basketball players who had to play by
a set of rules that made the game resemble a slow waltz. How times
have changed. The passing of Title IX, the emphasis on women's physical fitness, and the emergence of women athletes as role models has
redefined sports.*

The Northwestern University athletic department needed to add a new
woman's team in 2000 to comply with the guidelines of Title IX, a federal law that
ensures equal funding to both men and women collegiate athletic programs. The
department resurrected women's lacrosse, which had played nine seasons until
the team folded in 1991. This new version began play on the varsity level in the
spring of 2002 and quickly became a strong lacrosse brand. By 2005, the team
had not only attracted national attention to the school but won the NCAA national championship, the first for the university since the men's fencing team won in
1941. How did the team create its brand so quickly and so successfully?

First, the university hired a star coach, Kelly Amonte Hiller, and gave her
the authority to construct the team in her vision. Amonte Hiller compiled an
impressive record as a women's lacrosse player at the University of Maryland,
winning national championships and player of the year awards in both 1995
and 1996. She also had a star athletic pedigree that included her brother,
Tony Amonte, an NHL player and Olympic silver medalist, and her husband,
Scott Hiller, an All-American collegiate lacrosse player and the 2002 coach of
the year in Major League Lacrosse.[52] Based on her star-quality background,
Amonte Hiller admits, "I gave the program instant credibility. From day one
I've made this program my own and have been able to build it and shape it
exactly the way I wanted to."[53] Hiring Amonte Hiller and giving her the freedom to develop the team positioned the program as legitimate and provided
the foundation for future fan attention.

Second, Amonte Hiller used innovative and synergistic strategies to build
the team. Challenged with finding players in a region where lacrosse was underdeveloped, she recruited players with athleticism rather than traditional

lacrosse skills. She was setting a new standard for women's lacrosse that, while not as physical as the men's game, was somewhat of a hybrid. She felt that she could teach good athletes how to play lacrosse and mold them into the players that would fit her faster-paced style. For example, she initially discovered twins Courtney and Ashley Koester playing rugby on a university field. Several days later, she encountered the sisters again as they were running and approached them to ask about the possibility of playing lacrosse. They declined at first, but Amonte Hiller was persistent in her appeals and soon was teaching them the sport. The results were almost immediate for Amonte Hiller and the Koester sisters. Both became starters on the 2005 national championship team and Courtney, who played varsity basketball her freshman year at Northwestern, was a first-team All-American.

Finally, the Northwestern lacrosse team maximized its first-into-the-channel advantage to enhance its brand. Lacrosse, traditionally an elite eastern sport, is expanding rapidly into western regions and transforming into a more widely played game. The sport has become one of the fastest growing in the country with an increase of over 100,000 participants during the years 2001 to 2004. In addition, on the high school level, the sport has grown by 174 percent from 1994–1995 to 2003–2004.[54] The timing and decision to build a nationally branded lacrosse team in the Midwest during this participation boom placed Northwestern in a situation in which it could ride the wave of this emerging sport. As the sport continues to expand, Northwestern, as a pioneer in women's lacrosse in the Midwest, is capitalizing on an untapped and evolving market and potentially creating enduring and sustainable fan connections.

Northwestern Women's Lacrosse Team

Brand An athletic, aggressive, Midwestern-based team that redefined the sport of women's lacrosse. The lacrosse team set a new benchmark for players and fans and was in the same mold of similar teams that redefined style of play such as the super quick University of Miami football teams.

Transformation A strong star coach who, through celebrity, selection, and recognition of the sport's strengths and weaknesses, was able to mold a brand leader in a very short period of time.

Involvement An underdog type connects all the constituents to the emergence of a sport in an unlikely place.

Ethos The team has credibility through not only success but overcoming adversity of location, eastern biases, and historical precedent.

WHY ARE THESE SPORTS BRANDS SUCCESSFUL?

What do our successful sports brands have in common? Each has transformed into a strong, identifiable, and differentiated brand and is an example of how to execute two critical brand differentiation tools—*benchmarking* and *innovation*.

Benchmarking

The boundaries between professional, college, high school, and all other competitive levels of the sports industry have historically been fixed. Fans often had certain expectations of how a team, player, coach, or facility should operate on a particular level. It was once unthinkable that a high school football team would have a stadium with luxury suites and electronic scrolling advertisements or that a college women's lacrosse team would play a ferocious and physical style. In today's marketplace, however, the successful sports brands are often the ones that use other strong brands as a benchmark for their own brand. These can be competitors, higher-level brands in the same sport, or brands in a completely different sport. Driving the need for benchmarking is increasing competition, higher fan expectations, and the demand for sports brands to be aware of industry best practices and to integrate the most relevant qualities into their own brand.

Another aspect of benchmarking is searching beyond the sports industry for the best practices of other sectors. It is a mistake for any sport to become "sports-centric" and only view their products in a narrow context. For example, what are the retail brands from the fashion, electronics, and other consumer goods industries doing to attract and retain customers, and what elements of their brands can be applied to sports? Not unlike sports, these brands seek to create long-lasting brand loyalty and encourage their customers to spend more on their products. In addition, many of these retail brands are in competition with sports brands, and understanding how they interact with consumers is also an important factor in creating brand differentiation. In such a competitive marketplace, sports brands should be aware of the branding trends in other industries and benchmark when necessary to maximize fan connections and attract fans away from competitors.

The danger in benchmarking, however, is that sports brands will simply adopt many of the same strategies of competitors and lose critical differentiation as a result. In order to maintain distinction in the marketplace, sports brands must combine benchmarking with innovation.

Innovation

What is it about your brand that competitors can't emulate and consumers can't get anywhere else? In a competitive sports marketplace where fan attractions can quickly become commonplace and outdated, the need to innovate to attract and sustain fan interest has never been more critical. Differentiation in such a competitive marketplace is seemingly always at a premium, and fan expectations demand that brands be inventive in how they reach fans and sustain their interest.

Innovation can come from a number of sources—a new brand, unexpected partnerships, building a brand in an untapped market, or integrating the sports brand with other sectors. The potential innovation possibilities have expanded with the growth of media channels and available information, and the sports brands that can convert these new methods of communication into differentiated connection strategies will most often experience the greatest rewards. There is no better example than the sport of bass fishing, which was historically defined as intimate, isolated, and a nonspectator sport. As in the example of the CITGO Bassmasters Classic, the sport now combines strategies from many entertainment fields to emerge as a viewable and compelling sport for many fans.

Benchmarking and innovation work both interdependently and synergistically; the sports brand benchmarks what is working and then innovates to create differentiation. However, these differentiation tools are only successful when brand participants internalize the new positioning.

CONCLUSION

The cases in this chapter illustrate how effective branding can be in creating differentiation and connecting with fans. While these cases are important examples of transformation, they do not constitute the majority of sports communication and marketing practices. For the most part, branding in the sports industry is still a relatively young and growing practice. For too long, sports decision makers relied on a combination of winning, monopoly, and the fortunes of the sports marketplace to fill the stands and pump up the ratings. When the stakes are so high and the marketplace is so crowded, the sports programs that practice brand building in a systematic and strategic manner will endure. In the next chapter, we examine how the industry will unfold and what it means for both sports branding and the Elusive Fan.

Chapter

THE FUTURE OF
FAN CONNECTION

Fans have been standing outside Madison Square Garden since early afternoon in anticipation of the evening's basketball game—but the NBA's Knicks, NCAA's St. John's, or high school's McDonalds All Americans aren't playing. They're not looking for basketball in its purest form. They're not here to see team defense, offensive rebounding, or midrange jump shots. And they're not interested in who wins. They've come to the arena for a show, and it is Hot Sauce, Sik Wit It, Escalade, Half Man/Half Amazing, the Professor, and other nicknamed players who are the stars.

The sport is street ball, and the main event at Madison Square Garden is the And1 Mix Tape Tour. And1, a basketball shoe and clothing company, is the sponsor and organizer of the event, which combines sports, fashion, and music to create a multichannel fan experience. The tour has traveled to cities around the world since 2000, branding a basketball subculture and using media to grow the game. ESPN2 produced a reality series that awards an And1 endorsement contract and a permanent spot on the team for the next season; video-game maker Ubisoft created and distributed an And1 Street Ball game that features the tour's top stars; and numerous Mix Tape DVDs that fuse hip-hop music and street ball highlights have been released. The Tour has reincarnated the showtime of the Harlem Globetrotters, modernized the concept with popular programming formats, and created a brand that integrates a segmented lifestyle with an emerging sport.

The structure of the And1 Mix Tape Tour is in stark contrast to many of the industry's most successful and historically ingrained team sports such as baseball, football, hockey, and conventional basketball. In street ball, referees and rules are formalities; wins and losses are basically irrelevant; individual performances are the centerpiece; and the game is as much about entertainment as it is about sports. Although the sport doesn't fit within the traditional boundaries of structured and institutionalized games, it has become a widely popular and successful brand among its target audience—11- to 17-year-old basketball players. And1, fueled in large part by the tour, generated $180 million in revenue in 2004 and is the second most endorsed brand by NBA players next to Nike.[1] Combining a strong Internet presence with tour dates in international cities, the sport is also evolving into a global attraction. In addition, the Mix Tape DVDs have consistently been the top-selling sports DVDs in America, and ESPN2 has made the reality show a staple of its original programming.[2] In many ways, street ball and the And1 Mix Tape Tour represent a shift in what will define success in the future of fan connection. The tour is a textbook case in fan interaction, interrelated media platforms, and a multiple connection fan experience. Street ball is basketball's current version of sandlot baseball or two-hand touch football where players participate without the influences of parents or other institutional pressures.

However, games like street ball are not the only major changes facing the sports world. The days when one grew up with a sport and remained a lifetime fan can no longer be counted upon for fan connection. The participation ideal of a child starting to play basketball at the age of six, joining a number of school and park district basketball leagues and playing the game through high school, watching the sport on television with peers and attending a few games with parents, continuing to follow and play the game while at college, and finally as an adult becoming a lifelong season ticket holder for a professional franchise is increasingly disappearing. While there are still sports that rely upon a platform of participation such as basketball and baseball, which then lead to spending money to watch games at the college and professional levels, there are an increasing number of sports and sports-related activities that have no end game that could be defined as spectatorship. Sports such as dodge ball, table hockey, marathon running, and sports-related entertainment activities such as video games do not necessarily lead to becoming a spectator of that sport. Furthermore, there is an additional category of consumers which includes people who are watching sports in media or Internet-generated environments that vary from 30-second highlights to intense fantasy games that may or may not lead to attending a sporting event. In the United States, there are also sports such as soccer that have high participation rates that do not translate into fan interest at the higher levels of the sport and sports that have comparatively smaller participation rates but higher fan popularity such as American football.

All these various configurations of fan involvement present challenges to sports that need to generate revenue and an ardent fan base in order to survive. In evaluating what the most important drivers and implications for the next generation of sports decision makers are, there is a necessity to not only understand the technological and cultural trends that are creating such powerful forces in sports, but to begin to see them in a larger and more productive light that will allow for more prediction and profitability.

SIX FUTURE DRIVERS OF SUCCESSFUL SPORTS BRANDS

Although the total number of fans in the Elusive Generation is larger than ever, these fans are more difficult to reach, engage, and sustain. This combination makes the fan connection for sports brands even more difficult as the market evolves and changes. *The agile and forward-looking sport will constantly evaluate the following six drivers and undergo transformation in response to a changing and crowded marketplace.*

Driver One: Increasing Fan Interaction

The sports fan experience has changed dramatically as the industry has evolved over the Monopoly, Television, and Highlight Generations. Fans now have more access to sports information, and fan interaction with sports brands is increasing. Interacting with the fan, forming a personal relationship, and connecting on an emotional level are now key objectives of sports brands. It is conceivable that a fan of the MLS team Real Salt Lake could construct an entire day filled with information about the team from different channel encounters. The fan could read the *Salt Lake Tribune* sports section in the morning for news about the team, listen to sports talk radio about the previous night's matches on the way to work, check daily news and injury reports on Web sites during the day, unwind after work by playing an MLS video game as Real Salt Lake, watch the evening's game on HDTV or follow it on an Internet gamecast, and check fantasy soccer scores at the end of the night's games to see how his or her team fared. While a daily menu such as this one is hypothetical, it does illustrate the expanded communication environment for the sports industry. This fragmentation is what makes fans "elusive."

This new interaction potential requires sports decision makers to think not just about the fan's experience at the venue, but also to focus on the communication that takes place on a daily basis. These communication opportunities, whether they are newspaper stories or e-mail updates, all have consequences for how the brand functions in the marketplace. In a more traditional environment, sports brands had to manage fewer channels to be successful. Sports brands are now forced to understand the role of sports in their fans' lives in order to capitalize on the millions of sports impressions that reach fans through various channels. Those sports that can brand an interactive sports experience that integrates not only event attendance but the various media channels in which fans experience sports will be the winners.

Implication *Sports must brand interactive sports experiences.*
The marketplace has become so crowded that fan-based interactive experiences will be most successful in creating differentiation in the marketplace. Audiences are increasingly controlling their own communication environments,[3] and sports brands must provide a real incentive to get people out of their media-connected houses as the media experience will continue to be more inviting than attending a live performance. An interactive sports experience integrates

all the attendance, media, and participation components of a sports brand into a fan attraction. For example, imagine that the Minnesota Timberwolves are trying to sell season ticket packages and need to drive interest in attending games. An interactive innovation could include a series of events all driven off the team's asset base. The season ticket pass could include 10 home games in the stadium, three meet-the-player lunches or dinners, two pay-per-view special games with the Lakers, a private viewing of a sports film with Kevin Garnett as the host, and five games in which fans are sent a 20-person party game package to their home that includes stadium food, programs, and a phone call at the end of the game from one of the players.

A completely different strategy would be more externally driven and tie together different conferences, ages, and playing levels. The package might include two tickets to see the Michigan Wolverines, Detroit Lions, and the Michigan state high school football championship. The target could be the Detroit–Ann Arbor football fan who will receive, in addition to the game tickets, a complete football experience with a series of lectures on rivalries of Michigan football teams and a tour of the Michigan sports hall of fame in nearby Farmington. In both examples, the sports brands are orchestrating the experience and at the same time demonstrating goodwill by developing appealing experiences that fans are unlikely to put together themselves..

In these new experiences, everything is connected. In terms of ticketing, sports are now resembling auto assembly. They are often built on the same platform but have different features and amenities. Breaking fan experiences down into different levels and different price points and giving consumers their choice in how they interact with sports is a critical component of future sports branding success.

Driver Two: Expanding Star Power

The sports brand with star power has the potential to attract a premium for its product, move fans up the fan involvement ladder, and create long-term relationships. Star power also differentiates the brand in the marketplace, can communicate a competitive advantage, and is historically one of the most powerful connectors. Star power is necessary in order for all sports brands to achieve success because it increases the chances of forming profitable and sustainable connections with sports fans in the future.

A major change in the star power definition is the increasing understanding that star power includes more than just people. Star power also includes facilities, food, teams, places, and fan cultures. Orchestrating how the star will evolve and become integral to the brand is an essential task for sports brands. The decision of the Baltimore Orioles to include the longest building in the United States as part of the right field of their retro park, Camden Yards, was an example of star power influencing a facility's design. The Orioles further enhanced their brand by using brick similar to the edifice of the landmark building. It would have been just as easy to knock the building down and feature the downtown and harbor landscape as a backdrop for the stadium. But that's not star-power thinking. Management, looking for that star edge, differentiated its park from all the other parks in Major League Baseball and in doing so created a permanent star-power brand with a competitive advantage. When the Washington Nationals baseball team was launched in 2005, it threatened to erode a portion of the market for the nearby Baltimore Orioles baseball team. Baltimore economic consultant Anirban Basu, in evaluating the competitive picture, observed, "It's still a viable team, because Baltimore loves its baseball and Camden Yards remains a gorgeous park."[4] This example demonstrates a powerful redefinition of star power. Stars don't just have to be players, but whatever is chosen has to be understood and faithfully executed as a branding tool.

Implication *Discovering the sports brand stars and maximizing their impact is a matter of survival.*
While most sports brands have the potential to create star power, the reality is that many efforts fall short. Perhaps the owners are fearful that individual stars will leave their team or act badly or that management simply lacks the taste and judgment to identify the true stars. In other cases, there are good choices of various facility and technological star potential, but there is simply a lack of commitment to making it work. These points of view are no longer viable in a star-driven sports universe. It is essential that sports brands see developing the star as important as making sure that the rules are consistent or that the throwback jacket sheds water. Star power drives attendance, viewers, buyers, and ultimately profitability.

Fortunately, sports brands have a large range of options for building stars. This makes survival possible, especially because of fans' increasing acceptance of the expanded star universe. Sports brands can inventory their star possibilities, discover potential story lines and branding opportunities, and build the star power of their players, facilities, teams, events, or other sports products. Whether or not a sports product can become a star is dependent upon the sport's capacity threshold—the minimum skills required of the specific sector in the sports industry. For a facility, that might mean modernized amenities; for a coach, an ability to teach the sport and run practices; or for a player, enough athletic ability to be competitive during formal performances. If a product exceeds the capacity threshold, there is clear potential for creating, building, and developing story lines to maximize a star-powered sports brand. When the U.S. Bowling Congress decided to redefine its game, it chose Diandra Asbaty, an accomplished, articulate, and attractive bowler. She has become the star lever to elevate women's bowling from a small, second-tier sport to a major attraction.[5] The selection of Asbaty illustrates the star power principle at work—the U.S. Bowling Congress identified an athlete who surpassed the capacity threshold and positioned her in the channels to make an impact and build women's bowling as a sport.

Driver Three: Connecting to the Ever-Changing Youth Market

Reaching and connecting to young people will continue to be a central challenge for sports brands. Ideally, sports brands connect with young people while they're young and keep them as paying customers for the rest of their lives. With so many options in the marketplace for youth, creating this type of lifelong connection is more difficult than ever. For example, the after-school activities of an eight-year-old third-grader could include choosing from hundreds of satellite or cable television channels; playing violent, role-playing, or sports video games; surfing the Internet at high speeds and chatting on instant messenger; sending text messages or playing games on a cell phone; uploading MP3s onto a portable digital music player—all in a half hour. Combine this media multitasking behavior with the infinite number of messages aimed at young people by the food and beverage, fashion, music, and sports industries and other purveyors, and it's clear that the battle for the youth market's attention, time, spending power, and loyalty has never been fiercer. It will only become more relentless in the future.

What does this mean for sports? The connection process for youth and sports is not as straightforward as it was in the past. The overprogramming of children, parental concerns about safety, the specialization of sports participation, and the impact of new media are complicating this connective relationship. In the future, these four issues will continue to influence how the youth market functions, especially as the pressures to narrow participation choices increase and parents and children are forced to make decisions about which sport to play at younger and younger ages. In this complex youth environment, the sports brands that reach and connect with the youth market at critical decision points, maintain these relationships into adulthood, and continually adapt to new generations will survive and succeed.

Implication *Sports brands must continually adapt their products to changes in culture and technology.*

To say that the culture of youth sports has changed since the fifth-grade tackle football days of "1X to 3X through 45" is an understatement. One of the latest innovations is rapper Snoop Dogg's new football conference "Snoop Youth Football," which has turned Orange County, California, football upside-down. Snoop began as a "daddy coach" for his sons' team, the Rowland Raiders, and eventually served as the offensive and defensive coordinator during the Raiders' championship season. He gave the team custom-made DVDs commemorating the championship with his own recorded message and hosted the "Snooperbowl" at the 2005 Jacksonville Super Bowl, where 15,000 fans came to see the Raiders all-star team face a local team from the host city. After two years in this role, Snoop, seeking control over his youth football efforts, seceded from the Raiders to start his own competitive conference. Snoop's star power, aggressive recruiting practices, and financial support from corporate sponsorships and concerts featuring Ice Cube and the Red Hot Chili Peppers enticed many players to join Snoop's conference. The league's players were treated like professional football players as they traveled in a souped-up school bus with TV monitors that could show their game highlights.

The new league touched off a raging controversy in Orange County as many teams lost members to Snoop and organizers claimed that Snoop Youth Football was decimating their long-standing leagues. Sandy Gonzalez, an unhappy Rowland Raiders parent, complained, "He came here just so that he could take away from us what we'd taken many years to establish."[6] Emblematic of the new competitive wars in youth sports, the Snoop league signals yet another benchmark in youth participation. He has built a league in sync with contemporary youth culture, uses his star power to drive interest, and redefined youth football as "cool." Snoop's conference is the canary in the coal mine, a signal of the continuing luring and upgrading of what was once youth-driven, informal sports participation and a warning to sports brands that the players in this new league will have increased expectations for future spectator sports. It also foreshadows what is likely to be a strong sportsmanship and civility countermovement as communities become disenchanted with the excesses and seek to restore some reasonableness to sports expenditures and behavior.

It is essential for sports brands to manage the relationship between technology and youth. With cell phones, video games, instant messages, and other Internet communication forums, young people are living in a technology-driven social network that is unprecedented in communication history. Over 50 percent of teens have television sets in their rooms and about the same number manage their lives through their cell phones or Internet instant messaging.[7] The youth media culture has strong networks and much of their social cues come from peers via various messaging systems. This new communication and media environment also threatens to disconnect young people from their parents and close them off from traditional print media such as newspapers, magazines, and books. Despite these communication changes, the opportunities to reach youth are virtually limitless, and the channels are open in ways they have never been before.

How can the sports industry crack this often seemingly impenetrable youth universe? Sports brands must not only access the channels of youth communication but also adapt to the language, pace, and cultural codes that are embedded in this elusive market. To connect to the youth market, sports brands must not only become routine producers of their message but also must generate youth-focused content that utilizes the latest in research and distribution channels. For many sports brands, this means incurring greater cost and more responsibility for message development. This shift in message development and distribution will continue to realign the historically codependent relationship between sports and the media that formerly guaranteed coverage to sports. In this environment, reaching the youth market will find sports brands negotiating new partnerships, connecting to popular cultural trends, and adapting their story lines to an ever more demanding audience.

Driver Four: Delivering a Global Sports Brand That Is Profitable and Fan-Centered

Sports brands from all parts of the world are invading one another's markets, international matches are played in almost every sport, and barriers to becoming a fan of a sports brand in a country other than your own have been significantly reduced. Largely because of satellite and Internet technology, traditional location constraints on fans are becoming less of an obstacle. Although they can't easily attend Manchester United's game against Chelsea, Man U fans in China can follow the game on their cell phones or watch it at one of the team's branded restaurants. Expansion into global markets is not only creating new potential fans for sports brands but also is changing how the industry will operate in the future.

The globalization movement, however, is still maturing. The NBA, perhaps the fastest global mover, is still only developing its Basketball Without Borders program, through which players travel to foreign countries to teach the game and other life skills to impoverished citizens. The World Baseball Classic, baseball's world cup, is a recently developed event. And events such as the cricket and rugby world cups and other international competitions are still evolving into fully international attractions. In the sport of soccer, FIFA has expanded into global markets by taking its sport into new markets like Vietnam, which now has its own national team that plays internationally. In doing so, FIFA is creating fans in Ho Chi Minh City who will buy jerseys and hats and become part of the world soccer community. The globalization movement will be a key driver of sports brands in the twenty-first century, and those sports that retain their current markets and expand into both older and developing ones will have a competitive advantage.

Implication *Sports brands need to determine the desirability of entering the global market.*
Despite the buzz about globalization, there is much uncertainty about how to manage it. Is a global marketing strategy appropriate for the brand? Will global markets help or hurt the brand and at what cost? How can global markets be reached without alienating core domestic markets? How can the brand practically and efficiently expand? In the globalization process, answers to these and other questions must be analyzed carefully. The globalization of sports is in a constant state of change, and the challenges are everywhere. While there

302

has long been fan resistance to foreign expansion in such sports as cricket and soccer in the United States, there are also examples of overwhelming acceptance of sports such as basketball and soccer in China. The sports brands that can manage global expansion by sustaining core markets and implementing an international strategy in practical terms will succeed in the future.

The options for sports brands not to expand globally are rapidly declining. Sports have acquired much of the economic and political dynamic of long-standing industries such as automobiles, steel, and electronics. For a sports brand, the ability to hold market position is now more difficult, because attractive invaders can move swiftly into any territory through media channels, and now have the capacity to accompany this invasion with ground-level programs. The most effective defense to the globalization challenge for most sports is targeting potential international marketplaces and building bridges by better understanding their culture and adapting programs to fit their aspirations.

Driver Five: A Fan Base That Is Easier to Reach and Harder to Engage

New segmentation techniques have generated more information about consumers than ever before possible. From customer loyalty cards at the chain pharmacy that inventory product purchases, commercial Web sites that track customer preferences to digital video recorders that catalog the television programs people watch, decision makers are now constructing a more complete understanding of the buying habits of consumers. Their knowledge of consumers will continue to increase as technologies like radio frequency identification (RFID) and the global positioning system (GPS) that seamlessly track customers are increasingly implemented. In this new environment, decision makers might finally understand what customers want and create products that meet those expectations.

Sports decision makers now benefit from knowing more about their fans, but along with that knowledge comes the burden of making tough choices about which segments to target. The challenges are everywhere. Many sports brands are still dealing with issues of how to organize their data, let alone make the best use of the information. Others are trying to decide what channels to spend money on, which competitors to benchmark, and how to work with consumers who seem to have more information and less need for their services. This situation is made even more perilous because information is becoming so available and accessible to so many competitors. Thus the traditional advantages of having superior consumer research are slowly evaporating. In this marketplace, sports brands for the first time find themselves in danger of drowning in information, overwhelmed by choices, and fighting inertia to devise suitable segmentation strategies.

Implication *Sports brands must not only segment and target desirable audiences but they must be willing to manage unprofitable relationships.* It was more realistic for sports products to target mass markets when there were fewer competitors and fewer channels. Now sports fans are resegmenting into smaller and smaller markets. Connecting with these rapidly changing markets requires more interaction, more relationship-building, and, in general, a more fan-centered approach. The resources needed to connect with fans combined with fragmentation make it impractical for most sports brands to be everything to everyone. The sheer economics of turning a profit means that sports brands have to prioritize segments and, in some cases, end relationships with other market segments.

Even when there seems to be a consensus on how to get the most revenue from the most likely sources, the decision to move ahead can be overruled by other factors. It isn't always practical or possible for sports decision makers to turn away fans who want to pay money to watch their team play or who are taxpayers in the community that constitutes their home base. It is conventional wisdom that more dollars should be spent on the profitable markets and that markets with little potential should be abandoned. But segmentation in sports often presents a dilemma that other industries do not typically face. Inherent in many sports brands is the democratic ideal that everyone should be able to participate, go to the games, and share in the home team's fortunes and failures. The problem is that, while it is essential to make a profit, much of a sports brand's ability to function in the community is based on the goodwill and civic obligations required of the sport.

This doesn't mean that efforts to focus on avid or wealthier fans aren't important or can't be successful, but that in doing so the sports brand always runs the risk of alienating significant portions of the community. The political, social, and cultural responsibilities of sports make it difficult to ignore segments for profit reasons when a wide-based constituency is necessary to assure community acceptance. The majority of sports brands are place-connected and place-bound, whether they're the Boston Red Sox, South Dakota State Jackrabbits, or Chicago's Windy City Rollers. These connections enable the sports team to function in the home marketplace, and state legislatures, city councils, or regional districts can usually find ways to underfund, slow traffic, or withdraw police support. The effective sports brand will be strategic in making sure that, in serving target markets, the relationship between sports, place, and community is a priority.

Driver Six: Sports and Fan Relationships Are Ever-Changing

The danger of trying to compete in the volatile sports marketplace is always complacency. A successful sports brand can become overly satisfied with its position in the market and be wary of disrupting a successful enterprise. Lonn Trost, chief operating officer of the New York Yankees, one of the most valuable sports brands in the world, admitted, "We're always worrying. And we try to monitor and re-establish the brand and what it means. We really watch what the fans see. . . . You're never too old to remember the last time something negative happened, and then, the brand can dissipate like that."[8] Trost's comments will surprise no one who has been working in the sports business.

Fans will continue to be courted by other entertainment activities, restricted by time commitments to their families and occupations, and saturated by communication technologies. It is likely that changes in the marketplace will only intensify at an ever-quickening pace as technology proliferates and fans are under increasing pressure to find the resources and time to commit to anything. The term "moving target" describes the sports brand–fan relationship.

Implication *Transformation is an ongoing process.*
If the sports brand is not adaptable, it won't survive in the market. At the core of this book is the premise that sports brands must be willing and able to transform—not just once, but as a continual response to changing market expectations and competition. The popular sports brands today are by no means guaranteed a successful future. The culture evolves, media change, and new generations bond to different sports, all making the marketplace potentially volatile. Once-stellar and mainstream sports such as boxing and horse racing

declined, and formerly wildly popular sports such as indoor cycling have virtually disappeared. The once great Southwest Conference (SWC) has evaporated, and the hot, urban athletic jackets of Starter faded. There was also a time when Bo Jackson and Gabriella Reece could seemingly sell just about anything. Today, the most popular sports such as NASCAR, poker, and the NFL also are not immune to the forces of competition. Even sports superstars such as Maria Sharapova and Tiger Woods and iconic teams such as AC Milan and the New Zealand All Blacks may very well end up in decline depending on how well they handle the future. In this industry, nothing is fixed except change.

The controlling factor driving future transformation can be summarized in one word—*anticipation*. Effective sports brands won't just transform only when crisis has just about shut down the business. They will anticipate and respond before their competitors to the cultural, economic, and technological shifts in the marketplace. Whether the challenges come from competing entertainments, a breakthrough in technology, or global invasion of a traditional market, successful sports brands will always see themselves in transition.

CONCLUSION

The most Elusive Fans are just now being born. Millions of children and their parents will be making decisions about what sports to play, watch, and enjoy for decades to come. Some parents will hand their love of a sport down to their children, and the sport will remain in the family for another generation. Other children may be mentored by a sports specialist, embrace a sport not even discussed in this book, or choose other activities over sports. What we do know is the competition for fans of all ages will be unprecedented and communicating with them will require agile and market-driven sports brands. As each generation begins to stamp their identity on the culture, sports brands will always need to transform and find those connections that not only guarantee survival but intensify fan relationships. Sports decision makers must view their brands from this perspective and at the same time understand that any change must connect with the fan on the fan's terms. It is only through this lens that the Elusive Fan can be captured.

ENDNOTES

CHAPTER 1

1 "The Best-Paid Athletes," *Forbes*, June 24, 2004, www.forbes.com/2004/06/23/04athletesland.html, viewed September 6, 2005.

2 Erica Bulman, "From Backroom Operation to Billion-Dollar Industry, FIFA Comes a Long Way in 100 Years," *Associated Press Worldstream*, May 20, 2004 (Lexis Nexis).

3 Kurt Badenhausen, Jack Gage, Michael K. Ozanian, Maya Roney, and Jamie Sundheim, "The Business of Football," *Forbes*, September 1, 2005, www.forbes.com/2005/09/01/sports-football-gambling-cz_05nfland.html, viewed November 4, 2005.

4 Michael K. Ozanian, ed., "The Business of Baseball," *Forbes*, April 7, 2005, www.forbes.com/2005/04/06/05mlbland.html, viewed August 29, 2005.

5 Michael K. Ozanian, ed., "The Business of Soccer," *Forbes*, April 1, 2005, www.forbes.com/2005/03/30/05soccerland.html, viewed August 29, 2005.

6 "ARU Negotiates Removing World Cup Profit Cap with IRB," *Agence France Presse*, April 16, 2003 (Lexis Nexis).

7 Monte Burke, "X-treme Economics," *Forbes*, February 9, 2004, www.forbes.com/business/global/2004/0209/058.html, viewed November 4, 2004.

8   "Sports Licensing White Paper," SGMA International, 2005 edition.

9   "The State of the Industry 2005," SGMA International, 2005 edition.

10 Gene Menez, "The $20 Million Stadium Boom," *Sports Illustrated,* May 16, 2005, vol. 102, iss. 20, p. 68.

11 Ellen Gamerman, "Rah, Rah, EKG! Teams Fight Injuries Pro-Style," *Wall Street Journal*, November 19, 2005, p. 3.

12 Karlyn Barker, "NFL Tries a Big Play for Fans on the Mall," *Washington Post*, August 31, 2003, p. C1.

13 "Out of the Gates: NTRA Approves '04 Budget," *Sports Business Daily*, March 3, 2004, www.sportsbusinessdaily.com/index.cfm?fuseaction=article.main&articleId=832 23&keyword=Gates,%20NTRA, viewed September 29, 2005.

14 Shannon Mortland, "Cavs Ramp It Up," *Crain's Cleveland Business*, June 30, 2003, p. 3.

15 Adam Kress, "New Promos Aim to Boost D-backs' Sagging Attendance," *The Business Journal of Phoenix*, May 9 2005, phoenix.bizjournals.com/phoenix/stories/2005/05/09/story7.html?page=3, viewed February 2, 2006.

16 Clint Hale and Jennifer Bellis, "City Officials Still Bullish on Alamodome for MLS," *San Antonio Express-News*, June 16, 2004, p. 1C.

17 "NCAA Study: Expenses Outweigh Revenue in Most Division I-A Conferences," *Associated Press*, April 16, 2004 (Lexis Nexis).

18 The average costs are determined by the Fan Cost Index, a survey produced by Team Marketing Report. The average costs for MLB and the NFL are for the 2005 season, the NBA is for the 2004-2005 season, and the NHL is for the 2005–2006 season. See www.teammarketing.com/fci.cfm for past and current surveys and information on methodology.

19 "Different Leisure Activities' Popularity Rise and Fall, but Reading, TV Watching, and Family Time Still Top the List of Favorites," *The Harris Poll* #97, December 8, 2004, www.harrisinteractive.com/harris_poll/index.asp?PID=526, viewed October 17, 2005. The hours cited in this poll are the median number of hours Americans spent on leisure in 1973 and 2004.

20 Mark Yost, "A Detour Off Nascar's Fast Track," *Wall Street Journal*, September 28, 2004, p. D10.

21 "Superstudy of Sports Participation," SGMA International, 2005 edition.

22 Douglas Brown, "With Action Sports, It's a Whole New Ballgame for Fathers, Sons," *Chicago Tribune*, July 7, 2004, p. 1.

23 "Forbes Magazine Says NHL Didn't Lose Nearly as Much as Stated the Last Two Years," *Associated Press Worldstream*, November 12, 2004 (Lexis Nexis).

24 "Superstudy of Sports Participation," SGMA International, 2005 edition.

25 Bruce Weber, "Splat! Splat! It's Paintball, on the Rise," *New York Times*, November 16, 2004, p. A16.

26 "Recreation Market Report," SGMA International, 2005 edition.

27 Chris McNamara, "A Mission Possible: Paintball Warfare," *Chicago Tribune*, November 3, 2005, p. 9B.

28 A reaction to more sophisticated technological innovations can be seen in the rise of minor league baseball. The inexpensive parking and game tickets and low-tech format all trigger nostalgia for simpler times. Minor league baseball drew 40 million fans in 2004. See Alan Schwarz, "Not Just Peanuts," *Newsweek*, May 9, 2005, p. 36.

29 James B. Twitchell, *Living It Up: America's Love Affair with Luxury* (New York: Simon and Schuster, 2002).

30 Rhonda L. Rundle, "Hospitals: 'We Hope You Enjoy Your Stay,'" *Wall Street Journal*, November 22, 2004, p. R5.

31 Nicholas Negroponte, *Being Digital* (New York: Knopff, 1995).

32 For television viewing audience see Jim Jenkins, "Stat Corner: Women and the NFL," *Sacramento Bee*, October 29, 2004, p. C9; for attendance data see "NFL Sets Another Attendance Record," *Associated Press*, January 5, 2005 (Lexis Nexis).

33 "Highlights from Sports Media & Technology Conference," *Sports Business Daily*, November 15, 2005, www.sportsbusinessdaily.com/index.cfm?fuseaction=article. main&articleId=98429, viewed November 17, 2005.

34 Laura M. Holson, "Can Hollywood Evade the Death Eaters?" *New York Times*, November 6, 2005, p. 1.

35 Robert Putnam, *Bowling Alone: The Collapse and Revival of American Community* (New York: Simon and Schuster, 2001).

36 Ibid.

37 "NSGA Select Sport Participation Since '90: Inline Leaps," *Sports Business Daily*, July 25, 2001, www.sportsbusinessdaily.com/index.cfm?fuseaction=article. main&articleId=57716&keyword=nsga%20select%20sport%20participation, viewed October 18, 2005.

38 Alvin Rosenfeld, "Fun Is Gone, Kids Now Must Play Games," *Chicago Tribune*, February 8, 2004, p. 3.

39 Charles Fishman, "The Smorgasbord Generation," *American Demographics*, May 1999, p. 54.

40 Ibid.

41 Bob Condor, "No Joy in Sportsville," *Seattle Post-Intelligencer*, September 30, 2004, p. C1.

42 Emilie Le Beau, "Winning Isn't Everything," *Chicago Tribune*, October 14, 2003, p. 10.

43 "American Time Use Survey Summary," www.bls.gov/news.release/atus.nr0.htm, viewed October 18, 2005.

44 Michael K. Ozanian, ed., "The Business of Soccer," *Forbes*, April 1, 2005, www.forbes.com/2005/03/30/05soccerland.html, viewed August 29, 2005.

45 Denis Campbell, "Will the Glazers Lose Their Shirts?" *Observer*, May 15, 2005, p. 9.

46 Michael K. Ozanian, ed., "The Business of Soccer," *Forbes*, April 1, 2005, www.forbes.com/2005/03/30/05soccerland.html, viewed August 29, 2005.

47 "Football's New World Order," *Observer Sports Magazine*, June 6, 2004, p. 53.

48 www.manutd.com/mumobile, viewed August 29, 2005.

49 "Man Utd Launches First Fantasy Football Game," *New Media Age*, July 21, 2005, p. 5.

50 Alan Cowell, "A Horse, a Soccer Club, and the Tampa Bay Bucs," *New York Times*, February 28, 2004, p. C1.

51 Benjamin Morgan, "Manchester United Fires Up Marketing Machine in China," *Agence France Presse*, April 21, 2004 (Lexis Nexis).

52 Austin Murphy, *The Sweet Season: A Sportswriter Rediscovers Football, Family, and a Bit of Faith at Minnesota's St. John's University* (New York: Perennial Currents, 2002).

CHAPTER 2

1 William Nack, "The Long Count," *Sports Illustrated,* September 22, 1997, sportsillustrated.cnn.com/magazine/features/si50/states/colorado/flashback/, viewed September 25, 2005. The actual attendance has been debated with some accounts as low as 104,000.

2 "The TV Sports Report," *Media Insights*, April 2005. This is a special report on the television sports industry published by Magna Global USA.

3 Teddy Greenstein, "Ratings Off, Ebersol Sees Upside," *Chicago Tribune*, February 21, 2006, p. 4.

4 www.baseball-almanac.com/prz_qrr.shtml, viewed December 11, 2004.

5 Christopher H. Sterling and John Michael Kittross, *Stay Tuned: A History of American Broadcasting*, 3d ed. (Mahwah, New Jersey: Lawrence Erlbaum Associates, 2002), p. 864.

6 Mary Ann Watson, *Defining Visions: Television and the American Experience Since 1945* (Belmont, California: Wadsworth Group), p. 9. The 60 percent figure is an approximation of total sports programming in 1947.

7 Brian Wise, "The Music of Spheres," *New York Times*, September 11, 2005, p. 1.

8 "Broadcasting and Entertainment," www.collegejournal.com/researchindustries/researchindustries/entertainment-v.html, viewed October 31, 2005.

9 Correspondence with Artie Bulgrin, senior vice president, Research & Sales Development, ESPN, June 29, 2005.

10 Jim Dent, *The Undefeated: The Oklahoma Sooners and the Greatest Winning Streak in College Football* (New York: Thomas Dunne Books, 2001).

11 Murray Sperber, *Shake Down the Thunder: The Creation of Notre Dame Football* (Bloomington: Indiana University Press, 2002).

12 Bernard Wysocki Jr., "It's a Living: For a Pro Sports Psychologist, Life Is a Nonstop Consultation," *Wall Street Journal,* September 20, 2005, p. B1.

13 www.pbfn.org/ot-magazine.asp, viewed September 20, 2005.

14 "Top Soccer Clubs Show Interest in 9-Year-Old," *Chicago Tribune*, January 28, 2005, p. 2.

15 Stefan Fatsis, "The Battle for the NFL's Future," *Wall Street Journal*, August 29, 2005, p. R1.

CHAPTER 3

1 Daniel L. Wann, Merrill J. Melnick, Gordon W. Russell, and Dale G. Pease, *Sport Fans: The Psychology and Social Impact of Spectators* (New York: Routledge, 2001), pp. 28–50.

2 Hilary Cassidy, "What 'Drives' Their Obsession?" *Brandweek*, April 4, 2005, vol. 46, iss. 24, p. 30. See also www.gsdm.com.

3 Ibid.

4 Robert Passikoff, "N.Y. Yankees Aside, Winning Isn't Only Key to Fan Loyalty," *Brandweek*, November 6, 2000, vol. 41, iss. 43, p. 32.

5 Sarah Ellison, "P&G Chief's Turnaround Recipe: Find Out What Women Want," *Wall Street Journal*, June 1, 2005, p. A1.

6 Viv Bernstein, "For Nascar, No Gamble in Dealing with Lottery," *New York Times*, August 21, 2005, p. 8.

7 Jon Swartz and Michelle Kessler, "Online Bettors Furiously Ante Up for March Madness," *USA Today*, March 18, 2005, p. 1B.

8 During the 2006 season only 18 teams competed. The New Orleans VooDoo suspended operations due to Hurricane Katrina.

9 Joseph Pereira, "Arena Football Finds Its Footing after Some Fumbles," *Wall Street Journal*, June 10, 2005, p. A1.

10 "Electronic Arts Will Produce an Arena Football League," *Brandweek*, January 17, 2005, vol. 46, iss. 3, p. 10.

11 Emily Lambert, "Play for Keeps," *Forbes*, June 6, 2005, vol. 175, iss. 12, p. 158.

12 "AFL 101: Fans' Bill of Rights," www.arenafootball.com/ViewArticle.dbml? DB_OEM_ID=3500&KEY=&ATCLID=99182, viewed October 19, 2005.

13 Pereira.

14 Seth Schiesel, "Watching Titans Battle on Screen and Keys," *New York Times*, September 12, 2005, p. E1.

15 Stephen Ohlemacher, "No Sweat for U.S. Sports Fan," *Chicago Tribune*, December 21, 2005, p. 11.

16 Lee Jenkins, "Doubles' Jeopardy Is Focus of Lawsuit," *New York Times*, September 3, 2005, p. D2.

17 Stefan Fatsis and Jon Weinbach, "Front-Office Fireworks," *Wall Street Journal*, November 7, 2005, p. B1.

18 Christie Cowles, "MLB Pitch, Hit & Run Crowns Champions," *MLB.com*, July 12, 2005, mlb.mlb.com/NASApp/mlb/news/article.jsp?ymd=20050712&content_id=1127662&vkey=news_mlb&fext=.jsp&c_id=mlb, viewed August 23, 2005.

19 Ibid.

20 Christie Cowles, "Pitch, Hit & Run Visits Spring Camp," *MLB.com*, March 1, 2005, mlb.mlb.com/NASApp/mlb/news/article.jsp?ymd=20050301&content_id=953866&vkey=spt2005news&fext=.jsp&c_id=mlb, viewed August 23, 2005.

21 The Fan Involvement Ladder was adapted from Rein, Kotler, Hamlin, and Stoller, *High Visibility*, 3d ed. (New York: McGraw-Hill, 2006), pp. 94–104.

22 Ross Forman, "Autographs, Cards Draw 40,000 Collectors," *USA Today*, July 21, 2004, p. 3C.

23 Michael Kahn, "Sneakerheads Show Sole Devotion to Footwear," *Reuters*, September 28, 2004, www.signonsandiego.com/news/features/20040928-0500-life-sneakers.html, viewed October 20, 2005.

24 Matt Krupnick, "Bonds' 700th Home Run Ball Sells for $804,129 at Auction," *Contra Costa Times*, October 28, 2004 (Lexis Nexis).

25 eBay auction price, January 24, 2005.

26 www.go-star.com/antiquing/hwagner2.htm, viewed January 24, 2005.

27 Andrew Herrmann, "In World of Collectibles, Baseball's in a League of Its Own," *Chicago Sun-Times*, December 11, 2005, p. 11A.

28 Gary Parrish, "'Blue Crew' Aiming to Bring Spirit to U of M Games," *The Commercial Appeal*, October 21, 2005, p. D1.

29 Rochelle Steinhaus, "Tennis No Stranger to Stalkers," *Court TV*, March 28, 2001, www.courttv.com/archive/trials/hingis/tennis.html, viewed November 5, 2005.

CHAPTER 4

1 Jon Yates, "Sox Fantasies for Sale," *Chicago Tribune*, July 31, 2005, p. 1.

2 Charles Odum, "Rookies Helping Braves End Seven-year Decline in Attendance," *Associated Press State & Local Wire*, August 15, 2005 (Lexis Nexis).

3 "Denver Broncos," www.profootballhof.com/history/team.jsp?franchise_id=10, viewed February 24, 2006.

4 Jacob A. Riis, *How the Other Half Lives: Studies Among the Tenements of New York* (New York: Charles Scribner's Sons, 1890).

5 Jeffrey Stanton, "Coney Island—Nickel Empire (1920s–1930s)," naid.sppsr.ucla.edu/coneyisland/articles/nickelempire.htm, 1997, viewed September 27, 2005.

6 Notre Dame was 18th in the 2006 *U.S. News & World Report* annual ranking of national universities. See www.usnews.com/usnews/edu/college/rankings/brief/natudoc/tier1/t1natudoc_brief.php, viewed November 15, 2005.

7 Teddy Greenstein, "The Weis Way: Be It Play-calling, Recruiting, Uniforms or the Media Guido, 'Hands-on CEO' in Total Command of Notre Dame Football," *Chicago Tribune*, November 4, 2005, p. 1.

8 From Aristotle's Rhetoric translated by W. Rhys Roberts in Patricia Bizzell and Bruce Herzberg, *The Rhetorical Tradition: Readings from Classical Times to the Present*, 2d ed. (Boston: Bedford/St. Martin's, 2001), p. 181.

9 Ibid.

10 From Cicero's Book Two of *De Orator* translated by E. W. Sutton and H. Racham in Patricia Bizzell and Bruce Herzberg, *The Rhetorical Tradition: Readings from Classical Times to the Present*, 2d ed. (Boston: Bedford/St. Martin's, 2001), p. 328.

11 For more information on the Johnson and Jeffries fight and the life of Jack Johnson, see Ken Burns's film *Unforgivable Blackness: The Rise and Fall of Jack Johnson* (2005).

12 Stew Thornley, "Pay Days," stewthornley.net/millers_paydays.html, viewed January 18, 2005.

13 Ibid.

14 Matt Richtel, "Private Sector; Applying Science to the Casino," *New York Times*, November 3, 2002, p. 2.

15 Thomas Hoffman, "Harrah's Bets on Loyalty Program in Caesars Deal," *Computerworld*, June 27, 2005, vol. 39, iss. 26, p. 10.

16 Jon Van, "How the Uncanny Gets into Marketing," *Chicago Tribune*, July 24, 2005, p. 1.

17 Correspondence with Artie Bulgrin, senior vice president, Research & Sales Development, ESPN, June 29, 2005.

18 Ibid.

19 "The First Intercollegiate Game," www.scarletknights.com/football/history/first_game.htm, viewed January 20, 2005.

20 Michael Hiestand, "Red Sox Nation Buys Big into Team's Success," *USA Today*, January 20, 2005, p. 14C.

21 Michael Hiestand and Jeff Goodman, "Trophy Takes Emotional Tour of Mass. Towns," *USA Today*, January 20, 2005, p. 14C.

22 Clint Swett, "Games that Click: Sports Video Gaming Has Become a $1.2 Billion-a-Year Business that Thrives on Loyal Fans and Close Ties to Professional Leagues," *Sacramento Bee*, April 2, 2005, p. D1.

23 Gemma Tarlach, "Wrestling Fans Get to Flex Their Muscles," *Milwaukee Journal Sentinel*, September 28, 2004, p. 10.

24 "First-Ever WWE Fantasy Game to Be Offered by World Wrestling Entertainment," *Business Wire*, September 14, 2004 (Lexis Nexis).

25 Nesha Starcevic, "Report: Players Could Have Been Involved in German Soccer Scandal," *Associated Press*, January 28, 2005 (Lexis Nexis).

26 Kristie Rieken, "NCAA Bans Baylor Men's Basketball Team from Nonconference Play," *Associated Press*, June 24, 2005 (Lexis Nexis).

27 Lorne Manly, "Redskins Try to Become the Messenger," *New York Times*, January 7, 2006, p. D1.

28 "Super Bowl Draws Fewer Viewers," *CNN.com*, February 7, 2005, www.cnn.com/2005/SHOWBIZ/TV/02/07/media.superbowl.reut/, viewed February 21, 2005.

29 Allan Kreda, "Fox Charges Record $2.4 Million US for 30-Second Super Bowl Advertisements," *Vancouver Sun*, December 30, 2004, p. D4.

30 Jim Armstrong, "Japanese Fans Celebrate Suzuki's Historic Hit," *Associated Press*, October 2, 2004 (Lexis Nexis).

31 Ian Rowley, "Japanese Baseball: Old and Slow," *BusinessWeek*, September 27, 2004, p. 26.

32 Brian Bremmer, "In Japan, Baseball's Chance to Homer," *BusinessWeek Online*, June 7, 2005 (Lexis Nexis).

33 Norimitsu Onishi, "Forget the Fans: It's Bean Ball in the Boardrooms," *New York Times*, August 25, 2004, p. A4.

34 "Struggling Japanese Baseball Turns to Internet Whiz Kid for Revival," *Agence France Presse*, November 2, 2004 (Lexis Nexis).

35 Jim Allen, "Japanese Players Get On Board," *The Daily Yomiuri*, September 17, 2005, p. 24.

CHAPTER 5

1 The stages of transformation were adapted from Rein, Kotler, Hamlin, and Stoller, *High Visibility*, 3d ed. (New York: McGraw-Hill, 2006), chapter 8.

2 Jeff Benedict, *Out of Bounds: Inside the NBA's Culture of Rape, Violence, and Crime* (New York: HarperCollins, 2004).

3 Melody Gutierrez and Clint Swett, "Hunting for Title, Fans," *Sacramento Bee*, September 17, 2005, p. A1.

4 Robert Johnson, "Courting the Lazy and the Klutzy," *New York Times*, January 23, 2005, p. 7.

5 Paul Gutierrez, "Angels Just Hate to Say Goodbye," *Los Angeles Times*, September 26, 2005, p. D1.

6 Adrian Dater, "The Lane Rangers Revitalized: PBA Tour Takes Wing and Rides Again," *Denver Post*, December 1, 2004, p. D-01.

7 Liz Clarke, "NASCAR Changes Under Scrutiny," *Washington Post*, January 21, 2004, p. D1.

8 Emma Daly, "Soccer Team of Century Enters Age of Marketing," *New York Times*, August 15, 2003, p. W1. Real Madrid turned a profit for the first time in 40 years in 2004.

9 Luis Arroyave, "Expect Storied Year," *Chicago Tribune*, January 4, 2006, p. 2.

10 Daly.

11 William Kates, "Schayes Remembers Day 50 Years Ago When Shot Clock Was Born," *Associated Press*, August 9, 2004, sfgate.com/cgi-bin/article.cgi?f=/news/archive/2004/08/09/sports1524EDT0338.DTL, viewed July 26, 2005.

12 Jeff Zrebiec, "'Prime Time' Turns Down the Volume," *Baltimore Sun*, September 5, 2004, p. 1D.

13 Correspondence with NLL director of marketing Matt Miller, August 26, 2005.

14 Lacy J. Banks, "Lougherys Launch Indoor Lacrosse Team," *Chicago Sun-Times*, February 17, 2006, p. 118.

15 www.singaporebadminton.org.sg/AbtUs.asp, viewed July 28, 2005.

16 texastech.collegesports.com/trads/text-mission.html, viewed July 28, 2005.

17 www.bowlingmembership.com/hsbusa/aboutus.asp, viewed July 28, 2005.

18 Louis Effrat, "Pro Football's Defining Moment," www.nytimes.com/packages/html/sports/year_in_sports/12.28.html, December 28, 1958, viewed October 20, 2005.

19 Sarah Hollander, "Force of Gravity Games Felt Today," *Plain Dealer*, June 2, 2005, p. B3.

20 Genaro C. Armas, "Dialed-down Gravity Games Heads to Sports' Mecca in Rural Pa.," *Associated Press*, June 24, 2005 (Lexis Nexis).

21 "Gary Young Grabs Gold in Bike Park Competition at OLN's 2005 Gravity Games, Presented by Saturn," oln.dayport.com/nw/article/view/1025/?tf=OLNPressCenter_articles.tpl&UserDef=true, July 14, 2005, viewed January 11, 2006.

22 Clayton M. Christensen, Scott Cook, and Taddy Hall, "Marketing Malpractice: The Cause and the Cure," *Harvard Business Review*, December 2005, pp. 74–83.

23 Correspondence with Artie Bulgrin, senior vice president, Research & Sales Development, ESPN, June 29, 2005.

24 Sean Gallagher and Larry Barrett, "Case 093 Shoe Fits," *Baseline*, November 1, 2003, p. 44. Sales increased to $1.3 billion in 2002 from $560 million in 1997, which amounts to a 131 percent increase.

25 Robin Brownlee, "Team on the Run," *Edmonton Sun*, July 24, 2004, p. SP1.

26 Darcy Henton, "Beep Beep: Hockey Season in Edmonton Takes Off Without the NHL's Oilers," *Canadian Press Newswire*, October 16, 2004 (Lexis Nexis).

27 Robin Brownlee, "Beep, Beep! See Ya!; Road Runners Suspend Operations," *Edmonton Sun*, June 5, 2005, p. SP1.

28 Phone interview with Angie Sit, director, Marketing & Promotions, University of Oregon, September 2, 2005.

29 Henry C. Jackson, "Europe's Soccer Clubs Make Asia Pitch," *Wall Street Journal*, August 13, 2003, p. B5A.

30 Damon Hack, "PGA Points Race to Make the Rich Richer," *New York Times*, November 3, 2005, p. D6.

31 Richard Sandomir, "It's 'My NHL,' and Peter Puck Has Left the Building," *New York Times*, September 21, 2005, p. D6.

32 Carol Slezak, "Shock and Awe: NHL Doesn't Miss a Beat," *Chicago Sun-Times*, January 27, 2006, p. 121.

33 Judd Zulgad, "Wild Ratings Increase on Regional Networks," *Minneapolis Star Tribune*, December 16, 2005, p. 2C.

34 Tim Cleland, "Classes Not the Ruin of Hoosier Hysteria," *The Star Press*, www.thestarpress.com/articles/5/014526-4445-034.html, viewed October 26, 2005.

35 "IHSAA Partners with Comcast, Bright House Networks & Insight," www.ihsaa.org/media/2005-06/102505.Television.htm, October 25, 2005, viewed October 26, 2005.

36 Mark Hyman, "$10 Million a Year? No Thanks," *BusinessWeek*, May 5, 2003, p. 73.

37 Lawrence Donegan, "Money Men Poised to Pitch for a Slice of Wie's Talent," *The Guardian* (London), April 30, 2005, p. 20.

38 Bobby Verwey Jr. and James P. Herre, "My Shot; Michelle Wie Is a Great Player, But Does She Have the Heart of a True Champion?" *Sports Illustrated*, March 28, 2005, vol. 102, iss. 12, p. 34.

39 Damon Hack, "With Fanfare and Dollar Signs, Wie Becomes a Professional," *New York Times*, October 6, 2005, p D5.

40 "Musharraf Is Welcome," *The Hindu*, March 10, 2005, www.thehindu.com/2005/03/10/stories/2005031007930100.htm, viewed March 10, 2005.

41 John Shaw, "Kerry Packer, 68, Australia's Media Magnate," *New York Times*, December 27, 2005, p. A21.

42 Joanna Slater, "Cashing in on Cricket," *Far Eastern Economic Review*, March 6, 2003, vol. 166, iss. 9, p. 32.

43 "Cricket Puts Best Foot Forward," *Marketing*, July 14, 2004, p. 17.

44 Orrin E. Klapp, *Heroes, Villains, and Fools: Reflections of the American Character* (San Diego: Aegis, 1972).

45 Mike Lopresti, "Another Patriot Act: New England Dumps Eagles 24-21," *USA Today*, February 6, 2005, www.usatoday.com/sports/football/super/2005-02-06-patriots-eagles-game-story_x.htm?POE=NEWISVA, viewed October 20, 2005.

46 Ibid.

47 Ed Hinton, "So Good, So Young," *Chicago Tribune*, February 9, 2005, p. 2.

48 Richard Dyer, *Stars* (London: British Film Institute Educational Advisory Service, 1979), pp. 104–108.

49 Michael Schuman, "Louisville Slugger Museum, KY., A Smash Hit with Baseball Fans," *Boston Herald*, September 5, 2004, p. 48.

50 www.sluggermuseum.org/index.aspx, viewed February 12, 2005.

51 Denis Horgan, "Hey, Batter, Batter, Batter, Batter," *Hartford Courant*, October 31, 2004, p. F1.

52 "Biography of Famous Wrestler Gorgeous George Part 1," www.trivia-library.com/b/biography-of-famous-wrestler-gorgeous-george-part-1.htm, viewed January 8, 2006. This Web page was reprinted with permission from "The People's Almanac" by David Wallechinsky and Irving Wallace, copyright 1975-1981.

53 Gary Hook and David Leon Moore, "Skiing 'That Blows People's Minds' Takes Off," *USA Today*, February 9, 2005, p. 9C.

54 Chuck O'Donnell, "This Man Was Babe Ruth," *Football Digest*, December 2002, www.findarticles.com/p/articles/mi_m0FCL/is_4_32/ai_94123521, viewed February 25, 2006.

CHAPTER 6

1 Dan Baynes, "On the Warpath: History of the Haka," *Bloomberg*, October 25, 2003, www.rugbyheaven.smh.com.au/articles/2003/10/24/1066974312130.html, viewed October 21, 2005.

2 Paul Temporal, *Branding in Asia: The Creation, Development, and Management of Asian Brands for the Global Market* (Singapore: Wiley, 2000), excerpted from www.brandingasia.com/cases/case3.htm, viewed November 1, 2005.

3 Robin Rusch, "The World's Greatest Sports Brand?" *brandchannel.com*, March 19, 2001, www.brandchannel.com/features_effect.asp?pf_id=27, viewed March 3, 2005.

4 Ibid.

5 "DAPER Brand Focus Groups to Help Decide the Look of MIT Athletics," mitathletics.collegesports.com/genrel/120904aab.html, December 9, 2004, viewed March 14, 2005.

6　"USTA Open Series Announcement Transcript," www.usopenseries.com/news/full-story.sps?iNewsid=58614&itype=6679&icategoryid=553, April 20, 2004, viewed March 14, 2005.

7　See www.olsonzaltman.com/oza/zmet.html, viewed November 14, 2005.

8　David Kiley, "Shoot the Focus Group," *BusinessWeek*, November 14, 2005, p. 120.

9　"What Is the Best Logo?" www.sportsmarketingsurveys.com/vsite/vcontent/page/custom/0,8510,5045-145453-162669-28703-111279-custom-item,00.html, viewed November 1, 2005.

10　"Pro Sports 'Image Survey' Reveals Which Sports Have Best Image, Role Models," *PR Newswire US*, December 14, 2004 (Lexis Nexis).

11　Alex Brown, "Maybe Not Good Cricket, But Great Fun," *Sydney Morning Herald*, February 18, 2005, www.smh.com.au/articles/2005/02/17/1108609350349.html?oneclick=true#, viewed November 14, 2005.

12　Jerry Potter, "Rolling Out New Black Ball Lights Up Telephones at Nike," *USA Today*, February 8, 2005, p. 8C.

13　Margaret Talbot, "Why, Isn't He Just the Cutest Brand-Image Enhancer You've Ever Seen?" *New York Times Magazine*, September 21, 2003, p. 31.

14　www.dylanoliver.com/press.php, viewed February 17, 2005.

15　Kelly Cuculiansky, "At Age of 6, Louisville's Oliver Already Is 'Like a Pro,'" *The Courier Journal*, June 13, 2005, www.courier-journal.com/apps/pbcs.dll/article?AID=/20050613/SPORTS/50613001, viewed November 14, 2005.

16　See Oliver's Web site, www.dylanoliver.com.

17　Gina Chon, "VW's American Road Trip," *Wall Street Journal*, January 4, 2006, p. B1.

18　Bill McGuire, "Where the Cars Are the Stars," *AutoWeek*, October 10, 2005, p. 56.

19　www.americanlemans.com/schedule/2005_Schedule.aspx, viewed February 17, 2005.

20　Dave Caldwell, "European-Style Auto Racing Is Taking Hold in United States," *New York Times*, February 16, 2005, p. C17.

21　1836 was the leading vote-getter, receiving about 20 percent of the 11,000 entries. See Bernardo Fallas, "Team Will 86 Its 1836 Name," *Houston Chronicle*, February 15, 2006 (Lexis Nexis).

22　Bernardo Fallas, "Soccer Faithful Get in the Spirit of 1836," *Houston Chronicle*, January 26, 2006 (Lexis Nexis).

23　Simon Romero, "What's in a Brand Name? Houston Just Found Out," *New York Times*, January 27, 2006, p. C4.

24　Bernardo Fallas, "Goodbye 1836, Hello Dynamo," *Houston Chronicle*, March 7, 2006 (Lexis Nexis).

25　Ken Denlinger, "In Name Game, Fans Prefer None of Above," *Washington Post*, February 12, 1996, p. A1.

26 Josh Barr, "Fans Turn Noses up on Proposed Names," *Washington Post*, February 5, 1996, p. D4.

27 Jerrold Kessel, "On the Couch/White as Brown Remains a Delight," *haaretz.com*, February 18, 2005, www.haaretz.com/hasen/spages/541847.html, viewed February 19, 2005.

28 "Jimmy Gets Saucy with Name Change," *BBC*, February 8, 2005, news.bbc.co.uk/sport1/hi/funny_old_game/4245973.stm, viewed February 18, 2005.

29 Tom Silverstein, "Fans Love 'He Hate Me,'" *Milwaukee Journal Sentinel*, January 30, 2004, www.jsonline.com/packer/prev/jan04/203873.asp, viewed November 8, 2005.

30 "Carolina Panthers' Rod 'He Hate Me' Smart Expresses His 'Love' for Charlotte and Alltel," *Business Wire*, September 2, 2005 (Lexis Nexis).

31 Correspondence with Tara Preston, University of Michigan, Athletic Media Relations, August 29, 2005.

32 Correspondence with Steve McClain, University of Florida Sports Information, August 29, 2005.

33 "One-Size-Fits-All Dress Code Draws Some Divergent Views," *ESPN.com*, October 19, 2005, sports.espn.go.com/nba/news/story?id=2197012, viewed October 25, 2005.

34 Deborah L. Vence, "Serves Them Right," *Marketing News*, February 1, 2005, p. 13.

35 Simon Hattenstone, "Football: Happy Birthday David—But Where Did It All Go Wrong," *The Guardian* (London), May 2, 2005, p. 16.

36 Matthew Herek, "Bills, Seahawks to Feature New Looks in '02," *Sporting Goods Business*, July 2002, vol. 35, iss. 7, p. 20.

37 "Unveiled: The New Logo of the Iraqi Olympic Team," www.iraqcoalition.org/pressreleases/20040403_olympic.html, April 2, 2004, viewed March 14, 2005.

38 "Traveler, USC's Mascot," usctrojans.collegesports.com/trads/usc-m-fb-mas.html, viewed August 29, 2005.

39 Sarah Lyall, "In London, a Very British Bid for the 2012 Games," *New York Times*, February 17, 2005, p. D1.

40 Cris Prystay and David Pringle, "London Wins Olympic Bid with Emotional Appeal," *Wall Street Journal*, July 7, 2005, p. A2.

41 "Meet Coach Paterno," www.psu.edu/sports/football/Paterno/paternobio.html, viewed February 2, 2005.

42 "History of IDBF," www.dodge-ball.com/site/, viewed February 25, 2005.

43 Paul Hayward, "Racket Technology Threatens Tennis," *Daily Telegraph*, July 5, 2003 (Lexis Nexis).

44 Roger Dobson and Rachel Dobson, "Slow Balls Please," *Sunday Times* (London), June 22, 2003, p. 7.

45 "ITTF Happy at Results of Rules Changes," *Xinhua General News Service*, May 25, 2003 (Lexis Nexis).

46 Owen Slot, "Phelps the Fallen Idol Proves that Sorry Need Not Be the Hardest Word," *London Times*, November 13, 2004, p. 116.

47 Daniel de Vise, "Dazzled Fans Forgiving of Phelps after Md. Swimmer's DUI Arrest," *Washington Post*, November 14, 2005, p. C8.

48 Gady A. Epstein, "Athletes' Gold Is Beijing's," *Baltimore Sun*, March 2, 2005 www.baltimoresun.com/news/nationworld/bal-te.diver02mar02,1,1699595.story, viewed March 2, 2005.

49 "China to Pardon Shunned Athletes for Games," *China Daily*, February 17, 2006, www.chinadaily.com.cn/english/doc/2006-02/17/content_521435.htm, viewed February 26, 2006.

50 Jon Weinbach, "When Players Don't Pay," *Wall Street Journal*, June 17, 2005, p. W1.

51 Bob Foltman, "Hawks Reach Out to Reclaim Fans," *Chicago Tribune*, July 26, 2005, p. 3.

CHAPTER 7

1 www.hartfordwolfpack.com/community.php, viewed March 3, 2006.

2 Bruce Berlet, "With NHL Out, Wolf Pack Try to Step In," *Hartford Courant*, February 27, 2005 (Lexis Nexis).

3 John Reinan, "Wolves Hope to Spur Ticket Sales with New Marketing Campaign," *Minneapolis Star Tribune*, October 27, 2003, p. 7D.

4 Ann Meyer, "Marketing Latest Field to Get Ideas, Attention from Blogs," *Chicago Tribune*, July 25, 2005, p. 3.

5 www.nba.com/blog/, viewed August 14, 2005.

6 Theresa Howard, "Investors Can Capitalize When Companies Score Sports Sponsorships," *USA Today*, October 14, 2005, p. 5B.

7 Michael McCarthy, "Allstate Seeks Net Game with New Ads," *USA Today*, August 29, 2005, www.usatoday.com/sports/college/football/2005-08-29-allstate-ads_x.htm? POE=SPOISVA, viewed August 31, 2005.

8 William McCall, "Nike 4Q Profit Growth Beats Expectations," *Associated Press Online*, June 27, 2005 (Lexis Nexis).

9 Michael Barbaro, "Cricket Anyone? Sneaker Makers on Fresh Turf," *New York Times*, January 28, 2006, p. B1.

10 Dean Foust, "Greg Norman: All Business," *BusinessWeek*, November 14, 2005, p. 124.

11 Dramatic reality was adapted from Rein, Kotler, Hamlin, and Stoller, *High Visibility*, 3d ed. (New York: McGraw-Hill, 2006), pp. 123–131.

12 Michael Hirsley, "Solace on the Mat," *Chicago Tribune*, March 27, 2005, p. 8.

13 The major sports story lines were adapted from *High Visibility*, 3d ed. pp. 128–130.

14 Aristotle's Rhetoric translated by W. Rhys Roberts in Patricia Bizzell and Bruce Herzberg, *The Rhetorical Tradition* (2nd ed.), (Boston: Bedford/St. Martin's, 2001).

15 Tony Schwartz, *The Responsive Chord* (Garden City, NY: Anchor Press, 1973), p. 26.

16 Schwartz, p. 93.

17 Claus Ebster and Michael Kirk-Smith, "The Effect of the Human Pheromone Androstenol on Product Evaluation," *Psychology & Marketing*, September 2005, vol. 22, iss. 9, pp. 739–749.

18 Alain d'Astous and Jonathan Deschenes, "Consuming in One's Mind: An Exploration," *Psychology & Marketing*, January 2005, vol. 22, iss. 1, pp. 1–30.

19 Hilary Cassidy, "What 'Drives' Their Obsession," *Brandweek*, April 4, 2005, vol. 46, iss. 14, pp. 30–34.

20 Ron Lemasters Jr., "Feeding the Beast," *NASCAR.com*, January 12, 2005, www.nascar.com/2005/news/business/01/12/media.beast/, viewed August 13, 2005.

21 www.ballparksofbaseball.com/nl/SBCPark.htm, viewed August 13, 2005.

22 www.packers.com/stockholders/, viewed August 30, 2005.

23 B. Joseph Pine II and James H. Gilmore, *The Experience Economy: Work Is Theatre & Every Business a Stage* (Boston: Harvard Business School Press, 1999).

24 Joe Pine and James Gilmore, "Brand Strategy Briefing: Experience Is Marketing," *Brand Strategy*, November 8, 2004, p. 50.

25 Qiu Haixu, "In China, Sports Take Flight," *Wall Street Journal*, August 11, 2005, p. B3.

26 Suzanne Vranica, "Buzz Marketers Score Venture Dollars," *Wall Street Journal*, January 13, 2006, p. A11.

27 Amy Merrick, "Gap Deploys 'Viral' Online Promotion to Pump Up Sales," *Wall Street Journal*, August 10, 2005, p. B1.

28 Kortney Stringer, "On the Rebound, NBA Seeking a Lift," *Detroit Free Press*, June 10, 2005 (Lexis Nexis).

29 "Hook 'em Horns! University of Texas Runs Internet-Based Video Magazine Campaign Series to Promote Longhorns Football," *Market Wire*, August 2, 2005, press.arrivenet.com/tec/article.php/677057.html, viewed August 30, 2005.

30 Gavin O'Malley, "Texas U's Vmag Now a Weekly," *MediaPost Publications*, September 20, 2005, publications.mediapost.com/index.cfm?fuseaction=Articles.san &s=34223&Nid=15573&p=262728, viewed November 9, 2005.

31 "Wigan First Club to Team Up for Viral Meshcards," *Precision Marketing*, February 18, 2005, p. 3.

32 Ian O'Connor, "Giambi Swings and Misses with His Apology," *USA Today*, February 11, 2005, www.usatoday.com/sports/columnist/oconnor/2005-02-11-oconnor_x.htm, viewed October 25, 2005.

CHAPTER 8

1 Matt Lockhart, "An Up and Down Game," *Charleston Daily Mail*, June 25, 2004, p. P1C.

2 Kortney Stringer, "Going Off-Course," *Wall Street Journal*, April 18, 2005, p. R5.

3 www2.ncaa.org/sports/winter/gymnastics/mens/, viewed November 9, 2005.

4 "Olympic Sports Decline on Campus," *Seattle Times*, May 12, 2004, p. D3.

5 "WUSA Plans Summit as Revival Hopes Continue," *Associated Press*, May 13, 2004 (Lexis Nexis).

6 "World: Europe Olympics Bidding Shakeup," news.bbc.co.uk/1/hi/world/europe/262130.stm, January 25, 1999, viewed April 18, 2005.

7 John R. Wooden and Steve Jamison, *Wooden on Leadership* (New York: McGraw-Hill, 2005); Lou Holtz, *Winning Every Day: The Game Plan for Success* (New York: HarperBusiness, 1998); Joe Torre and Henry Dreher, *Joe Torre's Ground Rules for Winners: 12 Keys to Managing Team Players, Tough Bosses, Setbacks, and Success* (New York: Hyperion, 1999).

8 Jack Carey, "Big East Hopes New Members Help Bruised Football Image," *USA Today*, July 1, 2005, p. 11C; Rob Biertempfel, "Tranghese Has Stuck by the Big East," *Pittsburgh Tribune Review*, October 30, 2005 (Lexis Nexis).

9 Anthony Schoettle, "IRL Ratings Continuing Their Skid," *Indianapolis Business Journal*, November 1, 2004, vol. 25, no. 34, p. 3.

10 Tom Gage, "National Pastime Strikes Out with Black Athletes," *Detroit News*, April 10, 2005, www.detnews.com/2005/tigers/0504/10/A01B-145339.htm, viewed October 22, 2005.

11 Jeffrey M. Jones, "The Disappearing Black Baseball Fan," *Gallup Poll News Service*, July 15, 2003 (Lexis Nexis).

12 "Girl Sports Hit Their Stride," *USA Today*, April 18, 2005, p. 1.

13 Levon Sevunts, "Roll Out the Barrels: Hunters Aim to Halt the Sport's Decline," *The Gazette*, October 3, 2003, p. A9.

14 Bernard Lefkowitz, *Our Guys: The Glen Ridge Rape and the Secret Life of the Perfect Suburb* (New York: Vintage Books, 1998).

15 golobos.collegesports.com/facilities/nm-the-pit.html, viewed April 15, 2005.

16 Jeff Carlton, "The Tipping Point," *Albuquerque Tribune*, March 9, 2005, p. A1.

17 Jeff Carlton, "Attendance Lowest Ever," *Albuquerque Tribune*, November 17, 2004, p. B1.

18 Correspondence with Scott Dotson, associate athletic director, facilities, University of New Mexico, September 2, 2005.

19 Jeff Carlton, "Students Get Pit Section," *Albuquerque Tribune*, April 20, 2005, p. B1.

20 James U. McNeal, *Kids as Customers: A Handbook of Marketing to Children* (New York: Lexington Books, 1992).

21 Emilie Le Beau, "Winning Isn't Everything," *Chicago Tribune*, October 14, 2003, p. 10.

22 See the Maine Center for Sport and Coaching (www.sportsdonerightmaine.org/index.jsp); National Alliance for Youth Sports (www.nays.org); Positive Coaching Alliance (www.positivecoach.org).

23 Reed Albergotti, "Get Your Mind in the Gutter," *Wall Street Journal*, January 14–15, 2006, p. P6.

24 Ana Beatriz Cholo, "Hockey Moms Face Off for Fun of It," *Chicago Tribune*, January 19, 2006, p. 1.

25 Clint Swett, "Games that Click: Sports Video Gaming Has Become a $1.2 Billion-a-Year Business That Thrives on Loyal Fans and Close Ties to Professional Leagues," *Sacramento Bee*, April 2, 2005, p. D1.

26 Ronald Grover, "Trading the Bleachers for the Couch," *BusinessWeek*, August 22, 2005, p. 32.

27 See David Schrank and Tim Lomax, "The 2005 Urban Mobility Report," mobility.tamu.edu, May 2005, viewed January 23, 2006.

28 Ron Rapoport, "Few Saw It Coming, but Broncos the New Pick," *Chicago Sun Times*, January 18, 2006, p. 113.

29 David Paddon, "Five-year Contract Has Kangaroo Media Jumping for Joy," *The Gazette*, August 10, 2005, p. B1.

30 Seth Sutel, "CBS to Buy College Sports Network CSTV," *Associated Press State & Local Wire*, November 3, 2005 (Lexis Nexis).

31 Michael Hirsley, "Hawks Brass Angry, Sad," *Chicago Tribune*, February 17, 2005, p. 7.

32 Ron Sirak, "Martha and Hootie: Three Years Later," *Golf World*, April 7, 2005, www.golfdigest.com/majors/masters/index.ssf?/majors/masters/20050407sirak.html, viewed May 5, 2005.

33 "Martha in the Middle," *The Observer (London Guardian)*, April 6, 2003, observer.guardian.co.uk/osm/story/0,6903,928674,00.html, viewed May 5, 2005.

34 "Seventy-Six Sosa Bats Found to Be Clean," *ESPN.com*, June 5, 2003, espn.go.com/mlb/news/2003/0604/1563115.html, viewed May 5, 2005.

35 Ibid.

36 Comments by the Rev. Jerry Thorpe in "Community Reactions—10 Years Later," *Odessa American*, October 30, 1998, www.oaoa.com/specialsections/fridaylights/reactions.htm, viewed May 5, 2005.

37 Compiled by Katelin Trowbridge, "1990," *Odessa American*, December 23, 1999, www.oaoa.com/twentieth/1990.htm, viewed March 3, 2006.

38 Susan Serrano, "ECISD Academic Performance Rosier in 1998," *Odessa American*, October 30, 1999, www.oaoa.com/specialsections/fridaylights/academics.htm, viewed March 3, 2006.

39 Sharon Silke Carty, "Ford Uses Net to Get Customer Feedback," *Chicago Sun-Times*, April 11, 2005, p. 2A.

40 "ESPN's Coverage of NFL Draft Earns Record Nielsen Ratings," *Sports Business Daily*, April 27, 2005, www.sportsbusinessdaily.com/index.cfm?fuseaction=article. main&articleId=93496&keyword=nfl%20draft, viewed October 22, 2005.

41 L. A. Lorek, "NBA Marketers Are Scoring Big in China," *San Antonio Express-News*, June 18, 2005, p. 1C.

42 Jim Frederick, "The Beast Goes East," *Time Asia*, June 2, 2003, www.time.com/time/asia/2003/bob_sapp/story.html, viewed March 4, 2006.

43 Selena Roberts, "Boxing May Benefit from Unlikely Accomplices: Women," *New York Times*, April 10, 2005, p. 1.

44 "Most Classic Viewers Ever in 2006," *ESPN.com*, March 2, 2006, sports.espn.go.com/outdoors/bassmaster/classic/news/story?page=b_classic_ratings_release, viewed March 6, 2006.

CHAPTER 9

1   Rachel Blount, "The Hits Just Keep Coming for Moss," *Minneapolis Star Tribune*, May 8, 2005, p. 24C.

2   "National Rating for Kentucky Derby Down Slightly," *Associated Press*, May 12, 2005 (Lexis Nexis).

3   Allan Kreda, "NBC's Kentucky Derby Ratings Dip Slightly Amid Record Wagering," *Bloomberg*, May 8, 2005, www.bloomberg.com/apps/news?pid=10000103&sid=a84VFj1qaFow&refer=us#, viewed May 9, 2005.

4   Peter Kafka, "The Hot Shot," *Forbes*, July 4, 2005, www.forbes.com/free_forbes/2005/0704/116.html, viewed October 28, 2005.

5   Ibid.

6   Mark Cuban, "I Own Phil Jackson," www.blogmaverick.com, posted February 8, 2006, viewed March 4, 2006.

7   www.blogmaverick.com

8   Greg Boeck, "Vibrant Owners Shake Things Up in NBA," *USA Today*, January 18, 2005, p. 2C.

9   Bob Ryan, "Gathering Is Evidence Brennan Went out on Top," *Boston Globe*, April 2, 2005, p. F1.

10 Jill Lieber, "Happy on Air, on Court," *USA Today*, November 3, 2004, p. 1C.

11 Teddy Greenstein, "Coaching Not the End for Vermont's Class Act," *Chicago Tribune*, February 14, 2005, p. 1.

12 www.uvm.edu/~sportspr/mens_basketball/coaches/brennan.html, viewed August 12, 2005.

13 Lieber.

14 Ibid.

15 Matt Vautour, "The Coach Is Also a DJ," *Georgia Magazine*, March 2004, vol. 83, no. 2, www.uga.edu/gm/304/Pro3.html, viewed August 12, 2005.

16 Michael Lewis, *Moneyball: The Art of Winning an Unfair Game* (New York: W. W. Norton, 2003).

17 Dave Hoekstra, "It's Time to Talk Beane Ball," *Chicago Sun-Times*, March 21, 2005, p. 106.

18 Ibid.

19 Bill Shaikan, "New Regime in Oakland Is Counting on Beane," *Los Angeles Times*, April 1, 2005, p. D12.

20 www.astropitch.com/an/, viewed March 3, 2006.

21 www.athleticsnation.com/story/2004/9/20/23714/6909, viewed May 19, 2005.

22 Shaikan.

23 Gene Menez, "The $20 Million Stadium Boom," *Sports Illustrated*, May 16, 2005, vol. 102, iss. 20, p. 68.

24 Jack Bell, "A State Big Enough for Both Footballs," *New York Times*, August 2, 2005, p. C20.

25 Laurie Fox, "Dragon Merchandise Flying off the Shelves," *Dallas Morning News*, March 12, 2005, www.dallasnews.com/sharedcontent/dws/news/city/Tarrant/stories/031305dnnordragonshop.97aff0.html, viewed May 19, 2005.

26 Schuyler Dixon, "Southlake Carroll Dominating Texas High School Football Again," *Associated Press State & Local Wire*, August 19, 2005 (Lexis Nexis).

27 Tom Nichols, "Kingpin," *Wired Magazine*, September 2004, www.wired.com/wired/archive/12.09/kingpin.html, viewed March 7, 2005.

28 Julie Bick, "The Microsoft Millionaires Come of Age," *New York Times*, May 29, 2005, p. 5.

29 www.pba.com/home.asp, viewed March 8, 2005.

30 Nichols.

31 "Track History," www.daytonainternationalspeedway.com/track/TrackHistory.jsp, viewed May 19, 2005.

32 www.daytonausa.com/about/index.jsp, viewed May 19, 2005.

33 Jackie Franzil, "NASCAR Wows Fans with Daytona Renovations," *UPI*, February 15, 2005 (Lexis Nexis).

34 Ken Willis, "Avoiding Autograph Seekers, Sipping Daytinis in the Bistro," *Daytona Beach News-Journal: Speed Magazine*, February 16, 2005, www.news-journalonline.com/speed/special/2005/oldandnew/willis.htm, viewed November 10, 2005.

35 Mike Schneider, "Daytona Fans Getting Access to Drivers," *Associated Press Online*, February 17, 2005 (Lexis Nexis).

36 Franzil.

37 Rodney McKissic, "Retro Is All the Rage," *Buffalo News*, May 17, 2004, p. D8.

38 David Butwin, "Baseball Flannels Are Hot," *Sports Illustrated*, July 6, 1987, vol. 66, p. 105.

39 Randy Pennell, "In the World of Cutting-edge Fashion a Philadelphia Company Goes Old-School," *Associated Press*, June 5, 2003 (Lexis Nexis).

40 Jamey Eisenberg, "Throwback Jerseys Honor Athletes," *Cox News Service*, May 28, 2003 (Lexis Nexis).

41 Pennell.

42 Don Steinberg, "Sports Clothier Finds Victory in NBA Dress Code," *Philadelphia Inquirer*, October 21, 2005, www.philly.com/mld/philly/sports/12960563.htm, viewed November 12, 2005.

43 Eisenberg.

44 McKissic.

45 Pennell.

46 Steinberg.

47 Bob Harig, "Kohler's Vision May Be a Fixture for Majors to Come," *St. Petersburg Times*, August 8, 2004, p. 1C.

48 Gary D'Amato, "Whistling Straits on Course to Host PGA Championship," *Milwaukee Journal Sentinel*, January 22, 2005 (Lexis Nexis).

49 www.pga.com/pgachampionship/2004/course_overview.html, viewed June 2, 2005.

50 Gary D'Amato, "Wisconsin Has Become Major Force on National Golf Scene," *Milwaukee Journal Sentinel*, May 26, 2005 (Lexis Nexis).

51 Phil Rosenthal, "The Other Monday Debuts," *Chicago Sun-Times*, September 6, 2004, p. 31.

52 "About Coach Kelly Amonte Hiller," www.amontesports.com/kelly.php, viewed June 7, 2005.

53 Adam Rittenberg, "Amonte Hiller Engineers Wildcats' Rapid Rise," *ESPN.com*, April 20, 2005, sports.espn.go.com/ncaa/news/story?id=2040577, viewed June 7, 2005.

54 Pete Thamel, "Lacrosse Is Crossing into New Territory," *New York Times*, May 30, 2005, p. D1; "The Fastest Sport on Two Feet," *New York Times*, May 30, 2005.

CHAPTER 10

1 Alexander Wolff, "The Other Basketball," *Sports Illustrated*, June 13, 2005, vol. 102, no. 24, p. 66.

2 Ibid.

3 Tom Zeller Jr., "A Generation Serves Notice: It's a Moving Target," *New York Times*, January 22, 2006, p. 1.

4 Childs Walker, "The Orioles Are Hot, But the Fans Are Cool," *Baltimore Sun*, July 10, 2005, p. 1A.

5 Erik Brady, "Asbaty Strikes Down Bowling Stereotypes," *USA Today*, November 15, 2005, p. 3C.

6 Steven Barrie, "League of His Own Creates Waves," *Chicago Tribune*, August 18, 2005, p. 10.

7 Jeffrey Zaslow, "Moving on: Plugged in, but Tuned Out," *Wall Street Journal*, October 6, 2005, p. D1.

8 Richard Sandomir, "Yankees Are No Longer Best Show on the Road," *New York Times*, August 5, 2005, p. D1.

INDEX

Index

Index

Positive Coaching Alliance, 241
Pound, Dick, 235
Prefontaine, Steve, 227
Premium, for brands, 100
Price, Mike, 45
Prince, 207
Princeton University, 109, 115
Procter & Gamble, 56
Professional Bowlers Association (PBA), 75, 126, 276–278
Professional Golfers' Association (PGA) (*see* PGA)
Profitability analysis, 139–140
Projective techniques, in brand testing, 161
Protrade, 89
Pujols, Albert, 227
Pulford, Bob, 247–248
Putnam, Robert, 18–19
Pyle, "Cash and Carry," 34

Q rating, 163–164
Quiksilver, 49

Rabin, Yitzhak, 172
Racing Romeo, A (movie), 34
Racket ball, 68
Radio, 16–17
  advertising on, 35
  satellite, 44
  sports coverage, 33, 70, 269
  test markets and, 166
Ralph Engelstad Arena (University of North Dakota), 148
Randwick (Australia), 83
Rawhide (movie), 34
Reagan, Ronald, 33, 180
Real buyer role, in fan decision making, 76–78
Real Madrid, 24, 95, 126, 175
Real Pro Wrestling, 210–211
Real Salt Lake, 296
Red Sox Nation, 110–111
Reebok, 138, 207
Reece, Gabriella, 306
Reeves, Rosser, 98
Remember the Titans (movie), 72
Renewal strategies, 219–220
Resource availability, 130
Responsiveness, to fans, 199–200
Rice, Grantland, 33, 101
Rick Hendrick Motorsports, 149–150
Rickard, Tex, 105
Riggs, Bobby, 41, 134, 227
Riis, Jacob, 97
Ripken, Cal, Jr., 228

Risk transformation, calculated, 194–195
Rivalry, in sustaining connections, 259–260
Robinson, Jackie, 129, 227
Rockne, Knute, 46, 101, 102, 175
Roddick, Andy, 183
Rodman, Dennis, 141
Rodriguez, Alex "A-Rod," 173
Rodriguez, Ivan, 74
Roenick, Jeremy, 151
Rogge, Jacques, 235
Role modeling, in brand actualization, 193–194
Roller derby, 35, 40, 135, 240
Roller hockey, 11, 241
Romanowski, Bill, 227
Ronaldo, 126, 150
Rooney, Wayne, 228
Rose, Pete, 112, 227
Rosenfeld, Alvin, 19
Rosenhaus, Drew, 46, 147
Rounders (movie), 70
Rowland Raiders, 300–301
Royal Ascot, 156
Rozelle, Pete, 123–124
Ruettiger, Daniel "Rudy," 227
Rugby, 5, 10, 83, 148, 157–159, 288, 302
Rule changes, 27–28, 127, 143, 145–146, 165, 211
Russell, Bill, 155
Rutgers University, 109, 115
Ruth, Babe "the Babe," 23, 33, 85, 175, 228, 280–281
Ryan, Nolan, 281

Sabol, Ed, 38
Sabol, Steve, 38
Sacramento Kings, 15
Sacramento Monarchs (NBA Kings), 172
St. Anthony's High School (New Jersey), 148, 193
St. John's University (Minnesota), 25
St. Louis Browns, 227
St. Louis Cardinals, 13, 99, 175–176
St. Louis Rams, 191–192
St. Paul Saints, 105–106, 107–108
Samaranch, Juan Antonio, 234–235
San Antonio Spurs, 257
San Francisco Giants, 215–217
Sanders, Deion, 129–130
Santa Anita, 156
Saperstein, Abe, 31–32
Sapp, Bob "the Beast," 257–258
Saratoga, 156
Sarver, Robert, 267
Savoy Big Five, 31
Scandals, 113–114, 124, 185–187, 225–226, 234–235, 237–238, 250–252

About the Authors

Irving Rein, Ph.D., is a Professor of Communication Studies at Northwestern University's School of Communication. He is an internationally known expert in public communication and popular culture. He is a communication advisor to numerous highly visible places, organizations, and individuals. He has authored 12 books, including *High Visibility*, a groundbreaking study of image making. He also serves on Major League Baseball's Commissioner's Initiative for the 21st Century and is a member of the Advisory Board for Northwestern University's Master of Arts in Sports Administration.

Philip Kotler, Ph.D., is the S. C. Johnson Distinguished Professor of International Marketing at the Kellogg School of Management. He has been honored as one of the world's leading marketing thinkers and has received honorary degrees from 10 foreign universities. He is the author of 35 books, including *Marketing Management*, the most widely used marketing book in graduate business schools worldwide, and over 100 articles. He has been a consultant to IBM, General Electric, AT&T, Bank of America, Merck, Motorola, Ford, and other global corporations and places.

Ben Shields has done consulting work for a number of organizations on communication issues. His expertise is in sports and technology, and he is currently a doctoral student in communication studies at Northwestern University.

DATE DUE

AG 22 '07			
SEP 17 2007			
SEP 17 2007			
GAYLORD			PRINTED IN U.S.A.